D1458132

Human Response to Tall Buildings

COMMUNITY DEVELOPMENT SERIES

Series Editor: Richard P. Dober, AIP

URBAN ENVIRONMENTS AND HUMAN BEHAVIOR: An Annotated Bibliography/Edited by Gwen Bell, Edwina Randall, and Judith E. R. Roeder

DESIGNING FOR HUMAN BEHAVIOR: Architecture and the Behavioral Sciences/Edited by Jon Lang, Charles Burnette, Walter Moleski, and David Vachon

ALTERNATIVE LEARNING ENVIRONMENTS/ Edited by Gary J. Coates

BEHAVIORAL RESEARCH METHODS IN ENVIRONMENTAL DESIGN/Edited by William Michelson

ARCHITECTURAL PSYCHOLOGY/Edited by Rikard Küller

MAN'S PERCEPTION OF MAN-MADE ENVIRONMENT/Sven Hesselgren

INSTRUCTIONAL MEDIA AND TECHNOLOGY: A Professional's Resource/Edited by Phillip J. Sleeman and D. M. Rockwell

NEIGHBORHOOD SPACE: User Needs and Design Responsibility/Randolph T. Hester

ENVIRONMENTAL KNOWING: Theories, Research, and Methods/Edited by Gary T. Moore and Reginald G. Golledge

PLANNING BUILDINGS AND FACILITIES FOR HIGHER EDUCATION/UNESCO

THE URBAN NEST/Anne-Marie Pollowy

DESIGNING THE OPEN NURSING HOME/Joseph A. Koncelik

METHODS OF ARCHITECTURAL PROGRAMMING/ Henry Sanoff

HOUSING MESSAGES/Franklin D. Becker

BARRIER-FREE ENVIRONMENTS/Edited by Michael J. Bednar

HUMAN RESPONSE TO TALL BUILDINGS/ edited by Don Conway

ENCLOSING BEHAVIOR/Robert B. Bechtel

EDRA Conference Publications

EDRA 1/Edited by Henry Sanoff and Sidney Cohn

EDRA 2/Edited by John Archea and Charles M. Eastman

ENVIRONMENTAL DESIGN RESEARCH, Vol. I: Selected Papers/Edited by Wolfgang F. E. Preiser (EDRA 4)

ENVIRONMENTAL DESIGN RESEARCH, Vol. II: Symposia and Workshops/Edited by Wolfgang F. E. Preiser (EDRA 4)

MAN-ENVIRONMENT INTERACTIONS: Evaluations and Applications, Parts I, II, and III/Edited by Daniel G. Carson (EDRA 5)

RESPONDING TO SOCIAL CHANGE/Edited by Basil Honikman (EDRA 6)

THE BEHAVIORAL BASIS OF DESIGN, BOOK 1/ Edited by Peter Suedfeld and James A. Russell (EDRA 7)

THE BEHAVIORAL BASIS OF DESIGN, BOOK 2/ Edited by Peter Suedfeld, James A. Russell, Lawrence M. Ward, Françoise Szigeti, and Gerald Davis (EDRA 7)

CDS/34

Human Response to Tall Buildings

Edited by

Donald J. Conway

Dowden, Hutchinson & Ross, Inc.
Stroudsburg Pennsylvania

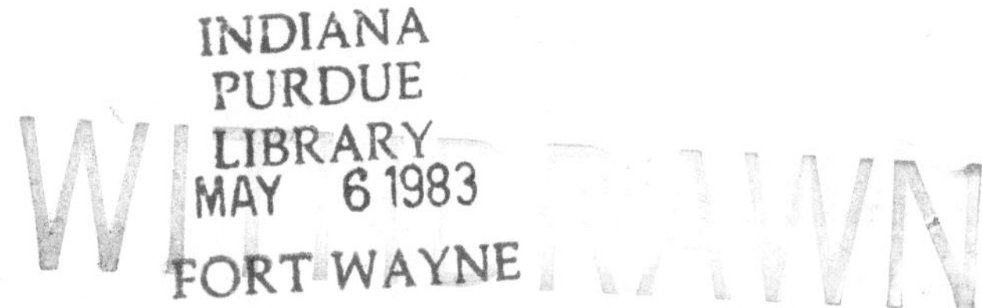

Community Development Series, Volume 34
Library of Congress Catalog Card Number: 76-58917
ISBN: 0-87933-268-9

77 78 79 5 4 3 2 1
Manufactured in the United States of America.

Library of Congress Cataloging in Publication Data

Main entry under title:
Human response to tall buildings.
(Community development series; v. 34)
Proceedings of a conference sponsored by the Office of Research Programs, American Institute of Architects, and the Joint Committee on Tall Buildings and held in the Fall of 1974.
Includes index.
1. Tall Buildings—Psychological aspects—Congresses. 2. Architecture—Human factors—Congresses. I. Conway, Donald, 1931- II. American Institute of Architects. Office of Research Programs. III. Joint Committee on Tall Buildings.
NA6231.5.H85 301.31 76-58917
ISBN 0-87933-268-9

Series Editor's Foreword

Some words from someone who knows the technical questions is probably the best way to begin this foreword.

Fazlur Kahn has served as structural engineer for two of the five tallest buildings in the world—the Sears Tower and John Hancock Center, both in Chicago. He developed a building concept that enables tall structures to be erected at per-square-foot costs comparable to shorter and squatter buildings. "Today, without any real trouble, we could build a 150-story building", Kahn says. "Whether we will, and how the city will handle it, is not an engineering question, it is a social question."

Human Response To Tall Buildings addresses his question and other similar issues. This important book acknowledges that tall buildings cannot be ruled out as a future building type. How then can we make them better? Better from the viewpoint of user, viewer, owner, and neighbor. Better as architectural symbols, urban design elements, convenient shelters for economic transactions that require high densities.

Timely? Boston is not likely to have another skyscraper in the coming decade. New York seems to be overbuilt, as does Atlanta and Minneapolis. But Des Moines just opened a soaring structure that can be seen from the cornfields miles away, strongly marking central city. Similarly sized metropolises are expecting to build tall and splendid edifices. News clips from Texas have many references to planned high-rise buildings. Not all of these are commercial enterprises. Housing and institutional uses can be well fitted into these structures. Multi-use mixes are not unusual anymore. A further round of urban development interest nationally may follow the opening of Detroit Plaza, a collection of skyscrapers clustered together and intended as an anchor for downtown. So there is no dearth of opportunities to do something better, to take advantage of the insights and experiences gathered by Don Conway in this book.

Accordingly, we are thus pleased to include this reference work in the Community Development Series which has the purpose of facilitating the exchange of information and advice among professionals concerned with the built environment. CDS publications include state-of-the-art books, handbooks and manuals. They are offered to planners, architects, landscape architects, engineers and others who would benefit in having such knowledge in readily convenient format. Philosophically, the books are not bound by traditional theory nor do they presume to establish a philosophic framework for all professional practice. There are themes that identify the series, however, and those who read this foreword should note the conceptual framework within which *Human Response to Tall Buildings* fits.

CDS books are concerned with active user and client involvement in problem defining and problem solving; systematic searching out of patterns, relationships and behavioral settings as a prelude to design. They reflect a high regard for physical interdependence of communities; ecological ethics; an interest in not just finding appropriate solutions, but also in establishing ways and means for having those solutions implemented. Touching, as it does, all these objectives, the work of Conway and associates is thus a welcomed addition to the Series.

Richard P. Dober, AIP

Contents

Introduction

The current American mythology about human response to tall building ranges from "tall buildings are awful and should be outlawed for human habitation to "tall buildings are just great and appear to be the wave of the future." The difficulty with this mythology is precisely that: It is all mythology.

In the past, those who have been concerned with the design, building, and management of tall buildings have had little reliable knowledge to use in making their decisions. If nothing else, the task of research can be looked upon as supporting or refuting mythologies such as these with empirical knowledge. One of the tasks of the office of Research Programs of the American Institute of Architects and the Joint Committee on Tall Buildings is the dissemination of knowledge about the man-made environment. Thus, it seemed to make sense, in the fall of 1974, for both these offices to collaborate in sponsoring a conference entitled "Human Response to Tall Buildings."

The intent of the conference was to bring to the surface whatever empirically derived research existed on this theme. As the reader will soon discover, the evidence of the reports tends to support both the "terrible" and "great" views of tall buildings. If anything, current research indicates such things as: The physiological stresses from sway and movement of tall buildings are real; the psychological reaction to tall buildings varies widely from occupant to occupant, depending on purpose and function in the building and sociocultural background.

The reports presented in these proceedings indicate areas of caution for the designer and manager of tall buildings and they seem to refute the notion that "all tall buildings are bad for all people in all circumstances."

We have included the sketches and notes made by architect C. William Brubaker during the Conference in "Sketchbook Notes," following this Introduction, to help the reader understand and get the flavor of the dialog and discussion that took place over those two days. Not only do these notes add a welcome visual addition to our book but the reader benefits from both the accuracy of the notes and the (often witty) insights of a keen mind with many years of practical architectural experience as well.

We start by attempting to put the entire subject of tall buildings into perspective vis-à-vis general urban development. Dr. Lynn Beedle, the chairman of the Joint Committee on Tall Buildings, and cosponsor of the conference, clearly points out the need for going beyond the physical and engineering concerns that have marked tall building research in the past. Future research, according to Dr. Beedle, must be broadened to include the characteristics of the internal environment of tall buildings and the impact of that environment on its users. Obviously, as Dr. Beedle points out, there is the larger issue of tall buildings and their development in the general scheme of things in a total cityscape. All of this is neatly summed up when Dr. Beedle says, "... Planning and design of tall buildings is concerned with much more than the safe and economical structures or energy efficient systems that engineers deal with. It is also concerned with more than the aesthetic solutions of the architect. It is intimately concerned with the complete life system of our society that is becoming so rapidly urbanized."

Lest we forget that research is not without its problems, David Cooperman, in his overview chapter, points out the difficulties and in some cases the scientific questionability of research on so complex an issue as human response to tall buildings. It is clear that both as individual structures and as parts of the urban scene tall buildings do represent complex systems. On this basis Cooperman points out the need to approach research on tall buildings (or any complex social system) from the more formal mathematical and statistical analysis of complex systems rather than the simplistic notion of collecting users responses along some number of variables. As a case in point the often criticized work of Oscar Newman, upon which his defensible space concept is based, is once again reviewed by Dr. Cooperman.

The call for increasing sophistication in research methods, evidenced in Dr. Cooperman's chapter, is a firm indication of both the current strength and weaknesses of human-environment research as well as an indicator of how far this field of study has come in the mere fifteen or twenty years since its recognition as a formal field of study. That there are weaknesses in the current methodologies ought to be acknowledged, and yet the body of knowledge being produced by these methods is a quantum jump in the knowledge resource available to design professionals and decisionmakers when compared to twenty years ago.

In order to deal with the question of human responses to tall buildings, we have divided the subject matter into three topical areas. The first, "The Tall Building and Its Neighborhood," attempts to assess the effect that the tall building has on both its immediate surroundings and the community in which it is placed. The focus in this section is essentially from the ground level. The articles deal with the consequences of intensive commercial high rise development. In San Francisco we find that the blocking of view from adjacent tall buildings plus the creation of "canyons" have significant impact on the character of the surrounding community and the responses of human beings at ground level. In Chicago we find that studies are under way to test the effect of tall buildings on land values, traffic congestion, and a broad range of social pathologies such as murder, suicide, and child abuse. In Maryland we find, from a study by a sociologist at the University of Maryland, that student undergraduate responses to high-rise dormitories seem to vary with age, sex, race, and class differences. These dormitory residents, as a group, however, seem to develop an awareness of the lack of greenery and vegetation in their high-rise dormitories. While there was some concern throughout the group for fire safety, females appeared to have a greater fear of potential fire than did males.

Finally, in this section researchers at the Center for Social Research in Bethlehem, Pennsylvania, used a combination of subjective responses and statistical analysis to probe the emotional response of over 330 people to high-rise and low-rise apartments and single family homes. By and large, their studies tend to show that familiarity or prior experience with either high-rise living or on-the-ground living has a direct relationship to how desirable one considers these buildings as places to live.

Thus what begins to emerge from this first section of the book are a number of warnings and caution notes to those who would build and those who would design tall buildings. To the builders the message seems clear—a tall building placed in a setting of relatively low building blocks out desirable views. If residents from the surrounding community find that familiar traffic paths now wind their way around a new tall building they will resent the new building. The guiding principle here seems to be the preservation of lines of sight from existing buildings to desired end points, such as an important view or a neighborhood park. When a tall building is placed in a setting in which it is surrounded by other tall buildings, the same principle of preservation of lines of sight from existing buildings seems to hold. An additional cause for dissatisfaction in the surrounding community seems to arise when a new building creates a "canyon like" affect at ground level. This can happen either by blocking off the end of a street or by completing the fourth side of any already blocked street to create a solid box of tall buildings.

In the second part of this book, called "Housing and the Livability of Tall Buildings," we attempt to deal directly with the most pressing and perhaps controversial issue of all in regard to tall buildings, that is: what is it like to really live in a tall building high up off the ground? The authors in this part cover the entire human life cycle from childhood through adulthood and aging in their studies of human resonse to tall buildings.

From Canadian researchers, for example, we find that children's play must be looked at as part of their overall development. From this perspective the opportunity for children to play out of doors goes beyond the question of play. It is a more critical issue in that it either provides, or deprives, children of the opportunity to socialize with other children. Thus, for both children and adults, the high-rise question is one of opportunities for socializing, which most usually occurs at ground level in play areas, rather than a question of indoor vs. outdoor play.

At the opposite end of the spectrum, researchers from Philadelphia, with a long history of studies of elderly housing, report the findings of a national survey from 154 federally assisted housing projects for the elderly. From this national survey a number of indicators of well-being and satisfaction for the elderly were derived and factor analyzed for their relative importance. In this analysis issues such as friendship, participation in activities, personal morale, and the number of contacts with family members were used as indicators of well-being and satisfaction. By-and-large the studies found that size of community was directly associated with friendship scores, sense satisfaction, and participation in activities. Small communities had distinctively higher ratings on these indicators than large communities. As for building height itself, this tended to be associated with lower mobility, and somewhat less satisfaction than living close to the ground.

Between these two extremes, of children on the one hand and elderly on the other, we attempt to look at adults, and particularly working adults, and their reaction to high-rise living. From studies in Atlanta and Chicago we learn that for the most part working adults without children agree that high-rise living provides many desirable features. Included in these are the "all in one" aspects of social life, convenience to entertainment and recreation, and desirable downtown shopping. This is not to say that these research efforts show high-rise living to be totally satisfactory for working adults, and a number of drawbacks and cautions for the designer and developer are presented in these studies.

In view of the diversity of occupants of high-rise housing and the sometimes conflicting research findings, it is no wonder that someone would attempt to identify some "key indicators" of housing satisfaction. That is, indicators that would provide reliable predictions of resident satisfaction across the entire spectrum of high-rise and low-rise dwellings. This is exactly the nature of the work that has been undertaken for the past four to five years by researchers at the School of Architecture at the University of Illinois. The basis for this work has been a massive study of thirty-seven housing developments in ten states. Though the work is still in progress, some hints of the key indicators of satisfaction are beginning to emerge. Among these are the type of building in which people live and the quality of its management. Both of these are seen as very high predictors of resident satisfaction. As this important work progresses, and other reliable predictors emerge, both designers and managers will be provided with powerful new tools to guide their efforts.

To conclude this part on housing we attempt to address ourselves directly to those who must make design decisions. Based on many years of research and analysis of housing research literature, Clare Cooper Marcus and Lindsay Hogue present us with a series of invaluable guidelines and tips to designers. Those who must make day-to-day design and management decisions about high-rise housing will find this section of the book to be the most useful of all.

In the last part of the book, but certainly not the least important, we address the question of emergency situations in tall buildings. In this section, "The Response to Emergency," we present reports on both human response and technical response to emergency situations. From the disaster research center at Ohio State University we learn, from twenty-five years of study of human behavior under very extreme stress, that the human phenomenon of panic is, in fact, very rare. What appears to be the case is that many more misconceptions about panic behavior prevail than are warranted. A serious issue that emerges from this discussion is the question of assumptions about human behavior during emergency situations that prevail in building codes, fire codes, and in the minds of designers. For example, how well do the assumptions about human behavior during emergency situations made by building officials and designers match real behavior? One wonders, after reading these research studies, whether or not some well-meaning provisions in codes and regulations might not even exaggerate an emergency situation! Clearly this question of fit between assumptions and the reality of human behavior during building emergencies is an area in need of a great deal of research.

From the Earthquake Engineering Research Institute we find that efforts are beginning to be mounted to address the specific question of what people do in tall buildings during earthquakes. In a similar fashion studies in Maryland, New York, and California are beginning to identify actual human behavior during fires in buildings. Researchers at the National Bureau of Standards, and elsewhere, working under contract to the General Services Administration, present information about a variety of fire warning systems for the occupants of tall buildings. In these studies both the traditional communications means of exit signs, etc., plus the more innovative verbal communication systems have been developed and tested. These studies of the differences in occupant reaction to vocal instructions coming over a public address system, as opposed to the old fire gong, provide important insights into the orderly control of humans and their evacuation from tall buildings during emergency situations. Additional studies from Canada and California deal directly with the process of building evacuation through vertical circulation routes, i.e., by stairways and elevators. Contrary to current belief and many regulations, researchers from the Department of Architecture at the University of California indicate that elevators may indeed be the fastest, safest, and most feasible means for evacuating people from buildings. Obviously this challenge to existing assumptions has to be evaluated and tested in future research.

In summary, the parts of this book attempt to bring to the surface as much reliable research knowledge as was feasible in the context of a two-day conference. Three important aspects of tall buildings are discussed and presented in depth and, indeed, some of the mythological fog about tall buildings does seem to be clearing away.

Don Conway, A.I.A.

HUMAN RESPONSES TO TALL BUILDINGS

SYMPOSIUM AT
SEARS TOWER, CHICAGO
JULY 17-19, 1975

SPONSORED BY
THE AMERICAN INSTITUTE OF ARCHITECTS
AND THE JOINT COMMITTEE ON TALL BUILDINGS

SKETCHBOOK NOTES —
C. WILLIAM BRUBAKER, PERKINS & WILL ARCHITECTS

HUMAN RESPONSE TO TALL BUILDINGS

Session 1

Friday, July 18

sponsored by
The American Institute
of Architects
and the
Joint Committee on Tall Buildings
(American Society of Civil Engineers, and
the International Association for Bridge
and Structural Engineering)
... sponsored by the National Science Foundation

Don Conway – chmn.
Director, Research Programs
American Institute of Architects

Lynn Beedle, Ph.D.
Lehigh University
Chmn., "Joint Committee
on Tall Buildings"

– "Joint"
means architects and engineers

concerns of the "Joint committee"
include economics
technology
social values

The suburbs boomed ..
metropolitan areas grew ..
agricultural land disappeared ..
centers were linked to
homes with expressways ..
... tall buildings
were a response to
1) desire for higher density
2) shortages of land

note responses to
emergency, fire,
motion,
other people

Joint Committee
has published 100 volumes
.... wants to identify
needs for future
research.

4 Ages –
1. Age of Crafts
2. Industrial Age
3. Scientific Age
4. and now ... The Age of Awareness!

Joe Fujikawa (Office of Mies)
chmn., Chicago Committee
on High-Rise Buildings

Session I Friday morning, July 18

"THE TALL BUILDING AND ITS NEIGHBOR"

Bruce Graham, chmn. (SOM)

... more interest since "Towering Inferno" film.

People in different parts of the world respond differently to tall bldgs....

In Houston, tall office bldgs are accepted but not apartments

In Chicago, tall apts are accepted (as are tall office buildings) especially along the lake.

In some areas, tall buildings are not acceptable.

Chicago's "South Loop" study in progress.. will be high density, include tall bldgs

More environmental damage by trailers & tract development and research is needed for those low density options.

High-rise buildings provide energy-efficient no-spread options for some citizens.

Sears Tower ... "the world's tallest."

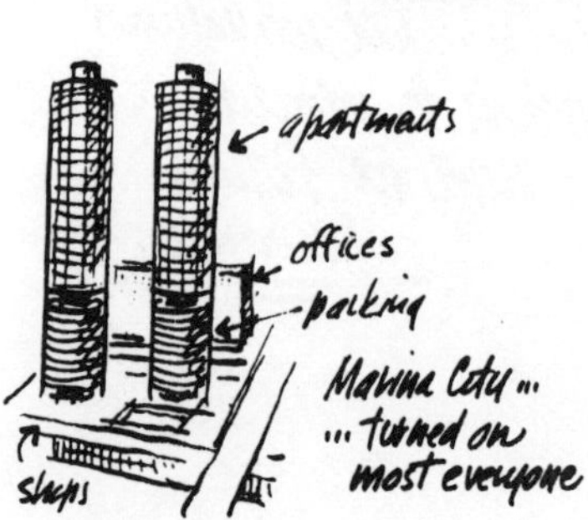

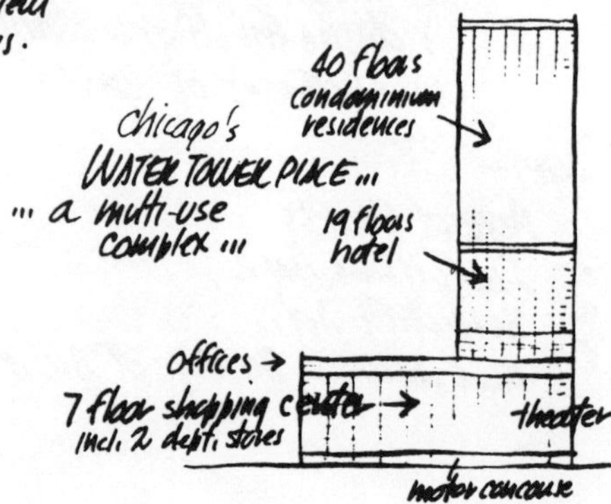

David
Dornbusch

a canned slide show & music
on San Francisco's
"changing face"

citizens concerns
" loss of unique character
" visual pollution (however, most liked the high-rise skyline from a distance)
" excessive size
" blank walls along walks
" mechanistic architecture
" loss of rich older buildings
" loss of feeling of hills (proposal = emphasize hills)
" loss of views (new, higher buildings blocking others' views)
" views from the street ~~damaged~~
due to closing off of views →
by large new structures
" views from residences
greater concern

Use of parks "
influenced by tall bldgs
which block access
cast shadows
cause wind conditions
at street level

wind

Tall Bldgs
concentrate development and automobiles & air pollution.
(transportation problems, obviously, must be solved concurrently.)
(BART services a small percentage of the San Francisco area's population)

CUB – However, many people in San Francisco don't need an automobile...
" concentration makes it possible!

H.A. Simon
- U. of Illinois

"The Impact of High-Rise Structures on the Community"

... 50/50 singles/couples
few children
go to work via car, bus, & walking (esp. Hancock)
police, fire, shopping, security, etc.
considered adequate by most
people liked views, being close to shops, or to work,
people disliked rather little.

for current research ..
(Economics, sociology, political science, engineering departments joined forces ..

studied John Hancock Bldg (condo)
and residential towers (rental)
on Lake Shore Drive
incl. land values
crime
traffic congestion.
etc.
by surveying via telephone

however, these are well-to-do people with choice
" of course they'll live where they are happiest.
-CWB

G. Moss Haber
-U. of Maryland

" The Impact of Tall Buildings on Users and Neighbors "

people liked views, scenery, convenience, recreation opportunities, etc.
people disliked "impersonality" ... facelessness ... isolation
waiting for elevators
lack of greenery
fear of fire
tall buildings generally
improvements suggested — "more creative design" (less impersonality)
more greenery
better elevators

Roy Herrenkohl
-Lehigh Univ

"Influences on the Attractiveness
of a Residential Setting
as a Place to Live"

K. Nichols — Goddard
"User Study:
Urban Office Bldgs:
View Variables"

"... most people want a window
and view outward

"... not having a view, many people
working in an office
seek out views during the day.

... views from lower floors are, of course,
more closely related to the
out door environment.

... views from upper floors
tend to be unrelated

conclusion - windows and
views aren't "essential"
but most people want windows &
outside views

method: 76 slides of
different types of housing
shown to respondents
who rated them.

types: high-rise apts
mobile homes
low-rise apts
row-houses, or twin
temporary (tents, campers)
garden apts
single-family

both "familiarity" and
"desireability" rated
and ranked

(people were most familiar
with single-family homes.
→ new, unfamiliar settings
may not be considered
to be desireable.)

ominous alternative -
projected image
of clouds &
birds.

Discussion

An architect =

" why can't the sociologists give us fast answers (in a day, not in months) based on their background + experience ?

(... will a year of "study" really produce a better answer ?)

On density and quality of the environment =

" high rises can be good or bad
" low density " " " "
" design and landscaping and other factors determine quality + desireability.

"... obviously, cooperation is needed ..
"... scholars can help designers.

note inconsistency ....

"HIGH-RISE" definitions vary ...

6 stories ?

15-20 stories ?

40-60-80 stories ?

← as Lake Point Tower, Chicago

cus-

however, how about a richer-mix –

← tower apts

balcony apts

town houses

terrace apts

(too often, design is limited to one type, endlessly repeated .... as public housing)

"HOUSING AND LIVABILITY OF TALL BUILDINGS"

SESSION II

Friday afternoon, July 18

Dan Levin
McHugh-Levin,
developers
Chicago

The social problems for high-rise design are not unique.
Sociology studies won't tell us how to design ...
("Management mistakes" give tenants something to do.)
The design problem is complex .. with no simple answers ...
.. a key factor is "feeling of entrapment" in a high-rise ...
.. but citizens make trade-offs, sometimes choose the option of living in a high-rise, to gain convenience, excitement, glamour, etc.

High-rise living does not and will not satisfy everyone.

Tom ~~Dors~~ Kavanagh, chmn.

"USER NEEDS: EVALUATING HOUSING FOR LOW & MODERATE INCOME FAMILIES"
– James Anderson, U. of Ill.

using the common matrix: for methods and variables

	Occupants	Managers	Researchers	Architects	Community
Physical characteristics					
Occupants					
Management					
Community					

"It is not clear that high-rise housing is an unsatisfactory building type"

... for higher income groups, for singles, for elderly, & for convenience ...
tall buildings can be highly satisfactory.

"ELDERLY PEOPLE IN TALL BUILDINGS"

-Lucille Nahemow
Philadelphia Geriatric Center

Complex methodology ..
included "indices of well-being"
- friendship in housing
- housing satisfaction
- morale
- mobility (or "motility")
- family contact
- activity participation

... however,
why are such buildings usually ordinary & ugly?
- CMB

"' Key question—
"' should we build high-rise structures for elderly people?
" first, for whom? (urban, rural?)
where? (city center, small city?)
how much? (high or low income?)
why? (what motive for considering high-rise?)

1) public or private
2) size of community
3) number of people in project
4) height of buildings (high rises are usually built in central cities.

"' size of project and height of buildings seemed to be of little significance

most public housing in the USA—
is housing-for-the-elderly.

high-rise bldgs. are more likely to have tenant organizations, better medical services,

high-rises in suburban settings often less acceptable.
(probably since people came from single-family houses.)

in the central city, however, the high-rise form is often "natural" now.

" Quality of building "
rated by HUD
1) grounds & landscape quality;
2) well-maintained & attractive buildings

note
great concern for fire safety ...
& fear of entrapment
many people express desire for a second way out
" a fire escape.

"VERTICAL VILLAGE = THE WORLD OF A HIGHRISE COMPLEX" (Carl Sandburg Village) in Chicago

... a lively presentation.

Gerda Wekerle
York Univ, Toronto

set task: to find out why people moved to Sandburg, & how they like it.

Sandburg is heavily singles (since 1963), well-educated, upper-income.

The young singles ("pre-family stage") are quite happy with the complex.

Some are aggressive, social, and know many other residents (but not all are so socially active.)

Sandburg's pool, tennis, etc. supported by extra fees... Tenants complained about the extra charges.

No pub .. no convenient hangout .. no indoor all-year pool.

Generally, satisfaction much-influenced by management's responsiveness ... ... Sandburg management is punctual in service & maintenance ... (but tenants look upon management as a remotely-controlled bureaucracy.)

The 1960's high-rise apartment boom gave many young people a new option — for a clean, secure, predictable apartment.

So, projects like Sandburg helped to create a new kind of market .. for young singles.

(Earlier, options were living-at-home, or in rooming houses.)

benefits from a superb location ... adjacent to high-cost richer-mix Gold Coast ... (which made Sandburg rents seem low.)

... the tenants like the design .. ... physical environment.

"SOCIAL NETWORKS IN CEDAR-RIVERSIDE"

D. Coopersmith
U. of Minn.

... COMPARTIVE ANALYSIS OF NETWORKS IN TALL BLDGS.

... on network analysis & mathematical modelling to measure social networks in tall buildings.

D.S.–
Oscar Newman's "Defensible Space" is a secondary look at data with inconvincing statistics, proving nothing.

At Cedar-Riverside (Minneapolis' new, controversial "New Town in Town")
the architect asked for "social reasons" for building forms,
(having already determined orientation, engineering, etc. reasons.)

In comparing high & low-rise..
... note that inter-action is screened in high-rises
(while its quite visible in low-rises)
... are high-rises good or bad for children?
..."territoriality" is for the birds!

"RESIDENTIAL RESPONSES TO HIGH-RISE LIVING"

notes on student housing in tall buildings

Greenberg
Wayne State U.

residents of higher floors felt
more security, quiet, satisfaction
as apt. density increased,
tenants were more dissatisfied
as expected length of occupancy increased,
satisfaction increased.

"COLONY SQUARE =
AN AFTER-OCCUPANCY
USER-NEEDS EVALUATION"

Bob Young
Georgia Tech

Purpose of study –
... to measure achievement
" to give users a voice
" to develop guidelines for
future multi-use complexes.

Survey results –
criticism of hotel interiors
criticism = noise from plaza
during events
(as AIA convention.)

recommend other rich-mix
multi-use complexes
recommend multi-use development
at MARTA rapid transit stations.

not enough shops open so far
general satisfaction with the complex
no complaints about height
most people think it does not
conflict with downtown,
2½ miles away.

Also – analysis of high-rise for
the elderly ...
... in some conflict with
other studies in this conference.

Atlanta has many
multi-use complexes
incl. Colony Square
with permanent
residential population.

Colony Square
has a "public square," 2-level plaza,
2 office towers
25 story hotel
3 14-16 story residential towers.
... 264 units.

Unfortunately,
the plaza is usually empty.
(In contrast, in Chicago, the
plazas at First National Bank,
& Civic Center – are very busy.)

"Colony Square"
Atlanta

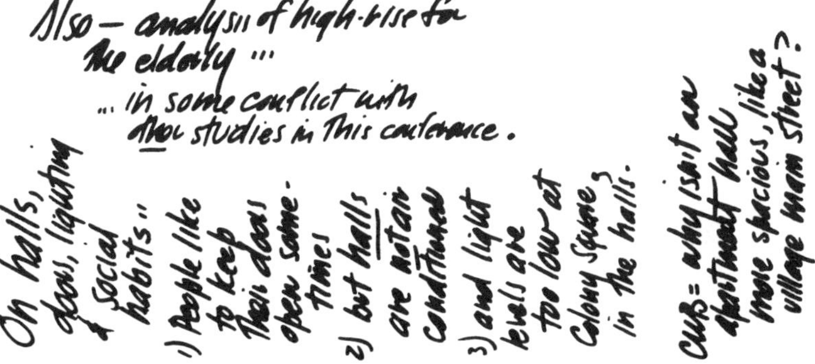

On halls, doors, lighting & social habits:
1) People like to keep their doors open sometimes
2) but halls are not air conditioned
3) and light levels are too low at Colony Square, in the halls.
CUB: why isn't an apartment hall more spacious, like a village main street?

"THE RESPONSE TO EMERGENCY"

SESSION III

Saturday morning, July 19

Joseph Fitzgerald – chairman
Commissioner of Buildings
Chicago

Dangerous conditions ...

- Crowded stair wells ...
  a stopping of movement ...
  plus smoke ...

Chicago, as other well-run cities, works hard to keep its building codes up-to-date.

New ordinance in Chicago –
... requires manual voice system controlled by fire dept. thru-out high rise floors (only in corridors in apartments)

New fire code for high-rises ... also considers how people might move when threatened by a fire (or should they stay in their apartments or offices?)

Should elevators be used during a fire?
Problems = smoke filled shafts
= electronic failure due to heat or water
= automatic elevators don't allow control of destination.

Architects plan primarily for fire emergency ...

... the Sears Tower has one of the most advanced fire protection systems.

... One must also ask – what would be the human response to an approaching tornado?

So far, a tornado has not hit a high-rise

... Or what response to a bomb threat?

... or an airplane collision with a tall building.

Also = large crowds in public meeting places, as sports arenas. " can create special problems.

"High-Rise Fire Safety = Human Response"

Gene Williams
U. of Okla.
Byron Hollander
Oaklahoma City Fire Dept.

the new concept = Fire Safety Management
... with architects, engineers, managers, fire officials, building authorities, etc
... working together.

Fires in buildings still destroy property and life.

(The 3 primary causes of fires are 1) men 2) women, and 3) children!

Modern buildings are superior in many ways but inferior in other ways —
.. as suspended ceilings, punched holes
.. as smoke-generating plastics
.. as insistence on higher structures
(allowing spread of fire & smoke.

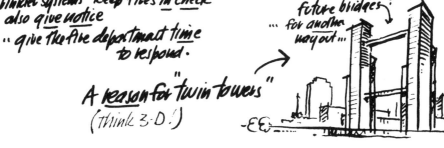

In an emergency..
... people head for the elevators (even tho they should not)
... it's too late, then, to "educate" the tenants, as by recorded messages.

(fire truck ladders reach only about 75 feet..)

75'

... instead, Tenants must be "educated" carefully before emergencies occur.
(.. should be the responsibility of building management.

Sprinkler systems keep fires in check
... also give notice
.. give the fire department time to respond.

A reason for "twin towers"
(think 3-D!)

-EE

"High Rise Fire Safety .." continued

what about helicopters?
... wind, heat, panic make use very limited.

How can fuel load (added by tenants) be controlled?
... lease conditions.

Wouldn't outside elevators be safer — since both heat & smoke would be dissipated

Casper Hegner's suggestion

" EMERGENCIES IN TALL BUILDINGS "
... THE DESIGNERS RESPOND TO THE HUMAN RESPONSE "

Eileen Duignan-Woods
~~HUD~~ GSA — mechanical engineer

the new-super-tall skyscraper (an engineering accomplishment) is dangerous

"total evacuation is not the answer"

an alternative = "refuge areas"
use air-conditioning systems to pump out smoke
use vocal messages
use smoke detectors, phones
sprinklers, alarm boxes, etc to sound the alarm.

Federal Building in Seattle is completely sprinklered compartmented vertically and horizontally

(and Chicago's Federal Bldg. has a "modified Seattle system")

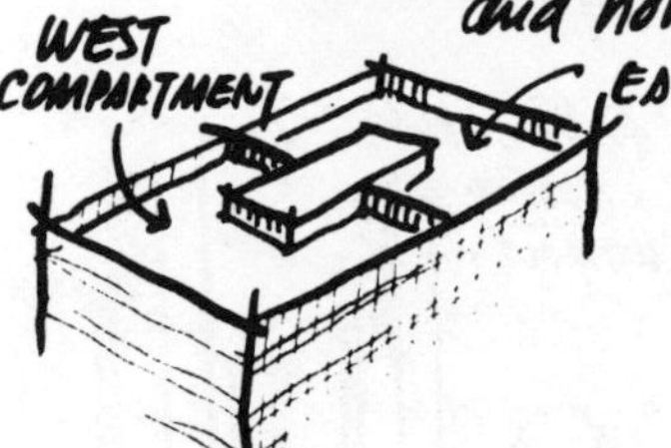

"MOVEMENT OF PEOPLE IN BUILDINGS"

- J.L. Pauls
National Research Council of Canada

efficiency of evacuation movement is determined by both
1) design, and
2) building management
" seldom sophisticated
(but remember how airlines do it)

total evacuation
has been traditional
" speed decreases with density"
(note studies with 44" exit stairs ... 2 units wide ..
as stair gets loaded with people,
movement slows down ..
& could even stop.)
flow down a stair varies with stair width

smoke moves up shafts
fire

partial evacuation = "selective evacuation"
often makes more sense
sometimes people in danger area
should move up or down to a safe floor.

stadiums & other sports facilities are often high rise too
can be over 100' high

"HIGH-RISE EMERGENCY COMMUNICATIONS"
Robert Glass
Nat'l Bureau of Standards

1. Detection problem
2. Recognition problem
3. Discrimination problem

people should be encouraged to use stairs
(but Sears Tower has signs to discourage use of stairs)

exit signs (often at ceiling, where smoke accumulates)
can be re-evaluated

this way ⇒
to the egress

"ELEVATOR PERFORMANCE "
UNDER CONDITIONS OF EMERGENCY"

– V. Bazjanac
U of Calif-Berkeley

Codes & design discourage or prohibit use of elevators, in a fire emergency.
However, since fires don't usually start in elevator shafts, elevators could be used for evacuation.

U. of C-Berkeley simulated conditions .. studied elevator performance
1) considered zones for partial evacuation as 3 floor zones
2) considered total evacuation (as required for bomb threats)

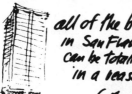

all of the buildings studied in San Francisco can be totally evacuated in a reasonable time.

(Alcoa Bldg would require 25 minutes for evacuation.)

(The huge Bank of America bldg. could be emptied in 12 minutes with use of elevators)

note: S.F.'s controversial tapered TransAmerica Bldg has, logically, decreasing population on upper floors.
= very safe, due to fast evacuation time.

Design suggestions: 1. overlap elevator zones
2. pre-plan for emergencies
3. establish refuge areas

"PANIC BEHAVIOR = SOME EMPIRICAL OBSERVATIONS"

E.L. Quarantelli
- Ohio State Univ.

I. people seldom "break down" in high stress conditions ...
only a few succumb to panic flight (ignore anecdotal stories)
generally, behavior is acceptable and predictable.

II. generally human behavior under stress is not bad.

however, in rare cases of panic behavior —
"un-checked fear" .. anticipation of what might occur whether there is real danger or not
flight from specific danger (non-social, but not anti-social)

conditions for panic flight =
1. perception of possible entrapment (while avenues of escape are evident)
2. sense of helplessness
3. feeling of social isolation (one's own actions are essential) feeling that

"SOCIOLOGICAL IMPLICATIONS OF DISASTERS"

E. Hass
- U. of Colorado

" panic, looting, helplessness, price gouging, etc. are not common (tho get generous media coverage)

tall buildings can provide safe refuge in natural disasters ..

→ hurricane →

" are usually safer in storms, floods, earthquakes even
(during earthquakes, what do people do? stay put? flee to streets?)
... note that fire danger increases following an earthquake.

"NEW DIRECTIONS FOR RESEARCH ON HUMAN RESPONSE TO TALL BUILDINGS"

Session IV

Saturday afternoon
July 19

Robertson Short, Jr.
Pres., Chicago Chapter
Bldg. Owners & Managers Assn.

NEEDED RESEARCH:

On vertical transportation =
technically good
but little sociological study of
cab size, speed, multiple stops

On window size =
for years, most assumed that
maximum glass area was
best for rental, therefore "best."
Now, that's in conflict with
energy conservation.

On revolving doors =
(used to combat "stack action")

On lighting =
re-evaluation due

On vandalism =
mostly in toiletrooms, narrow corridors.
" why?
" but none on the Plaza.

Don Conway, Director
AIA Research Programs

Although large amounts of money are expended for research in USA & other countries, very little on architectural, engineering & planning research.

Threats increase ..
(damage & bomb threats)
" certainly planning & design will be affected.

Fire Safety program of films attracted only 10% of people in the 60-story building.

Restaurants, shops, events, seem to contribute general satisfaction.

Zoning requires setbacks & plazas which destroy life of the street, by eliminating shops, crowded walks, etc.

Next — more all-year public spaces.

SOME SPECIFIC NOTES ON NEEDED RESEARCH — from Groups E & F.

Rankin — new devices for escape *
Booth Ext. Escape Corp (& principal of an elem. school)!

Vetter — U of Cal. how to get individual bldg. owners interested & financially supportive. * ***

Fitzgerald — Chicago Dept. of Bldgs. how people will react in an emergency = GSA has done some research on their canned messages.
- will they go horizontally or up, even if instructed.
- helicopter rescue?
- optional exit ways? ⟵ related **

Jacobs architect — Calif. note parallels to ocean liner (which has life boats) ... we need building "life-boats" ** ... as external elevators protected by water curtains.

... international cooperation needed. **

LeMeLu — (Tall Bldgs. Joint committee)
... agree, information from other countries needed.

Ed White architect N.C. .. state has a new code.

Jake Pauls researcher, Canada — more on movement of people in buildings

Mario Paparoni engineer .. Venezuela — how do weather conditions influence design & fire safety. * & how do materials, character, openness influence?

Randy Zisler teacher, Princeton — how bad are fires in large bldgs? * ... The public doesn't know either. ... studies should be more accurate in accounting.

... comments from everyone around the table ...

It's rather difficult to design for behavior if the architect doesn't know the behavior.

Kim Prentice
U of Ill.
.. why are sprinklers so expensive?
.. what are the alternatives?
.. new ideas for fire safety systems.
** NEEDED RESEARCH

Helmut Cahn
CF Murphy architects
.. little "research" in architecture
because it's applied for new buildings.
good reminder ↗
.. but codes vary everywhere
.. we need unified codes
.. need cost data (as for Seattle Federal Bldg.) *
.. research & design should be more closely related.

V. Bazjanac
Berkeley ..
.. need more money for research

Bob Young
Otis Elevator
.. what should be done with elevators
in case of fire? (we've heard
both sides today.) ** ← no answers yet!
(that decision would then influence design ...
as = where is the best position for
elevator cores?)

Norm Kornsand
Rolf Jensen Assoc. Consultants
consider
.. alternative people-moving systems ("life boats")
i.e. = other ways out
... smoke control! (how can we design systems
to control it.) *
... plastics affect on fires (not limited to high-rise design)

Gilda Haber
U. of Maryland
.. 1) Schools should teach fire safety.
2) closer ties with fire-fighters *
3) international cooperation valuable
4) alternate routes of escape via
hanging gardens - bridges! **
↖ towards 3-D urban design

Vince Waropay
USG Co.
.. for unified codes
.. toxicity studies important (but ~~comp.~~ expensive)

Caspar Ulequer [uncertain reading]
VA

NEEDED RESEARCH

1. .. human reaction to signage (incl. exit signs) *
2. .. incentives for control of "fuel load" *
3. .. where do fires start in tall bldgs. **
4. .. human reactions to windowlessness *

(good topic for all buildings, high and low.)

Kowalczyk .. use of escalators, elevators, stairs, etc?

Howard Eberhard, engineer
California

comments on research methods =
1) whatever, research should be well-defined — what are the objectives
2) evaluation essential ... especially where humans are involved.

Eugene Haas
sociologist
U. of Colorado .. involve sociologists, architects & engineers in multi-disciplinary studies — to see "how humans respond." *

D. Sfintesco
from Paris
.. active in Joint Committee
.. working on a new code for European nations.

C. Wm. Brubaker – how does the tall bldg. measure-up in war time? (note: for radio-active fallout, it's a good shelter)

San Paolo catastrophe unlikely in some cities. (don't make parallel assumptions.)

in research what are the goals? ** (historic data may show only great safety ..)

education of people in high-rise buildings most important. **

statistics lacking – **
... what are casualty records for high vs low buildings?
... some feel safer in tall buildings.

GROUPS E & F – D. Sfintesco (chairperson) and C. Wm. Brubaker (chairperson)

Part I

Commentary and Overview

1

Tall Buildings and the Quality of Urban Life

Lynn S. Beedle
Lehigh University

One of the earliest statements of the thrust of the Joint Committee on Tall Buildings was: "A better urban environment through improved planning and design of Tall Buildings."

What is the relationship between tall buildings and the urban setting? Do they affect urban life? Can better skyscrapers really improve the urban environment? The two are intertwined more than we realize. If the tall buildings are "good," the urban environment is improved. If they are "bad," hardly anything can be done to improve the city. And the answers to the posed questions have to do with what it is that we are calling "good" and "bad."

I remember a visit to Chicago some years ago when the First National Bank was just being completed. My reaction was: "How out of place. This beautiful building with flared base standing against the older straight-sided buidings. And so close." I wasn't noticing the building nearly as much as I was its setting in Chicago's local environment. I ignored the beauty of the building itself. I was judging by another standard, namely its interaction with other parts of the city, and in this case the adjacent architecture.

What I did not know (but could have guessed from what I knew of the advanced state of Chicago's approach to tall buildings) was that the larger "plan" for the bank went considerably beyond the walls. Thus, when I visited Chicago at a later time, I was greeted by a beautiful plaza, crowded with people in noontime activity, the upward curving sweep providing an impressive transition from the street to the building itself, the whole setting providing a pleasant accommodation to the rest of the immediate environment. The effect was exhilarating.

As Mrs. Ada Huxtable said, "What counts overwhelmingly today are the multiple ways any building serves a complex and sophisticated set of environmental needs. What is it part of? How does it work? How does it satisfy the needs of men and society as well as the needs of the client? How does it fit into the larger organism, the community? What does it add to, or subtract from, the quality of life?"

Japanese architect Yoshitake put the same idea in

another way in the form of a challenge: "The present society is calling for a new social morality on the side of architects and engineers. We need a new principle . . . considering . . . those who do not use a building but who are influenced by it."

And Fazlur Khan, structural designer of the Sears Tower and Chicago's Hancock Center, said: "The reason for the great height of the Sears Tower is, more than anything else, the need to provide an attractive environment at street level."

So when we say "good" and "bad," in connection with skyscrapers, we do not mean the structure alone or the architecture alone (even though these do occupy a great deal of attention of the Joint Committee). We are, also, and maybe most importantly, talking about their "planning and design" in a larger context.

On the one hand, there is the internal environment. Is it planned and designed both to account for (or to capitalize upon) that unique quality, "tallness"? Besides the normal concerns that apply to all buildings this can cover such things as (a) vistas and views from windows and balconies and associated orientation with regard to adjacent buildings, (b) internal courtyards and access to individual units, (c) creation of a "sense of place" both of internal regions and for individual units, (d) tallness criteria as regards occupancy category (the desire of families with small children to be close to the ground), and (e) a consideration of life style of those who are perhaps not yet accustomed to city living.

On the other hand, there is the external environment. The tall building is part of the urban system, a system whose quality it creates. Thus, the planning and design must necessarily include not only structure and architecture, and, as we have noted, the adjacent buildings and street space, but also the interface with people's *interest* at the street level (first floor shops and amenities), with the transportation system (whether by foot or by aircraft), with business and residential activity, with the cultural life of the city at its center, with the basic urban services of power, sanitation, water supply, and even with the "impact" of the skyscraper on the cityscape from outside the city walls.

As Kavanagh has said, it even extends to the surrounding communities and affects adjacent cities: "It [planning and design] is a matter of evaluating the contribution which the highrise building makes to the urban environment, its effects on the local, community, and regional life, on land use and even space use, on the social and human factors, and the need for communications, contact, choice, opportunity, and mobility which underlies the very existence of cities."

So the "planning and design of tall buildings" is concerned with much more than safe and economical structure of the engineer, energy-efficient systems, and esthetic solutions by the architect. It is intimately concerned with the complete life system of our society that is becoming so rapidly urbanized.

Since the statement made at the beginning of this chapter about the thrust of the Joint Committee implies a positive answer (the quality of urban life *can* be enhanced by improving its skyscrapers), the basic research question becomes "How"? How can tall buildings be improved to meet this need? What methodology is required?

In the MONOGRAPH on tall buildings, the Joint Committee is collecting answers from all over the world. Its findings are being disseminated not only to the design team but also to the decisionmakers. We are identifying some specific research needs so that the "how" may be better approached.

The success with which we apply what we now know and deal with the problems we see ahead governs more than we may realize at first glance. It governs the future of what is called, in a much-abused phrase, the "quality of urban life."

2

Social Research on Tall Habitats: A Critique and Proposal for Network Analysis

David Cooperman
University of Minnesota

INTRODUCTION

Published work on social aspects of tall buildings is highly varied in research design, style, methods, and conclusions. It ranges from highly impressionistic assertions about tall building effects based on ethnographic types of observations to secondary analysis of data utilizing multiple regression statistics. Studies have been carried out by scholars from a variety of social and design sciences, and with varied purposes. There is clearly no consensus on methodological problems nor on techniques for their resolution. Hence, it is not surprising that current research may be lacking in those qualities that would systematically advance our knowledge. This has serious implications for policy and design decisions. Planners and architects faced with planning building projects perforce may adopt gross recommendations based on inadequate, incomplete or irrelevant studies. Should this situation continue the lag between valid knowledge in the field and the rate of tall building development is likely to grow wider in the coming years.

Most research on the social aspects of tall buildings is problem oriented and often motivated by beliefs or fears that tall buildings per se cause social morbidities, such as crime, delinquency, or mental illness. Consequently many studies are primarily efforts to validate preconceived conclusions. Too often the research reports assume argumentative form. Yet, appropriate statistical tests to confirm the logic of such arguments may be lacking. Research may consist of single case studies or of several low- high-rise building descriptive studies with percentages and frequencies of inhabitants' responses reported by building height or type on such variables as degree of satisfaction, differential interaction of children, etc. Simple univariate statistics are often used as a basis for inferences and absolute differences are employed as compelling evidence in support of a particular position. Such findings are clearly unwarranted. Bivariate statistics—a simple, logical requisite for investigating such questions—may yield more specific information about relevant variables associated with the alleged effects of building height. In the absence of such basic procedures it is impossible for valid knowledge to be cumulative and any attempt at replication can only suggest what should have been done originally. The problem of reaching valid inferences is further complicated by a number of confounded variables used in this type of research.

Confounded Variables in Tall Building Research

The following is a brief list of ways in which independent variables can be confounded or uncontrolled unless more complex research designs or more powerful tests are administered:

1. *Physical Mobility and Tall Building Effects.* Many studies have been carried out on the poor or near poor who have moved from a low-rise, dilapidated dwelling to a public tall building project. The neighborhood of origin may have been characterized by different degrees of population homogeneity and social organization. Any of several effects of the move itself may be confounded with the effects of building height. Hence, moves which are socially dislocating, no matter what the building design, might elicit a negative response to the building. Moves involving choices on the part of the relocated resident are likely to result in less antagonism to the new unit no matter what the height than if tall buildings are the only possible alternative to a forced relocation.

2. *Financial Cost and Satisfaction.* Housing preference surveys invariably indicate that the type of preference for most families is the single house on individual lots. Often this response is interpreted inappropriately as demonstrating a general antipathy to tall buildings. (Low rank on a preference scale is not the same as a negative value). Moreover, since a single family house often represents a sizable amount of financed equity while an apartment unit is still considered conventionally as a rental unit, respondents will tend to have differential psychological investments which correspond to their economic investments. Responses to unit preference questions can be linked to attitudes to the unit design only when such variables have been controlled.

3. *Subjective and Objective Data.* A more general question can be raised at this point, namely, the degree to which subjective data, such as attitudes, expectations, perceptions, and evaluations may be confounded by an investigator with association, behavior, and interaction. Michelson's research suggests that such variables exhibit different quantitative values. Expectations and attitudes that people report about tall buildings do not correspond with their actual behavior (Michelson 1974). A wide array of methodological problems and possible solutions have been noted by social scientists and this literature may be useful in disentangling confounded variables of this type in tall building research (Deutscher 1973).

4. *Density, Design, and Tall Building Habitats.* Population densitites may vary with increased building height, depending on the type and scope of density measures used and depending on building, project, and unit design. Where such measures as floor area ratio or building density vary directly with height, controls should be introduced to distinguish potential effects of each on the dependent variable (Cooperman 1974). Different densities in surrounding urban environments may also be confounded with tall building effects.

An important theoretical point should be considered here. A full causal explanation of any general tall building effects must await the development of more confirmed theories of behavior-design relationships than we have at present. Our *impressions* are that density variables probably do not act directly, when they intervene at all, to produce or inhibit various social effects (see also Carnahan et al. 1974). Likewise, design characteristics of a building may not produce an independent effect on a dependent social variable. This only underscores the logical necessity of distinguishing between density and design variables at the concept formation stage in doing research, in order to prevent ambiguity and error later.

5. *Social-Cultural Variables and Tall Building Effects.* We often assume that both morbidity effects, if

any, and satisfaction measures vary at least by socioeconomic status, by stage of age-family cycle, by ethnic group status, housing experience, and socioeconomic aspiration. Yet almost all of the research extant on social morbidities has been done on impoverished people in public housing projects. In Great Britain the studies focus on estate housing, in Hong Kong and Singapore on mass public housing, and in the United States on large public housing projects. Empirical studies published on middle class inhabitants' reactions or attitudes toward tall buildings indicate possible significant differences from those of lower status groups (Höweler 1973; Michelson 1974; Wekerle and Hall 1972; Wekerle 1974). Nonetheless, the state of our current knowledge affords us no way of asserting whether *in fact* socioeconomic status differences are at work, or which of them and to what degree, and why.

It may well be argued that no one study carried out at levels of financial support common to such work can afford to include sufficient numbers of different control variables to avoid the confounding errors noted, nor would it be practical to obtain sufficiently representative samples of population as well as tall and small building designs to definitively answer these troublesome questions. A first toward understanding where we are, however, would be to recognize that when findings are limited by research design parameters, inferences drawn from the research are likewise limited. More than this, we should recognize certain limiting conditions inherent in current approaches and methods.

Methods and Their Limits

Like much of social scientific work in general, research in this applied field is likely to be carried out in one or some combination of three methods: survey research, including questionnaires and interviews; observation, including participant observation; and secondary analysis of data. Each approach has its value and its limits, even when carried out well. More significantly, however, all invariably use aggregate data. Information is gathered about individual responses or observed individual behavior, background, or demographic characteristics, and then aggregated in some set of statistics or generalizations. The results are then often used to make inferences about social interaction, community structures and processes, and these are narratively related to a tall building habitat. It seems obvious that such logical leaps are hardly defensible and that however valuable such studies are they cannot explain interaction or community processes.

The values and limits of research methods have been described at length in the methodological literature of the social sciences and need not be elaborated here. A few examples, however, are in order as general illustrations of issues in contemporary research and guides to future work.

Cross-sectional survey research

Cross-sectional case studies, even when well designed, administered, and analyzed, cannot yield vital information about ongoing behavior in such a manner that building height can be singled out as a significant variable. Interview and mail questionnaire responses at best tap attitudes or reports at a comparatively narrow time segment. Yet, it seems reasonable to hypothesize that with regard to both "normal" associational processes and social morbidities, a single time measure can barely begin to yield knowledge about how building height and design are causally involved with behavior. Longitudinal panel techniques and/or observational methods have typically been used to check survey research findings; but they have serious limitations of their own.

Observational research

This technique has been widely used, especially in gathering information about children's play habits in tall building habitats. A singular methodological problem in such research lies in the difficulty of generating random or representative samples. Conventionally, children are first observed at play and thereafter identified as residing at high- or low-rise levels. Or, if samples of respondents are first drawn for an interview schedule in some stratified or random manner, and subsequently observations are made on subsamples of children, the final samples of children broken down by other control variables may be too small to yield significant results. It should be noted that most extant research generally avoids such sampling questions by resorting to ad hoc observations of numbers of subjects which the researcher believes or asserts are large enough or representative enough to confirm the observer's conclusions. Most often, such impressionistic observations are linked to a general response pattern of mothers revealing their apprehensions about loss of supervision or visual contact with children because of building height. At best, inferences drawn from such a combination of survey and observational research may serve as hypotheses for further examination. Any or all of the confounding errors previously noted may operate to greater or lesser degree to obscure underlying processes.

Quasi-experimental controls and objective testing

One study in particular should be mentioned here because of the combination of sophisticated research design and methods used. Höweler compared the cognitive, social and emotional behavior of children living in single family houses with those living in tall buildings. Two groups of 132 children each were chosen from six different neighborhoods in Malmö, Sweden. They were matched so that background characteristics such as age, sex, father's occupation and income, length of residence, and number of siblings were controlled. The children were then tested using a projective test (Rosenzweig Picture-Frustration Test), they were given a scholastic achievement test, their parents were interviewed (using a closed-ended, rigorous schedule), and their teachers provided systematic assessments of personality traits and behavior characteristics. The children were then systematically observed at play areas. The data were analyzed (factor analysis of scholastic achievement data, extensive statistical tests on data from teacher's observations), reliability and validity analysis completed in the context of quasi-experimental design criteria. (Campbell and Stanley's classic 1963 work was used.)

> The results indicate very few clearly-definable differences between children living in the two different kinds of residential areas. Clearly definable differences are only discernible when frequent visits are made to the various playgrounds: children living in areas of multi-storey blocks of flats visit playgrounds more frequently than children in areas with one-family houses. Other differences are normally found in one age-group only. Some of the differences are further supported by results from the other age-groups: these results also point in a similar direction [Höweler 1973, p. iv].

Secondary analysis of data

Data generated for purposes unrelated to those of later researchers may be useful if, and only if, such data are amenable to the statistical analysis required by later research purposes. Aggregated data are notoriously resistant to disaggregation and reaggregation to make it fit different purposes. An example of such a study is Oscar Newman's *Defensible Space.*

The data base consisted of crime rates, and demographic and building design characteristics from 100 or 133 New York City Housing Authority Projects for 1969. (The number of project cases varies in different results reported.) Newman's basic empirical finding is given as, "Crime rate has been found to increase almost proportionately with building height, as illustrated by figure 15" (Newman 1973, p. 27). The figure cited, however, does not support the author's contention. Quite the contrary, it invites attention to the inherent weaknesses in such studies. The figure is a scattergram plotting felony rate in crime per 1,000 population against building height in number of floors (grouped in categories of different number of floors, not people!) for 100 buildings of uniform type "visible as a separate entity from the surrounding community." The sample drawn, then, cannot be said to represent the population of all New York City housing projects and the findings should be appropriately qualified. The resultant scatter of cases in the figure *does not* cluster along a linear slope representing means. In fact, the scatter of cases is so broad that visually it would appear any correlation is extremely weak. The regression line *implied* in the figure by asterisks represents only the means of X values (building height). No least squares criteria are applied. Nonetheless, the finding as written, stating an "almost" proportionate increase of Y as X increases implies the regression equation, $Y = a + bX$, and a positive correlation is asserted. The multiple regression analysis examined independent variables other than building height, such as various design factors and socioeconomic characteristics. The tables published in Appendix A of the book are most ambiguous. At best they may be interpreted to suggest that of all variables related to crime in tall buildings, height may account for a small portion of the variance, but only in combination with other variables. Most importantly, however, the authors of the Methodological Appendix correctly note that some problems in using stepwise multiple regression analysis (and some "other difficulties") ". . . would tend to make initial proof of any hypothesis concerning physical environment and crime rate rather difficult, utilizing this statistical approach" (Newman, p. 231). The stated problems include extensive multicolinearity among variables. This alone should preclude *any* valid inferences from being drawn from such secondary analysis.

The theoretical problems present in *Defensible Space* have been described previously (Cooperman 1974, p. 93). At several places Newman notes that upper and/or middle income people have successfully lived in tall buildings (although no evidence is presented on this point). In general, however, extensive physical design recommendations are made in the book to reduce crime and based on the assertion, "It is the apartment tower itself . . . that is the real and final villain of the piece" (Newman, p. 25).

Review

Thus far, we have noted that research which attempts to test out arguments about tall buildings and morbidity effects is fraught with problems in design, methodology, and technique. Given adequate research resources and assuming application of more rigorous or exacting research criteria, advances might be forthcoming in the development of empirical generalizations. Several lasting difficulties remain with such work, however. As previously noted, the use of aggregate data on individual characteristics can only provide the most indirect explanations for phenomena which are essentially interactional or behavioral. Second, empirical findings correlating morbidity pattern with building height or design for certain groups of people may be lacking in any theoretical framework which would explain the generalizations, or from which independent, testable measures can be derived. There is a vast logical difference between the following: (a) alleging a correlation between building height and crime, or between height and community disorganization and then afterward asserting an ad hoc untested allegation about why this should be, and (b) constructing a theoretical set of statements from which alternative hypotheses may be derived to test the statements under adequate controls. Such a theory is likely to be based on asssumptions about "normal" social processes (i.e., which explain forms of interaction in universal terms). Any predictions about morbidity effects are thus logically entailed in the general or partial theory rather than remaining unrelated to general behavior processes.

If we do not proceed toward some larger theoretical understanding, researchers may well attempt to devise more and more sensitive research designs incorporating more and more independent variables which may be suspected of accounting for some fractional variance of a morbidity pattern. Inevitably, causal path analysis would be used. This is to say that it is likely that a large number of factors are involved in tall building social behavior processes and sophisticated statistical models can be hypothetically advanced to discover them. There is, however, an alternate research strategy which we would recommend for development along with relevant statistical methods.

NETWORK ANALYSIS

Under conditions of causal complexity, mathematical models can be most helpful in describing logically ideal formulations of real processes. In network analysis a technique exists which permits explanation of social interaction over a wide range of levels of abstraction. At comparatively descriptive levels, friendship, kinship, and neighboring relationships can be *logically* related, and for tall building research purposes the structural plots of such ties can be contrasted with physical design maps reflecting building structural parameters. At theoretical levels of abstraction, digraph theory "can serve as a mathematical model of the structural properties of any empirical system consisting of relationships among pairs of elements" (Harary et al. 1965, p. 2). Matrix algebra is valuable in computing both general characteristics of models, such as the density, boundary, and structure or cluster type, and specific characteristics of elements, such as adjacency and reachability of any one element to others, and path lengths. Measures may also be designed to report the relative strength of bonds. Hence, the formal properties of social relationships may be calculated and theoretical propositions derived.

In tall building research (as in other research on social relations) points represent individuals and lines (or paths) represent relationships (or ties). Digraph theory begins with four undefined terms and four axioms logically relating sets of points and lines to each other. From these, theorems and corollaries are derived which describe such network properties as *connectedness* of points (adjacency and distance, for example) and path lengths. In social research such models can be highly suggestive of human interaction. Figure 2-1, taken from Mitchell, exemplifies three contrasting prototypical structures for a group of five.

Other matrices, such as *reachability* and *adjacency* provide basic structural information about networks. There is a growing technical literature in this field and such significant concepts as *network density* are in the process of being refined. (See, for example, the excellent article by Niemeijer, "Some Applications of the Notion of Density to Network Analysis," 1973.) While the recent development of network analysis owes much to such British social anthropologists as J. A. Barnes and J. C. Mitchell and others centered at the University of Manchester, sociometric studies which focused on residential structures and formal urban neighborhood research carried out twenty-five years ago were moving in similar directions (Festinger et al. 1950; Caplow and Forman 1950). Interestingly, the work by Caplow and Forman is often cited in support of a strong architectural determinist position. The milieu of that work was a low-rise, attached unit project for post-World War II veterans and their families. The population was homogeneous on almost every significant demographic and life style characteristic. With more advanced techniques now available it would be interesting to repeat the research under varied conditions with regard to population mix and building heights.

We cannot here discuss the numerous technical questions involved in conceptualizing, reporting, scoring and analyzing tall building networks. Briefly, the following should be noted:

1. The direction and linkages of the paths may be either constructed along single types of relationships (kinship or friendship or neighboring), or they may be plotted with regard to several types of ties to describe multiplex relationships. In the latter case, the use of a composite score, such as Caplow's Neighbor-

hood Interaction Scale, provides a means of analyzing general behavioral relationships. Shorter time interaction, such as conflict, can also be drawn as *action sets.*

2. A snowball interviewing procedure using a limited number of questions is a most economical way of gathering information on networks—or, if sampling errors are to be avoided in retrieving network data across a population, appropriate sampling procedures have been devised by Niemeijer (1973).

3. While computer analysis is necessary to handle large amounts of network data, a simple alternative exists for manipulating matrices up to 50 X 50 in size, which is economical and does not require special skills or computer access (Garbett 1968).

The Uses of Network Analysis

Physical structures are comparatively fixed and durable envelopes setting rough categorical limits to contained social relationships which vary in structure and process over time. Does building height *determine* specific relationships? Longitudinal network studies can provide accurate answers across a range of characteristics and quantitative values. This promises some closure to general design-behavior questions.

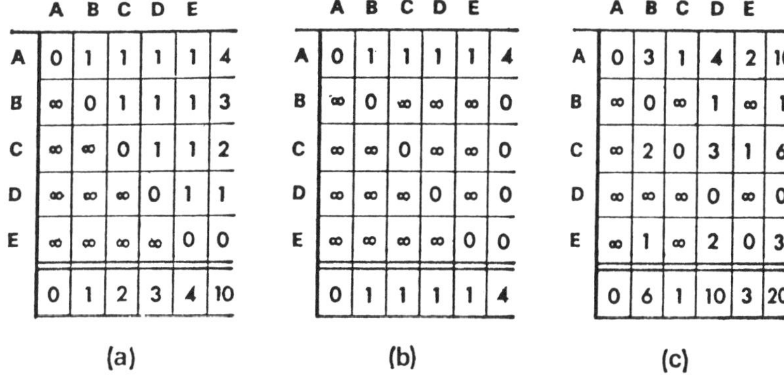

(a)

	A	B	C	D	E	
A	0	1	1	1	1	4
B	∞	0	1	1	1	3
C	∞	∞	0	1	1	2
D	∞	∞	∞	0	1	1
E	∞	∞	∞	∞	0	0
	0	1	2	3	4	10

(b)

	A	B	C	D	E	
A	0	1	1	1	1	4
B	∞	0	∞	∞	∞	0
C	∞	∞	0	∞	∞	0
D	∞	∞	∞	0	∞	0
E	∞	∞	∞	∞	0	0
	0	1	1	1	1	4

(c)

	A	B	C	D	E	
A	0	3	1	4	2	10
B	∞	0	∞	1	∞	1
C	∞	2	0	3	1	6
D	∞	∞	∞	0	∞	0
E	∞	1	∞	2	0	3
	0	6	1	10	3	20

The symbol ∞ indicates that the point at the head of the column cannot be reached from the point at the head of the row no matter how many steps are traversed.

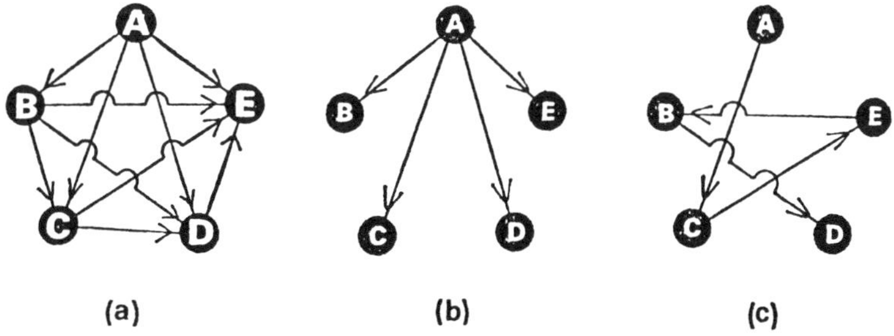

Figure 2-1
Network analysis. Reprinted with permission from *Social Networks in Urban Situations*, edited by J. Clyde Mitchell. Manchester: The University of Manchester Press, 1969, 1975 and Humanities Press, Inc., New Jersey, 1975. Copyright © 1975 by the Institute for African Studies.

Multi-unit residences have been used as partial indices of urbanism. Arguments abound that tall buildings themselves are more compatible with some life styles than with others and that they are especially antipathetic to families with children. Comparative network studies can provide objective, quantitative data on social interaction under varying population-design characteristics.

Arguments and questions about the type and degree of community relationships extant among tall building habitats can be clarified with this technique. A singular advantage is that ideological and nonanalytic conceptions of community are easily avoided. Moreover, definitional issues which have clouded recent urban community research (such as how are communities distinguishable from one another) are resolvable by reference to measures of network structure, or even by visual examination of linkages (see Craven and Wellman 1974). On this question, current research on social networks in the Cedar-Riverside new town, Minneapolis, indicates the presence of social networks varied in size and structure (density, distance, cluster linkages). Some networks are comparatively closed and short, comprising subcommunal clusters in the neighborhood; others reach radially across the neighborhood into other sectors of the Twin Cities area. A range of different types of structures is present including complex forms resembling the simpler three models given in Figure 2-1. The nine interconnecting buildings vary in height from 4 to 39 stories. Some 1,000 households contain about 2,100 people ranging widely in income, age, family structure and life style. There is no evidence as yet that building height significantly affects network structures.

Family and domicile relationships can be analyzed in broader network contexts. Bott's classic findings on conjugal role distinctions in networks of different degrees of connectedness can be tested in varied design and population characteristic situations (Bott 1971). Children's play networks can be related to parental structures. In general, the complex of familial, surrogate family, neighboring, and friendship patterns in urban areas can be sharply described. (For a study of family networks in Edinburgh, which highlights some of these points, see Cubbitt 1973.)

Statistical tests can be made of relationships between social morbidity rates for crime, delinquency, mental illness, etc., and network types. Controls for building height and design would then provide direct tests of interaction variables and design characteristics in relevant theoretical contexts. For example, the degree of network closure can be measured and related to crime rates, yielding tests of hypotheses about isolation, social controls, and building ties.

Social ties in residential structures can be compared with formal and informal networks in tall office buildings to discover if, at all, similar height conditions affect networks, regardless of their social function.

Research Designs of Tall Building Network Studies

Network analysis is a general technique which can be used (and has) in any number of ways. Tall building habitats are particularly appropriate for investigation because of the high potential of human interaction given a comparatively large population within a building. If network density is conceived as the percentage of actual interaction over the potential relations then we can assume that tall buildings will tend to be characterized by low measures of network density. As Niemeijer hypothesizes, "it is more difficult to organize a dense pattern of relations in a large group of people than in a small group" (Niemeijer 1973, p. 50). (On this point, in more general terms, see Michelson 1974, p.169.)

One fruitful approach would be to calculate for comparative tall building populations, densities that might be expected if people were randomly related to one another (random mesh) over a total building network. If examination of actual densities reveals departures from random mesh models, "one would suspect that some systematic factor is operating" (Niemeijer 1973, p.50).

A sample research project

Our research project design incorporates several features noted above. Random network calculations are to be made of tall building populations in several cities representing different demographic-life style characteristics. It is anticipated that differences in associative predispositions will be found, say, between a retired set of people with life experiences of richly textured communal interaction, on the one hand (North Miami Beach condominium dwellers) and single students whose socialization into housing indicates a previous history of comparatively low-rise, low network density (Minneapolis, Cedar-Riverside new town residents). Several other urban areas are included in the sample. Actual networks are then calculated as noted above. Comparisons are to be made (a) between ideal random models and actual behavior and (b) between corrected density scores for people at different floor levels. Examination of other network characteristics, such as clustering, is also planned.

Michelson's work, previously cited, is extremely suggestive concerning this kind of research, although his study did not use these techniques directly, but rather indicated the need for using both subjective and objective methods. He writes,

> . . . the "objective" picture is one of lack of isolation among apartment dwellers. They are no more isolated, according to the various measures here, than are those living in other types of dwellings. There are, however, different *paths* to friendship as a consequence of the wife's family-employment status, which in turn tends to coincide largely with the selection of housing and location—so much so that in practical terms these factors must all be considered simultaneously. Women living in high-rise apartments by and large meet even their local friends through *communities of interest* rather than through *territorially based neighborhoods.* While they have friends in their local areas, the local area itself is not a factor in originally making acquaintances [Michelson 1974, p. 169].

CONCLUSION

We agree with Michelson about the need for analyzing both subjective and objective data in tall building research. (This is clearly not to be confused with arguments about the comparative worth of "subjective" and "objective" methods.) Network analysis, we believe, can enrich our knowledge of contemporary urban life by detailing its "crystalline" structures and by explaining behavior with reference to such structures. It cannot provide direct information about subjective, emotive aspects of urban life (but see Mitchell 1973, p.27). Nor can it replace well-designed and appropriately qualified survey, observational and secondary data analysis. But it is compatible with other theories of potential value in this field, such as exchange theory (Mitchell 1973, p.25). When used either as simple logical plots of relationships, or as abstract mathematical formulations, it is highly heuristic with regard to new design-behavior hypotheses. As such, it may well aid in the development of ultimate research strategies for the future.

REFERENCES

Boissevain, J., and Mitchell, J. C. (eds.). *Network Analysis. Studies in Human Interaction.* The Hague: Mouton, 1973.

Bott, E. *Family and Social Network.* 2nd edition. London: Tavistock Publications, 1971.

Campbell, D., and Stanely, J. *Experimental and Quasi-Experimental Designs For Research.* Chicago: Rand McNally and Company, 1963.

Caplow, T. "Definition and Measurement of the Ambience." *Social Forces* 34 (October 1955).

Caplow, T., and Forman, R. "Neighborhood Interaction in a Homogeneous Community." *American Sociological Review* 15 (June 1950):357-366.

Carnahan, D.; Guest, A.; and Galle, O. "Congestion, Concentration and Behavior: Research on the Study of Urban Population Density." *The Sociological Quarterly* 15 (Autumn 1974): 488-506.

Cooperman, D. "Density, Design and Social Organization." In *Man-Environmental Interactions, EDRA 5,* edited by D. Carson, vol. 1. Environmental Design Research Association, 1974.

Craven, P., and Wellman, B. "The Network City." In *The Community, Approaches and Applications,* edited by M. Effrat. New York: The Free Press, 1974.

Cubbitt, T. "Network Density Among Urban Families." In *Network Analysis. Studies in Human Interaction,* edited by J. Boissevain and J. C. Mitchell. The Hague: Mouton, 1973.

Deutscher, I. *What We Say/What We Do.* Glenview, Illinois: Scott, Foresman and Company, 1973.

Festinger, L.; Schachter, S.; and Back, K. *Social Pressures in Informal Groups.* New York: Harper and Brothers, 1950.

Garbett, G. "The Application of Optical Coincidence Cards to the Matrices of Digraphs of Social Networks." *Sociology* 2, 3 (September 1968): 313-331.

Harary, F.; Norman, R.; and Cartwright, D. *Structural Models: An Introduction to the Theory of Directed Graphs.* New York: John Wiley and Sons, 1965.

Höweler, M. *En Studie av Barn Från Låghus–Och Höghusområden.* (*A Study of Children from Lowrise and Highrise Areas.*) Lund, Sweden: Pedagogiska Institutionen, University of Lund, 1973.

Michelson, W. "The Reconciliation of 'Subjective' and 'Objective' Data on Physical Environment in the Community: The Case of Social Contact in High-Rise Apartments." In *The Community, Approaches and Applications,* edited by M. Effrat. New York: The Free Press, 1974.

Mitchell, J. C. "Networks, Norms and Institutions." In *Network Analysis. Studies in Human Interaction,* edited by J. Boissevain and J. C. Mitchell. The Hague: Mouton, 1973.

Newman, O. *Defensible Space.* New York: Macmillan Publishing Co., 1973.

Niemeijer, R. "Some Applications of the Notion of Density to Network Analysis." In *Network Analysis. Studies in Human Interaction,* edited by J. Boissevain and J. C. Mitchell. The Hague: Mouton, 1973.

Wekerle, G. "Vertical Village: The Social World of a Highrise Complex." Ph.D. dissertation, Northwestern University, 1974.

Wekerle, G., and Hall, E. "High Rise Living: Can The Same Design Serve Young and Old?" *Ekistics* 33, 196 (March 1972): 186-191.

Part II

The Tall Building and Its Neighborhood

3

The Impact of High-Rise Structures on the Community

H. A. Simon
University of Illinois

INTRODUCTION AND OBJECTIVES

An interdisciplinary study on the impact of high buildings has been in progress at the Circle Campus of the University of Illinois since January 1974. The study is supported by a grant from the National Science Foundation. Participating departments include economics, energy engineering, political science, sociology, and systems engineering. The Survey Research Laboratory on campus has assisted in conducting an interview survey of residents in two high buildings in Chicago as part of the study.

The main goal of the study has been to identify and examine those impacts that are important in their influence on the quality of city growth. Improved understanding must engender opportunities for enlightened planning so that on the one hand deleterious and on the other beneficial effects can be predicted ahead of time. The ultimate goal, which goes beyond the capacities of this study, would be the development of a mechanism which makes all the relevant information on impacts readily accessible in a concise, easily understandable form for planning purposes. This study will answer some of the questions that are pertinent for planning purposes, will probably pose a number that should be answered, and will provide a framework within which such information can be collected.

STUDY DESIGN AND METHODOLOGY

In a multifaceted problem of this kind it pays to conceptualize its components in a clear and simple manner. The impacts are most conveniently categorized as, economic, environmental, political, social, and technological. Human response to these impacts may be expected from several clearly identifiable groups. Again for convenience, these groups may be categorized into, users, nonusers, developers, and planners.

Users comprise those people who either live or work in the building. The building is of course designed to satisfy the needs of those who will use it. Nonusers do not make use of the building but are impacted by its presence in a variety of ways. Several subcategories of nonusers may need to be distinguished, including nearby residents and people engaged in commerce. Another broad category of nonusers includes service personnel who may fight fires, control crime, deliver mail, pick up garbage, manage, clean, or maintain the building and its equipment. Residents either in the user or nonuser class may require further subdivision by age, socioeconomic level, or ethnic or religious identification.

Developers include also the financiers, architects, and builders, who achieve their livelihood in part by providing a usable structure. Although their interests are essentially economic, they are constrained by the acceptability of the impacts that their structures bring about. Some of this is formalized in building codes, but much depends on the experience and good judgment of the developers.

Finally, the planners endeavor in their decision-making role to interpret what is best for the city. They in their turn respond to the pressures arising from each of the impact categories.

Each of the above groups uses a different ordering of priorities in evaluating situations concerning high-rise buildings. A developer will accentuate economic return, while a resident user may feel that comfort and proximity to place of work are paramount. The resident nonusers, however, may be most concerned by neighborhood congestion.

To complicate the picture further it must be recognized that certain impacts are short term and primary by nature. An example would be the additional congestion that can occur as soon as a building is put into use. Others are longer term and may arise as part of feedback process. Hence experience of congestion in some areas may cause a social response in others that will eventually influence the zoning ordinances governing those areas. As another example, the occurrence of high-rise buildings in one area may engender improved transportation facilities serving that area so that in the long run congestion is relieved.

The impacts and responses are revealed by a number of measures. It is apparent from the above description that the number of measures needed to reveal every impact and response combination is extremely large. This study, while endeavoring to recognize the full perspective of the problem, is concentrating on only a few measures.

The approach of the current study makes use of two types of resource: The first may be termed primary data and includes data that are readily available now either in published form or on tape. Secondary data are not readily available, are usually diffuse in character, and require considerable effort to gather them into a meaningful form.

To assist in assembling information in the latter category required by the project team, a series of interviews were conducted with the residents of two large Chicago buildings. The first is the John Hancock Building, located at 175 East Delaware, which has forty-eight floors of apartments out of a total of ninety-five and is mixed commercial and residential. The second is the building at 2800 North Lake Shore Drive, which has 666 units and is forty-two floors high. The latter building is completely residential. The interviews were conducted by the Survey Research Laboratory, which completed 150 interviews at each building; forty-one questions were asked covering many areas including trip information, location motivation, living conditions, and political activity.

Different methods are being used by the groups within the project and each of these is discussed briefly below.

Economics

Professors H. W. Bowman and J. F. McDonald of the economics department are examining the impact of high-rise structures on land values. Olcutt's Blue Book of land values is being used to determine the magnitude of the change and also the extent to which high-rise buildings are caused by increased land values and the extent to which they are the source of high land values. They are also examining the change in transportation patterns, and automobile ownership resulting from a movement to a centrally located high-rise building. This latter problem is being tackled through the results of the questionnaire. From the same source it is hoped to study the influence of environmental amenities as a factor in determining whether or not the central city can compete with the suburbs. Certain anomalies in the distribution of land values in Chicago as a whole are also being studied to determine their relationship to the intensity of development associated with high-rise structures.

Sociology

Professor D. Amick is looking at the occurrence of social pathologies such as murder, suicide, and child abuse and their relationship, if any, to population density and the location of high-rise buildings. The areas studied will be derived from census tracts in which people and buildings can be located using a computer program known as ADMATCH. Relationships between the incidence of pathologies can be studied using ecological characteristics such as median income, education, and racial composition as control variables.

Resources drawn on include the 1970 Census of Population and Housing, the coroner's office, the police department, the Department of Children and Family Services, and the City Office of Buildings.

Political science

Professor J. Cook and F. P. Scioli are concerned with the political impacts arising from policy decisions made by public and private decision-making bodies. With this motivation they are trying to assess the extent to which political impacts of high-rise buildings have been evaluated by social science researchers.

Systems engineering

Professor F. G. Miller is concentrating on the whole question of traffic congestion. Where possible he will be using traffic counts from before and after a building's construction to assess the impact. He will also be attempting to obtain realistic estimates of the traffic congestion to be anticipated in a number of cases where high rises are currently being proposed. Finally it is hoped to examine the cordon count history of the city of Chicago as a whole in an endeavor to separate out the influences of high-rise structures.

Energy engineering

The author, and principle coordinator of the project, is looking at technological impacts of various types including impacts on water supply, energy supply, and sewage disposal. The pertinent data in areas such as these are extremely diffuse and difficult to assemble, even with the excellent cooperation afforded by most city departments.

As each particular impact is unearthed it becomes clear that the results are not very meaningful unless they can be seen in a much broader context both in space and time. The impact of one large building in Chicago on the water supply system is likely to be very small. However this can only be truly judged if the current status and future plans for the water delivery system are understood both in the area near the building and also in the city as a whole. A similar argument applies, by analogy, to other delivery systems on the urban scene.

Controls on the type of growth permitted by the city are reflected in the city zoning ordinances. This is another area to be studied to try and determine the influences exerted both on and by high-rise buildings.

FINDINGS

It is still too early to report the findings achieved under this study. As already mentioned, the interviews of residents of the two buildings chosen have been completed. In general the interviewing work went well. The refusal rate averaged only 12 percent and most respondents were both cooperative and interested. The data collected have been analyzed and are now being used by the project team for correlative purposes.

The land values, social pathologies, traffic congestion, zoning ordinance, and delivery system studies are proceeding independently.

IMPLICATIONS FOR ENVIRONMENTAL DESIGN

The implications of a study such as this one could be far-reaching. The benefits of high-rise buildings apart from the economic return to the developers and builders can be great from the point of view of tax returns to the city and commercial development. On the other hand, there may be a considerable penalty in certain areas due to change of social mix, increased congestion and crowding, and additional operating cost. The city must be concerned about the future directions implicit in its planning process. The models derived from this study should help in this regard partly through the relationship revealed between such variables as land values or social pathologies and intensity of development, and also by an identification of the components and people that comprise the total environment.

4

The Impact of Tall Buildings on Users and Neighbors

Gilda Moss Haber
University of Maryland

INTRODUCTION

This chapter deals with a study of individual and neighbor responses to tall buildings. The objective of the study was to explore attitudes toward tall buildings of a group of potential users, namely college students. Mainly we explored what this group of people liked and disliked about tall buildings, and if age, sex, race, and class had anything to do with their attitude towards tall buildings. Significantly different attitudes to tall buildings were found between men and women, white and black, higher and lower income groups. Since there had recently been a popular movie dealing with tall buildings, *Towering Inferno*, we also asked if people had seen it and if they thought it affected their feelings about tall buildings. The results of this research should be viewed as exploratory and as a guide to further research.

METHODOLOGY AND THE SAMPLE

This demonstration experiment was initiated by the author, but carried out in the course of, and with the help of, a class on "The City," Sociology 473, at Maryland University. A pilot study was done on 260 students in three classes using an open-ended question asking people to list things they liked and disliked about tall buildings. A content analysis was done on the list of responses, and a questionnaire was made up from it, which included twenty-two items under the heading, "things liked about tall buildings," and eighteen items listed under the heading "things not liked about tall buildings." Added to these two lists of items were questions on age, sex, race, approx-

My thanks to my students, particularly those in Sociology 473, "The City," for their hard work and enthusiasm; Dr. Kenneth C. W. Kammeyer, chairman of the sociology department, for computer funds; and to Mrs. Gladys Graham, secretary of the sociology department, for having this chapter typed. Thanks also to Dr. Robert Wehrli, chief, Architectural Research Section at the National Bureau of Standards, and to Edward Budnick for editorial comments on earlier drafts of this chapter.

imate family income, father and mother's education, marital status, and intended family size. Respondents were asked how many stories they thought constituted a tall building, if there are tall buildings in their neighborhood, and their reactions to them. Their opinions were sought as to whether tall buildings should be restricted by height, place, or by specific function. They were asked if they had seen *Towering Inferno* and how it affected them. Finally, they answered open-ended questions on what they thought would improve tall buildings.

A random sample of twenty classes totaling 300 students was drawn from the five-thousand course offerings in the spring 1975 catalog at Maryland University at College Park. Permission of the instructor was sought to have the questionnaire distributed. Where it was refused the class was dropped from the sample. In addition, the dean of graduate studies approved the study as being acceptable to standards required for research on human subjects under the law, in accordance with current university research procedures.

Students from the author's classes handed out the questionnaires and coded the responses. A simple computer analysis was designed for this exploratory study of responses on "things liked and disliked" about tall buildings; then cross-tabulations with chi squares and Pearson's rho were made to determine significant differences on items liked and disliked, by age, sex, race, and class.* Social class was measured by declared approximate family income and father's education. We also examined the relationship between living or working near tall buildings and reaction to them. We tested for relationships between seeing *Towering Inferno* and attitudes to tall buildings, perceived height of tall buildings, and preferences for tall buildings. Only those cross-tabulated variables having a chi square of 0.05 or less are discussed in this chapter.

*For those unfamiliar with the use of chi square and Pearson's rho, chi square measures whether a more-than-chance relationship occurs between two variates; Pearson's rho examines the intensity of this relationship.

A DESCRIPTION OF THE SAMPLE

The sample was composed of 300 undergraduate students at the University of Maryland, College Park Campus, with the following distribution on age, sex, race, and marital status: Sixty-six percent were between the ages of twenty and twenty-five, and about 17% each were under twenty or over twenty-six, to about age forty maximum. Forty-one percent of the sample was male and 55% female; the sex of 4% of the sample could not be determined. Eighty-four percent of the sample were white, 12% black, and 1% oriental; and 3% called themselves "other." The campus lists about 6% unknown on race, which may be the extra 6% blacks in this sample. Blacks and other non-whites were combined for analysis. Comparisons on the basis of race therefore are usually phrased in terms of white and non-white, with blacks forming the majority of non-whites.

The student respondents came from a variety of majors categorized under six major headings: agriculture and life sciences (8%), arts and humanities (17%), behavioral and social sciences (25%), human and community resources (6%), and combined in mathematics, physics, science, and engineering (6%). The remaining 6% who answered regarding major were undecided; 31% did not answer as to major.

Seventy-one percent of the sample were single, 17% married, 7% engaged. Regarding approximate family income, 11% checked less than $10,000, 40% $10,000-20,000, and 44% over $20,000; 78% of the sample were unmarried and probably stated income of their parents. The very low incomes of under $5,000 more likely represent the newly married students struggling to make it on their own, their spouses' earnings, or self-supporting students.

Regarding birthplace, 5% were born in a rural area, nearly 20% in a small town, and nearly 50% in a city. Twenty-five percent were born in a suburb. However, an estimated 50% born in small towns and cities moved out to the suburbs. The group is therefore probably upwardly mobile and affluent. Since this is a state college with nearly 90% of the undergraduates being state residents, it can be assumed that many moved out of the major cities of Baltimore and Washington, D.C.

The sample, therefore, is composed of a largely single, young, white population, with a representative number of people, compared to campus statistics, in each major. About 50% are socially mobile in the sense of having moved from city and small towns to the suburbs. They are mainly Maryland residents. Mean family income is about $25,000 per annum; this probably represents the combined income of a working father and mother. The counties around the college, Prince George's and Montgomery, have among the highest per capita incomes in the nation. Fifty percent of the parents have a college education, ranging from lower to advanced degrees.

QUESTIONNAIRE ON TALL BUILDINGS

Respondents were asked to indicate at what height they thought a building *began* to be tall. There were five choices, 6-10, 11-20, 21-30, 31-40, and over 40 floors. The findings suggest that there was a relationship between how tall a person thinks a tall building is, and liking height, feelings of safety, liking steel, feelings of prestige and power, and feeling close to stores. On the dislikes end, there was a relationship between the perception of what height makes a building tall and fear of fire; feeling the skyline is spoiled; that concrete and glass are disliked as materials; that there is annoyance with neighboring tall buildings; and finally, that there is a particular story or stories of a tall building most "comfortable for occupancy and that the location of this story(ies) depends upon how tall the respondent feels the tall building is. Only a few of these findings will be discussed here.

FINDINGS

The findings will be reported in the following order:

1. A listing of items liked and disliked by respondents in rank order
2. A discussion of those items liked and disliked, on the basis of age, sex, race, and class, where X^2 had a p of 0.05 or less significance
3. The relationship between having neighboring tall buildings and liking or disliking tall buildings
4. Materials liked in tall buildings
5. A summary of the findings and implications for environmental design or management of space use
6. Respondents suggestions for improving tall buildings.

Findings on Things Liked about Tall Buildings

A ranked listing of things liked about tall buildings

Table 4-1 lists the items presented in the questionnaire for respondents to circle, under the headings "things liked about tall buildings."

Obviously, "liking the view of scenery" and "be-

TABLE 4-1
Things Liked About Tall Buildings

Things Liked in Tall Buildings	*Percent of Respondents Saying They Liked this Item in a Tall Building*
Like view of scenery	80
Like to see far	63
Economical on space	38
Tall buildings are aesthetic	18
Convenient, near stores, each	18
Like height	14
Good for social life, meeting people	13
Like facilities	11
Good for recreation, no responsibilities	11
Like feeling of prestige or power	9
Quiet	7
Reasonable rent	4
Safe	2

ing able to see far" were things liked about a tall building. Thirty-eight percent of respondents were aware of the spatial economics of tall buildings. After this, the responses on things liked about tall buildings dropped sharply until a low of 2% indicated liking tall buildings because they are safe. As will be seen later, safety factors were the most frequently criticized, and most often by people who had seen *Towering Inferno*.

"Liked" variables—by age, sex, race, and class

There is a significant difference between those under twenty and those over twenty regarding liking to see the view or scenery from tall buildings. Those over twenty checked that they like the view more often than those under twenty (Table 4-2). Sex might also account for aesthetic appreciation, although a higher proportion of college women are older than the men, with many returning to college after marriage and children. In this study, women like views from tall buildings significantly more often than men do (Table 4-3).

In another study by this author (1974) on response to room by sex, it was found that males responded in terms of creature comforts, i.e., whether the seat was comfortable or whether the windows were sufficiently darkened for the satisfactory showing of movies. Females responded in terms of total arrangement of the rooms, and in terms of aesthetics, referring to color, materials, and appearance. In the 1974 study, women responded to the question "what do you like about this room" twice as often as men did, suggesting a greater involvement in the room. In the study reported here, though, men and women responded proportionately to their numbers in the sample. Overall findings suggest, however, that women enjoy appearance more than men do. Although sample analysis indicates that women like the view or scenery from a tall building significantly more than men do, they do not like height as an aspect of tall buildings as often as men do (Table 4-4).

The fact that men choose "liking heights" significantly more often than women regarding things they like about a tall building fits in with the stereotype of

TABLE 4-2
Age and Liking the View from Tall Buildings

	17-19		*20 & Over*		*Total*	
	#	%	#	%	#	%
Like view	36	69	205	83	241	80
Don't/NA	16	41	41	16	57	20
Total	52	100	246	109	298	100

$X^2_{1df} = 5.5, p < .02.$*
*Findings on cross-tabulations are only reported when X^2 is significant between .001 and .05.

TABLE 4-3
Sex and Liking the View from Tall Buildings

	Male		*Female*		*Total Responding*	
	#	%	#	%	#	%
Like view	69	56	115	70	184	64
Don't/NA	55	44	49	30	104	36
Total	124	100	164	100	288*	100

$X^2_{1df} = 6.4, p = < .01.$
*Totals vary from the number 300 according to the number of people who respond to that question.

TABLE 4-4
Sex and Liking Heights

	Male		*Female*		*Total*	
	#	%	#	%	#	%
Like height	27	22	11	6	38	13
Don't/NA	97	78	153	94	250	87
Total	124	100	164	100	288	100

$X^2_{1df} = 14, p < .001.$

men being bolder and braver and possibly with the Freudian interpretation of sexual pleasure from flying, for which height would seem to be a prerequisite. Males also liked tall buildings as symbols of prestige and power twice as often as women did.

More likely men are more mechanically oriented in this society than women and can see great heights without being as afraid of the dangers as women seem to be. On the issue of the safey of tall buildings, only five people in the total sample said that they liked tall buildings because they were safe, and all of those who checked this category were men. In addition, three of these five men were non-whites.

From the above information it appears that there is some difference between men and women regarding the aesthetic values of tall buildings, at least when the tall building is looked out of. But although women more often admire scenery, men more often like height.

Sixty-three percent of the sample said they liked tall buildings from the point of view of being able to see far. However, a significantly larger number of those twenty-one and under like a tall building because they can see far (Table 4-5).

One might try to explain this finding by saying younger people might be more idealistic and symbolically like to "see far," that as we get older we limit our horizons somewhat. This is a subjective interpretation of the author's. An unexpected difference in the sexes, however, is that women chose liking to see far significantly more often than men did. This, and the age factor, could only be explained by further research on sex differences in attitudes toward tall buildings.

To summarize, then, women, more than men like the view or scenery and also like to see far as aspects of liking a tall building, but they do not see it as safe. Men, also, but to a lesser extent, appreciate the view or scenery; they also like to be able to see far, but to a lesser extent than the women in the sample. Men like heights more than women do, and all of those who did answer that they liked the safety aspects of tall buildings were men. Women appear to like aesthetics; men, particularly non-whites, take more risks at least in their stated attitudes to tall buildings. Although 18% of the sample said they liked tall buildings because they were aesthetic, no significant differences were indicated due to age or sex. However, at the 0.10 level of significance on the chi square, there was an interesting class difference. Respondents whose fathers had a college education, particularly if the father had an advanced degree, liked the aesthetic aspects of tall buildings more than those whose fathers had less than a college education. Education, as a class factor, has some influence on the ability to perceive or be aware of aesthetic surroundings. Haber's study (1974) found that students with a higher paternal educational background were more critical of their environment than students with fathers who had less than a college education.

The last response to be discussed in detail on the list headed "things liked about tall buildings" is the

TABLE 4-5
Age and Liking to See Far

	21 & Under		*Over 21*		*Total*	
	#	%	#	%	#	%
Like to see far	123	67	68	58	191	64
Don't/NA	59	33	49	42	108	36
Total	182	100	117	100	299	100

$X^2_{1df} = 6, p < .02.$

TABLE 4-6
Sex and Liking to See Far

	Men		*Women*		*Total*	
	#	%	#	%	#	%
Like to see far	69	56	115	70	184	63
Don't/NA	55	44	49	30	108	37
Total	124	100	164	100	292	100

$X^2_{1df} = 6.4, p < .02.$

TABLE 4–7
Paternal Education and Seeing Tall Buildings as Aesthetic

	High School		College and Up		Total	
	#	%	#	%	#	%
Tall buildings are aesthetic	15	13	38	22	53	18
Not/NA	103	87	134	78	237	82
Total	118	100	172	100	290	100

$X^2_{1df} = 3.6, p < .10.$

TABLE 4–8
Race and Seeing Tall Buildings as Spatially Economical

	Whites		Non-Whites		Total	
	#	%	#	%	#	%
Economical	104	41	11	24	115	39
Not/NA	149	59	34	76	183	61
Total	253	100	45	100	298	100

$X^2_{1df} = 4, p < .05.$

response that tall buildings were economical in the use of space. Thirty-eight percent of the respondents checked that this was so in their opinion. There are some significant differences in response by race and by class, that is, by family income.

Whites answered almost twice as often as non-whites that they saw tall buildings as being economical on space (Table 4–8). Although this difference might be due to race alone, it could also be due to a class factor, since it is well known that the average income of non-whites is at least only 60% that of whites. Likewise as a class factor, non-whites receive less education than have whites. Further, those whose fathers have a higher education also perceive tall buildings as being more economical on space usage. Particularly those whose fathers had advanced degrees felt tall buidlings were more spatially economical (Table 4–9).

Summary

To summarize the main responses on things liked about a tall building: 80% responded that they liked the view or scenery from a tall building; those over twenty and women chose liking the view significantly more often than did those under twenty and men. This was thought to be due, perhaps, to the greater aesthetic development of people over twenty, and of women. Another possible reason might be the small amount of experience that younger people, who are also more frequently born in the suburbs, have with tall buildings. If this idea is correct then it suggests that those who have more exposure to tall buildings like them better. We would also like to examine whether perception of a tall building as

TABLE 4–9
Father's Education and Seeing Tall Buildings as Spatially Economical

	High		College		M.A.		Ph.D. etc.		Total	
	#	%	#	%	#	%	#	%	#	%
Economical	47	39	29	30	19	44	18	56	113	39
Not/NA	71	61	68	70	24	56	14	44	177	61
Total	118	100	97	100	43	100	32	100	290	100

$X^2_{3df} = 8, p < .05$

being over ten stories high leads people to like tall buildings more. These ideas will be explored after completing this section.

Men liked heights more than did women. The 2% who responded that tall buildings were liked because they were safe were all men, and most of those, non-white men. The under twenty-one people, and women, liked seeing far significantly more often than those over twenty-one and men. This might be attributed to idealism or good eyesight. Higher class respondents thought tall buildings were more economical on space, suggesting that education brings more awareness of community needs.

Findings on Things Disliked about Tall Buildings

Ranked in order of frequency of selection

The items listed under "what do you dislike about tall buildings" are listed in Table 4-10 by percentage of respondents. Forty percent said that if they had to choose between living or working in the lower, middle, or upper third of a tall building, they would choose the lower third. Seventeen percent said they would choose the middle third, 18% the upper third, 10% said they wouldn't live in a tall building at all, 2% that they would not work in a tall building at all.

TABLE 4-10
Things Disliked About Tall Buildings

Things Disliked in Tall Buildings	*Percent of Respondents Saying They Disliked this Item in a Tall Building*
Hate waiting for elevators	62
Miss greenery	61
Fear fire	55
Tall buildings are impersonal	52
Tall buildings are monotonous	44
It's hard to get outside tall buildings	41
Fear being stuck in an elevator	37
Dislike having no control over environment	31
Dislike heights	31
Neighbors are noisy	28
Feels isolated	27
Spoils skyline	25

Dislikes about tall buildings as related to age, race, sex, class, and perceived height of a tall building

We will examine those categories to which 50% or more of the sample responded as things they disliked about tall buildings. These items were waiting for elevators, missing greenery, fearing fire, feeling tall buildings were impersonal.

Hate waiting for elevators Examination of the sample indicates a significant correlation between income and hating to wait for elevators. Eighty-eight percent of the lowest income group (under $5,000 paid annually) hate waiting for elevators. Of the $10,000-30,000 income group, about 65% hate waiting for elevators. The $5,000-10,000 and over $30,000 income groups complain less, although still nearly 50% of them do complain about waiting for elevators. The explanation for the low and middle income high rate of complaints might be that these people really do suffer the most, especially low income groups, in elevator availability. There may be too few, or they may be frequently broken or both. Criminal attack while waiting for elevators may concern low income groups. However, only 3% of this sample earned under $5,000 and 8% earned $5,000-10,000. The high income group may complain less because it has less to complain about, living or working in well-run buildings. The $5,000-10,000 income group complains the least and this is either by chance, or there is some explanation for it. Perhaps these people have just moved into new buildings or to the suburbs and are relatively satisfied with their social and physical situation, so they complain less. All differences were significant at the 0.05 level of significance on a chi square test.

Sixty percent of the sample checked that they missed greenery. There was a significant difference in

TABLE 4–11
Income and Hating to Wait for Elevators (Income Is in Thousands)

	Under 5		*5–10*		*10–20*		*20–30*		*Over 30*		*Total*	
	#	%	#	%	#	%	#	%	#	%	#	%
Hate waiting	7	88	11	46	80	67	42	63	32	48	172	60
Don't hate waiting/NA	1	12	13	54	40	33	25	37	34	52	113	40
Total	8	100	24	100	120	100	67	100	66	100	285	100

TABLE 4–12
White and Non-White Response to Missing Greenery in Tall Buildings

	White		*Non-White*		*Total Responses*	
	#	%	#	%	#	%
Miss greenery	163	64	14	31	177	59
Do not miss greenery/NA	90	36	31	69	121	41
Total	253	100	45	100	298	100

$X^2_{4df} = 22, p < .001.$
Note: Chi square was done on 4 degrees of freedom and the table then collapsed.

response by whites and non-whites (Table 4–12). This difference may be due to a social class difference between whites and non-whites and/or due to more non-whites being from urban rather than suburban backgrounds and therefore missing greenery less. Non-whites may be more concerned with essentials than whether there is greenery or not. Whites probably expect more.

Fear fire Fifty-five percent of the sample responded that they feared fire in tall buildings. Women feared fire significantly more than men did (Table 4–13).

Women may be more safety conscious than men. Women work around fire more often than men,*

TABLE 4–13
Sex and Fear of Fire in Tall Buildings

	Males		*Females*		*Total*	
	#	%	#	%	#	%
Fear fire	57	46	106	65	163	57
Do not fear fire	67	54	58	35	125	43
Total	124	100	164	100	288	100

$X^2_{1df} = 10, p < .01.$

since women do the cooking and are familiar with small fire outbreaks and burns in the kitchen, and are concerned with combustible materials in the home and on their children's clothing. Thus it is entirely reasonable that women should be more concerned with the realities of fire, since they know of the frequency of outbreaks in the home. Perhaps, on the other hand, they simply fear fire more than men do.

Finally, those who perceive a tall building as only five stories high fear fire significantly less often than those who perceive a building as being tall when it is anywhere from six to over forty stories high (Table 4–14).

The *Towering Inferno* and fear of fire Finally, those who saw *Towering Inferno*, particularly women, were significantly more afraid of fire than those who did not see it. Either there was a predisposing factor, namely that people who were afraid of fire to begin with were more likely to see the movie, or the movie

*A male student has pointed out to me that some single men live alone and cook for themselves.

TABLE 4-14
Perception of Height of a Tall Building and Fear of Fire

	Five Floors		*Six-40+**		*Total Response*	
	#	%	#	%	#	%
Fear fire	22	48	146	58	168	56
Do not fear fire	24	52	107	42	131	44
Total	46	100	253	100	299	100

$X^2_{5df} = 13, p < .05$.
*The 6-40 floors categories were collapsed for a simpler table presentation, but the chi square was done on 5 degrees of freedom.

actually had the effect of making people more afraid of fire in tall buildings.

For those unacquainted with thc movie, it concerned the outbreak of a fire in a tall building, the subsequent damage to the building, loss of life, escape difficulties and thrills, the heroism of the firefighters, the widespread sex life of the architects and their assistants with women in the building, and the builder's cutting of corners in the cost of the electrical equipment which results in the fire. The firefighter hero ends by saying it's too bad there isn't more cooperation between architects and firefighters.

Impersonality and tall buildings Fifty-two percent of the sample checked that one of the things they disliked about tall buildings was that they were impersonal. Whites checked that they were impersonal significantly more than non-whites did (Table 4-15). A possible explanation of this finding is either that non-whites are more friendly with their neighbors, or non-whites are not as concerned with their living area as whites. Whites conversely might be more distant to their neighbors and also might react more strongly to their environment and be more demanding, as was shown by their higher rate of response than non-whites to missing greenery in a tall building. Higher income groups respond to physical environment more than lower income groups, in this study.

TABLE 14-15
Race and Impersonality in Tall Buildings

	Whites		*Non-Whites*		*Total Responses*	
	#	%	#	%	#	%
Tall buildings are impersonal	137	54	19	42	156	52
Not impersonal	116	46	26	58	142	48
Total	253	100	45	100	298	100

$X^2_{3df} = 11, p < .02$.
Note: Chi square was done on 3 degrees of freedom and the table then collapsed.

There was some difference in feelings that tall buildings were impersonal between those expecting to have no children and those expecting to have children. Those who stated they wanted no children did not feel that tall buildings were impersonal as often as those who wanted children (Table 4-16). Perhaps people without children find more of their satisfactions outside of a building. They are not as confined to it as are people with children. Those who either had or expected to have children might have felt the tall building was more impersonal compared to the neighborhood unit of small buildings or one unit family houses.

TABLE 4-16
Number of Children Wanted and Feeling Tall Buildings are Impersonal

	Want No Children		*Want 1 or More Children*		*Total Response*	
	#	%	#	%	#	%
Tall buildings are impersonal	24	49	97	53	121	53
Not impersonal	25	51	84	47	109	47
Total	49	100	181	100	230	100

Summary

To summarize, in responses where more than 50% of the sample responded to "things disliked" about tall buildings, 65% hate waiting for elevators, but the under $5,000 and the $10,000–30,000 income groups dislike waiting the most, possibly because they experience the most discomfort. It was suggested that perhaps the $5,000–10,000 income group is one which is coming up in social rank and/or is more suburban and is more satisfied, and the over $30,000 per annum income group gets the best service and so is more satisfied. Sixty-one percent responded they disliked having no greenery in a tall building. The majority of these respondents were white. Non-whites missed greenery only half as much as whites. This, we suggested, was either a class and/or an urban factor, where whites had more education and income, more frequently lived in suburbs and were therefore both more particular about environment and more often saw and expected greenery. Non-whites would have less choice in their environment, would more often be from the city, and would have less exposure to greenery due to lower income. Although there are, of course, middle income non-whites, the data here are not broken down by income and race.

Fifty-five percent of the sample feared fire in tall buildings, women feared fire considerably more often than men, and with reason, it was felt, since all women work intimately with fire, i.e., in the kitchen and know of its hazards, whereas comparatively few men work with fire. It takes an accident or an unusual event for men to see fires. Possibly this is one of the reasons that women were significantly more afraid of fire after seeing *Towering Inferno* than men were. Fifty-eight percent of the women and 32% of the men who saw it were more afraid of tall buildings after seeing it. Possible explanations are that women are more realistic about danger, women are more scared of danger, or that women admit to fear more easily than men do. In our society it is often considered unmanly to admit to fear. People perceiving a tall building as six floors and over feared fire more than those who perceived a tall building as consisting of five floors.

Fifty-two percent saw tall buildings as impersonal. Of these people, whites felt that tall buildings were impersonal more often than non-whites. People who intended having children versus those who intended having none saw tall buildings as more impersonal. Both of these could mean that those of higher socio-economic status and/or those more and more dependent on their living area seek more comfort from it.

Time and space do not permit a detailed discussion of the other aspects of tall buildings which people said they disliked. These were that tall buildings were monotonous inside, and hard to get outside of. They feared being stuck in an elevator, disliked having no control over their environment, disliked heights and the noise of neighbors, felt isolated, and felt the building spoiled the skyline.

Forty percent said they would choose the lower third of a building if they had to live or work in one, but about 17% each chose the middle and top third. Ten percent said they would never live in a tall building and 2% indicated they would never work in one.

Over 70% thought tall buildings should be used for offices only, and in already built-up urban areas; 7% of the sample said tall buildings should not be built at all.

Attitude to neighboring tall buildings Forty-eight percent of the 300 respondents said they had a tall building nearby. Nearly 70% of such people who had a neighboring tall building either lived and/or worked in a tall building themselves. Thus, people who have tall buildings in their neighborhoods appear to live or work in a tall building. About 34 percent of people who had a tall building in their neighborhood were annoyed by it. The remaining 66% were not annoyed by it. Since most of those who had a tall building neighboring theirs also lived or worked in a tall building themselves, this might explain their lack of annoyance. Another way to put it might be to say that people who use tall buildings do not mind having other tall buildings near them. However, twice as many whites (22%) as non-whites (11%) object to having tall buildings in their neighborhood. The difference has a chi square significane at the 0.05 level. As might be expected, people who are in favor of lower heights in buildings are significantly more annoyed by having neighboring tall buildings than those who are in favor of buildings being ten stories and up ($X^2_{5df} = 19, p < .01$).

Materials used in tall buildings As father's income went up, respondents' preference for glass as material for tall buildings increased ($X^2_{3df} = 10, p < .02$). Thirty percent of the women checked that they like glass in tall buildings, and 20% of the men did. Thus those from a more educated background, and women, like glass in buildings more than those from less educated backgrounds, or men. Men like steel almost twice as often as women. One might say there are building materials which are considered masculine and feminine. All of these differences between age, race, sex, and class reach the 0.05 to 0.001 level of significance on a chi square test. The taller people perceived a building to be to qualify as tall, the more often they like steel used as material. Twenty-two percent of these said they disliked concrete. Of these, whites (30%) disliked concrete significantly more than did non-whites (13%) and women (34%) disliked concrete significantly more than did men (15%). Those who perceived tall buildings as only five stories high disliked concrete very much more than people who perceived tall buildings as being anywhere from ten to forty or more stories high. The higher people perceived buildings as tall, the more they accepted concrete for use in tall buildings.

To try to summarize preferences on materials, 24% checked that they liked glass; higher class (qua education) and women liked glass in tall buildings more than lower class and men. Eight percent said they liked steel; of these, men and those perceiving buildings being tall at a ten-story minimum liked steel more than did women and those perceiving tall building beginning under ten stories. The greater one perceived height of a tall building, the more acceptable were steel or concrete.

The mean number of items checked for "like about tall buildings" was 2.7. The mean number of items disliked was 3. There was a significant difference in the total number of items checked as "things liked about tall buildings" and the total number of things checked in the dislike set of categories, by age, race, sex, class, and the perceived height of a tall building. Time and space does not allow for examination here of all of these differences. Just one will be presented as an example. Regarding the last category, perceived height of building, the taller people perceived the minumum height of a tall building, the more items they checked off as liking about tall buildings. Those who said a tall building began at forty stories had proportionately more positive check-offs under things liked about tall buildings. Those saying a tall building began at five stories had few positive things to say about tall buildings.

A CONTENT ANALYSIS OF RESPONSES TO THE QUESTION, "WHAT DO YOU THINK WOULD IMPROVE TALL BUILDINGS?"

The greatest number of responses to this question (50) were that buildings should be made safer, have higher standards and enforcement of building regulations, and more fire protection and fire escape routes in case of fire, earthquake or floods. One person suggested a moat should be built around tall buildings for protection against fire, another that fire escapes be reintroduced. Ninety percent of those who gave these responses had seen *Towering Inferno* and were apparently impressed by it. The next highest response (41) was a cry for more open space and greenery. Respondents suggested parks all around tall buildings, trees, plazas, landscaping, flowers, and "bringing the outside in," with roof gardens, whole floors of green areas, plants and flowers inside the building. Giving people extra outside space was suggested through more balconies and sundecks. The third concern was to lower the height of the buildings to a maximum of twelve stories, even using underground floors to reduce the height of buildings. Next people wanted more creative, varied, colored, aesthetic, classy designs for the outsides of tall buildings, and shapes other than "square slabs of stone." The next most frequently suggested improvement was for more, safer, and faster elevators, scenic and outside elevators, provisions for escape if elevators broke down.

Regarding the interior, people suggested safer wiring, better water and heating facilities, carpeting on stairs, and some comfortable and carpeted lounges in an area where people could socialize. They suggested larger windows, more skylights, more glass for light, less noise from neighbors, security measures for residents, and aids to the handicapped. They suggested internal shopping facilities like shopping plazas such as large hotels often have, interconnecting bridges between neighboring large buildings at the upper level, and easy access to mass transit systems. Some negative responses to this question were that nothing could improve tall buildings; they should not be built, should be torn down, bulldozed, razed, buried, blown up.

The largest number of responses concerned safety and escape routes. Most of these responses came from people who had seen *Towering Inferno*. The next largest response was on the strong desire for greenery and space, and aesthetic appearance and variety both outside and inside. There was, in my view, a surprising amount of participation and response to the whole research project and to this particular open-ended question from a young age group which does not now have to make decisions about living or working areas, for the main part.

SUMMARY AND IMPLICATIONS FOR ENVIRONMENTAL DESIGN AND THE MANAGEMENT OF SPACE USAGE

This research was based on the responses of 300 undergraduates at Maryland University to a questionnaire asking them about their attitudes toward tall buildings. The sample was a young, relatively affluent, middle class group, whose parents were more highly educated than the average American adult. As such, the results reflect the opinions and attitudes of this socioeconomic group rather than a cross-section of America. However, they do probably represent future homeowners, and people who, with their education and income, will have a say in environmental design and space usage.

The more salient responses about the impact of tall buildings were that the respondents enjoyed the view or scenery from tall buildings, enjoyed seeing far distances, recognized the spatial economy of tall buildings, and often liked the aesthetic aspects of tall buildings. There were considerable differences in responses by different age groups, by sex, race, class, and by how tall respondents thought a tall building was. Those under twenty-one and women liked the scenic view, and seeing far distances from tall buildings. Men liked heights and steel and concrete more than women did, and feared fire less than women did. After seeing *Towering Interno*, women were more afraid of fire than were men. Women and those with more educated fathers appreciated the aesthetics of tall buildings more than men and those with high school educated fathers.

A high percentage of people disliked waiting for elevators, and missed greenery and space around or in tall buildings. In diminishing order of response, people feared fire, elevator breakdowns, and felt tall buildings were monotonous. In almost all of these instances, groups who may be of higher socioeconomic status because they were white and/or their fathers had higher incomes had more complaints. The under $5,000 income group complained highly (88%) about waiting for elevators. The highest income group, over $30,000, complained least. It is thought that the lowest income group had the worst real housing and elevator conditions and the highest income group had the best, therefore the least complaints. Middle income people, $10,000–30,000, income also complained about elevators. Very few people saw tall buildings as safe, particularly anyone who saw *Towering Inferno*. Those who did see tall buildings as safe were all men.

Sixty-six percent of the sample did not mind

having tall buildings neighboring on their buildings, but most of these, 70% who answered that they did not mind, either lived or worked in a tall building themselves.

Whether people saw a tall building as under or over five stories had a great effect on their tolerance for tall buildings. Those who saw a building as tall when it was five floors high were much less favorable to tall buildings and to having buildings taller than five stories in their neighborhood. The higher a building was perceived as tall, the more appreciation there was for the positive aspects of tall buildings, and the more liking for heavy materials such as steel and concrete.

Implications derived from the findings on this research are that architects and engineers recognize the desire for safety, open space around tall buildings and green areas around and inside. Variety in external and internal appearance, in shape, size, and color, is desired by the respondents. A possible combination of bringing the green inside and clearing the outside area for fire trucks in case of fire would be to build inside courts and gardens. "Hanging gardens" connecting upper levels between buildings would serve a triple function of providing the desired greenery, socializing and recreation areas, and escape routes from one building to another in case of fire. Architects and engineers might consider improving public relations with a movie or advertising offsetting the dangers demonstrated in *Towering Inferno*, or demonstrating how architects work with the fire department in construction buildings.

Future research could concentrate on the needs of different age, sex, and class groups and the attitudes of those who think a five-story building is high versus those who think a ten-, twenty-, thirty-, or forty-story building is high.

Architects and engineers might take account of the different preferences among age groups, sexes, races, and classes when offering designs for buildings. Women, and those with higher incomes and education, are likely to be considerably more critical and demanding of safety, space, and greenery needs, as is this group of potential tall building occupants which is relatively affluent and aware of the need for fire safety, spatial economy, and beauty. Those with lower incomes could also be treated to good elevator service, exposed to the pleasure of green areas in inside courts, or "hanging gardens" between the upper levels of adjoining buildings.

REFERENCES

1. Gilda Moss Haber, "Response to Room by Sex, in College Classrooms," unpublished paper, 1974.
2. Juanita Kreps, *Sex in the Marketplace: American Women at Work* (Baltimore: Johns Hopkins University Press, 1971).

5

Human Response to Tall Building Motion

Mizuki Yamada
Takeshi Goto
Hosei University

INTRODUCTION

As a result of motion induced by severe earthquakes and wind, tall and flexible buildings affect the comfort of inhabitants. A long period and large amplitude are the peculiar properties of tall building motions. However, most research is based on periods lower than 1 second. It is the purpose of this chapter to investigate human response to tall building motion from a different angle with experimental measurements as follows:

1. Human Perception and Tolerance Threshold
2. The Swaying State of the Body
3. Acceleration Induced on the Body
4. Motion Effects on Human Task Performance
5. Motion Effects on Visual Performance
6. Physiological Reaction and Motion Sickness
7. Movement of Furniture and Fixtures
8. Difficulty of Ambulation.

Three experiments, numbers 1, 4, and 8, are just introduced here briefly because of space limitations, but they will be investigated along with some of the other experimental results in the final summary.

MOTION SIMULATOR

The motion simulator consists of a house 3.0 m × 3.0 m (approximately 10 ft. × 10 ft.) with 2.4 m (8 ft.) ceiling mounted on a platform 3.0 m × 6.0 m (10 ft. × 20 ft.) suspended by four vertical steel cables at the corners (Figure 5-1). The house is a wooden structure and has plywood finishing. It is connected to a 2 horsepower motor, incorporating a transmission gear, by steel rod. Two sides of the simulator are fitted with little wheels to prevent the platform from swinging freely in the orthogonal direction to the longitudinal one when being moved by the motor.

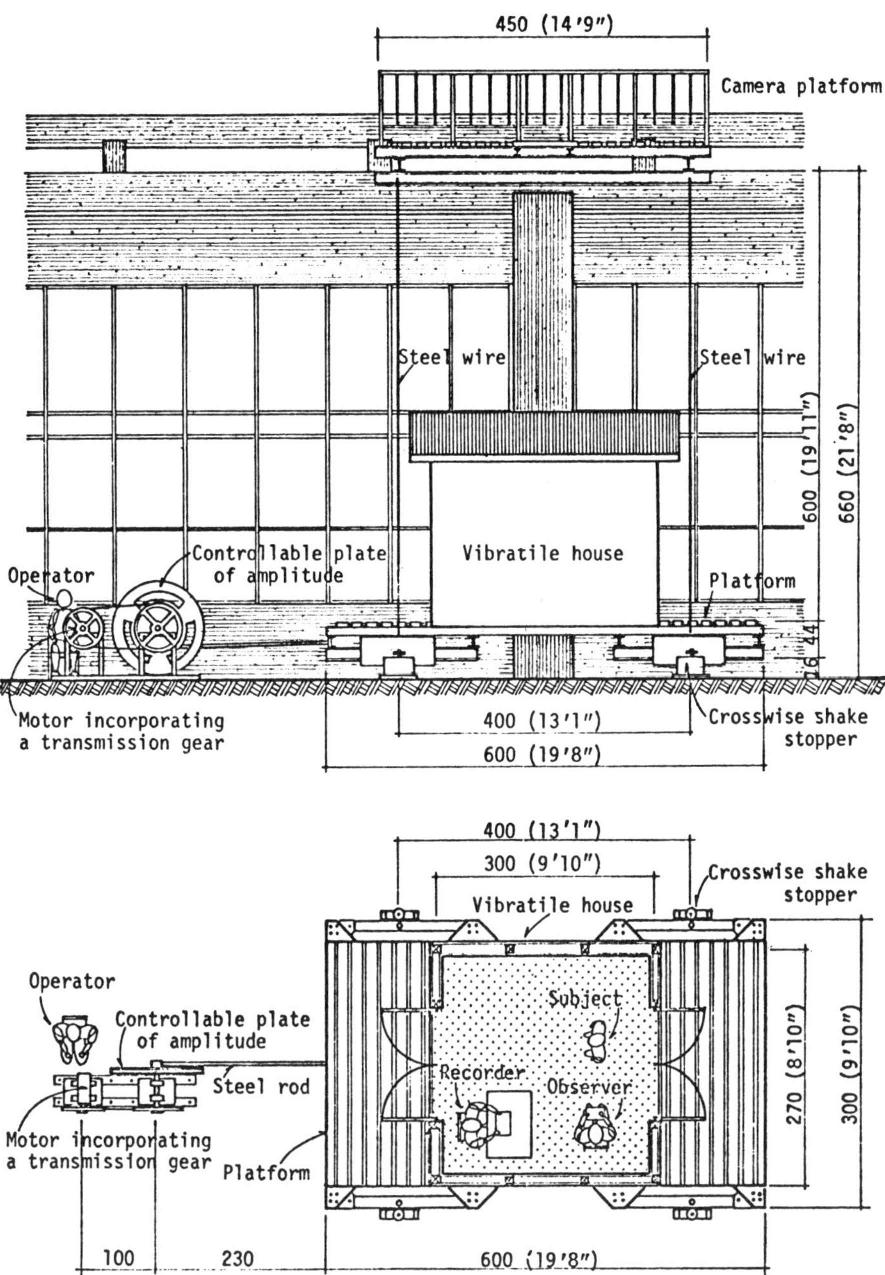

Figure 5-1
Motion simulator.

The results thus far obtained are based on the following conditions:

Period	: 0-10 [sec] (1/10-1/10 [Hz]), in linear variable.
Full Amplitude	: 1-100 [cm] (0.39 in.–about 3 ft. 3.3 in.), discontinues variation of every 5 cm (1.97 in.).

EXPERIMENTS

Experiment 1. Human Perception and Tolerance Threshold

Experimental design

Considering the psychological effects of building motions on inhabitants, the primary issue which we have to deal with at first will be perception and tolerance threshold. The perception and tolerance thresholds vary widely depending on the various factors: (a) individual difference, (b) sex, (c) age, (d) body posture, and (e) body orientation.

The experiment is designed in the form of an eleven factor analysis of variance (shown in Table 5-1) about the human perception and tolerance threshold.

Implements

The paper on which the three different subjective sensations are written, as follows, is put on the internal wall of the house.

Subjective Sensation I	: Imperceptible.
Subjective Sensation II	: Faintly and distinctly perceptible.
Subjective Sensation III	: More strongly perceptible and disagreeable.

TABLE 5-1
Experimental Factors for Human Perception and Tolerance Threshold

Sex	① *Male*			② *Female*
Age [years old]	③ 8-12 Childhood	④ 18-22 Youth	⑤ 45-55 Middle-aged people	18-22 Youth
Number of subjects	5	20	5	5
Body posture	standing	⑥ standing ⑦ sitting on a chair ⑧ sitting on the floor ⑨ lying on the floor	standing	standing sitting on a chair sitting on the floor lying on the floor
Body orientation	⑩ fore and aft ⑪ side to side			fore and aft side to side

TABLE 5–2
Period Pattern and Objective Amplitude in Experiment

Starting Signal — *The Start of Motion* ▼ … *The End of Motion* ▼ — *Ending Signal*

Period of motion [sec]		10	9	8	7	6	5	4	3	2	1	0
Duration of motion [sec]	30	30	30	30	30	30	30	30	30	30	30	30
The passing of time [min]	0.5	1.0		2.0		3.0		4.0		5.0		6.0
Objective amplitude [cm]	1, 5, 10, 20, 40, 60, 75, 100											

Experiment procedure

On a certain amplitude, one of the subjects is ushered into the house and asked to stand in the same direction to the longitudinal axis for a test on fore and aft motion. The subject has been previously informed that the experiment is a perception test of motion. There are no visual cues at all indicating motion inside the house.

Each experimenter takes his assigned place. Then the experiment is started with a signal. The simulator is operated according to a time schedule (shown in Table 5-2). The experimenter asks the subject to give his or her subjective sensation (using the list placed on the wall of the house) whenever this sensation to motion changes, and records the period at that time. After following the period pattern, the next item on the program is a side-to-side test.

Results

The threshold of perception occurs between zones I and II, and the threshold of tolerance occurs between II and III and in the subjective sensation mentioned above.

Table 5-3 gives the results of factors a to e described in the experimental design. A sign of inequality in the table stands for the relative sensitivity of different types under varied conditions.

TABLE 5–3
Relative Sensitivity Under Varied Conditions

Factors	*Results*
Sex	Female > Male
Age	Childhood > Youth > Middle age people
Body posture	Standing > Sitting on a chair > Sitting on the floor > Lying
Body orientation	Fore and aft > Side to side
Expectancy	Knew and experienced > Knew but no experience > No prior knowledge

Figure 5-2 is a graph showing the average threshold curves about eleven factors of perception and tolerance with the relation between period and acceleration. This figure shows that the tolerance threshold has quite a sensitive zone on the period. For instance, even if the acceleration is the same at about 65 cm/sec^2, the left side of the 5 second period boundary is in the subjective sensation III and the right side is in II.

On the other hand, there are the "Recommended Human Comfort Curves," which are proposed based on much investigation by Dr. Chang.[1] Those are shown with light lines (horizontal lines). A thin line located near the bottom of left side shows the average perception thresholds of five subjects, which have been obtained by Dr. Ishimoto.[2]

Finally, we correlated the subjective sensation and the value of the head's acceleration. The head acceleration of when the subjects feel each subjective sensation is plotted in Figure 5-3. From the figure it is seen that the subjective sensations are dominated by the head acceleration. It may be concluded that the human response to a large amplitude and long period of motion is decided by a person's head acceleration induced by the motion and not by the acceleration of the motion itself.

Experiment 2. Motion Effects on Human Task Performance

Experimental design

The experiment is designed to analyze to what extent motion has an effect on drawing lines, a typical example of a human task.

Implements

A desk, chair, and test paper (cf., Figure 5-4) for the subject to use are provided in the house.

Experiment procedure

The subject's task is to trace straight lines with a pen as well as regular squares and circles which are thinly drawn on a paper in advance. The test paper is put on the desk. One of the subjects is asked to sit on a chair in the house. First, the subject traces the three figures—a straight line, regular square, and circle—before the house is set in motion. During each tracing, the time required for tracing is timed by a stop watch. Next, the house is operated with a 10 second period of motion and the same tracing test is carried out again. The fore and aft and side-to-side tests are also performed, but in the case of the body posture factor the subject is only required to undergo the test sitting on a chair because the tasks are typical of desk work. Five young males are used as subjects.

Results

Figure 5-4 shows some samples of the results of the tracing test performed by one subject. Analyzing these results in detail, the grades of motion defect can be classified into three groups as follows:

Task Performance I : Subjects are able to trace normally.

Task Performance II : There is a little effect. Sometimes traced lines deviate from the base line which has been thinly drawn on the paper in advance.

Task Performance III : Traced lines deviate from the base line; subject can hardly trace at all.

The concrete samples of task performance are shown in each part of Figure 5-4 for your information. When we draw the border lines between each performance, I and II, and II and III, on a graph, they can be shown in 10 and 35 gal. (The graph is not in this

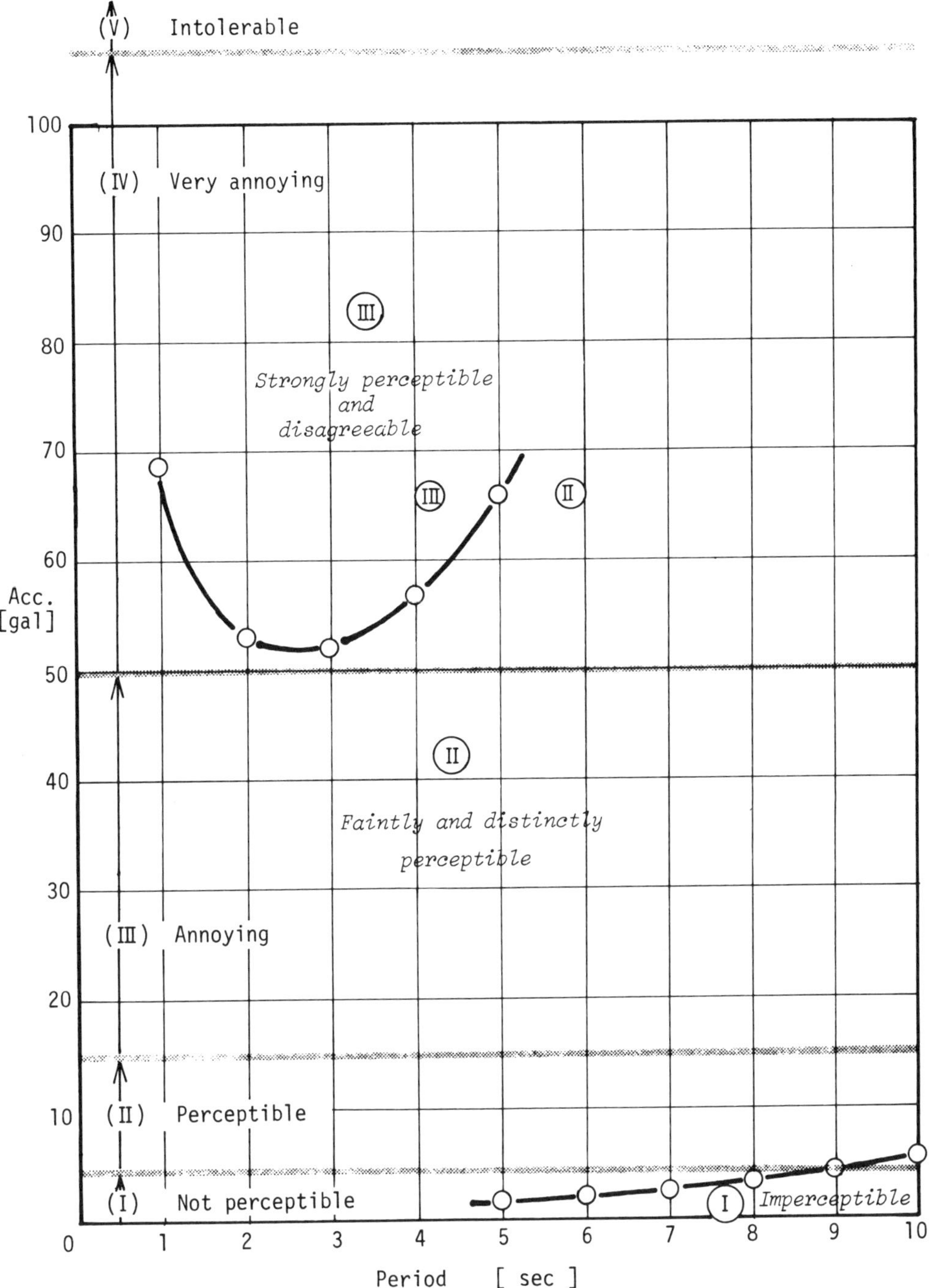

Figure 5-2
Synthetic average threshold on an acceleration graph.

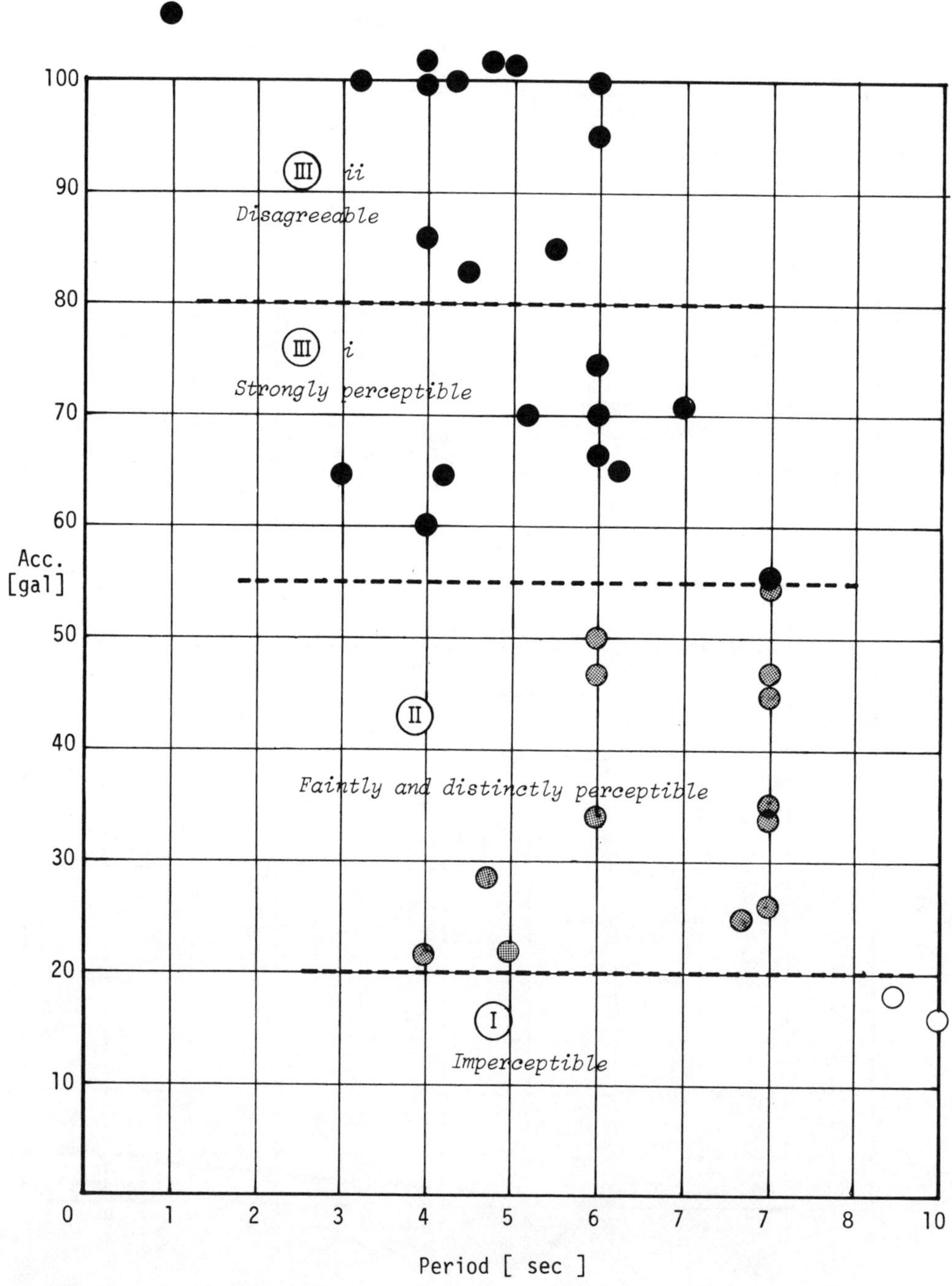

Figure 5-3
Correlation between the head's acceleration and subjective sensation.

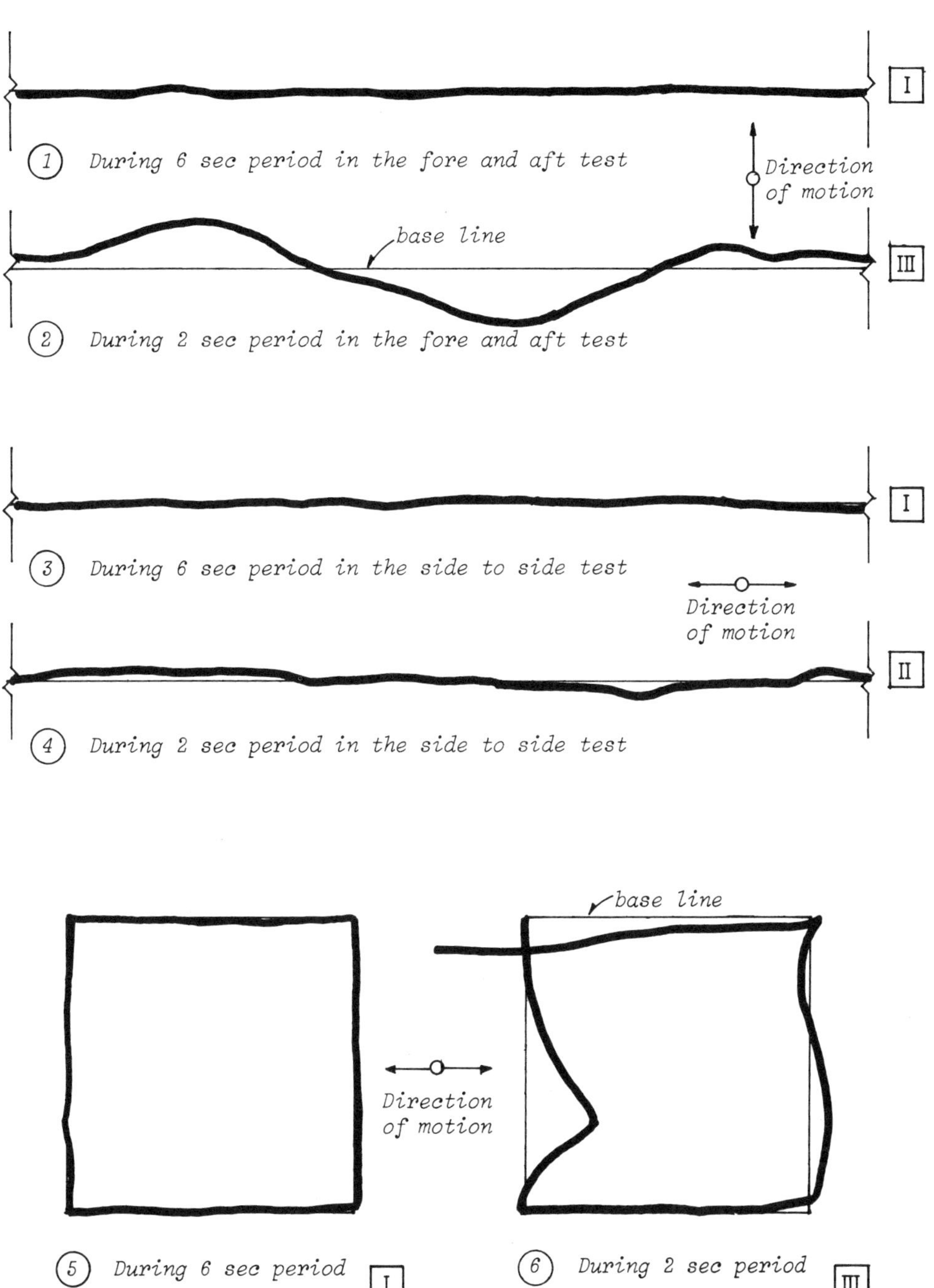

Figure 5-4
Samples of the results of the tracing test the amplitude is 20 cm (7.87 in).

chapter.) Thus we find that the human task performance during motion is decided by the floor acceleration.

Experiment 3. Difficulty of Ambulation

Experimental design

It is obvious that inhabitants may not walk well on a swaying floor and staircase. The experiment is designed to analyze the correlation between the magnitude of the motion and the difficulty of walking on the floor and going upstairs and downstairs, respectively. The difficulty of ambulation is analyzed by means of a motion picture camera filming the head and toes loci to the subject as he ambulates.

Implements

The motion picture camera and the motion analyzer are used here, and the roof of the house has been removed and a staircase is mounted on the platform.

The whole of the staircase is made of wood. It is composed of eleven steps and is surrounded on three sides by walls, but it does not have a ceiling or a handrail. The measurements of the staircase are 16.0 cm (6.3 in.) in rise, 28 cm (11.0 in.) in tread, and 120 cm (9 feet 11.2 in.) in width.

Experiment procedure

The camera is set on the camera platform above the house. Vertical and horizontal lines spaced 20 cm (apart 7.9 in.) are drawn on the floor and the walls. The lines are parallel to the sides of the floor. The center lines of the stripes are fiducial lines, which are a little bit thicker than the others. To a certain amplitude, one subject is ushered into the house and marks are put on the top of his head and on his toes. Then, he is asked to stand with the wall at his back on the longitudinal fiducial line for the fore and aft test. The subject is asked to walk on the fiducial line to the opposite side and back again twice to a metronome accompaniment in 84 step/min. (a little slower then the usual pace). While the subject is walking, he is recorded by the camera with a crank speed of 32 frames per second. The experiments for fore and aft and side to side are performed in this manner.

The subject is also asked to fill out a questionnaire about the four levels of difficulty, shown as follows with the ranking:

- I Quite normal walking or going (upstairs and downstairs)
- II Nearly normal walking or going
- III Difficulty in walking or going
- IV Inability to walk or to go

As the experimental method of going upstairs and downstairs corresponds with the one of walking, it will be omitted here.

Results

Figure 5-5 shows the head and toes loci when a subject walks on the floor during motion. From these figures the following results are obtained:

1. When the subjects walk in the same direction as the motion, they experience difficulty in keeping balance only in the fore and aft direction.
2. When walking at right angles to the motion, they experience difficulty in keeping balance in both directions, i.e., fore and aft and side to side.
3. The trends in (1) and (2) increase as the acceleration rises.
4. It is conceivable, for this reason, that the length of stride and width of stance are different. That is to say the stride when the subjects walk in the parallel direction to the motion is larger than the stance when they walk at right angles to the

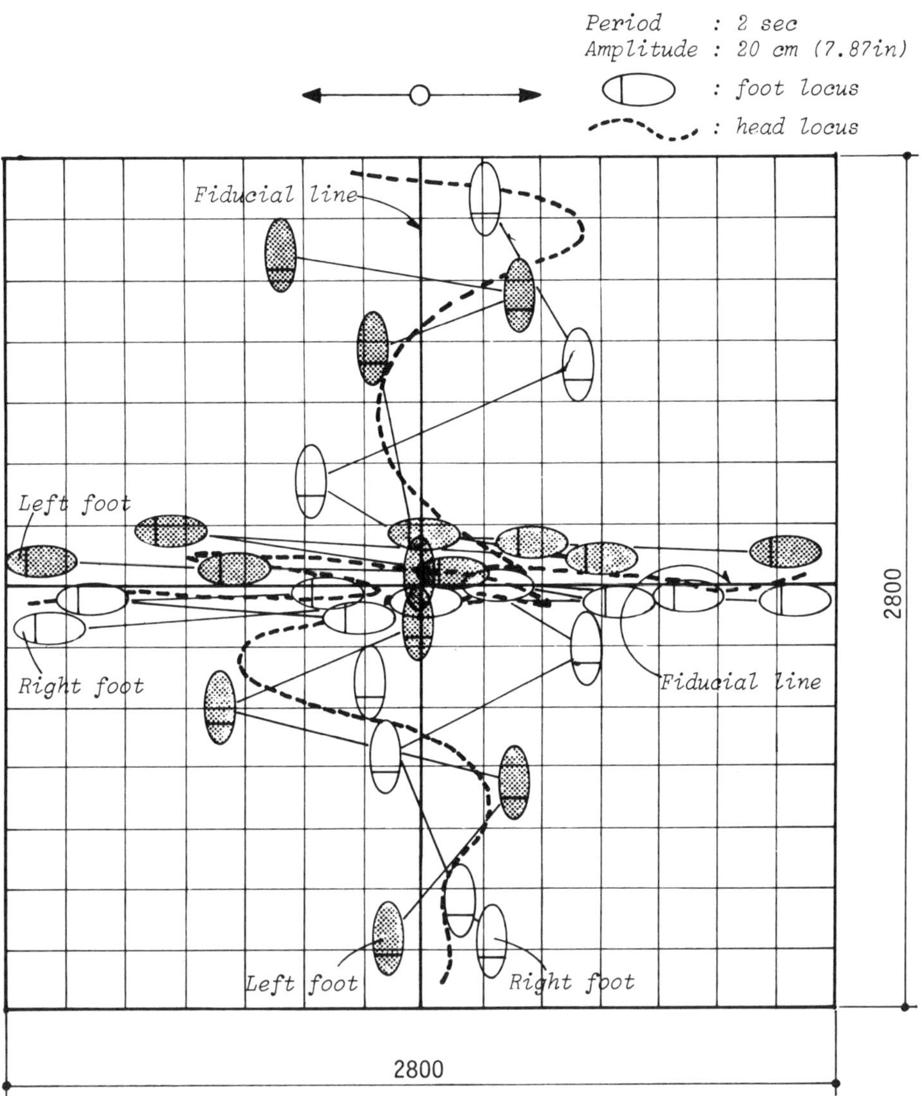

Figure 5–5
The divergences of the head and toes from the fiducial line.

motion. Therefore, it is easier to maintain stability walking in the parallel direction. One reason for this is the fact that the joints in the leg bend naturally in the direction of walking.

Incidentally, comparing the results in the difficulty of walking and difficulty of going upstairs and downstairs, most trends are quite similar. The performance lines of walking and going are found to be very close to each other under similar conditions. The final levels of the ambulation to the motion are based on the selection of the lower line in each zone.

INTEGRATION

The final results of the investigation to the many experiments are shown on a graph in Figure 5-6. The zones divided by lines or curves are designated as A to I for convenience.

A zone In the acceleration under 5 gal a human cannot perceive motion and his task performance and ambulation are not effected at all; furthermore there are no signs in interior surroundings.

B zone Between 5 to 10 gal some people can perceive motion. So we can say that there is a limit of human perception on tall building motions between the zones A and B. And in this zone, some of the furniture and fixtures which move easily, like chandeliers or water, begin to move slightly, but the movements are not observable except to a person who looks at them carefully.

C zone Between 10 to 25 gal most people are able to perceive the motion well, and there is a slight affect on desk work. When the motion continues for a couple of hours, there are some people who complain of suffering from motion sickness. But in this condition people can ambulate without hindrance.

D zone Between 25 to 40 gal desk work becomes hard for inhabitants, and at times it becomes almost impossible. But as for the ambulation, most people can walk and go upstairs and downstairs of their own will without too much difficulty. On the other hand, in the case of the movement of furniture and fixtures, the production of sound at 40 gal is considered to be the factor which strikes terror in inhabitants' heart. From the above mentioned, it may be said that there are common limits of difficulty of work and psychological response around 40 gal.

E zone All zones until now are subjected to acceleration on most items. But in this zone above 40 gal the effect by means of period begins to show, people perceive the motion strongly. And on the interior surroundings of the building, its change is perceptible clearly through the eyes and ears. Furthermore, standing inhabitants lose their balance and find it hard to ambulate of their own will.

F zone Over 50 gal the effective responsiveness by means of period becomes strongly marked. Most people will be in a state of tolerance and a state of inability to walk.

G zone G zone is a state in which people can strongly perceive motion but cannot ambulate of their own will. This zone is quite a dangerous one. Because, even during the same magnitude of motion as in this zone, in a real earthquake they might try to ambulate in an attempt to reach safety. They may fall down as soon as they start to ambulate in this zone where the sensitive response is located higher than the ambulatory response. From the investigation based on the zones of F and G, it is considered that there is a limit of ambulation around these zones.

H zone In this zone it seems that inhabitants can ambulate no further. They may naturally be in a tolerance state.

I zone Over 85 gal, as a few objects begin to fall down, it is expected that the inhabitants may be injured even if they remain still. So that the zone over 85 gal is undesirable for building motion, as we are concerned with the reactions and safety of inhabitants and not merely the construction of buildings.

A colligation of the investigation indicates it is better that the criteria for motion should be based on the human perception threshold when the motion is slight, because the perception threshold occurs before the other items in this sphere. But in severe motion it should not be based on human responsiveness, because the responsiveness is the most abstract factor compared with the others. It is quite possible that man's behavior and the motion of objects on the floor are absolutely restricted by the motion. It is supposed that inhabitants are thrown down violently or dashed against furniture, etc. Therefore, the criteria for the tall building motions should be considered from the limit of man's ambulation, movement of objects, and so on in the sphere of extreme motion.

CONCLUSION

We have tried to make a summary of various effects on tall building motion mainly based on experi-

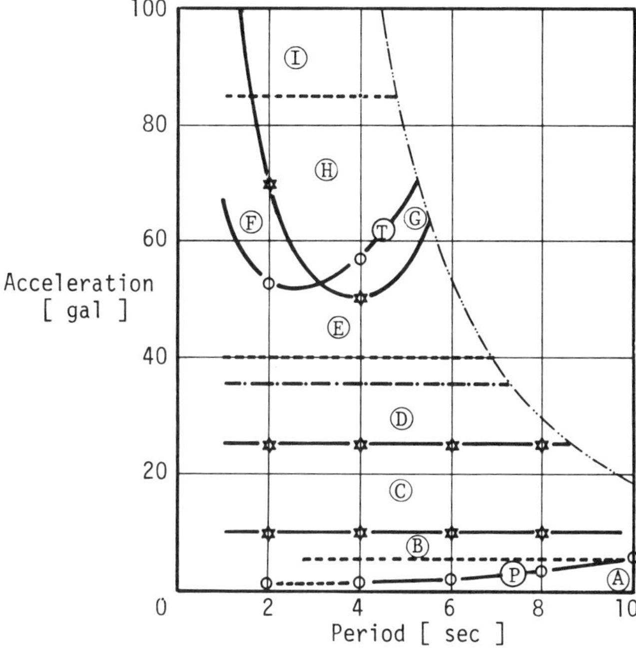

Ⓟ -Perception threshold

Ⓣ -Tolerance threshold

Ⓐ -Imperceptible & Normal ambulating

Ⓑ -Faintly perceptible & Objects begin to move

Ⓒ -Distinctly perceptible & a little difficulty in desk working

Ⓓ -Perceptible & a little difficulty in ambulating

Ⓔ -Strongly perceptible, begin to make sounds and difficulty in ambulating

Ⓕ -Tolerance

Ⓖ -Inability to ambulate

Ⓗ -Tolerance and Inability to ambulate

Ⓘ -Tolerance, Inability to ambulate, and Objects begin to fall down

Figure 5-6
Synthetic results.

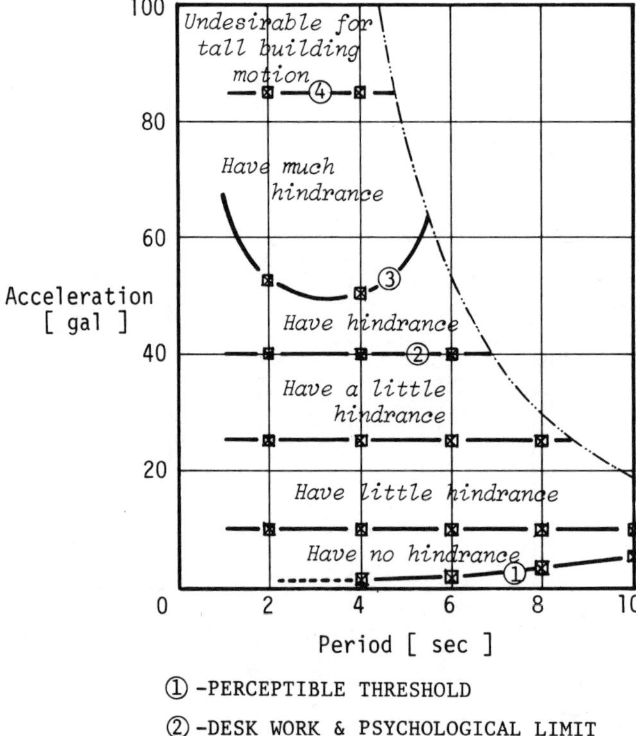

Figure 5-7
Criteria of tall building motions (period-acceleration).

mental methods. There are still many items concerning inhabitants which should be investigated. But it will take many years for these investigations to be finished completely. Therefore, we should like to propose the basic criteria in Figure 5-7 for information of design of tall buildings. Figure 5-7 is shown with correlation of period and acceleration, too.

When the buildings are designed, the important factors about their motion are considerable; not only the strength of the structure and economy of construction but also function and use. The performance of the motion will differ respectively between houses, hospitals, offices, warehouses, factories etc. For example, in houses and hospitals where rest, relaxation, and medical treatment are of primary importance, the performance of the motion for inhabitants and patients may be held in the zone of "Have a little hindrance" to the building motions which occur a few times a year as a result of severe wind and earthquakes. But under normal conditions the performance should be held under the perception threshold. On the other hand, in warehouses where people are not usually living, the motion performance may be held in the zone of "Have hindrance" because objects are not hindrance by motion in this zone.

Accordingly, referring to the design of buildings, it is desirable for the architect to know well the conditions and to investigate the various factors of the building and environment in each case, for instance, magnitude, duration, recurrence period, and other properties of motion at the place where the building will be built, in order to decide the correct limits of motion.

NOTES

1. F. K. Chang, "Wind and Movement in Tall Buildings," *Journal of the Structural Division, ASCE* (August 1967): 70–72.
2. M. Ishimoto and M. Ootuka, "Determination de la limite perceptible des secousses," *Bull. Earthq.* 11, 614 (October 1932):113–121.

6

Urban Office Buildings: View Variables

K. W. Nichols
Goddard College

INTRODUCTION AND OBJECTIVES

The high-rise office building is a firmly established part of the urban experience as evidence by both the permanence and sheer height of such recent structures as the Sears, Roebuck Building and the World Trade Center. It is most important to discover the sociological and behavioral responses this building type elicits, especially from the ultimate user. Due to energy conservation, security requirements, and improvements in artificially controlled interior spaces, windowless environments are increasing in number. Although office buildings are rarely without some window provisions, many interior spaces used by numerous people as workspaces, public lobbies, traffic corridors, conference spaces, and ancillary service spaces are without windows.

The high-rise office building environment is sufficiently unique in its physical and functional nature to merit investigation of height and view questions independent of studies pertaining to other building types, such as schools or housing. This building type deserves investigation not only due to its unique nature but also due to the fact that it is a widely experienced environment both in terms of time and numbers of people. Individual workers for the most part are contained within the building and stationed at particular workspace locations. The relationship of the building, the outside environment, and the individual is seldom discernible from either a viewpoint outside the building, due to scale differences, or a viewpoint inside the building, due to lack of view or height of the observer's location from ground floor.

The purpose of this study was to more specifically investigate attitudes and behavioral response of the individual worker in an urban high-rise office building to three variables concerning his view to the outside of the building. The first variable was the height from the ground floor to the floor level of the individual's workspace providing a view. An attempt was made to see if the worker experienced feelings of separation from the outside environment the higher the view was from ground floor level and what importance he attached to this.

The second variable was access or lack of access to a window view from the individual's workspace. Degree of importance of a window and reasons for importance were recorded to compare the attribute of view to other attributes provided by a window, such as daylight. An effort was made to see if the lack of a view to the outside was associated with feelings of enclosure beyond the factors commonly associated with enclosure. The study compared the responses of workers with and without windows by recording attempts to seek out window views and noting awareness of the outside environment. Attitudes about job satisfaction and productivity were also noted for both groups.

The third variable was the physical nature of a window which defines view quantity and perceptual accessibility. Variances in size, number, placement, and degree of transparency were studied as they related to degrees of felt enclosure.

The primary objective of the initial study was to identify relevant variables, test methods, generate hypotheses, and refine the direction for future study. Due to the exploratory nature of the study, statistical significance was not computed.

The rationale for relating the height of the available view from ground level to feelings of separation from the outside environment was less firmly based than is usual for scientific inquiry due to the lack of research into the effects of heights.

The presumption was that distance, in this case in the upwards direction, changes relationships, especially when there is a strong reliance on the visual mode of perception. Gestaltists say that people perceive parts and wholes mainly by the proximity of objects in the visual field.[1] The components making up the window view would be perceived in a manner similar to the object perception process. Of course, the proximity of most objects at ground level allows a more complete inspection of the visual field both in number and detail of objects; whereas views typical to higher floors of buildings usually offer only generalized patterns of movement and color even though vistas are wider.

Hall has scaled the type of interactions between people as a function of distance.[2] It is the contention of this author that distance is also a function in the type of relationship between an observer and his outside environment. How visual separation might relate symbolically to psychological separation cannot be guessed at this time. However, as Hall has said "at the distance people look like ants, contact with them as human beings fades rapidly."[3]

In addition Kohler has said that "due to our body systems for equilibrium and balance and due to the effects of gravity, people possess an innate sense of top and bottom."[4] If an individual is aware of the top and bottom of a building and if the factor of distance changes the visual relationship between the observer and the outside environment, it is possible that the individual might also experience an accompanying psychological separation. The ground floor level of a building is usually associated as the access point to the outside environment. It is at this level where it is possible to become a participant instead of an observer. A window view from the upper floors of the building might serve to remind the observer of the distance from the ground level, consequently reinforcing feelings of separation.

It was not the purpose of the study to substantiate the existence of psychological separation or to evaluate the effects such feelings would have on the worker. This must be left to future studies. However, it was the intention of the study to determine if workers felt that the height of the available view from ground level was related to visual separation from the outside environment and if so what importance they attached to this.

Subsequent to reviewing related studies on windowless spaces, it was predicted that a view to the outside environment would be considered a primary factor in assessing the importance of windows in the workspace. It was also predicted that workers in windowless spaces would experience feelings of enclosure.

Peter Manning, in his investigation of office buildings in Great Britain, found that "a slit of light was not sufficient; a window needed to be large enough to afford a view."[5] Theodore Ruys, in a study entitled "Windowless Offices," found that it was not the quality of view that mattered to the worker but the opportunity to look out.[6] Fitch added another dimension to the subject of enclosure when he noted that "instead of deep views of nature urban man moves in a shallow frame of man-made perspective. His horizon is usually limited by the surfaces of a room. With the advent of air conditioning and luminous environments there has been accumulating evidence of employee dissatisfaction or actual discomfort in windowless workspaces. Complaints were voiced of being cooped-up."[7]

It was thought that an extended view to the outside (not just an extended view) was a paramount physical consideration in regard to enclosure.

Of course the degree of felt enclosure of the workspace can be varied by the forms and size of the space and the number, placement, and size of the objects within that space. Variances in enclosure have previously been considered only in terms of breaking out of a static box form, reducing the density of a crowded space, or offering a physical opening. The characteristics of that opening or openings such as size, number, placement, and degree of transparency should also be considered.

STUDY DESIGN AND METHODOLOGY

Sixty questionnaires from volunteer participants were analyzed to determine the importance of window views and heights of views. Attitudes and preferences, awareness of the outside environment, the amount of use and type of use of windows were considered measures of the degree of importance. Extenuating factors inherent in the work situation, such as management policies or security and task requirements which might alter the workers' responses, were also identified by the questionnaire.

The respondents were asked to select the most important attribute of a window from a list of attributes given on the questionnaire and to note any other attributes not mentioned in the questionnaire. This information was then analyzed comparing the relative importance of view to other window attributes. The respondents were also asked to select from pairs of drawings illustrating various window attributes the window type they would most prefer in their workspace.

Attempts by the worker to seek out a window view if inaccessible in the workspace were considered indicative of the importance of a window view to that worker. Proshansky et al. said that "mentally and physically healthy individuals attempt to engage in positive interactions with their environment to satisfy their own needs."[8] It was thought that workers dissatisfied with windowless spaces would seek out views by taking trips whether job-oriented or non-job-oriented to other spaces within the building affording a view.

Respondents were asked to complete a time and space mobility log for three consecutive days. All movements from the workspace were recorded in this log, noting routes, destinations, number of trips, and times of trips. Reported trips were later categorized as to window access, presence of other workers, and job-task relatedness.

Observations were carried out to provide a corrective check on trips reported in the mobility log, use of windows, and extenuating circumstances which would alter behavioral response.

Respondents were also asked to select from pairs of drawings illustrating various window features such as size, number, and placement which drawing they thought represented the least enclosed workspace.

A series of photographs taken from different elevations within the building showing a single setting outside the building were included in the questionnaire. Respondents were asked to select the photograph they thought represented the most visual exposure to the outside environment. One of the possible answers to the above question was "no difference in degree of visual exposure between photographs."

The population selected for the study represented a cross-section of the total population of the participating organization in age, sex, rank, and job type. A cross-section was selected so that any variance in job satisfaction peculiar to one particular job type or department would not be a representative factor in response. The sixty participants used were all employed by the same organization in order to limit variables of management philosophy and employee relations.

Location of the participants' workspaces on either the lower or upper floors of the building (above floor level ten) and access to a window view in their workspaces were the two primary variables. The number of windows per workspace varied proportionately to the length of the perimeter wall defining the size of the space. Some spaces were shared by workers and some were private. Size of the workspaces varied. Ruy's study found that response to windows did not vary as function of the size of the room.[9] It was thought that if similar results were found in this study in regards to workers in windowless spaces reporting feelings of enclosure regardless of the size of their workspace, a lack of view to the outside could be considered a primary condition establishing enclosure.

In order to identify variables which might influence responses, results were analyzed according to both the total response and the categories listed below:

1. Claustrophobic Tendency
2. Acrophobic Tendency
3. Degree of Job Satisfaction
4. Private Workspace
5. Shared Workspace
6. Degree of Mobility (allowed and required by task)
7. Negative Environmental Aspects in Workspace (due to physical conditions or task requirements)

The building itself was a recently completed single tenant high-rise office building in center city Philadelphia. Special attention has been paid to the quality of the interior environment. Physical conditions such as heat, lighting, ventilation, and sound control were of high quality and uniform throughout the building. The building's provisions facilitated the work task and were conducive to the pleasure and comfort of the worker. In terms of quality and quantity of sensorial stimulation, there was sufficient variability provided by interior features to satisfy the worker's need. Hence any expressed dissatisfaction with windows or heights of view could be considered more directly related to those features rather than to a halo effect of dissatisfaction with other physical conditions.

The tinted solar bronze glass windows were nonoperable, the building's interior environment being artificially controlled. All windows were identical, measuring 15 X 7 1/2 feet and were repeated along the perimeter walls every twenty-five feet.

FINDINGS AND CONCLUSIONS

The results reported below cover the major findings of the study but do not include all the data computations or comparisons.

View Importance

1. 73% of all respondents felt it was important to have a window view to the outside available to them in their workspaces.
2. 82% of all respondents felt it was more important to have a view to the outside of the building than a view to the inside of the building.
3. 76% of all respondents said they would prefer a poor view to no view at all.
4. 82% of all respondents said that the presence of a window did not affect their ability to concentrate on their work.
5. 32% of all respondents selected view as the most

important feature of the window. (Five choices were provided as possible replies in addition to one blank reply to be completed by the respondent.)

6. 81% of all respondents felt it was important to know what was happening outside.

Reported attitudes on view importance showed no significant differences in responses between workers with windows and those without windows. However as a group, workers without windows felt that exposure to the environment outside the building was important more often than did the group of workers with windows.

The following replies were given to an open question asking the respondents to supply reasons they felt windows were important in the workspace. The replies are listed in the order of most often mentioned.

1. Affords daylight
2. Affords view
3. Avoids enclosure
4. Boosts morale
5. Creates cheerful, relaxing, enjoyable working conditions
6. Breaks monotony, enhances alertness for better work
7. Shows what is happening outside the building
8. Gives eye muscle relief

Even though more respondents mentioned daylight as the most important reason for a window, more respondents selected window types affording a view over window types offering daylight as the window types they would prefer in their workspaces and which related least to feelings of enclosure. Skylights, or numerous small windows, or windows placed above eye level were not the preferred selections nor did they lessen projected feelings of enclosure.

Use of Available View

1. 88% of respondents with window views reported they often checked on the view.
2. 100% of respondents with windows could describe the available view in detail.
3. 55% of respondents with windows observed the view from their desk position.
4. 33% of respondents with windows often walked to the window to observe the view.

Observation showed that workers with windows kept the window blinds open.

Seeking Views

1. 91% of respondents without window views in their workspaces reported they often traveled outside their workspace to or through other areas within the building which afforded a view to the outside.
2. 20% of the respondents with windows reported they often traveled outside their workspace to or through other areas of the building which afforded a view to the outside.

The number of reported trips did not change due to varying degrees of allowed mobility. Workers without windows did not register dissatisfaction with their jobs more than workers with windows. Workers without windows, however, did spend more time away from the work task due to the difference in the number of trips made outside their workspaces and due to the fact that not all trips were job-related.

Responses recorded by the respondents on the questionnaires and time/space mobility logs generally coincided with observation records. Observation records indicated much more traffic being made to areas with windows than to windowless areas even though lounges, Xerox and coffee rooms, mail conveyer stations, and bathrooms were all located in windowless spaces. The lack of traffic to the windowless areas just mentioned is particularly noteworthy when considering that the needs of the worker for variability and social interaction can often be met in such areas because modes of behavior typical to the workspace are relaxed.

Feelings of Enclosure

1. 52% of all respondents reported projected feelings of enclosure in windowless workspaces.
2. 72% of all respondents reported they disliked feelings of enclosure.
3. 63% of respondents in windowless workspaces reported feelings of enclosure.
4. 72% of respondents reporting claustrophobic tendencies stated they felt windows were important.

Size of the workspace or number of workers occupying the workspace did not alter responses regarding feelings of enclosure in windowless workspaces.

Window Properties and Degree of Enclosure

Respondents selected windows which were at eye level and which offered the greatest single total area of view as providing the workspace with the feeling of being least enclosed—that is, one large window gave the space a feeling of being less enclosed than two smaller windows. This was true even when the two smaller windows were located on different walls offering two different views and also when their combined area of glass was similar to the total area of glass of the single window. Skylights, opaque glass windows, or numerous slits of light did not lessen feelings of enclosure. Eye level access to view did.

Importance of the Height of View Access from Ground Level

1. 71% of all respondents felt it was important not to be visually separated from the outside environment.
2. 67% of respondents without windows said that the height of their workspace location made no difference either in terms of preference or feelings of separation from the outside environment.
3. 40% of the respondents who had worked on both the upper and lower floors of the building said that the height of their workspace made a difference to them.
4. 60% of the above respondents noting that height made a difference preferred workspaces located closer to ground floor.
5. 56% of all respondents reported they would prefer their workspaces located close to ground floor.

Height of View Access and Separation from the Outside Environment

1. 76% of all respondents selected from the photograph series the view closest to the ground floor as being the least visually separating from the outside environment.

Support for the assumed relationship between height of the viewpoint from ground level and feelings of separation from the outside environment was not more strongly indicated by respondents actually experiencing increased height of viewpoint due to their location on the upper floors of the building.

2. 71% of respondents selecting the view closest to the ground floor as being the least visually separating from the outside environment did not report acrophobic tendencies.

Influence on Results Due to Other Variables

No significant differences in results occurred due to the factors previously listed as possible variables: job satisfaction, private or shared spaces, size of space, number of workers per space, degree of mobility, and claustrophobic and acrophobic tendencies. In fact throughout the study users showed broadly similar patterns of response in assessing the quality and relative importance of environmental features.

One exception to this pattern occurred involving a group of workers experiencing physical aspects in their workspace and task requirements considered to be negative. The negative evaluation was due to numerous restrictions, high degree of supervision, and tight security conditions. The increase in the number of environmental aspects considered to be negative corresponded to a decrease in the number of efforts made by the workers to seek out views or to use available views. The workers were less aware of the physical aspects of the interior and exterior environment than were workers in more positively evaluated environments.

Workers reporting a high degree of job satisfaction recorded a higher degree of window use and trips to windows outside their workspaces than did workers reporting job dissatisfaction.

The ability to work effectively or the degree of job satisfaction were not investigated in relation to differences in the height of view access from the workspace to ground level.

Respondents recording claustrophobic tendencies consistently showed responses emphasizing the importance of view more than the total group of respondents or any other subgroup.

IMPLICATIONS FOR FUTURE RESEARCH

All findings are applicable to the participating organization but not necessarily relevant to other organizations housed in different buildings due to specific differences in management philosophies, physical conditions, and work activities. Further study is needed not only to include a wider population sample but to further clarify and substantiate effects of heights and view on the worker. These effects should be precisely measured in their relation to the worker's ability to work effectively and in relation to individual work goals. It is essential to continue research utilizing buildings of extreme height similar to the World Trade Center. Alternative research methods using workers in experienced spaces instead of simulation techniques similar to the photograph series used in this study should be employed prior to forming conclusions and applying findings to the design of the environment.

Further research is necessary to establish priority needs of the individual worker. This can be accomplished by comparing the importance of various physical features to each other and by comparing the relative importance of physical features to psychological and social conditions which recognize individual work goals and personality types.

The findings of this study pertaining to feelings of separation and enclosure were limited to the office building environment. The effects of windowless spaces and the heights of spaces from ground level need to be investigated in regard to other building types such as hospitals, mental health centers, or facilities where the user population is perceptually weakened, unstable, or restricted.

More broadly based criteria for quality environment emphasize consideration of features which encourage the individual to actively participate in his environment to satisfy his own needs. Perceptual experience and a degree of choice and control in the environment are consequently fundamental factors. Micro-environments which tend to isolate, limit, or remove the individual from the macro-environment should be questioned and investigated.

IMPLICATIONS FOR DESIGN, SPACE USE, AND MANAGEMENT POLICIES

Specific design and program factors dependent upon the findings of this study include the following considerations:

1. Consideration of window design and placement in terms of enclosure, view, and daylight.

2. Consideration of space layout, circulation, and wall system design to promote view exposure to the greatest number of users.

3. Consideration of management policies which

facilitate exposure to view in regards to workers placement and mobility.

4. Consideration of physical features which might compensate for the lack of view to the outside. These might include interior gardens, exterior balconies, or simulated view experiences via films, photographs, graphics, and recordings.

5. Consideration of physical features and conditions typical to the outside environment which might compensate for feelings of separation from the outside environment. Altering the controlled interior environmental features such as lighting and ventilation during the course of the work day is one possibility. Substituting ground level environmental features on the interior of the building and locating those features on the upper floors is also an alternative. This could be accomplished by programming particular floors higher in the building for a variety of uses other than office space. Such spatial uses might include public spaces open to the outside environment, interior courts, commercial spaces, and public service spaces for communication, education, recreation, and amusement. An alternative approach might deemphasize the attention to the building's interior and provide instead features offering direct experience and access to the outside environment from the higher floor levels. Connecting bridges, circulation spaces, and roof tops could be used to advantage in this respect.

6. Consideration by management of employee policies which either encourage active participation in the ouside environment by not providing extra services on the interior of the building or encourage participation and exposure to interior spaces provided with compensating physical features.

7. Consideration of space function and work task in relation to layout, floor location, visual barriers, and window provisions. Spaces used for group activities such as conference rooms, lunch rooms, etc., and spaces supporting a great deal of worker interaction such as large departments might be located on the higher floors of a building. Possibly the attention to the activity on the interior might compensate for feelings of separation from the outside environment by increasing perceptual and reality feedback. Workers with restricted mobility and interaction, located in private workspaces, or involved in negative work tasks might be located closer to ground floor level and provided with windows in their workspaces. Spaces on higher floors might be planned in a more open fashion, minimizing visual barriers and restrictions and offering views to interior areas. Interior areas which display a high degree of activity or are nonwork-related in function might also provide windows as a bonus feature emphasizing the interior space and bringing attention to its other amenities if located on higher floor levels.

8. Reevaluation of typical office space standards currently based on status and rank to be based in the future on the need of the individual worker.

These considerations need to be evaluated in terms of user experience over time in order to develop criteria for quality environment. Provision of environments responsive to such criteria, however, cannot in itself guarantee effective use of the environment. Users need to be educated as to the potential choices available to them and management needs to provide supportive programs and policies.

Planning for quality environment and effective use is not only an interdisciplinary endeavor among related professions but a shared experience in communication and education for those who design and provide the physical environment, the organizations who manage environmental use, and the ultimate user.

NOTES

1. W. Kohler, *Gestalt Psychology* (New York: Liveright Publishing Corp., 1920).
2. E. T. Hall, "The Anthropology of Space: An Organizing Model," in *Environmental Psychology*, edited by H. Proshansky, W. Ittleson, and L. Rivlin (New York: Holt, Rinehart, and Winston, Inc., 1970).

3. Ibid.
4. Kohler, *Gestalt Psychology.*
5. P. Manning, *Office Design: A Study of Environment* (Liverpool: Dept. of Building Science, University of Liverpool, 1965).
6. T. Ruys, "Windowless Offices," *Man Environment Studies Journal,* no. S–49 (1971).
7. J. M. Fitch, *The American Building: The Environmental Forces That Shape It* (Boston: Houghton Mifflin Co., 1972).
8. H. Proshansky, W. Ittleson, and L. Rivlin, *Environmental Psychology, Man and His Physical Setting* (New York: Holt, Rinehart, and Winston, Inc., 1970).
9. Ruys, "Windowless Offices."

7

High-Rise Buildings Versus San Francisco: Measuring Visual and Symbolic Impacts

Donald Appleyard
Lois Fishman
University of California, Berkeley

In San Francisco the controversy over high-rise buildings has been going on for over ten years, since the Fontana Towers, a pair of curved apartment buildings, were built on the shoreline blocking the view of the Bay from Russian Hill. During its evolution, the controversy drew in an ever increasing number of participants, as one new building after another became the focus of conflict. Each battle emphasized different aspects of high-rise buildings. The Fontana Towers interfered with the view; the Alcoa Building (1964–1966) was black with outside diagonal bracing; the Bank of America (1965–1966) was condemned for its dark color, the U.S. Steel Building (1969–1971) for its height, the TransAmerica Building (1969–1971) for its shape. As the visual and symbolic issues developed, the economic and social impacts were increasingly considered.

An examination of San Francisco's newspapers by Alcira Kreimer (1971) over the ten-year period reveals dramatic changes in San Francisco's image of itself.

> In the early 60's tall was positive: "I'm at home where the tall buildings grow. . . . I'll take the vertical city" [Herb Caen, July 1960]. In 1970 it is negative: "The entire concept of Manhattanization or 'verticality' seems old-fashioned [Herb Caen, September 1970].

Herb Caen, the city's leading columnist writing in the *San Francisco Chronicle*, in the early 1960s, became a leading antagonist by the 1970s. (Kreimer makes the point that the newspapers themselves, through their columnists, powerfully influence the image that people hold of a city.) In the high-rise controversy the image of each new building was shown to disrupt

This paper was originally presented at the Tall Buildings Conference in Mexico City, March 1973. It has since been revised. The authors wish to thank Professor Alcira Kreimer (now at MIT) for allowing them to draw from her unpublished term paper, "The Building of the Imagery of San Francisco," University of California, Berkeley, 1971.

We wish to thank the Chronicle Publishing Company and the *San Francisco Bay Guardian* for permission to publish Figures 7-1, 7-8, and 7-9.

the image of its setting—San Francisco, the stage on which it was to act. Increasingly, the new buildings were seen as foreign imports: "Manhattanizing," "plastic," "computerized," "artificial," "massive," "inhuman," "super-urbanized." The people behind them were seen as "outsiders." The buildings came, then, to be viewed as symbols. The picture of towering skyscrapers—gray, densely packed, and of exhibitionist design—scattered throughout the city is clearly at odds with the image that many San Franciscans hold of their city (Figure 7-1). San Francisco is still, perhaps romantically so, thought of by many citizens as a city of small, harmonious elements, a city which respects its natural topography, a glittering jewel on the San Francisco Bay. The high-rise buildings were contributing to its "rape," encirclement," and "Manhattanization." "There may be no Heaven but somewhere there is a San Francisco. . . . It's right here on what's left of the hills and valleys and alleys, living a half-life in the shadow of the tall buildings that scrape the sky till it bleeds" (Herb Caen, *San Francisco Chronicle* 1974).

Throughout this conflict the environmentalists have been pitched against the developers and their architects. Later the building unions joined the developers, while the environmentalists were joined by large numbers of people from the middle and working class neighborhoods. The arbitrating bodies—the Board of Supervisors, the City Planning Commission, and the Bay Conservation Development Commission—tended to change their positions throughout the controversy.

The population of the city today probably has a large majority in favor of some high-rise controls. An initiative subjecting each new high-rise building to a referendum received nearly 40 percent support in a public vote. The Urban Design Plan and its subsequent zoning ordinance controlling building height and bulk has been criticized mostly by those who think it not nearly stringent enough. Many would like to stop growth in the city altogether.

While this conflict has developed in San Francisco, concern about high-rise buildings has grown internationally. A building in Boston cannot be opened because pieces of the façade keep falling off; Londoners are unhappy about high-rise buildings since one partially collapsed. The series of disasters that have struck Manhattan have become partially associated either with high-rise buildings or high densities. Though isolated examples, these incidents build up a fear and dislike of high-rise buildings that is difficult to combat.

Behind the news reports and political conflicts concerning high-rise buildings lie their effects on the everyday lives of those who live in and around them. Do such buildings make the city more livable? Reason would say that they have positive as well as negative effects.

There is very little hard empirical evidence of the impact of high-rise buildings on people's lives. A few studies of the effects of high-rise housing on their inhabitants have been carried out (Newman 1972), but there has been almost nothing on the external impacts of high-rise buildings on cities (Dornbusch 1975). Much better predictions and simulations of impacts are needed *prior* to construction. Better understanding of public attitudes towards projects, full disclosure to the public of all possible impacts, and efforts to ameliorate impacts by cutting the size of projects, changing their location, or altering other qualities should be part of the process.

The National Environmental Policy Act of 1969 and the state of California's Environmental Policy Act together require that all new significant building projects be considered for approval only after the preparation of an Environmental Impact Report, disclosing all their possible effects on the environment. Professionals involved in planning or controlling high-rise development now have to attempt to assess objectively the environmental and socio-psychological impacts of each new building, but predictions of impact will be no more than guesses until substantive empirical research studies have been carried out.

STOP THEM FROM BURYING OUR CITY UNDER A SKYLINE OF TOMBSTONES

Both the above pictures are of downtown San Francisco. Same spot. Same time of day. Same weather conditions. The top one was twelve years ago. The bottom one, last year. San Francisco was once light, hilly, pastel, open. Inviting. In only twelve years it has taken on the forbidding look of every other American city. Forty more skyscrapers are due in the next five years. They are as great a disaster for the city economically as they are esthetically. Ask a New York taxpayer.

What can you do to stop it?

Contact SAN FRANCISCO OPPOSITION, 520 Third Street (second floor) or telephone 397-9220.

Figure 7-1
This ad, first appearing in the *Examiner* and *Chronicle* in October of 1970, was the first step in Alvin Duskin's campaign to enlarge the citizen assault on the U.S. Steel Building into a general attack on high-rise development throughout the city. More than 10,000 newspaper readers clipped coupons from the ad and sent them to City Hall.

MEASURING SOCIO-ENVIRONMENTAL IMPACTS*

How should we go about measuring socio-environmental impacts? The definition of socio-environmental impacts is a complex task, and can only be dealt with briefly here. Let us start with a number of defining propositions.

1. *The environmental impacts of high-rise buildings must account for their effects on different population groups.* Determining *population responses* to high-rise buildings is more important or at least as important as determining the *physical impacts*. The same environmental impacts may have an entirely different meaning from one population group to another. The population groups impacted by an office building include:

a. *the users*: executives, office personnel, visitors, janitors, merchants, building management, owners, etc.;
b. *neighbors*: neighboring building owners, office workers, neighboring households, the street public;
c. *the public*: the citizens of the city, their representatives, public agencies, interest groups, visitors from other cities.

This list is by no means complete, yet we can see that many people impacted by high-rise buildings presently have no say in their construction, nor do we know how they are affected by them.

2. *The impacts of different kinds of high-rise buildings, particularly office buildings, hotels, and apartment buildings may be so different in nature that they should be treated as quite separate enviromental issues.* Certainly the problems of a low income family living in a high-rise apartment tower are very different from those of an executive working in a high-rise office building, even if the buildings resemble each other externally.

3. *The external environmental impacts of high-rise buildings on surrounding neighborhoods and the city may be as important as their internal impacts on their inhabitants or office workers.* Indeed, the high-rise controversy in San Francisco has raged over the external impacts.

4. *The external environmental effects of high-rise buildings can be direct or indirect and cumulative.* The direct effects of a high-rise building may be the loss of old buildings and meaningful places, and view blockage, shadow effects, overlooking, etc., of the new building. The indirect effects may be increased *traffic* on the streets, in the subways, and *land use changes*—more high-rise buildings, restaurants, parking garages, etc. One building can therefore bring with it a *chain* of impacts.

5. *Environmental impacts are relative over time and between alternative choices.* The simplest relative measure is one comparing *before and after* conditions, that is, ambient environmental conditions before construction of the building and ambient conditions when the building has been built. A careful study of the environmental impact would examine conditions (a) before construction, (b) during construction, (c) immediately after the opening, and (d) after an impact stabilization period—if impact stabilizes.

The pre-construction period is usually the time when the negative impacts of a project are most acute. The eviction of an existing population, often of low-middle income, the tearing down of beloved buildings, places, trees, and views—all of these are sometimes felt as acutely as the loss of close friends and relatives (Fried 1963). The construction phase with its noise, dust, danger, and street blockage, while interesting to construction watchers (an exclusively male activity, according to a recent study

*Many of these concepts were developed in an empirical study of the environmental effects of a somewhat larger development project, the new Bay Area Rapid Transit (BART) system (Appleyard and Carp 1973). Later Donald Appleyard was on the Technical Advisory Committee for the San Francisco Planning and Urban Renewal Association's (SPUR) study of the environmental impacts of high-rise buildings in San Francisco (Dornbusch 1975).

[Yantis 1972]), can create misery for others, and occasionally put neighbors out of business. The opening period is a time when the image of the building—for better or for worse—is finally confirmed. Attention peaks. This is also a time when the occupants begin to crowd the local streets; use patterns change. The neighbors accept the new facility with pleasure or resignation. Finally, over the years the impact of a building may lessen as it becomes embedded in the changing urban fabric, absorbed into the public's image of its city.

Even measures of *before-after impacts* do not quite assess the relative impact of a new building, because other events may have occurred on the site had the building not been built. In other words, the *after*-conditions would have been different. In environmental impact studies the impact of *alternatives* for the same site—as well as *before-after conditions*—should be assessed, if that is possible.

6. *Cumulative impacts may be of more concern than the impacts of each successive building.* Alvin Duskin, a militant conservationist, showed the startling changes in San Francisco's skyline over the short period of twelve years in an advertisement in the *Examiner* and *Chronicle* (Figure 7-1). Ten thousand people clipped coupons from the ad and sent them to city hall. Images of an even more foreboding future followed. In a Sunday edition of the *San Francisco Chronicle*, two colored aerial photographs were featured. One showed the Bank of America and Trans-America towers jutting up through the San Francisco fog which enveloped the rest of the city. The second showed the same two buildings joined by the World Trade Center, the Chrysler Tower and other New York buildings—a forewarning of what could come. Another series of four cartoons put out by Ecology Action showed high-rise buildings gradually enveloping the city and ultimately Telegraph Hill. These doomsday images, though somewhat fantastic, trace out a trend which must be grappled with. The hidden effects of cumulative high-rise development—the vast consumption of energy, the generation of traffic, and sharing of city resources—may be even more severe.

DIMENSIONS OF ENVIRONMENTAL IMPACT

To measure environmental impact, the most reliable research strategy would look at large numbers of high-rise buildings in varying situations. A wide variety of *environmental measures,* such as height, bulk, shape, shadow, noise emissions, traffic generation, etc., would be taken for each one, and correlated with a wide variety of population *response measures* from users, neighbors, and the public.

The departing point for identifying relevant measures would be the series of concerns that various populations might be expected to have about high-rise buildings. For example:

1. *safety*: from fire, earthquake, falling objects, traffic hazards, crime, etc.;
2. *stress/comfort*: microclimate, noise, glare, shadow, air pollution, places to sit, crowding, other aspects of psychological stress;
3. *convenience*: changes in pedestrian and auto travel patterns, commuting times;
4. *privacy and territoriality*: intrusion on neighbors, provision or reduction of public territory through plazas, etc.; availability of building to the public;
5. *social interaction*: encouragement or disruption of neighborhood cohesion, interest group cohesion, worker morale, etc.; isolation of high-rise inhabitants from the city;
6. *visual disruption*: disruption through height, bulk, color, shape, scale, detail, blockage of views; "dead" street environments; signs/billboards;
7. *symbolism*: private versus public symbolism, associations attached to buildings, "dominance," "friendliness," etc.;
8. *maintenance*: levels of vandalism, cleanliness, trash in surrounding area.

SURVEY TECHNIQUES

The following techniques can be used:

1. *inerviews* seeking the public viewpoint; perceptions, evaluations and behavior of involved populations groups;
2. relevant *environmental measures* which affect people's attitudes taken from field analysis, aerial photos, and maps;
3. traffic, pedestrian, and street *behavior* from field surveys;
4. *census and other data* on the demographic structure of the impacted area, migration patterns, crime and accident statistics, traffic data, land use changes, land values, and rents.

THE VISUAL AND SYMBOLIC IMPACTS OF HIGH-RISE BUILDINGS

Let us focus here on the visual and symbolic issues, for they were central to the San Francisco controversies. Although "hard-nosed" professionals and the sociologically oriented consider the visual aspects of the environment to be trivial in comparison to technical and social issues, the fact is that the public is extremely sensitive to the visual environment, though as much for its symbolic as for its aesthetic quality. Matters of scale, color, shape, street character, and view affect a population's image of its city and of itself.* They convey powerful emotive messages which imply who runs the city, who dominates its environment, and the character of those in power. The following discussion provides some evidence of how San Franciscans responded to these qualitities, and describes some ways in which they can be defined more tangibly.

*Besides the evidence from the news media that these were important items, two interview surveys confirm their importance, one carried out by students at the University of California, Berkeley (De Casanova et al. 1972), the other by Dornbusch and Company (1975), who conducted the SPUR high-rise study.

The San Francisco Urban Design Plan (San Francisco, Department of City Planning 1971) dealt with many of these attributes in its guiding principles, but the only quantified measures, which became the basis for the later zoning ordinance, were those of *height* and *bulk*. They became the central measures simply because they could be quantified, even though they were not the only concerns of the public. The question is: Could there be other measures? For now, let us speculate a little.

Scale

As revealed in the media coverage in San Francisco at the time of the proposed U.S. Steel Building, San Francisco is acutely protective of its "civilized" scale. Again and again newspaper accounts, and editorial, feature, and commentary articles reiterated that it is the "little things" which count in San Francisco. The little things are seen as the real contributors to the quality of city life.

In these accounts, a civilized scale is equated with a "reasonable" scale, with the humanization of nature. Anything out of scale, violating the relation of man to nature and man to preexisting man-made form, immediately conjures up images of New York City. These images of New York tend to be very much like the portrayal of that city in the movie *Metropolis* by Fritz Lang—a vast, overbearing, overpowering city, mindless of the fragile humans who inhabit it. The high-rise buildings were variously described as "gargantuan," "colossal," "mammoth," "Big Ugly," and "monumental." One oft-quoted San Francisco commentator put it this way: "The old timers who knew what San Francisco was all about built their buildings to scale and made their city grow beautiful. The giants have passed on and now we have rich pygmies with ego problems." The status of being the "highest" has led to the absurdity of Chicago's three isolated gestures, the vying of San Francisco's Bank of America and TransAmerica, and the disruption of downtown Manhattan. In this status hungry quest, all civilized values and individual cities are sacrificed. Architects, control yourselves and your clients if you can!

How can scale be judged? It has both objective and subjective components. From a design point of view, buildings may be out of scale because they are too *tall*, dwarfing preexisting buildings into insignificance. Or they may be out of scale because they are too *bulky* for the block allotment in relation to other buildings. A new high-rise building may violate *the pattern of spaces and volumes* which give a block or a district its visual shape and character. In some cases it is the *detail* of high-rise buildings that is out of scale.

The public is quick to sense such violations. In San Francisco, for instance, the U.S. Steel Building, which would have stood over 500 feet at the Bay, was caricatured in the newspapers as a "steel giraffe," an ungainly, "out of scale" creature, disturbing to a sense of balance and proportion.

But a determination of scale also involves a subjective judgment. How do people feel when they are observing, walking past, working in, or experiencing the building in any way at all?

In downtown San Francisco, where many structures upwards of twenty stories have been built since 1967, a survey of employees in the Bank of America (De Casanova et al. 1972) showed a large percentage of them to feel personally *oppressed* by the buildings around them. Scale, then, implies a relation to human scale, not merely in terms of absolute height, but in terms of the whole "gestalt" which a person apprehends. How much of a building can be comfortably seen by a person at a given distance? To what extent does the building provide human-scaled amenities at its base to offset its tremendous height? How much "breathing space" is left around a building? How does it treat the prevailing street pattern and relate to surrounding older buildings?

Scale implies various relationships. *Human scale* implies a relation between the building and human figures. It also implies a relation with how much information the mind can process. *Neighborhood scale* relates new buildings with the scale of buildings in the surrounding neighborhood. High buildings, even if out of human scale, will be less disruptive in a neighborhood of high buildings than in one of small buildings.

The *change in scale* may be the most negative characteristic of high-rise buildings. These effects can be severe enough to ask: "Why does any building have the right to be out of human scale?"

Some experimental measures that could be the basis of design guidelines or controls have been proposed to study this matter of scale more closely:

1. *Relative height*. Hans Blumenfeld (1953), in a famous article on scale, suggested that the "maximum angle at which an object can be perceived clearly and easily is about 27 degrees, corresponding to a ratio of 1:2 between the size of the object and its distance from the beholder" (Figure 7-2). By this criterion buildings over about three stories are out of scale on most urban streets. Above this height, street inhabitants must crane their necks. Most people in the Dornbusch interviews confirmed they preferred to look at high-rise buildings from a distance. Were this to become a control measure, new buildings would have to be lower or stepped back in gentle gradations. Perhaps some of Soleri's buildings and Safdie's Habitat are the only large buildings that can meet such a criterion. If such a criterion proved too severe, a small percentage of exceptions could be allowed to rise above such height angles, so that the ambient scale could remain within bounds.

Another aspect is the relation of high buildings to

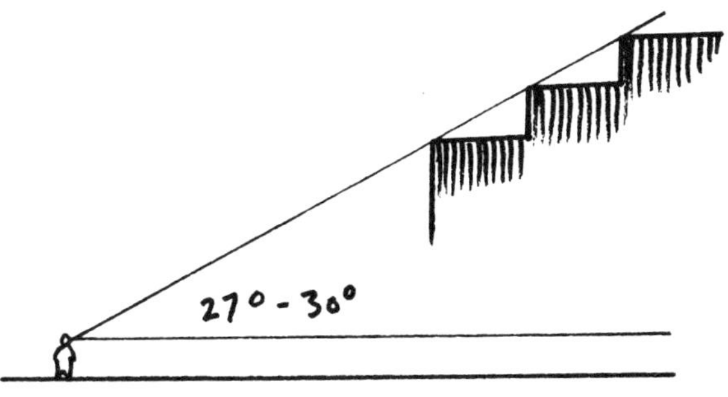

Figure 7-2
Relative height.

their neighbors. The outcry is sharpest when fifty- to seventy-story buildings are built next to three- and five-story structures. This is trauma more than drama. Limits on height relative to neighbors could comprise a more evolutionary control than the absolute height limits which were ultimately fixed upon in San Francisco.

2. *Relative length and bulk.* Buildings that are long horizontally without vertical breaks can disrupt the scale of a neighborhood of smaller ownerships (Figure 7-3). This was historically the technique for making buildings such as Versailles more monumental. If cities restricted the assemblage of small plots into large ones, their scale would be maintained. In San Francisco, the bulky high-rise buildings such as the Federal Building near city hall and the new Embarcadero Center are among the most dominating buildings in the city, especially since they are oriented east-west, creating massive shadowed façades over blocks to their north. In a small survey of building preferences, "slender" buildings were much preferred to massive ones. The controls of building bulk now written into the zoning ordinance seek to keep future buildings from being so bulky.

3. *Repetition.* In buildings that have too many components, such as thousands of similar windows, individual parts cannot be focused on because there are too many (Figure 7-4). There are limits to the amount of information we can process, and some buildings exceed those limits (Miller 1956). The individual parts become a texture and our attention is focused on the whole building, often as a meaningless, and always very large, entity. The human scale is lost and buildings are likened to "ant heaps" or "filing systems." A simple count of the number of similar parts, or a measure such as Krampen's (1974) type-token ratio, relating the variety of each detail, such as windows, to their total number, may supply us with a measured building scale (Figure 7-5). Any ways in which individual parts can be varied and grouped in smaller units will help bring attention back to them.

4. *Size of details.* If a building provides places to sit, normal size windows to look out of and into, humanly scalable steps, and doors that can easily be opened, then the building is likely to be in scale. Too many high-rise buildings have no detail at ground level to which human beings can relate. People are dwarfed and excluded from them. Architects of the Bank of America building consciously tried to recreate in their

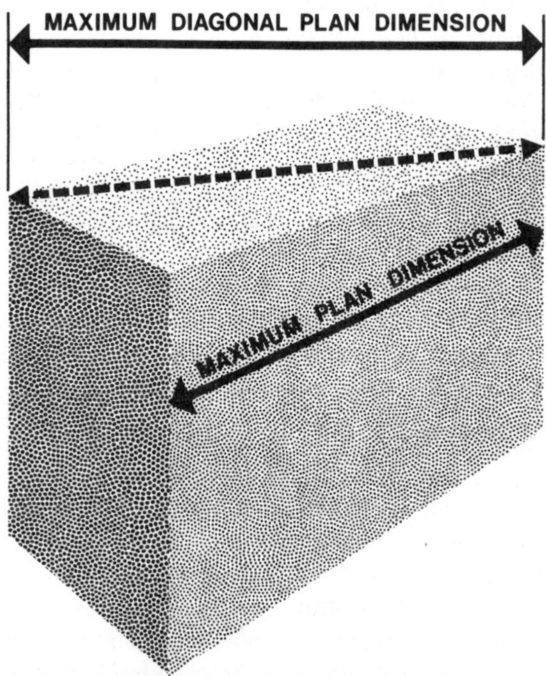

Note: The following measurements are used to determine whether a building would be excessively massive in relation to its surroundings:

Height: The height of existing, surrounding development. This would be the prevailing heights, not the exceptional ones.

Maximum plan dimension: The longest possible dimension along a building's side. This is taken from a building's plan at the height of surrounding development.

Maximum diagonal plan dimension: This, too, is taken from the building's plan and is measured at the height of surrounding development. It represents the longest possible dimension between the most separated points of a building.

Figure 7-3
Method of measuring building bulk.

VIEW OBSTRUCTION

note: Special height limits now exist in these areas.

ADVERSE SHADOW CONDITIONS

INAPPROPRIATE SCALE

Figure 7-4
Effects of massive buildings. Extracts from the San Francisco Urban Design Plan: Preliminary Project 8.

design San Francisco's bay windows. However, in a building fifty-two stories high, they are viewed more as "organ pipes" than bay windows.

There can be a conflict between these scale-creating characteristics. On a large building, windows, doors, and other details relating to the human figure will be so small relative to the overall building that they inevitably have to be repeated in large numbers. Ways of grouping them into conceptually manageable components may resolve this problem (Figure 7-6).

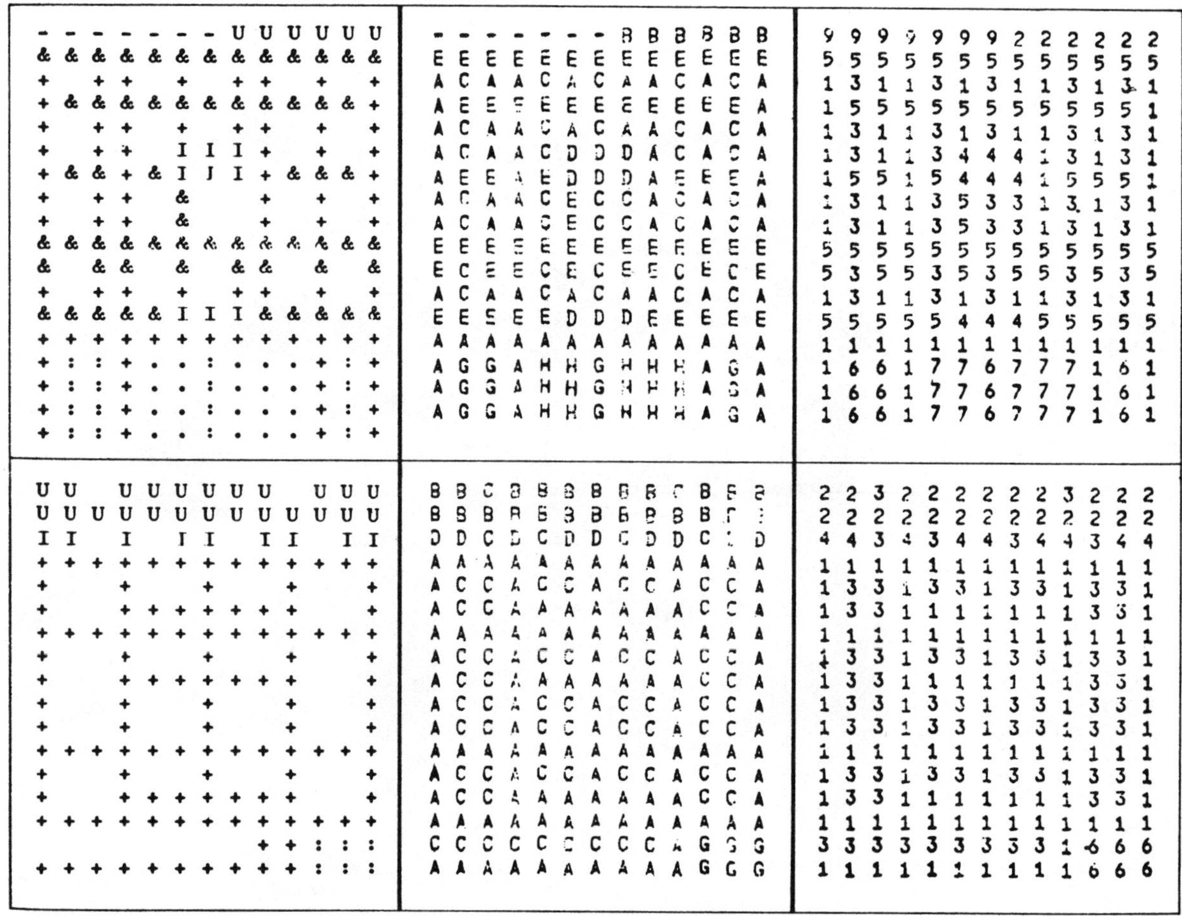

Figure 7–5
Three different versions of coding for two façades (from Krampen 1974).

Color and Tone

Some cities are thought of as characteristically lively, with paint-splashed dwellings and mosaic designs on facades; others are characteristically earth-toned. San Francisco is generally perceived to be simultaneously white and colorful. The predominant tonality of building façades has traditionally been cream-colored or white, occasionally perked up by a pastel fronting. The colorful element so often attributed to San Francisco is expressed through the actions of individuals upon the urban environment. *Individuals* are responsible for sprightly flower stands, gaily decorated Victorian homes, display awnings, garden plots, etc.

Thanks to the keepers of the flame—the colorful, the individual, the old San Franciscans (of whatever age), the dwellers in proudly restored Victorians, the clangers of cable-car bells, peddlers of street corner noises, writers of graffiti, the thousands of anonymous people who have a clearer vision of San Francisco than those who dwell in penthouses. Thanks to the little things that give The City its true tone and texture [Herb Caen, *San Francisco Chronicle*].

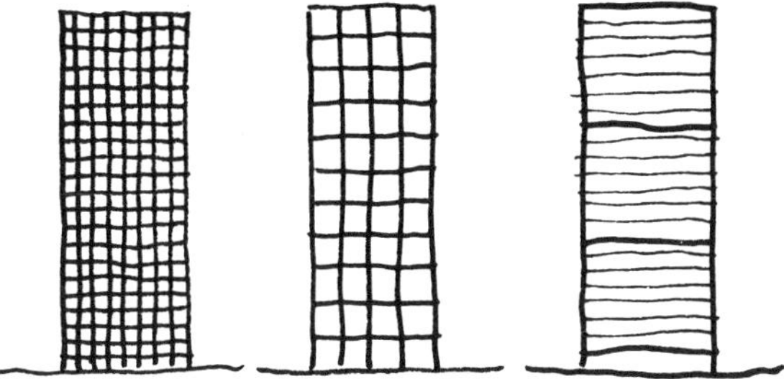

Figure 7-6
Scale-creating characteristics of buildings.

Most high-rises constructed since 1960 have respected this San Francisco tradition of light-colored buildings. In fact, one of the most recent, the new Hyatt House Hotel rising at the edge of famed Union Square boasts about how its cream color fits into the city image. What may happen when new high-rises do not respect the tradition of a given city can be illustrated by the now infamous case of San Francisco's Bank of America Building.

The Bank of America clearly violated the imaged norm on several counts. Not only did it sweep upwards to fifty-two stories, well above the twenty-odd-story buildings in its environs, but the Bank of America Building also presented a dark stone face to the public. The new brownish-black building was exceptionally conspicuous. Public reaction testifies just how out of keeping it was with other buildings around it. The media dubbed it a "monstrous" building thrown up by newcomers with *cold* New York hearts. Free descriptions of the building by people who work in the downtown area include such comments as "too large," "too drab and colorless," and "too dark for San Francisco." Even people working in the building, who might otherwise have cause to see it in a favorable light, describe it as "ominous," "like a tombstone," and "dark organ pipes reaching into the air."

Since the construction of the Bank of America, other dark buildings have shot up in San Francisco's downtown. Public reaction, as in the case of the Alcoa Building, ranged from irritation to outrage. Beneath the public outcry against dark high-rises lurks the fear that San Francisco is well on its way to becoming just another gray or black city, a Philadelphia, a Chicago, at worst a West Coast New York. The addition of each new dark-toned high-rise contradicts the treasured image of a sparkling San Francisco. Although color may not be a foremost consideration in evaluating potential high-rises in *other* cities, for San Francisco color *is* an issue.

In fact, *tone* appeared to be the more basic characteristic towards which many were reacting. The San Francisco Urban Design Plan set a range of tones which it considered appropriate. According to Allan Jacobs, former director of the Department of City Planning, architects are willing to go along on an informal basis with these Urban Design Guidelines.

Shape

The flurry of protest which greeted the designs for San Francisco's TransAmerica Corporation Building was, to a large degree, a reaction to the *idea* of a pyramidal building (Figure 7-7). The TransAmerica Building was the butt of countless jokes: it was pictured as a dunce's cap in newspaper and magazine cartoons; it has been called the Egyptian Embassy; it

was prophesied to be San Francisco's humiliation. Its shape was not consistent with the image of a "proper" downtown, as this was conceived by business-world leaders, employees, key public figures, and the citizens at large. It was not rectangular, predictable, and utilitarian, the way office buildings normally are thought to be. It did not economize on space. It was embarrassing. It made the city look silly. Although the TransAmerica now seems to be meeting with somewhat more acceptance, and fewer barbs, its stormy history underscores the need for respecting both the shapes of existing buildings and the public's image of the shape of their downtown.

Shape is a difficult quality to measure. Simple assessments of the singularity of building shapes have been made (Appleyard 1969), uniqueness in the local environment, in the neighborhood, or in the city as a whole being the basis for the scale. Degrees of difference from shape norms could be approximately measured, as a basis for a "look-alike" ordinance. The issue of attention will be discussed at greater length in the section on symbolism.

Plaza and Street Images

Within the confines of the "internal" central business district (CBD) environment, a new high-rise may bring about changes in images of the *street environment*. Plazas at the base of high-rises which create usable open space in the CBD can positively offset the image of downtown as a dark, dense jungle. Poorly designed, or purely cosmetic unusable plazas reinforce the image of downtown as an anti-human work-only area.

Much of the public dissatisfaction with the Bank of America, as judged by newspaper commentary, magazine articles, and interviews, rests with the design of the plaza. Although provided with a fountain and gay flower pots, the plaza itself faces northward and is submerged in shadow for the better part of the day. A recent random sampling of workers from the offices within the Bank of America indicated that they do not spend what they would consider "any time at all" in the plaza, not even at lunchtime. One merely has to observe for a brief time to realize that people just do not linger there. The public uses the plaza merely as a corridor, as a path to scurry from one place to another.

More successful plazas can obviously enliven the street environment, encourage people to gather, provide the setting for miniparks, sidewalk cafes, displays, vendors, etc. It is possible to survey those high-rise plazas in a city which do thrive and to ascertain the particular characteristics or bundle of characteristics which create a sense of amenity. Such an inventory can then be employed to evaluate the designs of proposed high-rise structures.

The *shadows* cast by a new high-rise may transform the character of surrounding streets, darkening them to the point where people consider downtown a gloomy, chilly place (Figure 7-4). Similarly, the character of streets may be altered by the creation of *dead areas* resulting from the siting of a new high-rise or from a decrease in patronage in surrounding establishments due to a change in block composition. The presence of these dead areas directly atttributable to high-rises has very real effects upon the public's sense of security in the downtown area. Any decrease in the sense of security may well influence the decision not to frequent the CBD in off-peak hours or to shun particular sections of it, even during the workday hours.

As with street plazas, the characteristics which make an area a "dead area" can be determined empirically. The first step, again, is to inventory the attributes of the area, to collect data about the physical environment. Then, by interviewing users of that area, it is possible to compile different sets of conditions which explain, produce, or are associated with particular public reactions. More likely than not, it is a *combination* of attributes which figure in the prevailing perception of an area. Unlit, long walkways, shielded from public view, may produce strong feelings of fear, for example.

View Blockage

In newspaper coverage of the period of the U.S. Steel controversy, the issue of view blockage overwhelmingly won first place as the most oft-mentioned concern. What was all the concern about? How are amenities reduced by view blockage, and who are the impacted peoples?

First, view blockage implies a reduction in the visibility of pleasing features which surround the city. The proposed U.S. Steel structure would have prevented many people in both residential and commercial areas from glimpsing the natural grandeur of the San Francisco Bay. Other high-rises block off other views: the Golden Gate Bridge and the hills of Marin County will no longer be visible to much of the city population because of increasing high-rise construction. The availability throughout history of these three views in particular—the bay, the bridge, and the hills—structured the image of San Francisco as the precious city by the bay. Indeed, San Francisco lore prides the city on being particularly attuned to its natural waterfront setting. A high-rise which cuts off a view of that setting obliterates the self-image of San Francisco as somehow different from all other waterside cities: "The bay blocked from view by a Waikiki wall of office buildings and hotels with a 'plastic park'."

As more tall buildings are constructed, the number of people who have views does not increase very much, while the number with blocked views increases a great deal. More people find themselves in offices which face directly into other office buildings, affording no view to speak of. Although nothing conclusive has been established, one study which interviewed workers with access to different kinds of views—wide bay views, partially obstructed views, totally blocked views—revealed that people with blocked views were very sensitive to their situation. They tended to be very concerned lest their view be further diminished in attractiveness and value. People who already had totally obstructed views tended to pull the curtains to avoid being reminded of their enclosed situation, but they too registered resentment about their boxed-in condition.

This feeling of being enclosed when deprived of a desired view relates directly to a third effect of view blockage. This is a reduction in the overall sense of *spaciousness* within the city. When natural corridors of vision down avenues or streets are impeded by bulky buildings; the city, for many people, becomes a closed container. This attitude was given expression in the tendency for many people interviewed to describe their experience in downtown as being trapped or feeling oppressed.

In assessing the quality of views, the *depth* and *width* of a view may be its most important attributes. But the level of *interest*, what it reveals about the city or the surrounding landscape, is also a factor. The value of *view direction* may also be important. North-looking views, where the sun lights up the view, may be more valued in northern climes; east and west views of sunrise and sunset are apparently valued highly in Japan, where protest is rising because these views are being obliterated. More experiments on the meaning of different views to different people is needed.

The impact of potential view blockage due to new high-rise construction can be measured if the value of existing views are known. A recent study principally concerned with the alternative impacts of different forms of urban development upon property values suggests just such a technique for evaluating the *amount* and *quality* of views.

The view evaluation technique drawn from the study by S. R. Winter (1971) requires that a particular site be analyzed by means of a computerized mapping system. Under such a system, the site in question, be it a small section of a city, an entire district, or the city itself, is broken down into cells of a fixed size. These cells are then easily identifiable and locatable on the map. Small cell size is favorable because it allows for the representation of individual properties, hence individual buildings, by single cells.

In this system, a view index is generated by using a computer program (called VIEWIT) designed to identify which cells (from the total matrix of cells) can be seen from a designated point, for instance, from a viewpoint on a particular floor within a building. Each visible cell is then scored according to its land use. The score for each floor of the building from which the view evaluation is taken is equal to the sum of the scores of all the cells visible from the elevation at eye level about that floor. The view index of the building as a whole, then, is the sum of the scores for each of its floors.

A ranking system has been established to score the views of different land uses which are seen from the viewing vantage point. Highest value is given to views of parks, open space, and ocean, equal to a value of 4. A ranking of 3 is awarded to views of residential areas. Street views are assigned a value of 2, commercial a value of 1, and industry is assigned a 0 value for view. In addition, whenever the edge of a site can be seen, as represented by glimpsing the horizon, the quality of the view is assumed to acquire the aspect of a *vista* and its value is thereby increased.*

In this way it is possible to quantify the view which is enjoyed by any present structure. But it is therefore also possible to quantify the *change* in value of view which would come about because of the introduction of an obstruction to the view area. Using this model for evaluation, the various mixes of height, bulk, and siting for proposed structures can be tested for the differential impact they would have on view from designated points and areas. The value of views added by a new high-rise could be compared with the value of views sacrificed by existing buildings.

When view indices were calculated for an area of San Francisco, they were found to have a higher correlation with assessed land values than any other factor. This partially confirms the fact that property loses value when its view is lost.

Clearly, the availability of such a method to assess the impact of view of proposed development would greatly aid in the determination of the most suitable and least disruptive sites for new construction.

*This technique can be employed as follows. The coordinates of the first viewing vantage point are identified within the computerized mapping matrix. The elevation of building height for that location are recorded. It is assumed that the observer is standing in the center of the building and that he can see in any direction without internal interference from the building he is in. Proceeding according to a pre-selected line of direction, each cell in the site falling along that line is examined. The elevation and building height of this next-in-line cell is recorded. The vertical angle required by the observer to see the cell is also calculated. The value of the land use is recorded and stored. This procedure is repeated for each cell in the chosen line of direction. The values of the visible land uses are added cumulatively. The process continues down the line of cells until the view limit is reached.

Similarly, a new line of direction is followed outward from the point of observation. This is repeated until all of the cells within the circular area bounded by the circumference of the view limit have been evaluated for angle of view and value of land use. The entire procedure is repeated for each floor of the building until ground level is reached. The total value of the view score for the building is summed and recorded.

Symbolic Disruption, Prominence, and Visibility

The symbolic image of the city is woven from a special blend of legend, reality, tradition, and memory. It is what attracts tourists, it is the stuff of travel blurbs, but it is also what many residents themselves savor about their city: the city of intimacy, the city of Victorians, the city of hills, the city by the bay, the fair city, the city of little old ladies, of taste, of charm, of cosmopolitan delights.

Buildings, too, are seen as symbols. In other words, when people are confronted with certain buildings, they interpret them as symbols of particular groups or of individual or social acts. They may think primarily of who owns them, who designed them, or who lives in them, and such inferences may well dominate the visual or architectural impacts of a building.

Architects and engineers are not always aware of this quality of high-rise buildings. They see the buildings as structures, functional spaces, or as sculptural forms, but many people see them more as the actions of large corporations, real estate developers, or public housing authorities. The more unique, large, and dominating a building is, the more clearly will it be distinguished from others, and the more it is therefore susceptible to symbolization.

An article in the *New Yorker* a few years ago described exactly how the role of a new high-rise apartment building named Kawaida Towers (a Swahili name) became a symbol of black intrusion into Italian territory in Newark, New Jersey, where its function as an apartment building was completely subordinated to its symbolic role.

> In the analysis of Italian political leaders in Newark, Kawaida Towers is not an apartment house for black people, but a power base for Imamu Baraka [local black leader].... Even the calmest Newark view of Baraka's motives would interpret Kawaida Towers as an attempt at a symbolic triumph—a demonstration that even in a supposedly Italian area it is black people who now have the political savvy and organizational ability to erect a flashy, tax-supported apartment building [Trillin, *New Yorker*, December 30, 1972].

Further on in this article the author suggested that this symbol may, indeed, hasten the movement of the threatened white minority out of the city. Symbols therefore have a lot of power.

The opponents of high-rise buildings in downtown San Francisco see the buildings in the same symbolic way: large corporations are coming in to take over San Francisco (Figure 7-8). In the context of this kind of thinking, environmental details of size, shape, and color are sometimes of less consequence than the question of whether there should be any large buildings at all. From the point of view of the younger conservationists, headed by Alvin Duskin, the aim is to stop them altogether, just as San Francisco stopped the freeways, a battle position in the effort to revolutionize environmental and societal values in the United States.

The issue can be phrased as a question: Whose buildings should dominate the public environment of a city? Should they be office buildings, residential buildings, civic buildings, hotels, or transportation terminals?

Again, it is not difficult to interview citizens to find out which kinds of buildings they think are most important in their city, and which ones they think should be accorded prominence. A study carried out some years ago on a Venezuelan city (Appleyard 1976) found that people were able to define which uses they thought most important to their city. Measures of the *prominence* of buildings are also possible. In that same Venezuelan city we found that the best known (not necessarily the best liked) buildings were those which were *visible* from major streets and at major intersections, were *unique* in their *form* qualities—shape, isolation, size, surface color, and texture—and were highly *used*. We developed a predictive model, which could predict how well known

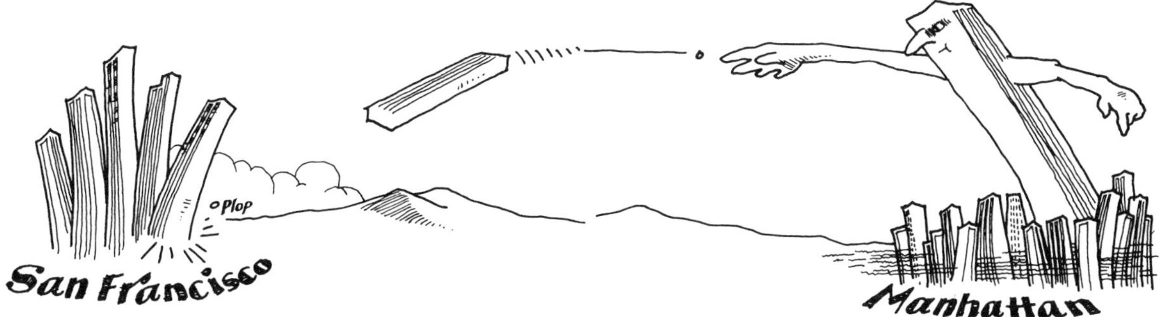

Figure 7-8
Cartoon by Louis Dunn from *The Ultimate High Rise* (Brugmann et al. 1971).

a building would be if we could measure its visibility, form qualities, and use level. The TransAmerica Building, on the basis of this model, always will draw extraordinary attention to itself, because in addition to its unique shape, it lies on the axis of Columbus Avenue, the most visible location in the city after the Ferry Building.

It is not surprising that the Bank of America and TransAmerica Buildings (until the Hyatt Regency came along) were the best known buildings in San Francisco. Highly visible buildings also polarize public emotions. In interviews carried out by Berkeley students, these two buildings were either the most liked or the least liked buildings in the city. Unfortunately; the new height controls will forever maintain their prominence.

The role of high-rise buildings in the *symbolic disruption* of a city's image has been an increasing source of public resentment. Just as the World Trade Center has disrupted the profile of lower Manhattan, the Hilton Hotel towers over Jerusalem, the ITT building transforms the skyline of Brussels, and the Montparnasse is overshadowed by a 56-story dark presence, so the U.S. Steel Building threatened the relatively coherent image of downtown San Francisco. This undermining of a city's identity can represent a loss that the public may view as intolerable.

Tall buildings also *devalue existing symbols*. Once heroic and respected buildings are reduced to toy-like dimensions—the Arc de Triomphe has been "conquered" by La Defense; the grandeur of London's St. Paul's is dwarfed by surrounding towers; the city's formerly great parks are perceptibly diminished by high buildings which intrude on their pastoral seclusion. Distances that along winding streets seemed considerable are now shown in a casual glance to be short. The devaluation of previous grandeur has only one arguable benefit. It makes the old city more "cute," "human," and endearing. In more and more cities the "old" is now perferred to the "new." Is it worth the cost?

If we can measure the prominence of buildings and develop a clearer idea of the public's symbolic goals for their city's environment, certain kinds of guidelines or limitations on the prominence of buildings are possible. The city could stipulate that no new building be more prominent than any other building of similar use. This might slow the trend to use buildings as "billboards" to advertise corporate entities. Another city might desire such diversity and encourage each building to be as prominent as it can, to give "life" to the public environment by openly revealing symbolic competition. Miami and Las Vegas have flourished on this unconscious policy, but not every city needs it.

Reducing the Uniqueness of the City

Each city wishes to be unique, but high-rise buildings from city to city are increasingly similar to each other. They are part of the trend towards homogenization of a world culture. Given photos of high-rise buildings, how many could tell to which city they belong? The fear that San Francisco is losing its uniqueness—with all that implies for the tourist industry, loss of city pride, deterioration of the quality of life, decline in property values—underlies much of the hue and cry against further high-rise construction. Each additional high-rise tarnishes the characteristic image of the city, making it less San Francisco and more like other cities. This is, of course, happening to London, Paris, Boston, Mexico City. Just as with building prominence, measures of city uniqueness and building conformity can be developed.

The choices here seem to be twofold. One is to prohibit new changes—to preserve what is valued, the uniqueness that exists. New buildings should be absorbed quietly into the unique setting, fitting harmoniously with its character. The other strategy is to create consciously unique buildings, and therefore a *new* uniqueness. This is much more risky and is unlikely to get much public support, unless a city feels it has already been homogenized. Cities without distinctive buildings may wish to go this path. The TransAmerica Building is an interesting case. It will further increase San Francisco's uniqueness, and therefore may be accepted over time, although most San Franciscans may feel their city is already unique. Look-alike Midwestern cities might greet unique buildings with more acclaim, although their relative impropriety might only pass muster in cities like Miami or Los Angeles.

High-Rise as Political Symbol

Will the attitudes emerging in San Francisco combine with the non-growth, think-small, anti-technology movement which has worldwide support, especially among the young, to form a powerful and pervasive anti-high-rise ideology that effectively halts their spread? This symbolic question may override utilitarian questions of safety, efficiency, and livability of each individual building. Such an ideology could be fueled by isolated disasters such as the collapse of a building in London, the peeling façade in Boston, another book by Oscar Newman, or more films like *Towering Inferno*.

Myth plays as powerful a role in environmental politics as in all politics and as Edelman (1971) has argued, myths are essential to keep constituencies together. High-rise buildings, huge though they are, could be no more than pawns in the game of power, a game in which professionals may have to choose sides on political as well as functional grounds (Figure 7-9).

Yet each city and country will still make its own decisions depending on how much its government—or people—identify with high buildings. In the 1950s, after an era of stagnation, Boston welcomed tall buildings. They symbolized a break-out from an oppressive situation. In the late 1960s, in the midst of a boom, San Francisco had had enough. Moscow is proud of its thirty-story Kalinin Prospect, Singapore boasts fifty-story skyscapers, Chicago vies for the highest of them all, but the struggles to stop them go on in San Diego, Portland, Paris, and Jerusalem.

San Francisco, basking in the dubious protection of its height and bulk ordinance, has now become quiescent.

> The last time a crowd rallied to protest the wrong building in the wrong place—U.S. Steel's 52-story tower on the waterfront—may literally have been the last time we shall see such a demonstration. Apathy is too lively a word to describe the mood of the city since then. The feeling is more one of justified helplessness [Herb Caen, *San Francisco Chronicle* 1974].

IMPLICATIONS FOR ARCHITECTS

Architects were to be found on both sides of San Francisco's controversy. Those involved in the design of high-rise buildings supported them, the local AIA chapter generally supported the height and bulk controls. A quote from the chief architect of one of the leading firms proposing a high-rise building illustrates an utterly different value set from those expressed in the newspapers: "If I had my way I'd tear [the Ferry Building] down tomorrow. It's the worst thing Arthur Brown ever did. It's nothing but a bus depot with a tower. In fact I'd tear down every building in town except the City Hall." This kind of arrogance deliberately devaluing the existing city may be accepted in Cleveland or Chicago, but it infuriated San Franciscans. It did not exactly endear architects to the public. Another example of the different worlds of architect and public: "They [the diagonal braces of the Alcoa Building] hold the building up and prevent it from falling down in an earthquake. That's a very good thing. Besides they remind me of a Franz Kline painting." Will the public understand such associations?

The architect usually designs his buildings for a physical environment whose meaning is unknown and therefore easily devalued. It is like working in a vacuum of meaning, perfectly illustrated by the gray-colored buildings which surround models of new building proposals. The San Francisco controversy was important because it brought out how other people felt about the city. The setting became alive.

Architects will, and should always, be torn between the demands of the "inside" and their clients, and the

Figure 7-9
The day the U.S. Steel Tower was turned down by San Francisco's Supervisors (SUPES) in favor of a 175′ height limit. *San Francisco Chronicle*, **February 18, 1971. ©1971 by Chronicle Publishing Co.**

demands of the "outside" and the public. For too long buildings have been designed from the *inside-out*. Façades have been seen as cosmetic, trivial. But this is the public's concern and the public is more important than an individual establishment. The public may in the future be demanding that buildings be designed as much from the *outside-in*. This view was generally supported by San Francisco's AIA chapter.

The visual qualities of high-rise buildings and the messages concerning power and identity which they send are not issues to be taken lightly. They are one of the chief means by which the profession communicates to the public. They are "read" more widely than the *AIA Journal* or *Progressive Architecture*.

The approach to the design of high-rise buildings suggested here seeks to base political and professional design decisions on a *knowledge* of public values and feelings. This is not to say that public views should be followed slavishly, but they should be known and respected. The method is to identify the environmental characteristics of high-rise buildings, relevant to the public, and the neighbors as well as the users: whether they be scale, shape, view blockage, color, prominence, or visibility.

Figure 7-10
Still from a film of a model simulating high-rise alternatives for San Francisco made in the Berkeley Environmental Simulation Laboratory.

Since there are not at present, and may never be, universal principles of what is acceptable and desirable, each city will have to identify its own character, its own valued qualities and places, and stipulate in which ways new buildings can contribute. Architects should play a leading role, but they must also *listen*.

In proposing projects they must also communicate clearly and openly the kinds of impacts their buildings will make on the city's environment. A notable feature of the San Francisco controversy was the emergence of "opposition drawings." While the proponents of the U.S. Steel Building showed it blending neatly into the city as seen from the air to the south of the Bay Bridge, opponents depicted the actual view from Telegraph Hill, which showed how it dwarfed the Bay Bridge. The later twenty-story Haas Towers on Russian Hill were not opposed until a local lawyer had them drawn onto several perspectives of Russian Hill. A neighborhood opposition group was immediately formed.

"Truth in simulation"—open disclosure to the public—may seem hazardous and unnecessary, but in the long run it may avoid deep and lasting resentment. Besides, it is the right thing to do.

REFERENCES

Appleyard, Donald. *Planning a Pluralist City: Conflicting Realities in Ciudad Guayana*. Cambridge: MIT Press, 1976.

Appleyard, Donald. "Why Buildings Are Known." *Environment and Behavior* 1 (December 1969):131-156.

Appleyard, Donald, and Carp, Frances. "Residential Environment Impact Study" (Part II, in six volumes). The BART Impact Management Documents, Final Report, Part II. Berkeley: Institute of Urban and Regional Development, University of California, Berkeley, 1973.

Blumenfeld, Hans. "Scale in Civic Design." *Town Planning Review* 24 (April 1953):35-46.

Brugman, Bruce B.; Greggar Slettland; the Bay Guardian Staff; and 52 other arch skyscraper foes. *The Ultimate High Rise*. San Francisco: San Francisco Bay Guardian Books, 1971.

De Casanova, Caroline Arrighi; Fishman, Lois; and Paula Silberthau. "Case Study." Unpublished paper for IDS 241, University of California, Berkeley, December 1972.

Dornbusch, David M., and Co., Inc. *Environmental and Social Impact of Intensive Commercial and High Rise Building Development in San Francisco*. San Francisco: Dornbusch, 1975.

Edelman, Murray. *Politics as Symbolic Action*. Washington, D.C.: Academic Press, 1971.

Fried, Marc. "Grieving for a Lost Home." In *The Urban Condition*, edited by Leonard Duhl, pp. 151-171. New York: Basic Books, 1963.

Krampen, Martin. "A Possible Analogy between (Psycho-) linguistic and Architectural Measurement—The Type-Token Ratio (TTR)." In *Psychology and the Built Environment*, edited by D. Canter and T. Lee. London: The Architectural Press, 1974.

Kreimer, Alcira. "The Building of the Imagery of San Francisco." Term paper, University of California, Berkeley, 1971.

Kreimer, Alcira. "Building the Imagery of San Francisco: An Analysis of Controversy over High-Rise Development." *1970-71—Environmental Design Research (EDRA IV), Vol. 11*, edited by W. F. Preiser. Stroudsburg, Pa.: Dowden, Hutchinson & Ross, 1973.

Miller, George A. "The Magic Number, Seven Plus or Minus Two: Some Limits on Our Capacity for Processing Information." *Psychological Review* 63 (March 1956):81-97.

Newman, Oscar. *Defensible Space*. New York: MacMillan, 1972.

San Francisco, Department of City Planning. *The Urban Design Plan for the Comprehensive Plan of San Francisco*. San Francisco, 1971.

Winter, Stuart R. "The Environmental Components of Property Value." Master's thesis, University of California, Berkeley, September 1971.

Yantis, John M. "Case Study." Unpublished paper for IDS 241, University of California, Berkeley, December 1972.

8

High-Rise Visual Impact

David M. Dornbusch
Pat M. Gelb
David M. Dornbusch & Company, Inc.

INTRODUCTION AND OBJECTIVES

In a study of some impacts of high-rise development on the visual environment of San Francisco, we surveyed opinions of how San Francisco high-rises look to residents and workers with views of the city's high-rise areas. Our objectives were (1) to survey the terms people use to characterize high-rise buildings and the primary criteria they use to evaluate structures in their environment; (2) to determine whether a cumulative score of attitudes toward the looks of high-rises based on responses to a variety of questions could be derived; (3) to investigate relationships between attitudes toward high-rises and characteristics of the population surveyed; and (4) to apply the results of the opinion survey to a comparative evaluation of the impacts of different forms of development alternatives.

STUDY DESIGN AND METHODOLOGY

Sample Selection Criteria

The primary criterion of selection of respondents to be polled in the high-rise visual impact survey was opportunity to view high-rise buildings in San Francisco as part of the ordinary visual environment. This attribute was considered essential if we were to monitor actual impressions of the visual environment using a self-administered questionnaire. Secondary selection criteria aimed at a cross-section of high-rise and low-

This chapter discusses part of a research study in which the impacts of urban growth and particularly tall building development in San Francisco were analyzed. The study was prepared for the San Francisco Planning and Urban Renewal Association and was sponsored by the U.S. Department of Housing and Urban Development, the Mary A. Crocker Trust, and the San Francisco Foundation. San Francisco Planning and Urban Renewal Association. *Impact of Intensive High-Rise Development in San Francisco: Step One-Part B, A Final Feasibility Report*, Vol. III, Appendix D-7, pp. 224–225.

rise residents, and of the San Francisco workforce in high- and low-rise buildings.

Using a topographic map of San Francisco, nine hillside residential areas were selected which face the downtown business and financial districts where most of the city's high-rise development is concentrated. Blocks were randomly selected from among these areas, and residents' names and addresses were obtained from *Polk's San Francisco City Directory*. The Polk's entries were then checked against the current San Francisco telephone directory to avoid erroneous mailings. The list of residents to be mailed questionnaire forms was then randomly selected, the number of recipients in each area determined from the proportion that area represented of the total of all residential areas selected. Both high- and low-rise buildings (buildings above and below ten stories) were included in the sample, and forms were mailed to equal numbers of men and women. A total of 290 questionnaires were distributed to residential areas.

Procedure was different for sampling from the commercial areas. Once again, a view of high-rise buildings was a primary criterion. In addition, we sought to survey a cross-section of the San Francisco workforce at all levels, and to include different kinds of firms. In order to obtain access to employees at all job levels, we made contact with personnel managers at several large firms, who applied a random selection procedure to their employee rosters to choose equal numbers of male and female survey participants. Managerial staff also distributed the survey forms for us, the number in each firm depending upon that firm's proportion of total employees in the commerical sample. We obtained the cooperation of four large firms, two banks, a retail department store and a hotel, located in high-rise and low-rise buildings (buildings above and below fifteen stories). A total of 286 questionnaire forms were distributed to commercial firms.

The selection criteria controlled were thought to be sufficiently inclusive of factors which might reasonably influence the kinds of responses sought. Anticipated sample size and structure were judged sufficient for the suggestive nature of survey results, since findings were not intended for use in a projection model. Survey responses were tabulated by David M. Dornbusch & Company staff, and results were analyzed using the Vogelback Computing Center Statistical Package for the Social Sciences.

A combined total of 576 questionnaire forms were distributed, and 201 completed survey forms were returned, a response rate of 35 percent.

Questionnaire Development

Final questionnaire development was based upon results of a methodological pretest, with additional comments and suggestions from technical advisory committee members, Daniel Yankelovich, Inc., consultant staff, and other survey design consultants. The revised questionnaire form was retested among some twenty individuals.

Cumulative attitude scoring was developed to provide for cross-tabulation with different respondent characteristics. To minimize subjectivity, each response earned a possible maximum of ± 1 point. Neutral, balanced, or qualified responses scored zero. A careful balance was maintained between the proportion of open and closed questions to avoid bias toward or against verbally proficient respondents. It was possible to score a total of ± 52 points.

No attempt was made to characterize nonrespondents. Comparatively few responses were obtained through follow-up telephoning, and these forms were not scored or weighted differently from earlier returns.

The questionnaire included several open questions, the product of our success with this format in the feasibility test and of our desire to obtain the fullest range of attitudes and of individual expressions of evaluation without predetermining responses.

FINDINGS AND CONCLUSIONS

The high-rise visual impact survey found that aesthetics is the most important evaluator of areawide quality for most respondents, and that high-rise developments are frequently at odds with respondents' aesthetic goals. Respondents' greatest objection was to high-rise buildings in residential areas.

Opportunity to view high-rise buildings as part of their ordinary San Francisco visual environment was a primary criterion of selection for survey respondents, and 89 percent of all respondents in our sample had such a view.

Specific survey results include the following:

1. Only 45 percent of those possessing views of high-rise buildings from home liked their view, while the high-rise view from work was liked by only 41 percent. Existing high-rise developments apparently improve the cityscape for the comparative minority of San Francisco residents and workforce respondents.

2. The greatest indifference to view opportunity (35 percent of respondents) was expressed toward views from respondents' workplace.

3. The most preferred vantage point for looking at San Francisco high-rise buildings was "from far away" (69 percent), while the vantage point most disliked was "from street level" (55 percent). These responses point up the need for most respondents, whatever their overall attitude, to achieve considerable distance from high-rise buildings before they can be perceived as visual amenities. The survey responses also indicate that high-rises are not necessarily viewed advantageously from other vantage points of height. While 48 percent of respondents liked to see high-rises from a hill, only 40 percent found them attractive from another high-rise building.

4. Sixty-two percent responded negatively when asked if they would choose a home in an area with high-rise buildings.

5. The concept occurring to most respondents most often when they look at high-rises in San Francisco was "loss of unique San Francisco character" (40 percent). Next most frequent were "economic growth" (38.5 percent), "desirable place to work" (36.5 percent), and "oversized for human environment" (32 percent). While these responses are inconclusive in themselves, they do point up the apparent conflict between two perspectives on the high-rise issue: aesthetics and economics. (Although, indeed, "economic growth" was not expressed as being exclusively positive.)

6. The median definition of "high-rise" buildings among respondents was 14.7 stories high, or taller.

7. Aesthetic issues were the primary determinants of respondents' valuations of the overall quality of both neighborhoods and commercial districts. Eighty-four percent cited aesthetics as the primary criterion for evaluating neighborhoods, compared to 75 percent who cited aesthetic issues as primary for commercial areas.

8. In comparison, economics ranked as a primary criterion among 37 percent of respondents for commercial areas, and among 28 percent for neighborhoods.

Discussion of Survey Findings

As previously noted, the survey aimed primarily at investigating how citizens characterize their environment, what terms they use to describe and evaluate high-rise buildings, and commercial areas or residential areas, in order to derive indications for future focused investigation. The following procedure was used to learn what were the evaluative criteria which were important to the lay population surveyed. Open questions permitted respondents to consider and describe their own neighborhood, the area most familiar to them, and then to evaluate San Francisco's downtown business and financial districts similarly. Respondents were then asked to summarize which factors helped them to make these judgments about each area. Factors included aesthetics, facilities, people, physical design, economic considerations, among others, and each factor was given a working definition. Finally, respondents were asked to list in order the three factors which were most important in helping them to evaluate each area.

Comparing the three most important evaluation factors for neighborhoods with those for business and financial districts reveals that certain criteria are found to be of primary importance, whether respondents applied them to evaluating residential or commercial environments. Where 84 percent of respondents cited aesthetics as one of the three most important criteria of judgment for neighborhoods, 75 percent also chose aesthetics as one of the three most important criteria for evaluating the business and financial districts. It should be noted that cross-tabulations of the criteria chosen as most important for neighborhoods against those chosen for the commercial areas reveal little statistical dependence. That is, the same respondents do not automatically choose the same factors, whatever the object of evaluation.

Among the 84 percent who chose aesthetics as one of the three most important evaluative criteria for neighborhoods, moreover, 57 percent chose aesthetics as the most important. A similar relation holds for the business and financial districts evaluations. Of the 75 percent who chose aesthetics as one of the three top criteria, 52 percent place it number one in importance.

The next most frquently chosen criterion for both neighborhoods and the business and financial districts was facilities available in the area. This factor was among the top three in importance for 70 percent of respondents when judging the downtown business and financial districts, and for 57 percent of respondents when judging their residential neighborhoods. Among those who cited facilities among the three most important factors for judging either area, it was most frequently ranked as second in importance (with 50 percent of mentions for neighborhoods and 46 percent of mentions for downtown).

While aesthetics and facilities available ranked first and second in importance for both residential areas and the downtown business and financial districts, the third evaluation criterion varied with the type of area. "People" received the next highest frequency of mentions for neighborhoods, with 45 percent of total responses; less than half of these (43 percent) ranked it second in importance. "Physical design" follows, with 40 percent of total responses and was ranked third in importance by 42 percent of those who included it in their top three. For the downtown business and financial districts, on the other hand, "physical design" is next in importance after aesthetics and facilities, with 48 percent of all respondents including it in the top three, and 45 percent of those ranking it third. "Economics" follows with 37 percent of all responses. Of those 37 percent who mentioned economics as one of their top three criteria of evaluation, 45 percent ranked it first in importance. "People" follows closely behind economics for the business districts, with 36 percent of all responses, and of these, 39.5 percent each chose it as second or third in importance.

Comparing these responses with the concepts most frequently brought to mind when respondents look at high-rise buildings yields some interesting indications. While the concepts most often associated with high-rise are either aesthetic or economic, the responses just discussed suggest that economics does not rank very high among the survey sample as a yardstick by which to judge a city district, whether residential or commercial. Economics is clearly more important to respondents when they are judging commercial districts than when their object is a residential area, though it is not considered very important in either case. Economics placed among the three most important criteria for only 28 percent of all respondents when judging their neighborhood, and 44 percent of these ranked it third, as compared to 37 percent when applied to commercial areas, as reported above. The main point is that aesthetics is mentioned almost twice as frequently as economics among the top three criteria for the downtown business and financial districts, and three times as often for residential neighborhoods. ("Prestige," "Location," and other criteria were mentioned infrequently, 14 percent or less of total responses, as important evaluators for either kind of area.)

These comparisons are derived from the distribution of responses of a comparatively small sample and are, moreover, initial findings of a preliminary attempt to categorize the criteria people use to evaluate different areas, and to determine the relative importance of these criteria. As such, these results are suggestive rather than predictive. Duplication of results in similar studies, in conjunction with rigorous restructuring of the different criteria to eliminate overlaps between them and to assure that no relevant factors are excluded, will be necessary before the findings can be implemented as an accurate predictive tool.

As a preliminary to querying respondents' evaluation criteria for the two different kinds of areas, we asked them to describe their likes and dislikes about their neighborhood and the downtown business and financial districts. The frequency with which different characteristics were named was tabulated from write-in responses to open questions. There was no limit to the number of features which could be named; however, responses were categorized to permit tabulation. Bear in mind that respondents were not presented with an array of features to choose from. All responses derive from individuals' own conception and recall. Our object in this initial attempt to monitor preferences was to discover which features were important to people without defining the terms of their response in advance. In context, it is not surprising that frequencies of response are small. Analysis of these responses is based upon minority consensus.

The bar graphs in Figures 8-1 and 8-2 summarize characteristics most frequently mentioned as liked or disliked in either area. Responses for different areas are compiled not to compare the different areas, but to note the kinds of features which are important to

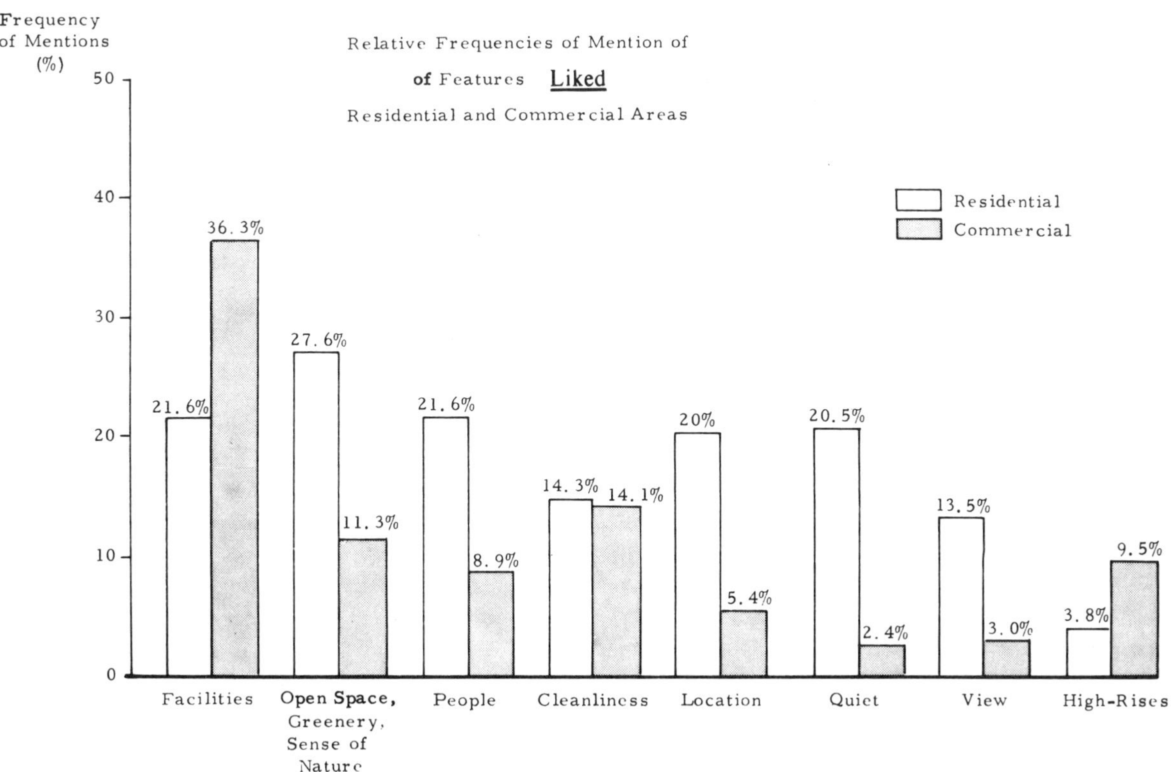

Figure 8-1
Relative frequencies of mention of features *liked*—residential and commercial areas.

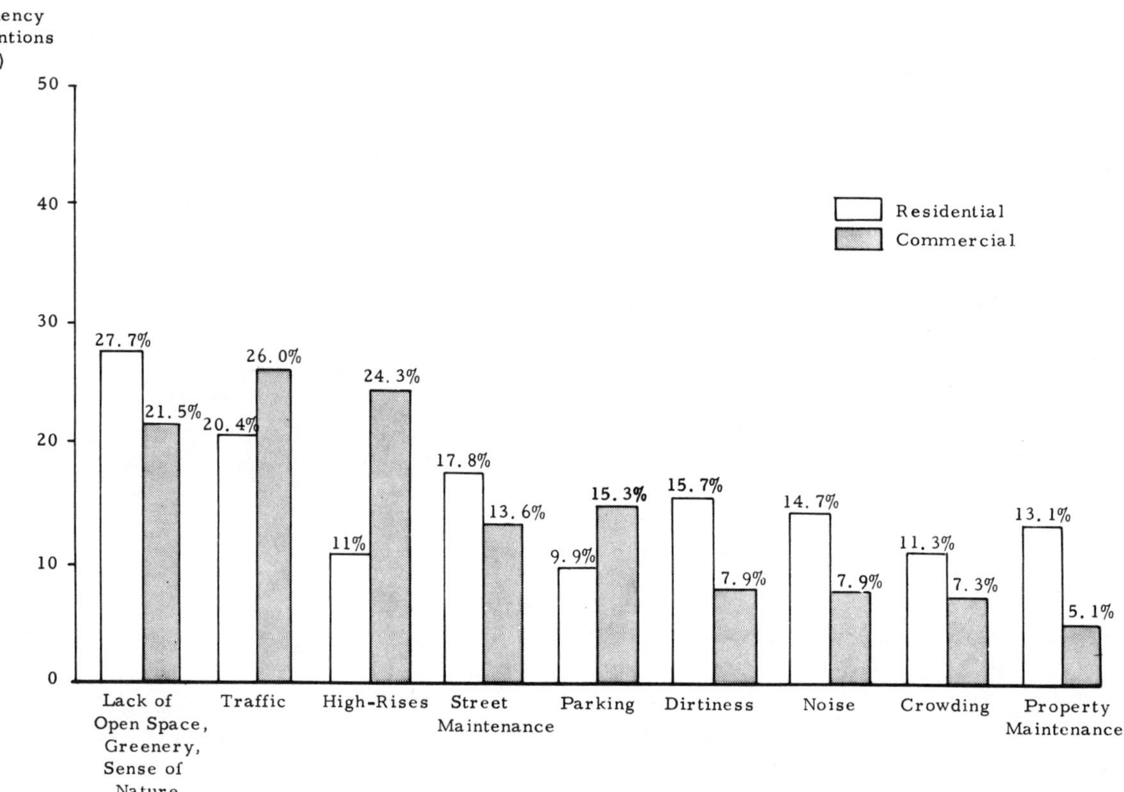

Figure 8-2
Relative frequencies of mention of features *disliked*—residential and commerical areas.

people in either area, as well as the relative importance of these features. Direct comparisons between the residential and commercial areas were not solicited, although the survey format necessarily involves application of similar measures to both kinds of areas. In fact, many respondents explicitly evaluated San Francisco's business and financial districts in terms of other city centers, while residential areas were compared to other residential areas.

Figure 8-1 presents features most frequently mentioned as liked in both residential and commercial area evaluations. Although the three or five most frequently mentioned features vary for the different kinds of areas, it also appears that both the number and extent of preferences in the commerical areas are less than in the neighborhoods. Facilities ranks above all other features as liked downtown, while cleanliness and open space, the next most frequently mentioned features, occurred to less than half as many people. For neighborhoods, on the other hand, five features clustered together as most frequently mentioned. Open space, greenery, and sense of nature, also at a premium downtown, appears to have most focus in the neighborhoods, followed by facilities and people next, and then by quiet and location. Among these features, open space, greenery, and sense of nature is perhaps most sensitive to impacts from increased high-rise development, although the remaining characteristics may receive indirect impacts.

Two features are mentioned frequently among

those disliked in both commercial and residential areas. (These dislikes are presented in Figure 8-2.) Traffic problems are singled out for complaints most frequently in the downtown districts, while they are mentioned second most frequently in the neighborhoods. Lack of open space, greenery, and sense of nature is the most frequently named dislike for neighborhoods, and is third in order of mentions for the commercial areas. Recalling that open space, greenery, and sense of nature is also the most frequently liked feature in the neighborhoods emphasizes its preeminence among amenities. High-rise buildings themselves are the second most frequently mentioned disliked feature for the commercial areas, while street maintenance is the third most cited complaint in the neighborhoods. These latter responses are perhaps influenced in the first case by the focus of the questionnaire as a whole and in the second by the timely controversy over street sweepers' salaries in San Francisco.

Although overall attitude scores were neither clearly positive nor negative toward high-rises, the majority of respondents surveyed, including many with attitude scores positive toward high-rises, would apparently not like to have high-rise buildings in their home neighborhoods. Asked whether they would choose a home in an area with high-rise buildings, 62 percent responded negatively, while only 17 percent answered "yes." The remainder considered that factors other than the mere presence of high-rises would figure prominently in their decision if the issue were actually confronted.

Cumulative attitude scores were derived as the sum of respondents' scores on individual survey questions. Attitude scores could be positive or negative, according to individual responses, and a maximum of ± 52 points could be scored. The distribution of cumulative attitude scores by decile group for the entire survey sample, presented in Table 8-1, is normal, with 66 percent of respondents falling within the five central deciles. This distribution expresses no overriding positive or negative result. The mean score is zero, or neutral. However, there are slightly more respondents scoring below zero (negative toward high-rise) than above zero (positive toward high-rise), and the mode (or most frequent score) is negative. But the difference is not sufficient to assume acceptance or rejection of high-rise in general.

TABLE 8-1
Cumulative Attitude Scores of Survey Respondents by Decile Groups

	Absolute Frequency	*Adjusted Frequency (%)*	*Cumulative Adj. Freq. (%)*
-39.5 through -30.0	14	7.0	7.0
-29.5 through -20.0	20	10.0	16.9
-19.5 through -10.0	27	13.4	30.3
-9.5 through -0.5	39	19.4	49.8
Zero	4	2.0	51.7
0.5 through 9.5	29	14.4	66.2
10.0 through 19.5	33	16.4	82.6
20.0 through 29.5	18	9.0	91.5
30.0 through 39.5	14	7.0	98.5
40.0 through 49.5	3	1.5	100.0
Total	201	100.0	

Valid Cases = 201.
Missing Cases = 0.
Mean Score = 0.

The normal distribution of attitude scores does indicate, however, the respondents were able to express themselves in the survey's terms and that the survey format did not bias opinions. Cumulative attitude scores provided us with a means of relating and discussing the different opinions of different populations within the survey sample.

Cross-tabulating attitude scores against the height of respondents' buildings of residence and work is noteworthy. For example, of the 190 respondents residing in buildings under ten stories tall (classed as low-rise) the majority have negative attitude scores toward high-rise buildings (see Table 8-2). However, there is only one high-rise resident respondent whose attitude score is nagative.* These trends are only

*Total sample = 201 respondents. Raw X^2 = 18.4472 with 9 degrees of freedom. Significance = 0.0303; one case undetermined. Note that 5 percent of our respondents reside in buildings ten stories high or taller, compared with approxi-

TABLE 8-2
Cumulative Attitude Scores Toward High-Rise by Stories in Respondents' Residence Building

Count / Row Pct / Col Pct / Tot Pct — *Stories in Residence Building*	-39.5 thru -30.0	-29.5 thru -20.0	-19.5 thru -10.0	-9.5 thru -.5	Zero	.5 thru 9.5	10.0 thru 19.5	20.0 thru 29.5	30.0 thru 39.5	40.0 thru 49.5	Row Total
Low-Rise (less than 10 stories)	14	20	27	37	4	29	29	16	11	3	190
	7.4	10.5	14.2	19.5	2.1	15.3	15.3	8.4	5.8	1.6	95.0
	100.0	100.0	100.0	97.4	100.0	100.0	87.9	88.9	78.6	100.0	
	7.0	10.0	13.5	18.5	2.0	14.5	14.5	8.0	5.5	1.5	
High-Rise (10 stories or more)	0	0	0	1	0	0	4	2	3	0	10
	0	0	0	10.0	0	0	40.0	20.0	30.0	0	5.0
	0	0	0	2.6	0	0	12.1	11.1	21.4	0	
	0	0	0	.5	0	0	2.0	1.0	1.5	0	
	14	20	27	38	4	29	33	18	14	3	200
Column Total	7.0	10.0	13.5	19.0	2.0	14.5	16.5	9.0	7.0	1.5	100.0

Attitude Scores (column headings)

Raw Chi Square = 18.44723 with 9 degrees of freedom. Significance = .0303.
Number of Missing Observations = 1.

suggestive, however, since our sample is small and includes few high-rise residents, while the difference between the majority with negative scores and the minority with positive scores in the low-rise buildings is slight. The trend is hardly surprising, however, since residence location is largely a matter of choice, and high-rise residents would be unlikely to oppose high-rise buildings on principle. The demand for high-rise living units (roughly 2 percent of total city units surveyed in 1972) compared to that for the majority of low-rise residences remains an issue.

Cross-tabulating respondents' attitude scores by height of work building reveals a similar trend (see Table 8-3). Our sample includes a large number of high-rise employees (workers in buildings of fifteen stories or more). Once again, a small majority of the low-rise workforce is negative toward high-rise buildings, overall, while the majority of the high-rise workforce is positive.†

The survey results also provide interesting details on those who possess the enhanced view opportunity afforded in the commercial areas. A cross-tabulation of our respondents' job classifications and evaluations of view from work is presented in Table 8-4. Of the six major employment groups classified, managerial staff and professional and technical workers stand the greatest chance of possessing a view opportunity in the commercial areas. Yet these individuals express

mately 2 percent of high-rise dwelling units citywide, as reported in a 1972 survey for the San Francisco Planning and Urban Renewal Association study, *Impact of Intensive High-Rise Development in San Francisco: Step One-Part B, A Final Feasibility Report*, Vol. III, p. 206.

†Raw X^2 = 13.9679 with 9 degrees of freedom. Significance = 0.1235; 26 respondents were unemployed; two cases undetermined.

TABLE 8-3
Cumulative Attitude Scores Toward High-Rise by Stories in Respondents' Work Building

Count Row Pct Col Pct Tot Pct					*Attitude Scores*						
Stories in Work Building	-39.5 thru -30.0	-29.5 thru -20.0	-19.5 thru -10.0	-9.5 thru -.5	Zero	.5 thru 9.5	10.0 thru 19.5	20.0 thru 29.5	30.0 thru 39.5	40.0 thru 49.5	Row Total
Low-Rise	.9	14	14	22	4	15	12	7	10	2	109
(less than	8.3	12.8	12.8	20.2	3.7	13.8	11.0	6.4	9.2	1.8	63.0
15 stories)	75.0	77.8	70.0	64.7	100.0	60.0	41.4	46.7	76.9	66.7	
	5.2	8.1	8.1	12.7	2.3	8.7	6.9	4.0	5.8	1.2	
High-Rise	3	4	6	12	0	10	17	8	3	1	64
(15 stories	4.7	6.3	9.4	18.8	0	15.6	26.6	12.5	4.7	1.6	37.0
or more)	25.0	22.2	30.0	35.3	0	40.0	58.6	53.3	23.1	33.3	
	1.7	2.3	3.5	6.9	0	5.8	9.8	4.6	1.7	.6	
	12	18	20	34	4	25	29	15	13	3	173
Column Total	6.9	10.4	11.6	19.7	2.3	14.5	16.8	8.7	7.5	1.7	100.0

Raw Chi Square = 13.96790 with 9 degrees of freedom. Significance = .1235.
Number of Missing Observations = 28.

their dislike or indiffference for the view as frequently as their liking for it. Almost twice as many managers are indifferent to the view as like it. There is also no clear preference for the view among professional and technical respondents. In fact, there are at least as many respondents who are indifferent to the view as those who like it for every job group but services occupations. Among this group alone, a liking for the view from work is expressed more than twice as often as indifference, and much more frequently than dislike. This group represents about 21 percent of the workforce surveyed, and about 7 percent of the San Francisco Central Business District workforce reported in 1970.

Several characteristics of the survey sample revealed no significant relationship to overall attitude score. There was no strong correlation between attitude toward high-rise and whether respondent lived in or outside of San Francisco, or owned or rented his or her dwelling. (Chi square tests higher than 0.5.) Length of residence in San Francisco was also not correlated with overall attitudes, nor were job classification, age group, or whether respondents had children living at home.

In sum, the findings of the high-rise visual impact survey indicate that respondents perceive no generalizable "high-rise question" to support or oppose. However, the survey responses do suggest that high-rise building developments frequently conflict with respondents' aesthetic goals. High-rise developments create views which more respondents dislike or ignore than enjoy, while they concentrate net viewpoints gained in the commercial areas where the greatest indifference to those views exists. It appears that people's overall valuation of an area depends heavily upon its aesthetic features, that areawide valuation, and hence, satisfaction, is most sensitive to impacts on aesthetic amenities. Although economic benefits

TABLE 8–4
Survey Respondents' Preference for View from Work by Occupational Group

Count Row Pct Col Pct Tot Pct			*Like View from Work*			
Job Classification	*No*	*Yes*	*Indif-ferent*	*Not De-termined*	*Not Appl.*	*Row Total*
Not Employed	0 0 0 0	0 0 0 0	0 0 0 0	0 0 0 0	24 100.0 85.7 12.1	24 12.1
Managerial	6 22.2 15.4 3.0	7 25.9 11.9 3.5	13 48.1 20.0 6.5	1 3.7 12.5 0.5	0 0 0 0	27 13.6
Prof. and Tech.	14 26.9 35.9 7.0	16 30.8 27.1 8.0	16 30.8 24.6 8.0	4 7.7 50.0 2.0	2 3.8 7.1 1.0	52 26.1
Clerical	9 25.0 23.1 4.5	10 27.8 16.9 5.0	17 47.2 26.2 8.5	0 0 0 0	0 0 0 0	36 18.1
Sales	4 28.6 10.3 2.0	2 14.3 3.4 1.0	7 50.0 10.8 3.5	1 7.1 12.5 0.5	0 0 0 0	14 7.0
Services	4 9.5 10.3 2.0	24 57.1 40.7 12.1	11 26.2 16.9 5.5	1 2.4 12.5 0.5	2 4.8 7.1 1.0	42 21.1
Self-Employed	2 50.0 5.1 1.0	0 0 0 0	1 25.0 1.5 0.5	1 25.0 12.5 0.5	0 0 0 0	4 2.0
Column Total	39 19.6	59 29.6	65 32.7	8 4.0	28 14.1	199 100.0

Raw Chi Square = 198.78175 with 24 degrees of freedom.
Significance = 0.
Number of Missing Observations = 2.

are clearly associated with high-rise by our respondents, aesthetics emerge as of overriding importance. The drift of these responses, particularly in the light of other study findings, suggests that satisfaction with the visual and living environment in San Francisco will decrease under high-rise forms of development unless they more explicitly address people's aesthetic objectives.

REFERENCES

Blumenfeld, Hans. "Scale in Civic Design." *Town Planning Review*, April 1953.

Craik, Kenneth H. "The Comprehension of the Everyday Physical Environment." In *Environmental Psychology: Man and His Physical Setting*, edited by Harold M. Proshansky, William H. Ittelson, and Leanne G. Rivlin. New York: Holt, Rinehart & Winston, 1970.

Festinger, Leon. "Cognitive Dissonance." *Scientific American* 207, 4 (October 1962):93-102.

Hayward, Scott C., and Franklin, Samuel S. "Perceived Openness-Enclosure of Architectural Space." *Environment and Behavior* 6, 1 (March 1974):37-52.

Hershberger, Robert G. "Toward a Set of Semantic Scales to Measure the Meaning of Architectural Environments." In *Proceedings of the Third Annual Environmental Design Research Association Conference, 1972*, edited by William Mitchell.

Lowenthal, David. *Environmental Assessment: A Comparative Analysis of Four Cities*. Publications in Environmental Perception No. 5. New York: American Geographical Society, 1972.

Lowenthal, David, and Riel, Marquita. *Environmental Structures: Semantic and Experiential Components*. Publications in Environmental Perception No. 8. New York: American Geographical Society, 1972.

Lowenthal, David, and Riel, Marquita. *Structures of Environmental Associations*. Publications in Environmental Perception No. 6. New York: American Geographical Society, 1972.

Moser, C. A. *Survey Methods in Social Investigation*. Melbourne, London, and Toronto: William Heinemann Ltd., 1966.

Oppenheim, A. N. *Questionnaire Design and Attitude Measurement*. New York: Basic Books, Inc., 1966.

Rabinowitz, Carla B., and Coughlin, Robert E. "Some Experiments in Quantitative Measurement of Landscape Quality." RSRI Discussion Paper Series: No. 43. Philadelphia: Regional Science Research Institute, March 1971.

U.S. Environmental Protection Agency, Office of Research and Development, Washington Environmental Research Center, Environmental Studies Division. *Aesthetics in Environmental Planning*, by Stanford Research Institute. Washington, D.C.: U.S. Government Printing Office, November 1973.

9

High-Rise Impacts on the Use of Parks and Plazas

David M. Dornbusch and Pat M. Gelb
David M. Dornbusch & Company, Inc.

INTRODUCTION AND OBJECTIVES

High-rise buildings located near or on the perimeter of a park can limit visibility of the park to potential users in the surrounding community. If people cannot see a park, they may not think to use it, and thus by cutting off views of the park, the high-rise buildings may limit use of the park. Tall buildings bordering a park can also cause shading and winds over the park space. We investigated the relationship between high and low buildings surrounding a park and park use and amenities by studying a variety of neighborhood parks and plazas in San Francisco.

Our study of the impacts of high-rise buildings on the use of parks and plazas in San Francisco had four primary objectives: (1) to learn whether high-rise buildings located near a park (or plaza) affect the size or shape of the area served by the park; (2) to determine whether visibility of a park is a significant factor in its use by the surrounding community; (3) to survey whether park users perceive any negative effects produced in the park by high-rise buildings—such as winds and shadows, or increased traffic and noise; and (4) to estimate how different forms of development will affect the use of parks and plazas in San Francisco.

We focused primarily on neighborhood parks and plazas principally serving the surrounding neighborhood community. Regional or district parks attract users from far too large an area to serve as good sites for studying local impacts. It is doubtful whether parks of the size and visibility of Golden Gate or Buena Vista would suffer severe negative effects from adjacent high-rise development. But smaller parks—even hilltop sites—might be significantly affected by tall buildings surrounding them.

This chapter discusses part of a research study in which the impacts of urban growth and particularly tall building development in San Francisco were analyzed. The study was prepared for the San Francisco Planning and Urban Renewal Association and was sponsored by the U.S. Department of Housing and Urban Development, the Mary A. Crocker Trust, and the San Francisco Foundation.

STUDY DESIGN AND METHODOLOGY

The Survey Method

Our estimate of proximate high-rise building impacts on the use of parks and plazas in San Francisco derived from a comparison of selected high-rise and low-rise area park characteristics. Data were collected by means of personal surveys of park users in the parks and plazas, to provide information on park user origins, frequencies of visit, travel time and visibility access to the park, height of residence and workplace, and park likes and dislikes. We also collected information on park users' transport modes, and asked what were their *usual* origins, travel times, and transport modes, so that we could verify the representativeness of our day-of-survey responses for ordinary park user practice.

Interviewing was performed in the parks and plazas by teams of two, rotating around the park at timed intervals in order to achieve equal representation of park users originating from all sides of the park. While one team member conducted the survey at a given point, the other tallied all persons entering the park at that point. These counts provided a check on the representation of park users interviewed within each park sector, and also provided the basis for estimating total park usership and the percentage of usership interviewed. The rotation method succeeded in interviewing comparable proportions of park users in each sector.

The length of time each team was stationed at a given point in each park was determined on the basis of the total number of park perimeter entrance points to be covered. Our goal was always to circle the entire park in one half-hour, in order to avoid underestimating peak usages during certain time periods. We used as many as three teams per park, depending upon the total number of entrance points and distance to be covered, again so as to allow the park to be circled in a half-hour (that is, where no individual team could circle the park in a half-hour and still achieve a reasonable proportion of interviews).

Teams were composed of one man and one woman, and jobs were traded during the survey to minimize sex or personality biases and fatigue. Relief personnel provided breaks so that surveying and park user count tallies continued uninterrupted. Surveyors included professional interviewers and planners and university students.

The interviewer was not to discriminate among potential respondents, but to approach for interview the first person (over approximately seven years of age) to enter the park at each given point when the interviewer was free to begin an interview. If several persons entered in a group, the interviewer was to choose the one on the right, left, or in the middle alternately, rather than make any other discrimination. Only persons *entering* the park were approached for interview. Subsequent interviews were attempted upon completion of each previous one. The interview took approximately three minutes to complete, and no new interviews were to begin during the last two minutes of the time interval at any entrance point so as to avoid delays in circling the park. The team member doing the park user tallies also kept track of the time.

Surveying in the field was preceded by formal training sessions in the Dornbusch & Company offices, and survey personnel were supervised in the field by Dornbusch & Company staff.

Surveying continued for three, four, or five midday hours on the weekend or during the week or both, depending on the usage patterns of particular parks and plazas.

Completed interviews were computer tabulated and analyzed by David M. Dornbusch & Company staff, using the Northwestern University Vogelback Computing Center Statistical Package for the Social Sciences.

Description of Survey Sample

We surveyed 629 park users among the parks and plazas studied. This total represents an 8.0 percent sample of all park users counted entering the park, and a 2.4 percent sample of total estimated usership for all parks. About 28 percent of those approached for interview refused to participate.

The survey sample included 70 percent male respondents. This distribution has two principle causes. The first is that the interviewers' selection rule meant an interviewer could theoretically interview any person entering the park alone, but could approach only one person from any group entering the park. Our surveyors found that not only were men much more likely to come to the park alone than women, but that female park visitors were very frequently in groups with other women (from which only one interviewee could be selected). Second, women refused to be interviewed much more often than men. This was especially true during peak lunchtime use in commercial area parks and plazas. However, analysis of a subfile of responses aggregated by sex group revealed no characteristic or consistent differences between the park use practices or preferences of males and females.

Approximately one-third of respondents were twenty-five years of age or younger. An additional 57 percent were between the ages of twenty-six and fifty; 12 percent were ages fifty-one or over.

In order to learn whether visibility access to the park or plaza influenced park use, we asked respondents whether they could see the park from their home or workplace. Where the respondent was a visitor to San Francisco, the questions were applied to their current residence and/or workplace in the San Francisco Bay Area.

We also queried respondents' travel times, transport modes, and place origin to the different parks studied, on the day they were interviewed as compared to their usual practice. Their responses provided us with a convenient check on the representativeness of our survey results, while they are interesting in their own right. Some 68.5 percent of all respondents had traveled ten minutes or less to reach the park on the survey day, compared to 63.4 percent for whom this was ordinary practice. An additional 8.6 percent had traveled between 11 and 15 minutes to the park, compared to 7.8 percent usually. This group brought to 77.1 percent the total of respondents who had traveled 15 minutes or less to the park on the survey day.

Respondents' transport modes on the day of survey were also similar to their usual transportation to the park. The large majority of park users surveyed (70.5 percent) had walked to the park, compared to 66.9 percent who usually walked. Automobiles were used by an additional 20.5 percent on the survey day, compared to 14.9 percent who usually came to the park by car. Public transportation was used by only approximately 7 percent of respondents, both on the survey day and usually.

Respondents' places of origin to the park on the day they were surveyed were quite similar to their usual origins to the park as well. The majority came from home: 51.5 percent on the day of survey compared to 57.6 percent who usually came from home. Another 24.3 percent had come to the park or plaza from work, compared to 24.6 percent who usually came from work. The most significant difference between respondents' place of origin on the survey day and usual practice was those coming to the park from shopping and services such as restaurants, retail stores, medical visits, etc. While 8.5 percent of respondents originated from such places on the survey day, it was the stated usual origin of only 1.3 percent.

Overall, the similarities between park visitor travel times, transport modes and places of origin to the park were certainly sufficient to verify the representativeness of the analytical tools developed from our survey responses.

On the basis of the park and plaza entrance point tallies of park visitors, we derived estimates of total usership for the parks surveyed during the hours and on the days of the surveys. These estimates, along with the numbers of actual visitors counted, are presented in Table 9-1, for their own interest. The large numbers of persons visiting these parks and plazas is remarkable, and serves to indicate the already high demand for open space in San Francisco, especially within the downtown commercial business district.

TABLE 9-1
Usership by Park or Plaza

Park or Plaza	*Day of Survey*	*Hours of Survey*	*Users Counted*	*Estimated Usership*[1]
Washington Square	Weekday	11-3	296	987
	Weekend	11-4	2,200[2]	7,333[2]
Sidney G. Walton Square	Weekday	11-3	543	1,900
	Weekend	11-4	167	585
Lafayette Park	Weekday	11-3	200	533
	Weekend	11-4	116	309
Alta Plaza Park	Weekday	11-3	147	392
	Weekend	11-4	165	440
M. Justin Herman Plaza	Weekday	11-2	1,267	4,223
	Weekend	11-3	1,073	3,577
St. Mary's Square	Weekday	11-2	450	1,125
Crown Zellerbach Plaza	Weekday	11-2	197	788
Maritime Plaza	Weekday	11-2	872	2,907
Duboce Park	Weekend	11-4	215	645
Totals			7,908	25,744

1. David M. Dornbusch & Company estimates based upon park entrance user counts during the time period named.
2. A well-publicized photography show drew an exceptionally large population on this day.

FINDINGS AND CONCLUSIONS

Summary of Principal Findings

The visibility of a neighborhood park or plaza was found to be a significant factor in its use by the surrounding community.

1. People who *cannot* see a park or plaza from home or work tend to visit it comparatively infrequently.

Generally, high-rise developments located within a neighborhood park's potential service area limit the extent and shape of that area.

1. Park users who come from behind high-rise buildings to the park tend to travel shorter distances and be fewer in number than those who originate from areas more open to the park.
2. High-rise buildings close to parks and plazas have some perceptible negative impacts upon amenities sought by park users, including sunlight and avoidance of wind.

Discussion of Findings—Parks

Our first analytical task was to compare the area containing the majority of actual park user origins to the park with a theoretical service area for each park. This theoretical service area is the area extending out and around the park for a walking distance corresponding to the time most park users surveyed took to get to that park. This distance was estimated on the basis of about 264 horizontal feet traveled per minute of walking time.* This theoretical service area was mapped for each park, and its boundary was adjusted for the competing attraction of other parks in nearby districts. We conducted a survey of park users in each of the parks to gather information on park user origins and travel time to the park. We then plotted all park user origins for each park, on the map showing the theoretical service area. Thus we could compare the two areas readily.

Although all of the park's theoretical service areas had relatively smooth perimeters, parks bordered by high-rise buildings exhibited very irregularly shaped areas of actual user origins compared to those of parks surrounded by lower buildings. Figures 9-1 and 9-2 illustrate this difference for a pair of hilltop parks of similar size, facilities, and communities served, Lafayette Park and Alta Plaza Park. The area around Lafayette Park (Figure 9-1) includes a considerable number of buildings over ten stories high, especially to the north, while the Alta Plaza Park area (Figure 9-2) has comparatively few tall buildings.† The figures illustrate theoretical service areas with radii 5 and 10 minutes walking distance to each park. The theoretical service area is flattened on the west of Lafayette and the east of Alta Plaza, since along this edge, a potential park user has an equal option to visit either park.

The heavy dark line encloses the majority cluster of actual user origins to the park. More isolated and distant park user origins are also depicted. Note that the actual service area (locus of user origins) of Lafayette Park (Figure 9-1) is considerably more irregular than that of Alta Plaza Park (Figure 9-2). Moreover, the irregularities of shape conform generally to the locations of the high-rise buildings. That is, Lafayette's actual service area generally flattens to the north, where most of the high-rises are, except for a few isolated and distant origins. The actual service area also extends much further toward the east and the south than towards the west and the north.‡ On the other hand, Alta Plaza Park's actual service area is comparatively regular, with user origins scattered fairly evenly around the park. The figures also reveal that fewer people come to the park from areas blocked by high-rise buildings than originate from the open sides of the park. The areas of park user origins for these parks during the week conform to the weekend patterns displayed.

We also surveyed and plotted park user origins compared to theoretical service areas for a number of additional *unpaired* parks, in and out of high-rise areas. Their results bear out findings for Lafayette and Alta Plaza Parks. While the boundaries of the area of actual user origins to the parks in high-rise districts do not conform so specifically to the location of the high-rise buildings as in the Lafayette Park case, still these areas are much more irregular than those of the low-rise area parks.

Moreover, while all of the actual service areas of the parks studied are smaller than their theoretical areas, the actual service areas of parks in high-rise areas generally cover a smaller percentage of the area they could theoretically serve than those of low-rise area parks.

We also found that park users who originate from behind high-rise buildings tend to visit the park somewhat less frequently than those who come from unblocked areas. This difference is most dramatically illustrated by again comparing the paired parks, Lafayette and Alta Plaza. Figures 9-3 and 9-4 present

*Rai Y. Okamoto, "Bart-Induced Urban Design and Architectural Impacts," prepared for the Metropolitan Transportation Commission's Phase I Land Use and Urban Development Study of BART Impacts, June 1974, p. 11; John A. Bruce, "The Pedestrian," in *Traffic Engineering Handbook,* edited by John E. Baerwald, 3rd ed. Washington, D.C., Institute of Traffic Engineers, 1965, p. 111. Walking was the principal mode of travel to the parks for the vast majority of park users surveyed.

†Ten stories is a reasonable definition for high-rise residential buildings by current San Francisco standards.

‡This area boundary is remarkably similar to that which was derived for Lafayette Park during our preliminary test of the analytical method and survey approach. Since the pretest was conducted over eighteen months previously, the similarity provides strong support for the final study results.

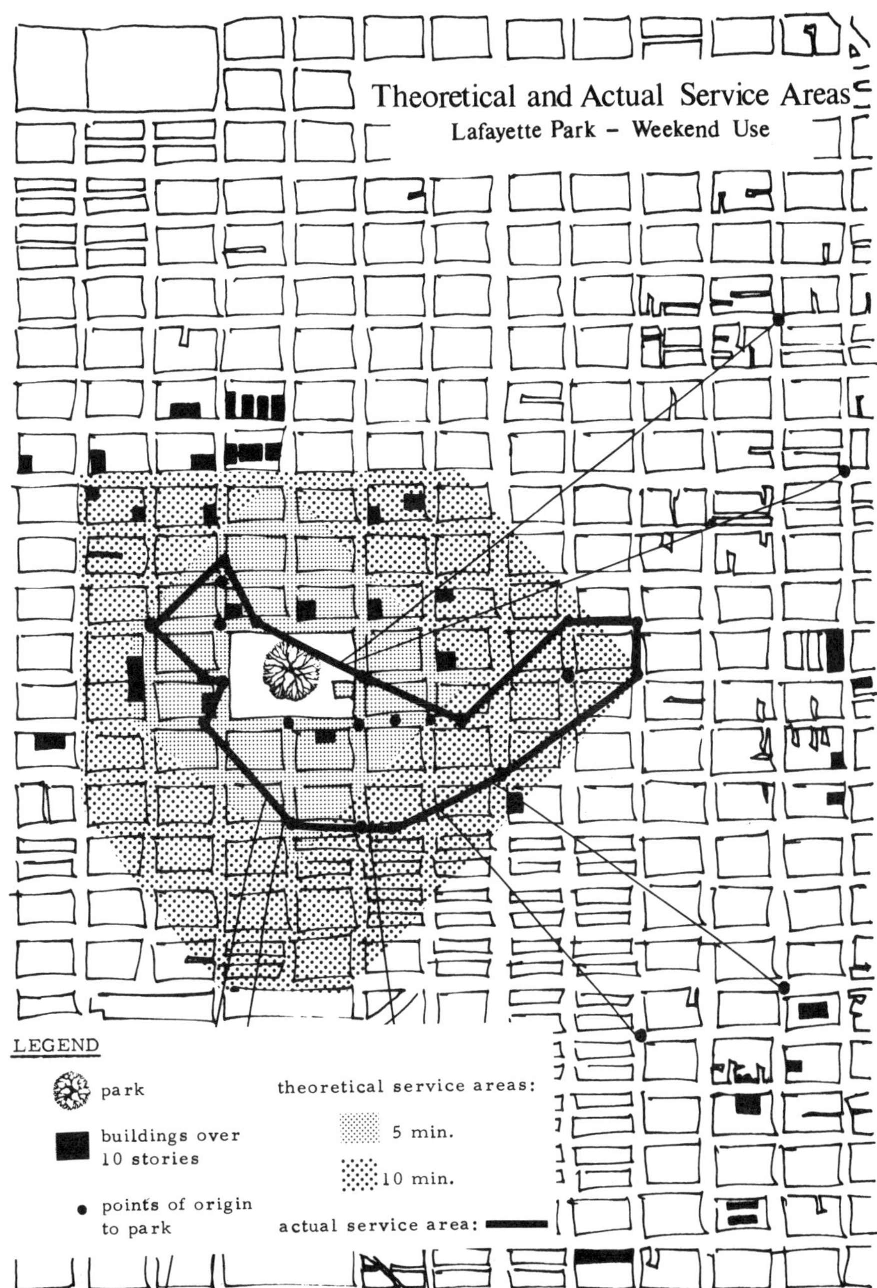

Theoretical and Actual Service Areas
Lafayette Park - Weekend Use
LEGEND
park
buildings over 10 stories
points of origin to park
theoretical service areas:
5 min.
10 min.
actual service area:

Figure 9-1

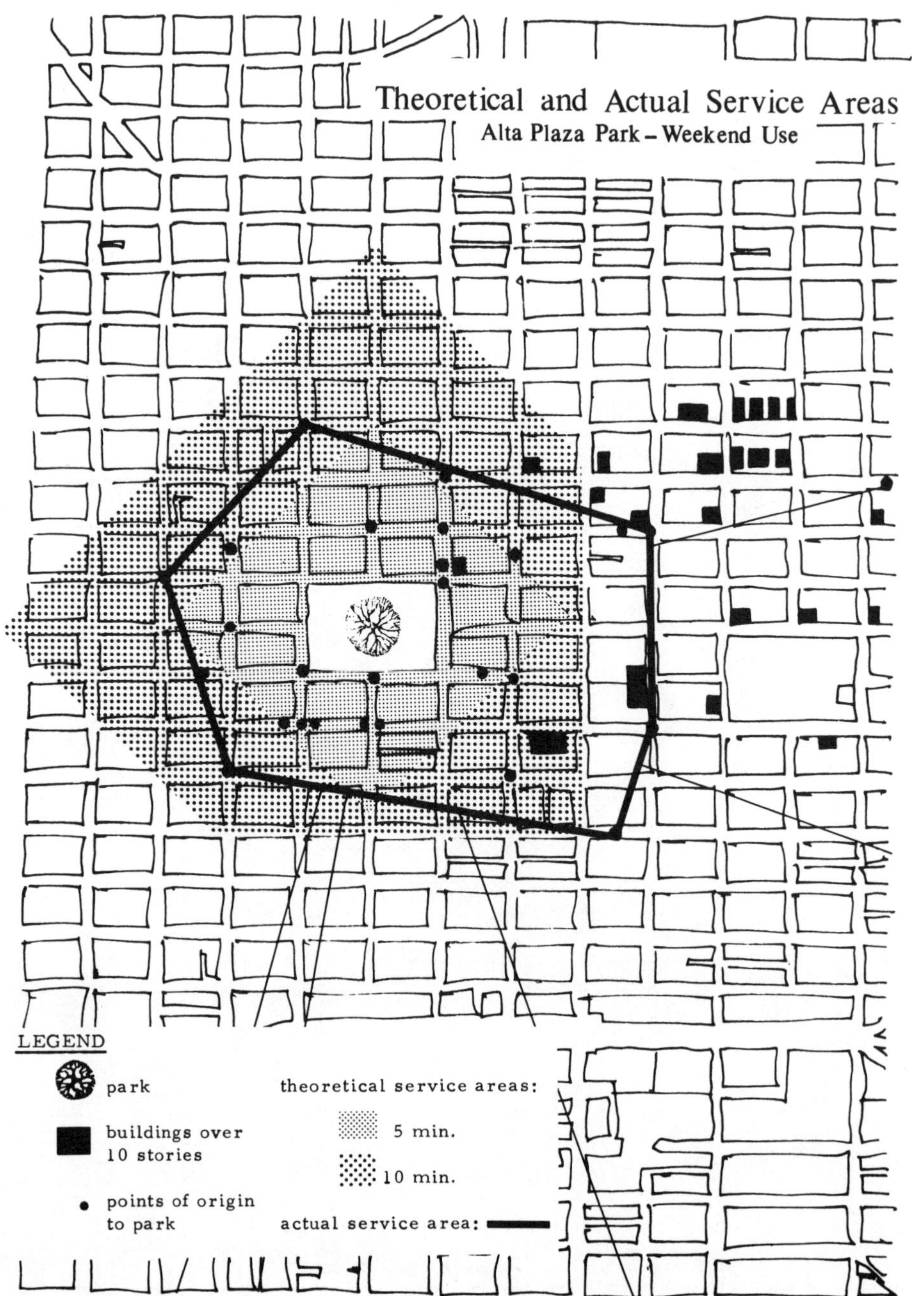
Theoretical and Actual Service Areas
Alta Plaza Park – Weekend Use
LEGEND
park
buildings over 10 stories
points of origin to park
theoretical service areas:
5 min.
10 min.
actual service area:

Figure 9-2

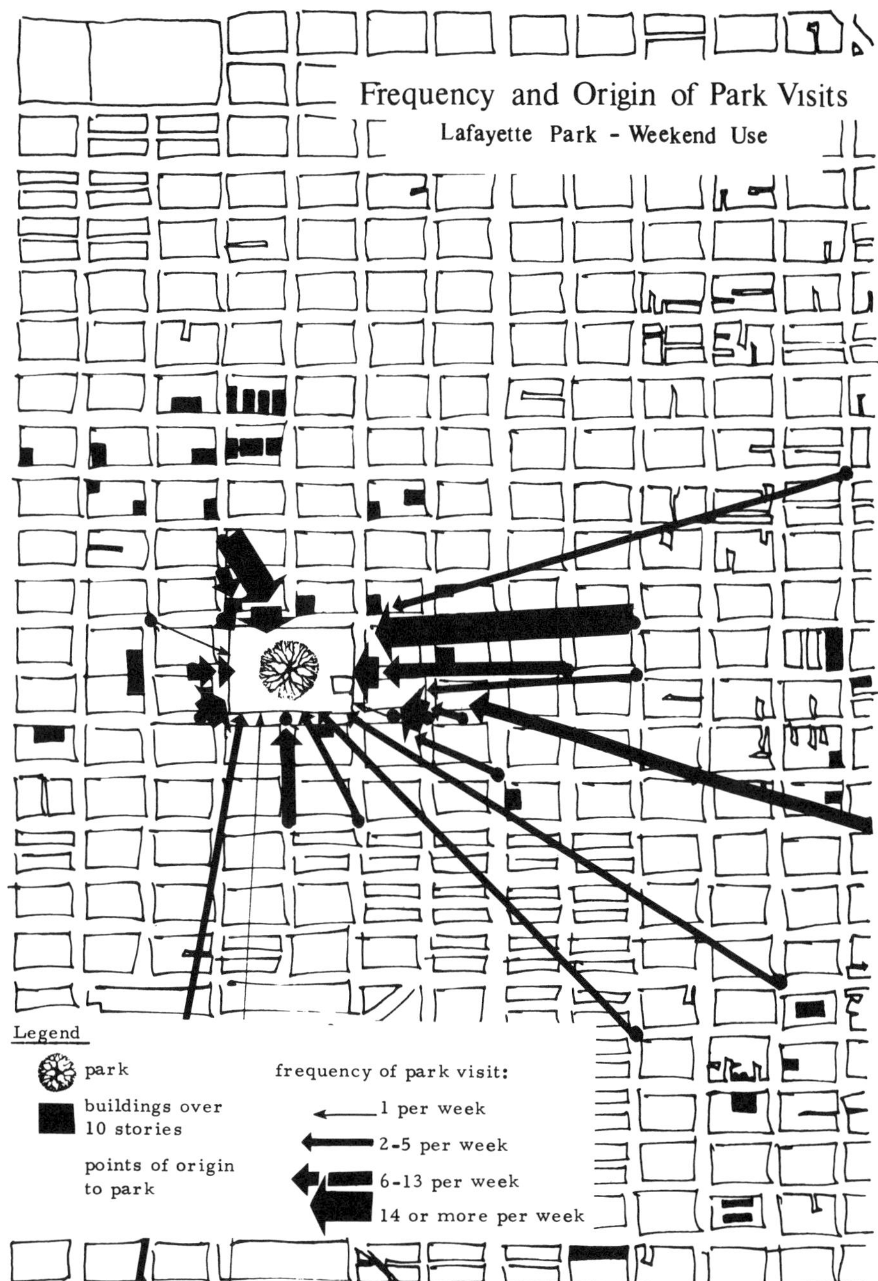
Frequency and Origin of Park Visits
Lafayette Park - Weekend Use
Legend
park
buildings over 10 stories
points of origin to park
frequency of park visit:
1 per week
2-5 per week
6-13 per week
14 or more per week

Figure 9–3

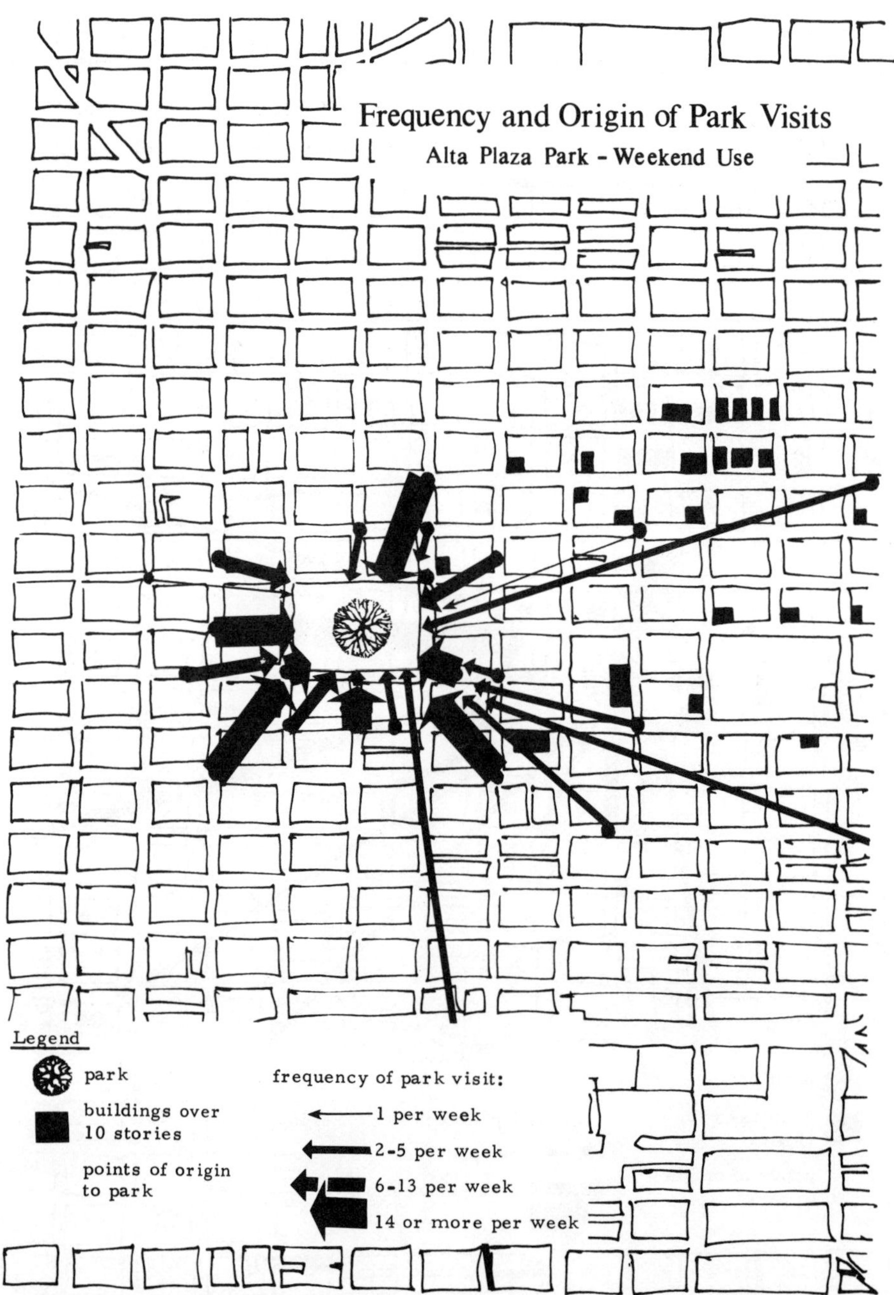
Frequency and Origin of Park Visits
Alta Plaza Park - Weekend Use
Legend
park
buildings over 10 stories
points of origin to park
frequency of park visit:
1 per week
2-5 per week
6-13 per week
14 or more per week

Figure 9-4

both the origin and frequency of user visits to these parks. Both parks are frequently used, and the most frequent visitors (6 through 13 and 14 or more visits per week) emanate from origins on all sides of the parks. But with a single exception, the most frequent visitors tend to travel shorter distances to Lafayette Park then do frequent visitors to Alta Plaza Park. On the north and west sides of Lafayette Park, the most frequent visitors tend to originate from the park's immediate perimeter, or from the high-rise buildings themselves. Very few very frequent visitors to the park originate from behind the high-rise buildings.

Although none of the other parks studied is visited as frequently by as many people as are Lafayette and Alta Plaza Parks, the differences between high- and low-rise area parks support the previous findings. First, the low-rise area parks are visited more frequently by more people than the high-rise area parks. Second, the most frequent visitors' origins are most evenly dispersed around the low-rise area parks than around the high-rise area parks.

Statistical analysis showed, moreover, that park users' frequencies of visit to the park are correlated with their ability to see the park from their home or workplace. Cross-tabulation of users' frequency of park visits with their ability to see the park from their home is presented in Table 9-2. A similar cross-tabu-

TABLE 9-2
Frequency of Park User Visits and Visibility Access from Home

TABLE 9-2 (Continued)

Count Row Pct Col Pct Tot Pct	*Ability to See the Park from Home*		
Frequency of Park Visits (Times per Week)	*Yes*	*No*	*Row Total*
Under 1	6 4.1 8.0 1.0	142 95.9 26.2 23.0	148 24.0
1 thru 3	16 7.9 21.3 2.6	186 92.1 34.3 30.1	202 32.7
4 thru 6	7 8.6 9.3 1.1	74 91.4 13.7 12.0	81 13.1
7 thru 9	20 25.3 26.7 3.2	59 74.7 10.9 9.6	79 12.8
10 thru 13	0 0 0 0	1 100.0 0.2 0.2	1 0.2
14 thru 20	14 37.8 18.7 2.3	23 62.2 4.2 3.7	37 6.0
Over 20	7 53.8 9.3 1.1	6 46.2 1.1 1.0	13 2.1
Unique Visit	5 8.9 6.7 0.8	51 91.1 9.4 8.3	56 9.1
Column Total	75 12.2	542 87.8	617 100.0

Raw Chi Square = 70.94078 with 7 degrees of freedom.
Significance = 0.
Number of Missing Observations = 12.

TABLE 9-3
Frequency of Park User Visits and Visibility Access from Work

Count / Row Pct / Col Pct / Tot Pct

Frequency of Park Visits (Times per Week)	Ability to See the Park (Plaza) from Work: Yes	No	Row Total
Under 1	11 9.7 11.5 2.4	102 90.3 27.9 22.1	113 24.5
1 thru 3	30 19.4 31.3 6.5	125 80.6 34.2 27.1	155 33.6
4 thru 6	25 35.2 26.0 5.4	46 64.8 12.6 10.0	71 15.4
7 thru 9	9 20.9 9.4 2.0	34 79.1 9.3 7.4	43 9.3
10 thru 13	0 0 0 0	1 100.0 0.3 0.2	1 0.2
14 thru 20	13 46.4 13.5 2.8	15 53.6 4.1 3.3	28 6.1
Over 20	1 14.3 1.0 0.2	6 85.7 1.6 1.3	7 1.5
Unique Visit	7 16.3 7.3 1.5	36 83.7 9.9 7.8	43 9.3
Column Total	96 20.8	365 79.2	461 100.0

Raw Chi Square = 29.66178 with 7 degrees of freedom.
Significance = 0.0001.
Number of Missing Observations = 168 (includes unemployed and retired persons and students).

lation of use frequencies against visibility of the park (or plaza) from work is presented in Table 9-3. In both cases, the proportion of park users who can see the park from home or work is small among those who visit the park comparatively infrequently. Among visitors who use the park once per day or more (7 to 9 times per week for home-viewed parks, and 4 to 6 times per week for work-viewed parks and plazas), the proportion of those able to see the park increases dramatically.* That is, if people cannot see a park (or plaza) from home or work, they tend to visit it rather infrequently, while those who can see the park from home or work tend to visit it more frequently.† The combined evidence of the service area and user origin and frequency maps and the statistical analysis strongly suggest that the visibility of a neighborhood park is an important factor in its use.

*In addition to the chi square test, a comparison test of the probabilities for achieving the proportion of respondents in each cell for different frequencies of visit was performed. Its results lend further support to the hypothesis.

†Home and work were the most frequent places of users' origins to the parks surveyed.

Discussion of Findings—Plazas

We also surveyed users at two plaza open spaces in the downtown area: Crown Zellerbach Plaza and M. Justin Herman Plaza.

Figures 9-5 and 9-6 show the actual service area of user origins to the plazas compared to the theoretical service areas of Crown Zellerbach and M. Justin Herman Plazas. As in the case of the high-rise area parks, Crown Zellerbach Plaza's actual service area is much smaller than theoretically possible, except for isolated visitor cases. Indeed, the majority of plaza users originated from very close by, an indication of the low visibility of the plaza area, which is below street level as well as amid tall buildings.

M. Justin Herman (Embarcadero) Plaza, on the other hand, possesses a considerable draw, which is dramatically illustrated by the representation of its weekend use in Figure 9-7. This attraction suggests that the plaza's visibility is conceptual as well as physical: people are aware of its presence because of its landmark features like the Vaillancourt fountain and the handicraft merchants.

The context of impacts here is that of two userships, the predominantly weekday workforce who need relaxation and lunchtime open space in the commercial area, and the weekend and leisure tourist and resident groups who visit the plaza as a sightseeing and shopping landmark. Additional surrounding high-rise buildings could cut off the plaza from a substantial section of the workforce, although their effects on the resident and tourist group should be less severe.

High-Rise and Low-Rise Populations and Available Open Space

The tendency for high-rise buildings surrounding a park to shrink the service area of that park is not necessarily a detriment, since the tall buildings locate more potential park users near the park. The net impact must be seen in terms of two primary factors: (1) the different populations involved (the high-rise residents or workers who can see the park and the low-rise residents and workers whose view access to the park is blocked); and (2) the areawide availability of open space for all those who seek it.

While new high-rise development reduces the extent of a given park's service to surrounding residents whose visibility access to the park is blocked, the high-rise residents do not necessarily replace the lost usership: park use may actually decline even while unsatisfied demand exists. Or, existing park space may be inadequate for the new demand. Thus, whether the park experiences any changeover in its usership from low-rise to high-rise residents, the current majority of park users will suffer.

Of the park users surveyed, the overwhelming majority were low-rise residents (95 percent).* The usership of parks located near enclaves of high-rise residential development also featured a large majority of low-rise resident park users, although the proportion of high-rise resident park users certainly increases (9.4 percent).

Where high-rise developments create pockets of high potential demand around park and plaza spaces throughout the commercial area, existing open spaces will reach their saturation levels very rapidly. Therefore, when new high-rise developments surround existing parks and plazas, additional parks and plazas must be created to serve that portion of the present usership which is blocked by the new buildings, the usership which is squeezed out by the new populations of park users, and the overall increase in demand that existing open space is inadequate to meet.

The trend in recent high-rise building development in San Francisco has been to provide plaza space available to the public at large, so there is a real possibility that plaza users cut off from existing open space can find alternative space. But parks are not adequately compensated for by the familiar kinds of

*Residential buildings under ten stories high were classed as low-rise; buildings ten stories or more were classed as high-rise.

Theoretical and Actual Service Areas
Crown Zellerbach Plaza - Weekday Use
LEGEND
park
buildings over 15 stories
points of origin to park
theoretical service area:
5 min.
actual service area:

Figure 9-5

Theoretical and Actual Service Areas
M. Justin Herman Plaza - Weekday Use
(Embarcadero Plaza)
LEGEND
park
buildings over 15 stories
points of origin to park
theoretical service areas:
10 min.
15 min.
actual service area:

Figure 9–6

Theoretical and Actual Service Areas
M. Justin Herman Plaza - Weekend Use
(Embarcadero Plaza)
LEGEND
park
buildings over 15 stories
points of origin to park
theoretical service areas:
10 min.
15 min.
actual service area:

Figure 9-7

office building plaza, since the plazas are usually smaller and less green than conventional parks, while their location exposes them to the negative impacts of surrounding buildings, like shadows and winds. An inventory of high-rise building plazas conducted for this study revealed that many offer only relatively low levels of amenity.

High-Rise Impacts on Amenities Sought at Parks

High-rise buildings around a park can have a variety of physical impacts on the park space, depending on their height and orientation around the park. We sought to survey whether park users perceived any of the effects of proximate high-rise developments by asking them what they liked and disliked about the park they were in. In order to avoid implicit bias, our interview questions were open-ended and did not suggest any specific preferences or dislikes to respondents. This format resulted in relatively small frequencies of any response. Future studies would probably obtain greater confidence levels by offering multiple-choice questions with the display of response options at least partly based upon the most frequent responses to this study. Since the open-ended questions did not allow us to focus on high-rise impacts specifically, the force of benefit or nuisance perception responses is considerably diluted.

Some characteristic differences between features of high-rise area and low-rise area parks were mentioned by our respondents, nonetheless. The most noticeable differences emerge from comparing the order of features mentioned as disliked among the two types of parks (see Tables 9-4 and 9-5). While lack of facilities was the most frequently named dislike in both kinds of parks, high-rise buildings, lack of greenery, and design are the next most frequently mentioned in high-rise area parks, compared to a slightly higher frequency of dislike for dogs and dog messes in low-rise area parks. The comparative frequency of mentions of high-rise buildings in the high-rise area parks is remarkable, given the open question format. Moreover, the greater the high-rise building presence, the greater the dislike for high-rises: St. Mary's Square, M. Justin Herman Plaza, and Crown Zellerbach Plaza are located amidst the densest high-rise development, and users of these open spaces express the greatest dislike for high-rises. Wind is mentioned more than twice as often as an annoyance in high-rise as in low-rise area parks. Lack of sunlight, although infrequently mentioned overall, is *only* mentioned as a problem in high-rise area parks, and again, is mentioned most often where shading is most significant. However, low-rise area parks are perceived as too small more often than high-rise area parks.

The array of features mentioned as liked is perhaps more telling as a general index of demand for quality open space in San Francisco than in terms of proximate high-rise building impacts on park space. Greenery is most frequently mentioned among likes for both groups of parks, and especially for high-rise area parks, in districts where the presence of nature is generally low. (As we have already seen, however, the high-rise area parks are apparently not green enough, since their lack of greenery is a frequent dislike.)

Appreciation of the fact that there is an open space is also very frequently mentioned, and once again, the highest frequency of mentions is among parks in high-rise areas where the need for open space is greater than in the low-rise areas of the remaining parks.

Quality of Open Space Provided by High-Rise Buildings

In addition to the negative impacts high-rise buildings can have on open space in San Francisco, it is also true that high-rise building developers frequently provide new open spaces for public use. The city planning code offers floor area ratio bonuses to developers who provide plazas and landscaped open

TABLE 9–4
Features Mentioned as Disliked – "Low-Rise" Parks
(% Frequencies of Respondents)[1]

	Lack of Facil-ities	Dogs	Too Small	People	Main-tenance	Design	Lack of Greenery	Noise	Wind	High-Rise Build-ings	Lack of Sunlight	No. of Respondents
Washington Square	18.1	19.0	20.0	16.2	11.4	11.4	10.5	12.9	4.8	3.8	0	105
Alta Plaza Park	29.7	21.9	6.3	9.4	9.4	18.8	4.7	3.1	7.8	1.6	0	64
Duboce Park	20.6	20.6	20.6	11.8	23.5	0	20.6	0	0	5.9	0	34
Totals	22.2	20.2	15.8	13.3	12.8	11.8	10.3	7.4	4.9	3.4	0	203

1. There were 279 responses, 203 respondents (1.37 answers per respondent); 86 interviewees (29.7% of total interviewed) expressed no dislikes.
Note: An average 10.8% of respondents also mentioned other dislikes; most of these were extremely park specific such as hours of service of given facilities; police patrols in parks also figured prominently among other dislikes.

TABLE 9–5
Features Mentioned as Disliked – "High-Rise" Parks and Plazas
(% Frequencies of Respondents)[1]

	Lack of Facil-ities	High-Rise Build-ings	Lack of Greenery	Design	Wind	Too Small	Main-tenance	People	Dogs	Noise	Lack of Sunlight	No. of Respondents
Sidney G. Walton Square	15.0	17.5	0	12.5	30.0	22.5	10.0	12.5	2.5	2.5	10.0	40
Lafayette Park	25.8	9.1	9.1	6.0	4.5	10.6	18.2	9.1	22.7	6.0	0	66
M. Justin Herman Plaza	15.5	25.9	41.4	22.4	1.7	3.4	3.4	8.6	1.7	12.1	0	58
St. Mary's Square	8.3	33.3	8.3	0	4.2	25.0	25.0	25.0	0	0	20.8	24
Crown Zellerbach Plaza	36.4	18.2	9.1	45.5	0	0	9.1	0	0	9.1	27.3	11
Maritime Plaza	13.3	6.7	23.3	43.3	36.7	10.0	0	3.3	0	3.3	6.7	30
Totals	18.3	17.5	17.5	17.5	12.2	11.8	10.9	10.0	7.4	6.1	6.1	229

1. There were 350 responses, 229 respondents (1.53 answers per respondent); 111 interviewees (32.6% of total interviewed) expressed no dislikes.

areas—among other building features—within the C-3 (commercial) zoning districts, up to a maximum of 15 percent of basic allowable gross floor area. Indeed, were it not for office building plazas, the downtown commercial district would suffer severe shortages of available open space.

However, the specification criteria for plaza and open space are sufficiently general to allow floor area ratio bonuses for plazas which vary greatly in their overall quality of service to the community. In fact, bonuses can be awarded, though at a lesser rate, to ground-level open space which is not actually accessible for use, if it provides street-level visual amenity "consistent with the purposes of the bonus system." The actual provisions of the code are as follows:

7. Plaza. The plaza shall be directly and conveniently accessible to the general public during all business hours common in the area, from either a street or alley with a minimum sidewalk width of five feet, a feature conforming to the standards of 5 or 6 above, or a permanent public open space. The creditable plaza area shall be located at least 20 feet inside the lot lines separating the lot from streets and alleys, shall have a minimum entrance width of 10 feet, and shall be at least 30 feet in its horizontal dimensions; space occupied by a feature conforming to the standards of 5 above may be counted for up to one-third of any dimension; however, no area credited under 5 above shall also be credited as plaza area. Up to two-thirds of the surface of the creditable plaza area may be occupied by planting, sculpture, pools and similar features, and the balance shall be suitable for walking, sitting and similar pursuits. Any building servicing requiring the presence of vehicles or goods in the plaza area shall be confined to times other than the business hours common in the area. Encroachments permitted by Section 126 of the Code for usable open space shall be permitted for the creditable plaza area.

Notwithstanding the requirements of this provision concerning accessibility or horizontal dimensions, landscaped open area located as herein provided at ground level, consistent with the purposes of the bonus system and readily visible from a street or alley or permanent public open space, may be credited as plaza area within the scope of the 15 percent maximum permitted for the plaza bonus in Table 1A [not shown in this chapter]; provided, that the bonus awarded shall be three square feet of floor area for each creditable square foot of such open area.*

*San Francisco City Planning Code, Chapter II, Article I, Section 112.3, b 7, p. 23.

Thus, while the code certainly attempts to encourage builders to provide open space, it does not deny bonuses for open space of even very limited use to the general public.

In order to derive some estimate of the extent and quality of open space which has been provided by high-rise developers in the downtown study area, we compiled an inventory of the plazas adjoining buildings in this area which are fifteen stories high or taller. The inventory was compiled on the basis of information gained from managers and other executive personnel of tall buildings listed by the City Planning Department, and through on-site measurement and inventory of plaza features. (Wind conditions at the plazas were estimated on the basis of methods derived for the winds analysis section of the large study.)

There are eighty-six buildings fifteen stories high or taller listed by the Department of City Planning within the downtown study area. Of these, only eighteen, or 21 percent, provide twenty-three plazas which are accessible to the general public. Although many of the high-rise building plazas are quite large, generally they are neither very green nor very sunny. (The average percentage of green area for all plazas listed is 16 percent; the average area shaded at noontime during the fall season, 47 percent.) Moreover, several are exposed to severe winds, and these negative features are predominantly owing to the configurations of tall buildings surrounding the plazas.

Careful design and orientation of plaza space can maximize greenery and available sunlight and minimize winds. But the overall density of development in the downtown area often poses nearly insurmountable obstacles to achieving optimum open space. Furthermore, as density increases, surrounding buildings become even more unavoidable, decreasing the chance for future plazas to avoid shadows. Therefore, although new development may offer some new open space and greenery at the same time that it increases the demand for it in this area, San Francisco's high-rise building plazas alone do not meet the demand for quality park space downtown, nor do they compensate users of existing parks for loss of present amenities or park space.

IMPLICATIONS FOR ENVIRONMENTAL DESIGN MANAGEMENT OF LAND USE

Negative impacts on the extent and frequency of park user visits when high-rise buildings border a neighborhood park suggest that restrictive zoning around neighborhood parks be imposed.

This study's results affirm that buildings surrounding a neighborhood park or plaza should be designed to preserve visibility access to the park and to minimize negative impacts on amenities sought at the park. Ideally, surrounding building heights should increase *away* from the park.

Development floor area bonuses should be awarded so as to secure new building plazas of optimum quality and usability. These open spaces should actually provide street-level public access, seating, comfortable paving surfaces and greenery. Planning departments should consider acceptability criteria for sunlight and shading of open spaces. Since high-rise buildings can also induce severe street-level winds, development bonuses—perhaps even building permits—might be denied where uncomfortable wind velocities would be exceeded around the proposed building for more than a small percentage of the time.

REFERENCES

Buechner, Robert D. (ed.). *National Park Recreation and Open Space Standards.* Washington, D.C.: National Recreation and Park Association, June 1971.

Ferris, Abbott L. "Types of Recreation Surveys." In *Recreation Research,* pp. 160-176. University Park, Pennsylvania: National Conference on Recreation Research, 1965.

Gold, Seymour. *Urban Recreation Planning.* Philadelphia: Lea & Febiger, 1973.

Molyneux, D. D. "A Framework for Recreation Research." In *Recreation Research and Planning: A Symposium,* edited by Thomas L. Burton. London: Allen & Unwin Ltd., 1970.

Moser, C. A. *Survey Methods in Social Investigation.* Melbourne, London, and Toronto: William Heinemann Ltd., 1966.

Oppenheim, A. N. *Questionnaire Design and Attitude Measurement.* New York: Basic Books, Inc., 1966.

Sapora, Allen V. "Ascertaining Interests for Recreation Program Planning." In *Recreation Research,* pp. 94-105. University Park, Pennsylvania: National Conference on Recreation Research, 1965.

Scherer, Ursula, and Coughlin, Robert E. "A Pilot Household Survey of Perception and Use of a Large Park." RSRI Discussion Paper Series: No. 59. Philadelphia: Regional Science Research Institute, December 1972.

U.S. Department of Agriculture, Forest Service, North Central Forest Experiment Station. *Outdoor Recreation Research: Applying the Results.* General Technical Report NC-9. Papers from a workshop held by the USDA Forest Service at Marquette, Michigan, June 19-21, 1973.

U.S. Department of the Interior, Bureau of Outdoor Recreation. *Outdoor Recreation Space Standards.* March 1970.

10

High-Rise Impact on City and Neighborhood Livability

Pat M. Gelb
David M. Dornbusch & Company, Inc.

INTRODUCTION AND OBJECTIVES

High-rise buildings impact upon the character of city districts and neighborhoods in two primary ways. Some effects result from the increased densities of people and motor vehicles generated by intensive development in a limited area. Other, perhaps more subtle, effects include the dramatic physical changes high-rise buildings produce by virtue of their size, their design, perhaps even their symbolism. The context of high-rise impacts on neighborhoods is one of contrasts, between the high-rise structure and surrounding low-rise buildings, and between the high-rise and low-rise populations. Not only does a high-rise building multiply the resident population on a block, but the high-rise residents may be very dissimilar to residents in the surrounding low-rise buildings, whom they suddenly outnumber.

Our study focused upon the relative livability of residential blocks with and without high-rise buildings. *Livability,* as operationally defined for this study, expresses the continuity between individual dwelling units and the rest of the block (including semi-private and public open areas as well as other dwelling units): the extent of territory residents perceive as home base. Involved in this concept are aspects of territoriality, or the extent to which residents individualize and defend their living spaces, as expressed in their visibility on the block and their use of outdoor areas as extensions of the individual dwelling unit. The tension between neighborliness and personal privacy is also an important component of this overall concept. We hypothesized that high-rise buildings, by changing the physical form of living space on the block, by closing down views and openness, by shadowing and overlooking neighboring

This chapter discusses part of a research study in which the impacts of urban growth and particularly tall building development in San Francisco were analyzed. The study was prepared for the San Francisco Planning and Urban Renewal Association and was sponsored by the U.S. Department of Housing and Urban Development, the Mary A. Crocker Trust, and the San Francisco Foundation.

buildings, and by increasing the resident population—especially if the high-rise tenants were very different from surrounding low-rise occupants—could impair the livability of the block.

We sought to monitor livability impacts by observing outdoor activities and behavior traces on the block as manifestations of the extent to which residents are comfortable about their home base. Would residents on the high-rise blocks take advantage of surrounding open areas as extensions of home territory available for their use to the same, greater, or lesser extent than residents on comparable low-rise blocks did? Would observers be able to monitor relative degrees of neighborliness by noting the frequency of conversations between residents and passersby? Would the physical features observed in the two blocks offer evidence of different degrees of security or concern with privacy and the safety of individuals and personal property?

To respect residents' privacy insofar as possible as well as to achieve conformity of observation technique among all study blocks, observers were restricted to the public walkway. This procedure to some extent limited the kinds of activities, features, and areas which could be monitored. Nonetheless, we were able to observe and record a wealth of detail. Activities which were hypothesized to be indicators of block livability and which were readily observable outdoors included: conversation groups, relaxation activities, "people watching," movable repairs and maintenance tasks, active recreation and children's play. These activities are defined in the methodology section of this chapter. Selected block features were also recorded, and these are also described in that section. Observation sites included residential blocks both near and far from the principal downtown commercial area.

STUDY DESIGN AND METHODOLOGY

Definitions of Activities Monitored

Activities observed and recorded in residential areas included conversation groups, relaxation activities, "people watching," movable repairs and maintenance tasks, active recreation, and children's play.

Conversation groups included verbal greetings between passersby, between passersby and residents, and between residents. These were moving or stationary conversations, and included communications between persons on different parts of the block, or in separate private spaces. All participants were tallied (excepting observation personnel).

Relaxation activities included sunbathing, lounging, reading or sleeping, as opposed to *people watching* or observing the passing scene, where the primary objective is to watch.

Movable repairs and maintenance tasks were those which allowed a choice of location. That is, gardening, house painting, fence repair, and the like must be performed at given locations. Portable mending operations as well as bicycle and motorcycle repair, for examples, are jobs which residents can perform in a variety of places, according to their preference. We focused on this latter group of tasks.

Active recreation is self-explanatory, including team sports, catch, Frisbee, jogging, and the like. *Children's play* included all recreation activity performed by children, excluding only pedestrian travel and conversation groups including children as passive participants.

The activity groups were considered to be mutually exclusive; that is, if people were observed playing catch and talking, they were logged under either of the two activities but not both. For consistency of observation, we decided that the predominant activity determined the categorization; thus, the case above would be logged as active recreation.

In the commercial areas, we focused principally upon relaxation activities and pedestrian traffic. Observers logged pedestrians according to whether they were hurrying through the block or traveling slowly so as to window shop or otherwise take advantage of the location. The distinction is somewhat subjective, but the differences between high- and low-rise blocks recorded in terms of this distinction are significant and consistent with other observation results.

Behavior Traces Observed

In addition to surveys of outdoor activities, observers noted and recorded selected block features or behavior traces as indicators of the extent of residents' perceived home base. These features included windows open to the view of residents within as well as others outside the dwelling unit, or shielded to limit the view from within and into private areas; fences shielding enclosed areas; signs posted to protect residents' privacy or establish territory rights, such as "do not disturb" or "no parking"; extra locks; and personal belongings left untended outdoors.

Structure of Observation Study

Three pairs of residential blocks were chosen for observation. The block pairs were matched insofar as possible in terms of city area, physical amenities and terrain, orientation, type of dwelling units and the socio-economic characteristics of residents. San Francisco 1970 Census data were used to verify our selection.

The high-rise residential blocks necessarily had higher resident populations than the low-rise blocks, with the high-rise site populations averaging 2.4 times those of the low-rise sites, although densities of persons per unit were comparable between high- and low-rise sites (average 1.6 persons per unit; maximum density 1.8 persons per unit, minimum 1.3 persons per unit). However, observed activities were two to three times as frequent on low-rise sites where the smaller populations reside.

It is impossible to determine the exact proportions of children residing on the observation block *face* from Census data. We attempted to choose sites so as to achieve comparability of residents under eighteen years of age over the entire block. The Golden Gateway block studied was singular for its large population and its minute proportion of resident children. But the advantages of including a totally designed high-rise living environment in our observations were thought to outweigh these disadvantages, since the majority of activities observed do not require juvenile participants.

The low-rise blocks featured predominantly two- and three-story buildings. The tallest building on any low-rise block was an older seven-story apartment building.

The high-rise blocks selected represent relative intensities of development, with proportionately greater high-rise floor space contrasting to surrounding low-rise units.

Two of the block pairs are in the Pacific Heights district, an area which has experienced much recent high-rise residential development, and which is a high-demand area for continuing residential development. The high-rise block of the third pair of sites is part of the Golden Gateway development downtown. Its low-rise partner is located on Telegraph Hill. Residents have predominantly upper-middle and upper incomes.

Four pairs of observation blocks were selected in the commercial area. We attempted to represent both high- and low-rise outdoor environments, and to achieve comparable motor vehicle traffic volumes and character of facilities offered on the members of a given block pair. Strict control of observation sites was impossible, since the presence (e.g., shadows) of high-rise buildings on one block frequently carries over to a proximate low-rise block, and traffic noise, exhausts, and other influences also exert a pervasive effect.

Observation teams of two were stationed on a block for several hours between 11:00 and 6:00 in the residential areas and between 11:00 and 4:00 in the commercial districts. We did not observe during the morning and evening rush hours. Residential blocks were each visited twice—once during the week and once on the weekend—and commercial blocks were surveyed once only during the week. Observation team members were rotated to minimize bias. Teams were made up of professional interview surveyors, planners, and university students. Formal briefing sessions preceded all field work. Each team had a prepared recording notebook for logging specific activities and features in focus. Break times were coordinated so that observations occurred simultaneously on all blocks.

FINDINGS AND CONCLUSIONS

The presence of a high-rise building on a residential block appears to have a negative effect on the livability of the block as measured by this study.

1. The high-rise residential blocks observed featured many fewer instances of people engaged in various activities outdoors than were observed on the low-rise blocks.
2. The low-rise blocks featured three times as many conversation groups and persons engaged in moveable maintenance tasks outdoors as the high-rise blocks. There were also more than twice as many people engaged in relaxation activities and children playing outdoors on the low-rise blocks.
3. The only instances of active recreation observed were on the low-rise blocks.
4. There were up to five times as many pedestrians with origins or destinations at the high-rises on the high-rise blocks as at all other buildings on the block.
5. Motor vehicle trips to and from the high-rise buildings also increased traffic on the high-rise blocks substantially.

High-rise commercial buildings also appear to have negative effects on the livability of downtown streets, by increasing pedestrian traffic volumes on streets within a concentrated area.

1. Observation data indicate an inverse relationship between the magnitude of off-peak pedestrian traffic volumes on commercial blocks, and the number of persons engaging in relaxation activities on those blocks (at high pedestrian traffic volumes).
2. While pedestrian traffic was not consistently heavier, it was generally faster on the high-rise commercial blocks than on the low-rise commercial blocks.

Primary Findings—Residential Areas

Table 10-1 presents observations recorded for all high-rise residential and all low-rise residential blocks for both observation days.

Although the high-rise blocks had an estimated *2.4 times more* residents on average than the low-rise blocks, the high-rise blocks featured only *one-third to one-half* as many instances of the outdoor activities displayed. The most striking differences appeared in the numbers of conversation groups (an index of neighboring and of mutual recognition among residents), and of people engaged in active recreation (an indication of residents' perception of the extent of outdoor "home territory" available for their active use).*

Because high-rise residential development dramatically increases the resident population in a limited area, it correspondingly reduces the proportion of people any single resident can recognize. This impact has ramifications for the block's social climate: the numbers and readiness of passersby to exchange greetings and the relative probability that any several individuals will know one another are factors which also affect the block's overall atmosphere of friendliness or anonymity.

The observation data tend to support this relationship, and they are consistent with similar investigations of neighborliness.†

Because high-rise development also concentrates traffic flows in a limited area, it can impact upon the extent to which residents will adapt the roadway or sidewalks for alternative uses. The absence of active

*Definitions of the activity categories recorded were presented in the Study Design and Methodology section.

†E.g., San Francisco Department of City Planning, *Street Livability Study: An Urban Design Study Background Report,* by Donald Appleyard, June 1970, found that higher traffic volumes could interrupt interactions between neighbors on a block, with consequences for block identity. Anne

TABLE 10-1
Numbers of Persons Engaged in Various Activities[1] – Residential High-Rise and Low-Rise Blocks Compared

	Conversation Groups	*Relaxation Activities*	*People/ Scene Watching*	*Repairs & Maintenance*	*Active Recreation*	*Children's Play*	*Total Persons*[2]
DAY ONE (Weekday)							
All High-Rise Blocks	43	9	7	0	0	7	66
All Low-Rise Blocks	138	5	28	1	3	16	191
DAY TWO (Weekend)							
All High-Rise Blocks	52	0	17	5	0	2	76
All Low-Rise Blocks	157	16	20	15	14	8	230
AVERAGES							
High-Rise Blocks	47.5	4.5	12	2.5	0	4.5	71
Low-Rise Blocks	147.5	10.5	24	8	8.5	12	210.5

1. See Study Design and Methodology section for definitions of the different activities.
2. Excluding pedestrian activity, other than activities specified.

recreation from the high-rise blocks observed in our study may result from increased motor vehicle trips to and from high-rise buildings. The data are inconclusive in themselves, since one of the high-rise blocks is developed above street level and has no vehicle traffic, and the largest through traffic volumes were recorded for one of the low-rise blocks (see Table 10-2).

Another factor in the choice of an appropriate area for active recreation is the extent of open space available, and it may be that the high-rise buildings limit the perceived openness on the block, cast shadows across potential play areas, or pose breakage hazards to a greater extent than do low-rise structures. The high-rise blocks also had fewer instances of childrens' play, an activity type which is subject to influences similar to those which affect active recreation.

Instances of relaxation activities were also greater on the average on the low-rise blocks, as were examples of movable repair and maintenance tasks performed outdoors, and of individuals engaged in watching the overall scene. It is not possible for us to specify the precise links in the chain of cause and effect which explain this difference between the high-rise and low-rise residential blocks studied. But the comparatively infrequent use of outdoor areas for home-based activities is nonetheless characteristic of the high-rise blocks for all activities observed.

Buttimer, "Social Space and the Planning of Residential Neighborhoods, *Environment and Behavior* 4, 3 (September 1972) found that a sense of belonging to the area was the most significant variable associated with residential environmental satisfaction.

TABLE 10-2
Average Motor Vehicle Traffic Counts: Residential Districts – High- and Low-Rise Blocks Compared

Blocks	*Through Traffic*	*Origin or Destination on Block*	
		At High-Rise	*Elsewhere*
Vallejo Street – High-Rise	401	64	52
Clay Street – High-Rise	108	53	60
Golden Gateway – High-Rise	no motor vehicle traffic		
Average: All High-Rise Blocks	255	59	56
Green Street – Low-Rise	564		63
Washington Street – Low-Rise	167		54
Montgomery Street – Low-Rise	motor vehicle traffic not recorded		
Average: All Low-Rise Blocks	366		59

Figures 10–1 and 10–2 offer a graphic representation of the observation data for a typical low-rise and high-rise block pair. The figures depict half of the individuals who appeared on the blocks throughout a five-hour observation period. This method of presentation helps to illustrate the relationship between the number, kind, and location of activities which take place on a block and the subtle quality we are calling its livability.

The low-rise site not only features a larger number of people engaged in various activities, but also illustrates the wider locational scatter of these activities. (The location of individuals in Figure 10–1 is based upon data from the observation log compiled in the field.) While people confine themselves predominantly to the sidewalks and front setbacks on the high-rise block, the low-rise block shows people using the front and sides of the lot, balconies, and the roadway in addition to the sidewalks. There are not only more individuals looking out windows and balconies to observe the passing scene on the low-rise than on the high-rise block, but these individuals also disperse themselves more than on the high-rise block. Where people were observing the scene on the high-rise blocks, the large majority were situated in or on the high-rises themselves. This distribution depends largely on the comparative populations in and out of the high-rise buildings, but it also has implications for the atmosphere on the block. Where street-scene observers scatter over the block, the effect is much less dramatic to other block residents than where the occupants of one or two buildings appear to be watching their neighbors. High-rise residents not only enjoy greater view opportunity than low-rise residents, but high-rises also overlook the private open and interior spaces of low-rise dwellings. The situation of high-rise building windows and continuous balconies can symbolically as well as actually invade the privacy of

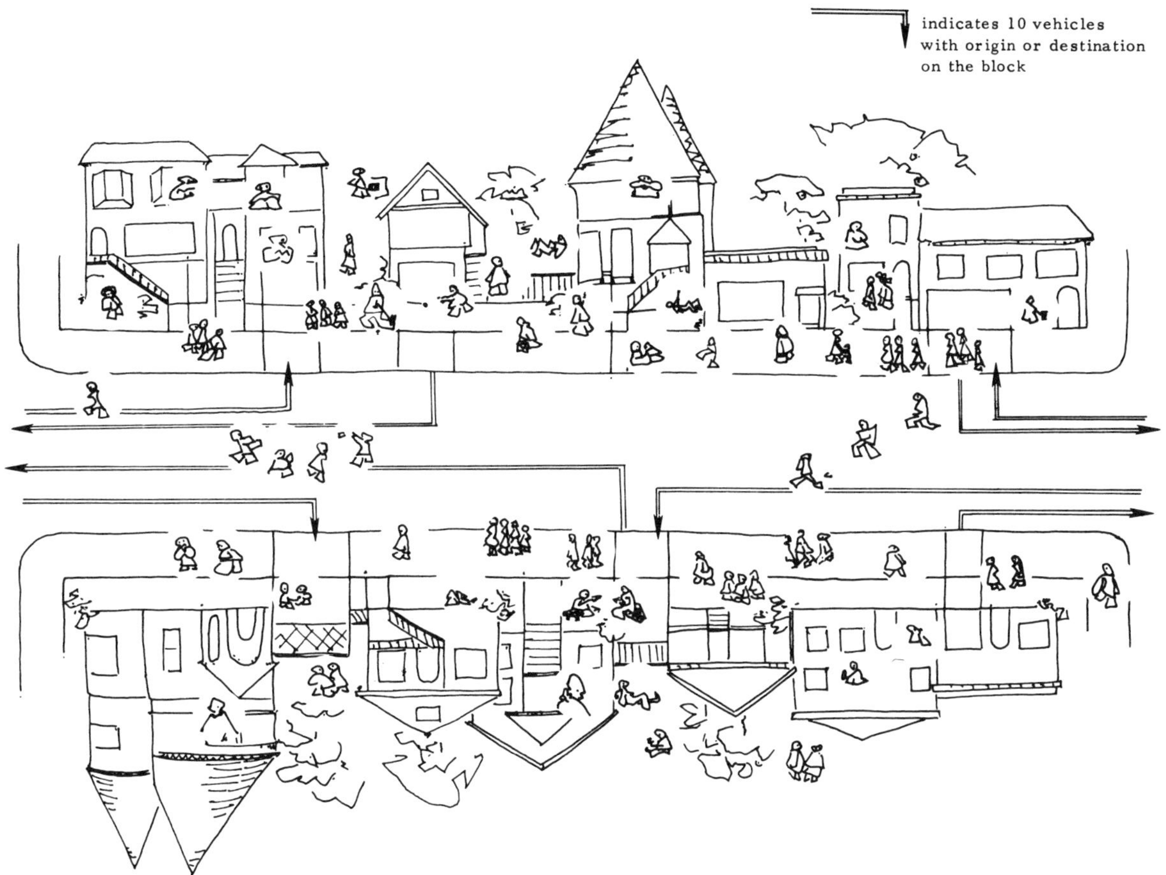

Figure 10–1
Residential block activities—low-rise.

other residents. The comparatively few instances of the various activities we observed on the high-rise blocks can result.

Finally, the figures illustrate the comparative crowdedness of the high-rise block with its large pedestrian loads. While the greater diversity and spatial range of activity on the low-rise block appear to indicate that residents perceive more of the space as available for their use, obviously activity in semi-private open spaces, sidewalk and roadway cannot increase indefinitely. After a certain level of activity is reached, density produces a diminishing return of enjoyable space. Crowding may be an important factor in the reduced use of open space on the high-rise blocks. Active recreation, children's play, maintenance tasks, and relaxation activities are much more likely to be disturbed by passersby on the high-rise blocks, while these passersby are also more likely to be unfamiliar persons than on the low-rise blocks.

An inverse relationship between the number of pedestrians and the number of persons engaged in relaxation activities on the block was suggested by the observation data collected in the commercial areas (see Figure 10-3 and its discussion). The same

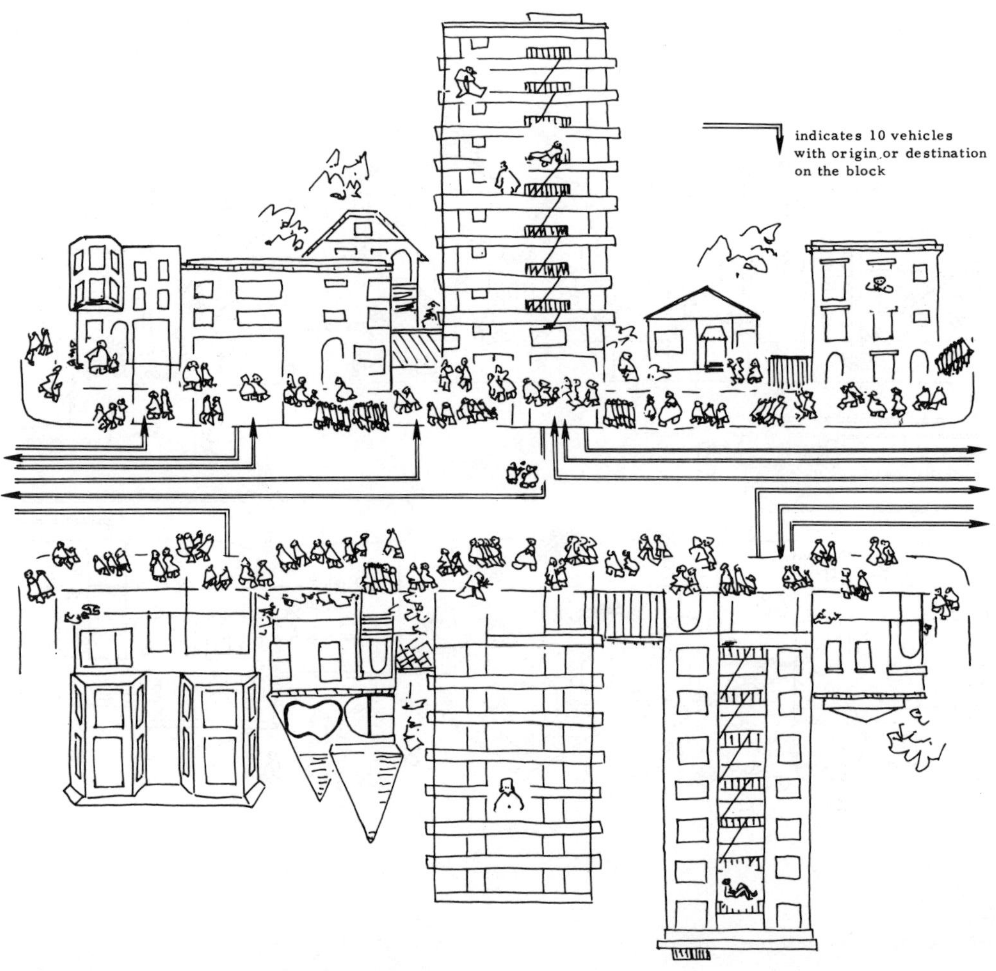

Figure 10–2
Residential block activities—high-rise.

relationship is likely to be operative for large pedestrian traffic loads in residential areas. If subsequent research efforts were to select additional observation sites according to population densities and then collect pedestrian traffic counts and activity observations, it should be possible to determine the extent of negative impact attributable to increased density. In this study, we focused on high-rise buildings specifically, and the impacts of increased population density are part of the more general effects measured.

Observation data also underscore the difference in the sizes of the high-rise and low-rise populations on the blocks studied. Except in the case of the Vallejo Street site, Table 10–3 shows that pedestrian trips to and from the high-rise buildings on the high-rise blocks averaged more than five times those to and from all other buildings combined.

Table 10–2 displays the comparative number of high-rise-oriented motor vehicle trips with those for all other origins and destinations on the block. It is

TABLE 10–3
Pedestrian Traffic: Residential High-Rise and Low-Rise Blocks Compared

	Through Traffic	Origin or Destination on Block	
		At High-Rise	*Elsewhere*
DAY ONE (Weekday)			
Vallejo St. (High-Rise)	41	31	67
Clay St. (High-Rise)	23	73	43
Golden Gateway (High-Rise)	59	110	38
Average Traffic All High-Rise Blocks	41	75	49
Green St. (Low-Rise)	55		88
Washington St. (Low-Rise)	88		96
Montgomery St. (Low-Rise)	116		126
Average Traffic All Low-Rise Blocks	86		103
DAY TWO (Weekend)			
Vallejo St. (High-Rise)	26	5	43
Clay St. (High-Rise)	25	260	15
Golden Gateway (High-Rise)	40	128	12
Average Traffic All High-Rise Blocks	30	151	23
Green St. (Low-Rise)	61		93
Washington St. (Low-Rise)	76		77
Montgomery St. (Low-Rise)	121		115
Average Traffic All Low-Rise Blocks	86		95

obvious that the high-rise buildings double the number of vehicles traveling to and from the block.

Time and budget constraints prevented our surveying the importance of outdoor activity in their neighborhoods to residents. This evaluation can vary for different people. Our study results are necessarily influenced by the kinds of residents settled in the areas observed. We had to study residential high-rise buildings where they exist in San Francisco, and the neighborhoods we observed feature predominantly upper-middle and upper income individuals who enjoy a wide range of activity options. Where residents are more isolated, less cosmopolitan, or simply poorer (as, for example, in high-rise project housing), the area around the dwelling unit becomes much more important as extended living and playing space.

We also do not know how many former residents had already moved away to escape the impacts of the high-rise buildings, or the extent to which those who moved were replaced by others less sensitive to high-rise proximity, although we do know from other study results that both effects take place. It is reasonable to assume that the observed differences between high- and low-rise blocks represent a conservative estimate of total impacts.

Additional Findings—Residential Areas

In addition to activities, observer teams also noted behavior traces which indicate the extent to which residents feel "at home" in their use of their dwelling unit and its surrounding area. Among these features

TABLE 10–4
Behavior Traces in Residential Areas — High- and Low-Rise Blocks Compared[1]

	Windows "Open"	*Windows "Closed"*	*Balconies Used*	*Balconies "Closed"*	*Fences "Closed"*	*Personal Belongings*
DAY ONE						
Vallejo St. (High-Rise)	25%	67%	41%	23%	50%	0
Green St. (Low-Rise)	33%	45%	47%	6%	18%	3 shirts, 1 hose, 1 mat, 1 bike
Clay St. (High-Rise)	20%	50%	34%	10%	60%	2 ladders, broom, shovel, dustpan
Washington St. (Low-Rise)	24%	48%	22%	13%	20%	1 hose
Golden Gateway (High-Rise)	24%	61%	7%	0	100%	0
Montgomery St. (Low-Rise)	41%	38%	40%	34%	31%	0
DAY TWO						
Vallejo St. (High-Rise)	26%	68%	45%	27%	50%	0
Green St. (Low-Rise)	18%	49%	32%	6%	18%	0
Clay St. (High-Rise)	28%	43%	27%	10%	44%	0
Washington St. (Low-Rise)	27%	42%	22%	13%	27%	1 shirt, 1 hose
Golden Gateway (High-Rise)	29%	50%	15%	7%	100%	1 bike
Montgomery St. (Low-Rise)	38%	45%	47%	39%	32%	2 pet bowls, 2 chairs, 1 mat, 1 sculp.
Averages:						
High-Rise	25%	51%	28%	13%	67%	1/block
Low-Rise	30%	45%	35%	19%	24%	2.5/block

1. Features of the high-rise buildings themselves are reported in Table 10–5.
Note: Window percentages do not total to 100%, since windows partially open or closed were not tallied.

were windows and balconies "open" or "closed," that is, windows or balconies which were covered to limit the view from within and into private spaces, or which were open to the view of residents within and passersby alike; fences which prevent viewing into the area they enclosed; and private belongings left unsecured outdoors.*

Table 10–4 reports behavior traces logged for high- and low-rise sites on both days of observation, with averages for all high-rise and low-rise blocks. The high-rise blocks were generally more "closed" in terms of window treatments and fences than were the low-rise blocks, although the differences in the proportions of "open" and "closed" windows were not dramatic. The difference in fences is more distinctive. While the low-rise blocks had a larger proportion of shielded balconies than the high-rise blocks, the low-rise blocks also featured a greater share of balconies which were evidently in use. The evidence of personal belongings left outdoors was meager, perhaps largely a function of the class of neighborhoods studied. But there were more unattended belongings on the low-rise blocks. This datum is not conclusive in itself, but it is supportive in the light of the activity observation findings.

It is interesting to compare features of the high-

*By "open" windows, we do not mean windows physically opened for ventilation, but the extent of visibility into and out of living quarters the window allowed.

TABLE 10-5
Features of the High-Rise Buildings on the High-Rise Blocks

	Windows "Open"	*Windows "Closed"*	*Balconies "Used"*	*Balconies "Closed"*
DAY ONE				
Vallejo Street	52%	23%	90%	0
Clay Street	40%	27%	13%	0
Golden Gateway	47%	44%	60%	14%
DAY TWO				
Vallejo Street	49%	24%	85%	0
Clay Street	66%	16%	13%	0
Golden Gateway	61%	31%	59%	10%

rise buildings themselves with those for the rest of the block. Observation teams tallied several identical features for the high-rise buildings, insofar as visibility permitted, and these tabulations are presented in Table 10-5. The most striking difference revealed by the data is that the high-rise buildings themselves are consistently more "open" than structures on the rest of the block. (Compare Tables 10-4 and 10-5.) The high-rise is less subject to invasions of privacy from passersby and neighboring residents, while the upper floors can command enhanced view opportunity. While the high-rise occupants enjoy their prerogatives of elevated open space, however, they perhaps also encroach upon the privacy of their neighbors. As we have seen, residents on the high-rise blocks use their open space less frequently, and for fewer activities than do those on the low-rise blocks.

We also recorded extra locks on doors, gates, and fences; signs posted to protect privacy or territoriality, like "do not disturb" or "no parking"; and areas planted for residents' privacy. However, comparison of tallies was not conclusive for the blocks studied.

Principal Findings—Commercial Areas

The major differences observed between high- and low-rise blocks in the commercial areas were the relative proportions of pedestrians travelling fast or slowly. Activities observed and recorded in the commercial areas are reported in Table 10-6 for the high-rise blocks, and Table 10-7 for the low-rise blocks. Summary data for each type of block are shown on the bottom line.

While similar pedestrian volumes were observed on high-rise and low-rise blocks, the large majority of pedestrians were rapidly passing through on the high-rise blocks (an average 85.5 percent of total pedestrian traffic), compared to a minority (46.2 percent) on the low-rise blocks. The proportion of pedestrians strolling, window-shopping, or otherwise traveling slowly through the block is correspondingly greater on the low-rise blocks: an average 53.8 percent compared to an average 14.5 percent on the high-rise blocks. Though few overall, there were also almost twice as many people observing the scene from windows on the low- than on the high-rise blocks, and the eleven individuals recorded were situated over all of the blocks studied. The six people recorded for high-rise blocks were all on the same block.

The numbers of persons observed in relaxation activities like sunning, lounging, or eating is generally comparable between blocks. The highest records of relaxation activities occur on both a high-rise and a low-rise block, with comparable pedestrian volumes. In fact, the high-rise block attracts the greatest number of relaxers of any block studied. This particular California Street block is noteworthy for its general

TABLE 10-6
Activities Observed – Commerical Area High-Rise Blocks

High-Rise Blocks	Motor Vehicle Flows	Pedestrian Traffic: Total	Pedestrian Traffic: Rapid Through Traffic	Pedestrian Traffic: Slower Traffic	Stationary Relaxation Activities	People Observing Scene from Windows	Total Persons
Sansome St. between Pine & Bush Sts.	5,500[1] vpd	2,155	1,554 (72.1%)	601 (27.9%)	41 (1.9%)[3]	0	2,196
California St. between Sansome & Montgomery Sts.	12,600[1] vpd	1,079	756 (70.1%)	323 (29.9%)	75 (6.5%)[3]	0	1,154
Montgomery St. between Pine & Bush Sts.	8,620[2] vpd	2,102	2,067 (98.3%)	35 (1.7%)	41 (1.9%)	0	2,143
Pine St. between Montgomery & Kearny St.	13,730[1] vpd	1,524	1,488 (97.6%)	36 (2.4%)	42 (2.7%)	6	1,572
Totals		6,860	5,865 (85.5%)	995 (14.5%)	199 (2.8%)[3]	6	7,065

1. Estimates of J.D. Drachman Associates for the SPUR Study, 1974.
2. Estimates based on 1965 evening peak traffic volumes reported in *San Francisco Downtown Traffic, Downtown Parking and Traffic Survey*, Part II, December 1970.
3. Percentage of all persons observed outdoors.

attractiveness, sense of spaciousness, and outdoor seating facilities. This block also featured the lowest percentage of rapid pedestrian traffic of all the high-rise blocks. The lowest record of people engaged in relaxation activities is on a low-rise block, and this block also carries the largest pedestrian loads recorded.

Sidewalk activities in commercial areas are perhaps primarily dependent upon the quality and variety of shops and facilities available and the number and needs of the majority of people who occupy these areas. The magnitude of pedestrian traffic volumes also seems to represent a significant influence. Indeed, the observation data suggest the assumption of a limit to the extent of relaxation activity which a downtown commercial block can support. The only blocks among those studied to exhibit significantly higher instances of relaxation activities than the others were blocks which offer sidewalk seating space, and which carry comparatively light pedestrian loads.

When pedestrian volumes are plotted against the numbers of persons engaged in relaxation activities for the eight blocks observed in our study, the inverse relationship illustrated in Figure 10-3 appears. That is, generally as pedestrian volumes increase, the number of persons observed relaxing on the block decreases. In the commercial areas, then, the presence of a high-rise building per se on a block does not appear to impact upon outside activity in the same way as in residential areas. The presence of high-rise buildings appears to be a more pervasive influence throughout the commercial area, rather than confined to the block or immediate vicinity. Instead, the sec-

TABLE 10–7
Activities Observed – Commerical Area Low-Rise Blocks

Low-Rise Blocks	Motor Vehicle Flows[1]	Pedestrian Traffic: Total	Pedestrian Traffic: Rapid Through Traffic	Pedestrian Traffic: Slower Traffic	Stationary Relaxation Activities	People Observing Scene from Windows	Total Persons
Montgomery St. between Jackson & Pacific Sts.	2,585 vpd	721	237 (32.9%)	484 (67.1%)	44 (5.8%)[2]	2	767
Front St. between California & Sacramento Sts.	5,435 vpd	1,077	628 (58.3%)	449 (41.6%)	67 (5.8%)[2]	3	1,147
Kearny St. between Pine & Bush Sts.	15,215 vpd	2,130	630 (29.6%)	1,500 (70.4%)	47 (2.2%)[2]	1	2,178
Kearny St. between Bush & Sutter Sts.	15,215 vpd	3,335	1,858 (55.7%)	1,477 (44.3%)	24 (0.7%)[2]	5	3,364
Totals		7,263	3,353 (46.2%)	3,910 (53.8%)	182 (2.4%)[2]	11	7,456

1. Estimates based on 1965 evening peak volumes reported in *San Francisco Downtown Traffic, Downtown Parking and Traffic Survey*, Part II, December 1970.
2. Percentage of all persons observed outdoors.

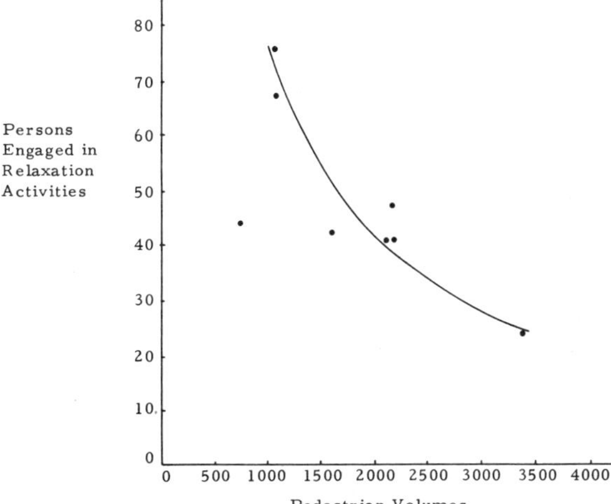

Figure 10–3
Empirical relation between persons engaged in relaxation activities and pedestrian volumes.

ondary impacts of increased population density on the block appear to contribute most significantly to the loss of its livability. Hence, the denser commercial development alternatives would limit people's options to use downtown street space for relaxation activities by increasing both the numbers of seekers of relaxation space *and* the nuisance impact of greater pedestrian volumes in more blocks.

IMPLICATIONS FOR ENVIRONMENTAL DESIGN AND MANAGEMENT OF LAND USE

Because of the negative effects which high-rise buildings have on a neighborhood's livability, it seems reasonable to control the design and number of high-rise buildings in and near residential areas to preserve preexisting neighborhood amenities.

Since there appears to be an inverse relationship between pedestrian traffic volumes and the number of persons engaged in relaxation activities at high pedestrian traffic volumes on downtown commercial blocks, efforts should undertake to moderate pedestrian flows and improve sidewalk amenities where increasing development will promote greater crowding.

REFERENCES

Anderson, Jeremy, and Lindall, Margaret. "The Concept of Home Range: New Data for the Study of Territorial Behavior." In *Proceedings of the Third Annual Environmental Design Research Association Conference, 1972,* edited by William Mitchell.

Appleyard, Donald, *Pre-BART Studies of Environment, Land Use, Retail Sales, Part II. Vol. VI, Rationale and Procedures for Collection of Behavioral and Environmental Data.* Berkeley, California: Metropolitan Transportation Commission, June 29, 1973.

Appleyard, Donald, and Carp, Frances M. "The BART Residential Impact Study: A Longitudinal Empirical Study of Environmental Impact." Working Paper No. 205/ BART 12. Berkeley: University of California, Institute of Urban and Regional Development, February 1973.

Atkisson, Arthur A., and Robinson, Ira M. "Amenity Resources for Urban Living." In *The Quality of the Urban Environment,* edited by Harvey S. Perloff. Baltimore: The Johns Hopkins Press, 1969.

Chapin, F. Stuart, and Hightower, Henry C. "Household Activity Patterns and Land Use." *Journal of the American Institute of Planners* 31, 3 (August 1965).

Cooper, Clare. "Resident Attitudes Towards the Environment at St. Francis Square, San Francisco: A Summary of the Initial Findings." Working Paper No. 126. Berkeley: University of California, Institute of Urban and Regional Development, July 1970.

Cooper, Clare; Day, Noel; and Levine, Beatrice. "Resident Dissatisfaction in Multi-Family Housing." Working Paper No. 160. Berkeley: University of California, Institute of Urban and Regional Development, March 1972.

Design and Environment 3, 2 (Summer 1972): *passim.*

Everitt, John, and Cadwallader, Martin. "The Home Area Concept in Urban Analysis: The Use of Cognitive Mapping and Computer Procedures as Methodological Tools." In *Proceedings of the Third Annual Environmental Design Research Association Conference, 1972,* edited by William Mitchell.

Great Britain, Department of the Environment. *The Estate Outside the Dwelling: Reactions of Residents to Aspects of Housing Layout.* London: Her Majesty's Stationery Office, 1972.

Great Britain, Ministry of Housing and Local Government. *Families Living at High Density: A Study of Estates in Leeds, Liverpool, and London.* London: Her Majesty's Stationery Office, 1970.

Gutman, Robert. "Site Planning and Social Behavior." *Journal of Social Issues* 22, 4 (October 1966).

Kaufman, H. "Is Territoriality Definable?" In *Behavior and Environment: The Use of Space by Animals and Men,* edited by Aristide H. Esser. New York: Plenum Press, 1971.

Lansing, John B., and Marans, Robert W. "Planner's Notebook: Evaluation of Neighborhood Quality." *Journal of the American Institute of Planners* 35, 3 (May 1969): 195–199.

Lansing, John B.; Marans, Robert W.; and Zehner, Robert B. *Planned Residential Environments.* Ann Arbor: University of Michigan, Institute for Social Research, Survey Research Center, 1970.

Lee, Terence. "The Effect of the Built Environment on Human Behavior." *Ekistics* 200 (July 1972):20–24.

Lee, Terence. "Urban Neighborhood as a Socio-Spatial Schema." In *Environmental Psychology: Man and His Physical Setting,* edited by Harold M. Proshansky, William H. Ittelson, and Leanne G. Rivlin. New York: Holt, Rinehart & Winston, 1970.

Leyhausen, P. "Dominance and Territoriality as Complemented in Mammalian Social Structure." In *Behavior and Environment: The Use of Space by Animals and Men,* edited by Aristide H. Esser. New York: Plenum Press, 1971.

Lyman, Stanford M., and Scott, Marvin B. "Territoriality: A Neglected Sociological Dimension." In *People and Buildings,* edited by Robert Gutman. New York: Basic Books, Inc., 1972.

Perin, Constance. "Concepts and Methods for Studying Environments in Use." In *Proceedings of the Third Annual Environmental Design Research Association Conference, 1972,* edited by William Mitchell.

Porteous, J. Douglas. "Design with People: The Quality of the Urban Environment." *Environment and Behavior* 3, 2 (June 1971):155–178.

Proshansky, Harold M.; Ittelson, William H.; and Rivlin, Leanne G. "Freedom of Choice and Behavior in a Physical Setting." In *Environmental Psychology: Man and His Physical Setting,* edited by Harold M. Proshansky, William H. Ittelson, and Leanne G. Rivlin. New York: Holt, Rinehart & Winston, 1970.

Proshansky, Harold M.; Ittelson, William H.; and Rivlin, Leanne G. "The Influence of the Physical Environment on Behavior: Some Basic Assumptions." In *Environmental Psychology: Man and His Physical Setting,* edited by Harold M. Proshansky, William H. Ittelson, and Leanne G. Rivlin. New York: Holt, Rinehart & Winston, 1970.

Sanoff, Henry, and Sawney, Man. "Residential Livability: A Study of User Attitudes towards their Residential Environment." In *Proceedings of the Third Annual Environmental Design Research Association Conference, 1972,* edited by William Mitchell.

Social Planning Council of Metropolitan Toronto. *Families in High Rise Apartments.* 1973.

Sommer, R. "Spatial Parameters in Naturalistic Social Research." In *Behavior and Environment: The Use of Space by Animals and Men,* edited by Aristide H. Esser. New York: Plenum Press, 1971.

Stea, David. "Space, Territory and Human Movements." In *Environmental Psychology: Man and His Physical Setting,* edited by Harold M. Proshansky, William H. Ittelson, and Leanne G. Rivlin. New York: Holt, Rinehart & Winston, 1970.

Strauss, Anselm. "Life Styles and Urban Space." In *Environmental Psychology: Man and His Physical Setting,* edited by Harold M. Proshansky, William H. Ittelson, and Leanne G. Rivlin. New York: Holt, Rinehart & Winston, 1970.

Studer, Raymond G. "The Dynamics of Behavior—Contingent Physical Systems." In *Environmental Psychology: Man and His Physical Setting,* edited by Harold M. Proshansky, William H. Ittelson, and Leanne G. Rivlin. New York: Holt, Rinehart & Winston, 1970.

U.S. Department of Housing and Urban Development, Office of Policy Development and Research. *Effects of Housing on Mental and Physical Health,* by Stanislav V. Kasl. June 1973.

U.S. Department of Transportation, Federal Highway Administration. *Highway Improvement as a Factor in Neighborhood Change, Vol. II, Changes in Social Interaction,* by Jon E. Burkhardt, Armando Lago, and Jerome Rothenberg. Springfield, Virginia: National Technical Information Service, March 1971.

U.S. Environmental Protection Agency, Office of Research and Monitoring, Environmental Studies Division. *An Anthology of Selected Readings for the Symposium on the "Quality of Life" Concept: A Potential New Tool for Decision-Makers.* Symposium held August 29-31, 1972, at Airlie House, Warrenton, Virginia.

Wilner, Daniel M., and Baer, William G. "Socio-cultural Factors in Residential Space." Los Angeles: University of California, Department of Political Science, March 1970.

Wilson, R. L. "Livability of the City: Attitudes and Urban Development." In *Urban Growth Dynamics in a Regional Cluster of Cities,* edited by F. Stuart Chapin, Jr. and Shirley F. Weiss. New York: John Wiley & Sons, 1962.

Part III

Housing and the Livability of Tall Buildings

11

Children in High-Rise Buildings

A. M. Pollowy
Université de Montréal

INTRODUCTION AND OBJECTIVES

Most parents, particularly those with small children, do not need "research" to tell them that children's play can be a problem. In this age of intense urbanization, of distant family ties, of frequent dwelling changes, the continuity and environmental security that children once knew does not exist any more. Instead of being raised in large extended families, knowing a number of loving caretakers, the child grows up in the small nuclear family, possibly (and more and more probably) in a high-rise, isolated in the cubicle of the urban dwelling. The problem exists, it is very real and some definitive measures must be taken. To this effect recommendations favor housing provision for families (particularly those with small children) in low-rise units or in the lower floors of a high-rise. Is that a solution, or could we consider that the problem of high-rise livability has been badly stated? If so, what are the options, the design implications?

In this chapter I shall attempt to answer these questions and propose some alternative performance guidelines to be used as an environmental design checklist. The supporting information is drawn from two sources: (1) environmental surveys or user studies concerning the adults' problem with children's play or with the adults' perception of children's play problems, and (2) psychological literature concerning child development and the child's interaction with the physical environment. This dual approach is essential if we are to understand the forces at play and their spatial consequences.

It may be necessary to clarify that I do not advocate a single-minded, child-based design principle. However, it seems obvious that an approach via a well-documented user group (the children) can provide valuable information which, if acted on, may alleviate both adult and child problems. Nevertheless, this approach implies some concepts which may be

This chapter is drawn from *The Urban Nest*, A. M. Pollowy, (Stroudsburg, Pa.: Dowden, Hutchinson & Ross, 1977).

debatable: It will be assumed, for the purpose of this chapter, that young children pass most of their time in or around the dwelling, looked after by an adult. As such, the dwelling, rather than a day care or community facility, acts as the center, the focal point of children's daily activities.

CHILD DEVELOPMENT AND DESIGN

Let us begin by acknowledging that children are important, and as a majority group in the most intense use of our housing stock, what they do is also important. Now let us go further, and recognize that children play wherever they happen to be, whether the space or condition is suitable or not. Generally, attitudes toward play vary within all types of building forms, showing that the character and success of individual schemes, from an adult's point of view, is not necessarily determined by physical factors. Attitudes are related to culture and personality, the individuality of the parent as well as of the child being extremely relevant in both their choice of dwelling (if choice exists), and in their adaptability to the dwelling condition. Environmental design enters into the situation as a facilitator or inhibitor of children's activities, and as such intervenes in both children's and adults' satisfaction. This implies that far from being an inconsequential background to activities, design has considerable influence over ease of childrearing, in terms of how appropriately and safely the physical environment is conceived for children's activities. Two factors seem to have the most affect on the child-physical environment situation: the age of the child* (i.e., stage of development) and the dwelling type.

*It has been noted that more mothers with at least one child under five than with older children appear to be concerned with play as a "great problem" (Great Britain 1969, 1973). Reflecting the greater strain of looking after pre-school children in general, and the need to keep a watchful eye on them when playing, this is evidently related to the early development of the child, their intense need to explore and learn.

Concerning child development, we are all quite aware of the physical growth pattern of children and of its design implications. Less known are certain specific aspects of psychological development, particularly as they relate to the use—and consequently the design—of the physical environment. To this effect I shall attempt to outline briefly four major interrelated topics: attachment, knowledge of the physical environment, exploratory behavior, and socialization.

Attachment

Carefully studied and described by Bowlby (1969), this is a "proximity-maintaining" behavior shown towards the mother or other familiar adults. From birth to eleven years "attachment behavior" remains a dominant strand of the child's life. It is the strongest in the first three years and during the second year, the young child has difficulty tolerating separation from mother or mother figure even for brief periods, any such separation being a major source of anxiety (Weiner and Elkind 1972). From the fourth year on, children are increasingly able to accept separation and/or surrogate attachment, evolving so that in the seventh year, they will start surrendering much of the previous dependence on parents or home. However, if this phase is to develop "normally"—to independence around the tenth or eleventh year—the younger children must be confident that contact with the "mother" can be resumed on short notice.

Knowlege of the physical environment

Knowledge or representation of the physical environment is gradually developed through childhood. Following largely the writings of the Swiss psychologist Jean Piaget (1967, 1969), I shall start with his phase II: the "pre-operational period," representing approximately ages 2–7 (i.e., as of the onset of relatively competent locomotion). During this period, the child begins to form mental representations of the environment and develops gradually a knowledge of the spatial properties of only those areas which were experienced through personal locomotion, the "action-space" of the familiar environment around the home. However this is still a very partial ability, e.g., the child can recall familiar routes but cannot reverse these routes in thought, implying that beyond a small familiar area, a child cannot return home without assistance (Hart and Moore 1973). The child uses a fixed system of reference, based on fixed elements in the environment. It is ". . . first centered on the child's home and later on a small number of uncoordinated routes, landmarks and familiar places" (Hart 1973).

With the onset of the "concrete operation period" (from about 7-10 years) the child's representation of the physical environment becomes more coordinated into comprehensive map-like representations of the environment, utilizing an euclidian system of reference (Hart 1973). The child can now reverse routes and the "action-space" is consequently enlarged.

Finally, with onset of the "formal operations period" during early adolescence, ". . . the child is not only able to mutually coordinate his thoughts about concrete objects and spatial relations, but is also able to reflect on these, and consider theoretically spaces totally abstracted from any concrete particulars" (Hart 1973). This implies that from this age on, children are able to think in terms of short-cuts, and are generally competent in the use of the physical environment.

Exploratory behavior

Exploration draws the child away from the "mother" and as such is antithetic to attachment behavior. Bowlby (1969) notes that: "A paradoxical feature of exploratory behavior is that almost the very same properties that elicit exploration elicit alarm and withdrawal also." What we can note from the above section is that exploration will be limited by children's ability to know, and therefore act in the physical environment. It starts with the first explorations of the home when the child becomes mobile (during the first year), when the special joys include discovering the contents of cupboards, drawers, etc., and continues with the child's increasing desire to range away from home to experience and explore everything in both the physical and the social environment.

Socialization

As represented in play, socialization with peers evolves from solitary play, to parallel play, to associative play, to cooperative play. In each, the relation to the peer group is different. In associative play (in the second and third years), children ". . . engage in games involving the others, but each one [is] intent only on his own bit . . ." (Millar 1968) and play-groups consist of three children at the most. Cooperative play rarely starts before the fourth year since it requires communication and the ability to attend to more than one person at a time (Millar 1968). By the fifth year however, children show a preference for a play-group of four or five children (Gesell 1940; Millar 1968). In the seventh year informal play-groups are formed by the children, and a transition to the later "gang-age" occurs.

We can see here that the evolution of the social play pattern affects the type of play as well as the size of the play-group. Also, Millar (1968) states that: "The familiarity of the context in which the play takes place is important too. . . . The extent to which the environment or the other children are familiar and not frightening, and whether the mother is present or not, are equally important when one is counting the spontaneous social contacts of human infants."

Design Implications of Developmental Information

Although some of the specific implications will become apparent as each particular "design" topic is discussed, some general notions appear. First, we could state that exploration and spontaneous socialization opportunities are closely linked and particularly crucial in the high-rise setting. Obviously, children will be allowed out much earlier in a "safe" environment, but from the child's point of view safety also implies the possibility of returning to the affective security of the home base.

Second, in function of children's ages, their mobility, their activities and their need for socializing, the radius of action increases and radiates from the dwelling to its immediate vicinity, to the neighborhood, and eventually to the entire community. Obviously, dwelling proximity and accessibility will be a key factor in where and with whom children play. In the period of early socialization, in order to encourage social development through play, the child should be able to contact other children and adults within close proximity to home. Up to the age of three years, and even after that if access to the outside is made difficult by either the dwelling location or the climate, the child's predominant play space will be within or immediately adjacent to the home. From the time of creeping to complete locomotion control by the end of the second year, this is the domain of the early discoveries. Somewhat later, in the third year where socialization with other children becomes spatially identifiable, play groups of rarely more than three children can be formed, and although they do not last long (Millar 1968), provisions for them should be made in the home or proximity.

Third, the more secure and expandable the early experiences can be, the more the child will feel a sense of autonomy within the physical environment. From a very early age up, until they are free and able to explore the larger environment, the dwelling and its immediate environs will greatly affect children's play patterns, and consequently their self-images as competent individuals.

THE HIGH-RISE COMPLEX

Having looked at "play" as a function of child age and development, let us turn to dwelling type. This consists of dwelling level, the building form, and the dwelling itself. In this section the first two shall be discussed.

Dwelling Level

It has been noted that generally, for families with children, the actual height of the dwelling seems to have little effect on attitudes to the play problem; those living very high being no more dissatisfied than those living on or near the ground. However, attitudes to play appear to be different from attitudes to living off the ground and the causes of play problems are not the same factors which influence attitudes to living off the ground.

Two specific concerns can be detected regarding dwelling level; first, whether the child can play outdoors and, second, the effects of being indoors (inside the dwelling). Looking at these problems another way, let us ask whether it is "fresh air" that is meant by outdoors or an opportunity to socialize, to explore, or possibly both. Also, what is meant by "indoors" if not the antithesis of the desirable "outdoor" element? Reading further does "outdoor" mean "on the ground," does "indoor" mean "up there, where it is isolated"? With these additional questions in mind, we shall see that some of the information that is available concerning "dwelling level" contains tacit notions that have to be decoded.

Starting with low-rise dwellings (where the least criticism is noted), observations indicate that a higher proportion of under-eleven's play outdoors in a low-rise setting than in either the mixed or the medium rise setting. Cooper and Hackett (1968) suggest that this phenomena may exist because even small children are more frequently allowed to play outside alone if they are within view of the dwelling. The most important contributing factor for playing outside for under-eleven's (frequency and duration) is ready and easy access (ground or second floor dwellings). "Proximity to the ground means that the mother and young child are less likely to treat the outside as a special outing but rather as part and parcel of normal home life and a continuation of the home environment (Great Britain 1973). Also, within typical high-rise apartment buildings, lower floor residents (ground to third) have been noted to be more satisfied than upper floor residents with respect to child supervision, since parents can see and direct their children through lower floor windows, while upper floor residents are beyond visual or calling distance.

It is obvious from the above that it may be less of an "indoor-dwelling" vs. "outdoor-ground-fresh air" dichotomy, than an interpretation of adults' and children's need for access to activity and socialization areas as well as supervision and contact. Consequently, if we attempt to look at the situation in performance terms, the height of the dwelling may be less of a problem cause than another symptom of the misplanning or the lack of planning for accessible group activity areas in the body of the high-rise.

Building Form and Access Areas

Limiting the discussion to the "internal" characteristics, the importance of the building form is related to the interior plan; as a building increases in height from walk-up to high-rise, there is an increasing amount of interior "semi-private" access areas, with an increased potential of use. In walk-ups and high-rises, three major types of building forms can be recognized, each having a specific type of access area: the point block or tower, where dwellings are clustered around the vertical access zones; the internal corridor block or slab, with a double-loaded corridor reached through vertical access zones; the balcony or deck-access block, with dwellings located on one side of an open corridor reached through vertical access zones. The importance of the building form stems from the use, misuse, or lack of use of its access areas. These are generally unifunctional, designed for circulation only, alternate uses being conditional or nonexistent. For families living in high-rises, the out-of-dwelling play of children depends on the cooperation of neighbors, on the physical safety of the child, on the perceived threat of danger from intruders (Newman 1973) and on general building regulations; all contributing to lessen the child's opportunities for dwelling-proximity exploration. To this effect, a study by the British Ministry of Housing and Local Government (1971) indicates that multistory blocks with internal access arrangements (i.e., point blocks and internal corridor blocks) are the least suitable types of building forms for families with young children.

Corridors

This space could be the main target for unsatisfactory design, their gloom and unimaginativeness discouraging children's play. Further problems are created by the allocation of non-soundproof doors to dwellings, leading to the necessity of understanding neighbors (who probably have children of their own), or to a definite "do not play in the corridor" policy. There are additional problems regarding corridors in high-crime areas where there is a fear of strangers, and to this effect Newman's (1973) work on architectural design for crime prevention provides numerous guidelines. However, one main issue flows through his comments: need for the surveillance of access areas from the relative safety of the dwelling. In our case, surveillance also means the supervision of children's play and the child's knowledge that security is close by.

So far, some of the problems general to most current high-rise access areas have been presented, yet one type, the deck- or balcony-access block, seems to provide some special conditions worthy of note. Studies by the British Department of the Environment (1973) present the following observations: that the pattern of play of children living on access decks is similar to that found among those living at ground and first floor levels; that the deck and access balconies fulfill the function for "doorstep play," particularly for children under five; that significantly more children play on wide access decks (10 ft.) than on the narrower decks or access balconies (5 ft. and 3 ft.); that wide decks are used almost as much in dry as in wet weather, the narrow balconies' use increasing in wet weather. On the negative side, Rothblatt (1971) and Anderson et al. (1973) have found that the most frequent complaint from residents is due to noise from children's play on the balcony or deck and lack of privacy; windows face onto decks and passersby can look into the dwelling unless precautions are taken. This latter condition also causes daylight penetration into the rooms to be less along the deck or the balcony than along facades, lighting being at times below the norm. It seems, however, that for the play of young children this planning type is more satisfactory than any other, although the few studies available (these being mostly from England) do not provide either conclusive evidence for that country or the possibility of transferred design to another, harsher climate.

As an alternative possibility in multistory housing, communal terraces or spaces (semi-outdoor or enclosed) could also be considered. However, if these are not located on all floors, they may prove unsatisfactory, since parents are reluctant to allow young children in unsupervised spaces; and again the young child does not want to be away from the home base for any extended time. Rothblatt (1971) states that they could also have the advantage of providing added opportunity for families to spend somewhat more free time together near the dwelling and providing space for work or other activities which may be difficult to perform within the apartment. His study also shows that ". . . when the terraces were used as play areas they partially compensated upper floor residents in overcoming the difficulties of supervising their children's outdoor activities. . . ."

THE DWELLING

In any discussion of the dwelling, two specific topics must be examined: the dwelling itself, and the relationship between dwellings.

Relationship Between Dwellings

There are three major factors to be considered: adjacency (horizontal and vertical), the grouping of dwellings, and the relative location of user groups within the complex. Since the grouping of dwellings is totally related to building form, the planning of access and service areas, this section will deal with the other two aspects.

Adjacency

Interpreted here as the acoustic condition between dwellings, it is one of the major problems facing families with children. Nicholson and Marsh (1968) noted that having to keep children quiet indoors for fear of disturbing neighboring residents is a primary concern. This is not to say that noise and license should be advocated, but rather that children's activities, singly or in group, tend to lead to a certain amount of exuberant behavior. Sound transmission, then, is not only a factor of conducted noise but of impact noise as well, one that can be most disturbing to lower floor residents.

Location of user groups

While families with children of a similar age group may be more tolerant of disturbances, one can certainly not say the same for adult or elderly households. A high priority for these users is privacy and quiet. Consequently satisfaction with their dwelling is directly affected by their location relative to children's "play areas." Obviously then, only adequate acoustic separation or the careful positioning of dwelling types (preferably both) will alleviate the problem. Primarily, dwellings for childless households should not be located in close proximity to family households (Great Britain 1973). Accordingly, a report by the British Department of the Environment (Great Britain 1973) states: "At high densities opting for a solution where all old people are housed on the ground may result in pleasing no one: it may fail to give them reasonable privacy, views and quiet; reduce the children's opportunities for ground-floor dwellings, and their ability to play without incurring the displeasure of neighbours." Although in appearance this is a clear-cut statement, we must note that it still relies on the previously mentioned premise that children's outdoor play implies on the ground. If however, we take a more global view, then dwelling positioning is less a question of level and much more one of relative location.

The Dwelling and the Child

This realm of private family space is the most frequently used play area for the urban child. Morning preparations, meals, family time and quiet times, day and night, it is in constant use, the intensity of use varying with the age of the child, with the season of the year, the time of day, with the general socio-cultural environment as well as with the overall physical plan of the dwelling and its immediate environs. For families with children, space and layout are the two most influential, critical factors in dwelling design.

Space

Concern for the appropriate use of the dwelling should be reflected in the allocation of children's play and activity space, areas considered in their own rights as would be a living room, a kitchen, a bedroom. This would represent a recognition that children as much as adults, have needs and rights within the domain of the dwelling, and consequently in planning provisions. This point cannot be too strongly emphasized, particularly because of the conflict situations that are likely to occur between children and adults in the very tight dwelling. Jephcott (1971) does not exaggerate by stating that "Sheer shortage of space means the child is liable to be nagged at for precisely what, at that age, he should be doing." We have the problem of spatial inadequacy and related social inadequacy presented by certain dwelling types. Spatial inadequacy presented has to be treated at the level of space allocation with a more humanistic and realistic area provision that we can find in today's norms: one child needs less space than two, or three, or more, but what the size of this space should be, or whether additional children require space on a proportionate basis is not known at this time. Government norms do not tend to be lavish, but they could and should provide directives. Would it be possible to eventually state that each child in addition to "sleeping area" of *N* sq.ft. also needs *X* sq.ft. of "play-space" located in a manner most appropriate to the age? Could we spatially recognize the necessity of children's activities? One could of course argue about the additional costs that such provisions would entail, and today, this concept of additional space for children is utopic in the dwelling of most residents.

Layout

This leads to the obvious problem of the typical dwelling, be it apartment or house, where the rooms intended for the children do not provide adequate play space and where consequently children's activities spread into the adult areas, creating a conflict with adult activities. How many have known that frantic picking-up before friends arrive, or the need for a quiet spot which is nowhere to be found. Perin (1972) very aptly pointed out that "One of the consequences of small spaces is that people—children especially—are unable to work cumulatively at the same activity, thereby less aware of the work process and deprived from seeing the consequences of what they had begun to do." Yet is it possible that given the available housing stock the use of spaces could be altered to better satisfy existing and changing needs rather than conform to established and non-realistic stereotypes? I would say yes, but only if designers plan for fexibility in the layout and if the users are willing to initiate alternate "plan-styles." To give a couple of examples, assuming that two or more children share a room for sleeping, would it be conceivable that one bedroom be set aside for play? Or, could the larger parents' bedroom provide the required additional space? Alternatives may be there, if we look for them.

At another level, alternatives are essential since information about the location of children's play in the dwelling seems to indicate that this may be a cultural factor as well as an effect of the layout—not only does the child have preferences (and these are influenced by the age of the child), but adult rules are imposed on activities and activity locations. If we consider developmental requirements, knowing children's desire and need to be near the mother figure in the early years, of the subsequent period of gradual exploration and movement away from the human home base, and of the period of adolescence in which ego establishment takes place, it seems evident that the activity pattern is likely to move from the common family space to the privacy of the "own room."

The common space

Adult users seem to prefer a separation of living and dining spaces, irrespective of price range, particularly if the dining-kitchen areas are combined. A separation of these two areas allows for two activities to take place simultaneously ("Low Income Family" 1967; Sauer and Marshall 1972) and seems to fit better with the life-style patterns of a large number of families. This is an important consideration, particularly since the combination of living-dining spaces, if there is no additional eating place in the kitchen, results in informalizing what may be considered a formal space or in formalizing an otherwise casual activity (Kurtz 1971). Since children do not tend toward formality, its imposition could again lead to unpleasant conflicts. Within the norms of minimal housing it is more difficult, if not impossible, to arrive at imaginative plans, but some general preferences are available from the abundant adult-user surveys.

While the size of the spaces is one factor in the activities that are likely to occur in them, their relationship to each other also affects use and consequently satisfaction. For example, if a direct connection exists between the living room and the kitchen space, this can play a large part in the use of both rooms, where the living-room may actually become an all-purpose room ("Flexible Dwellings" 1969) or a play space extension for the younger children. Consequently direct connections should be carefully looked at in function of their influence on "desirable" children's activity patterns. Also, new connections should be considered; for example since young children in particular prefer to play within sight and sound of adult activities, in a small dwelling we may consider placing the child's room *next to* and *opening into* the family space, so that the children can partake in their own activities, in their own area, while in the affective presence of the parent.

In the relationship of adult's and children's activities, the kitchen assumes a historically important position in life-style patterns. The great demand for multipurpose kitchens stems from socio-cultural conditions whereby it is used for many functions other than cooking: meals are taken there, friends are entertained there, people listen to the radio, and generally sit and chat (Raven 1967; Sauer and Marshall 1972). It had even been said that ". . . if people are satisfied with their kitchens, they tend to be satisfied with their homes . . ." (Raven 1967). Younger children have been observed playing in there the most, particularly if this space is the main adult activity space (Sauer and Marshall 1972). Today, when the image of the kitchen may be undergoing a radical alteration in function of the changing role and activities of women in society, we can no longer assume the kitchen to be the central activity area, the main focus around which most family functions occur, and to which, as such, children's activities and activity spaces can be related. The question asked today is more general: where does the adult who is in the home during the day, or when the child is there, spend his or her time—not necessarily the eating or meal preparation time, but the major amount of the day. Yet for appropriate activity space planning, the larger "kitchen" in which a multitude of other activities could occur may still be the most satisfactory location for adult-based child activities.

At this point, I could only conceive of a total re-evaluation of the concept of "kitchen" by users, planners, and government standards allocators: this space should be considered as a family activity space, part of its function being the required equipment and storage for the preparation of meals. This attitude allows for a larger margin (a margin which is nonexistent in today's planning codes) for user-based space definition within this area. As an "alternative" mechanism this is essential, particularly for larger families whose spatial requirements increase in all parts of the dwelling, and whose activity needs cannot be fulfilled with the provision of another minimum-sized bedroom. If, however, we must remain with small, minimal kitchens, the provision of appropriate, functional kitchens should be mandatory; spatial allocation must be realistically related to the general dwelling size (or household size), and it should take into consideration two people (adult and child or two adults working together).

Private spaces

The bedroom is conceived primarily as a sleeping-dressing area, yet it could and sometimes does fulfill a variety of other functions for the single child. If shared, a double study-bedroom produces difficulties if two children are to do their homework at the same time, so that consequently two alternative solutions have been advanced for the achievement of a multi-functional bedroom: (1) Where space is provided in addition to what is required for two single beds, clothes storage, personal storage, two chairs and a table (the use of two-tier bunks and built-in storage units would provide the extra floor space required to make a useful room) (Great Britain 1961); (2) Where bedrooms are reduced in size so that while preserving privacy for sleeping and dressing, a reasonably large space may be made available for joint use. Children can thus sleep with less disturbance than if they shared a double room, and the joint play area may be used in case of illness when more space is required (Great Britain 1961). The multiple use of the bedroom appears to be particularly important since all of the children play or read inside every day, and reading—as the need for privacy—increases as the child gets older. Considering that some parents complain of lack of space for play or visiting friends in the children's bedroom (Perin 1972), others indicate a definite preference for one bedroom per child, rather many small ones than few larger ones ("Low Income Family" 1967; Sauer and Marshall 1972). If such a general preference for individual small rooms does in fact exist, minimal bedroom standards would have to be revised and the room allocation principle based on two children sharing a bedroom questioned. Governments' minimal provision for a family of four (parents and two children) being generally two double rooms, unless children are of opposite sex or of very different ages, the family having two children of the same sex and close in age is spatially deprived. Such room allocation principles seem basically arbitrary. More appropriately, individual user choice should be allowed, and alternative solutions should be explored at the family decision level. In the open market, although more variations exist, there are still very few options: can one divide a room, add a door, or are not families limited to smaller-shared vs. larger-costlier dwellings?

The general location of bedrooms is also to be considered. Should all the bedrooms be grouped so that adult and child privacy are low but the parent can hear the young child in the night, or should there be a physical lock as advocated by Alexander (1967), in which case relative privacy may seem like isolation to the young child? Again more questions are asked than can be answered, and the individual designer has more decision responsibility than the user has choice. However in the case of larger families, where four or five bedrooms are needed, the parents' bedroom should possibly be at another level or otherwise acoustically private, this being particularly relevant if one parent works irregular hours and the sleep period conflicts with children's play ("Low Income Family" 1967).

IMPLICATIONS FOR ENVIRONMENTAL DESIGN

Reviewing the discussion on access areas in general, on children's need to explore and socialize close to the dwelling, it becomes an obvious conclusion that some play areas, with small equipment, should be provided within the immediate range of the dwelling and that others, more suited to somewhat older children should be distributed within the body of the high-rise unit. They do not have to be external, they could be semi- or completely enclosed (as is the case of play areas provided in shopping centers), but they have to be planned for. The access area acts as a bridge between the privacy of the dwelling and the public domain; developmentally it is an important activity space for children, it is the immediate extension of the dwelling and as such provides the terrain for the first home-based explorations and a secure vantage point for participating in and observing the activities of others. Ideally, play areas, particularly the one for older children, would be supervised by a play leader, while the smaller ones could rely on the informal surveillance provided by dwelling or service area proximity. For specific guidelines as to what is to be provided where, again it would have to be context specific, yet some notions may be obtained from some of the *better* outdoor playground or play area planning criteria. Generally, the following environmental performance guidelines are suggested in order to allow and encourage children's activities out of the dwelling:

1. Corridors and other access areas should be reconsidered as multifunctional circulation and activity areas, particularly where housing is to accommodate young families.
2. All spaces for the use of small children should be within visual and auditory distance of the dwelling.
3. "Play" areas should be informally supervised by a small group of tenants and should provide for socializing and exploring opportunities within the proximity of the dwelling.
4. The location of "play areas" should take into consideration children's ability to return to home base.
5. "Play areas" should allow for children to watch general activities within and/or outside of the building unit.
6. Where desirable, visual and acoustic privacy should be insured between access areas and the dwelling.

The following guidelines concern the relationship between dwellings and the dwelling itself.

1. Adjacent dwellings (horizontal and vertical adjacency) should be soundproofed for conducted and impact noise between dwellings.
2. Adult and elderly households should not be located within the immediate proximity of children's "play" areas, or of "family" dwellings.
3. Within the dwelling, common family spaces should be designed in function of young children's play areas. Desirable relationships are either positive or negative and this should be reflected in the openings between spaces and in the general layout.
4. Within the dwelling, play space provisions should be allocated to families with small children in proportion to the dwelling size, i.e., number of children housed.
5. The dwelling layout should allow for the flexible and alternate use of spaces.
6. Children's private space should be conceived as a multifunctional space: for sleeping and dressing as well as for playing and receiving friends. Privacy from the dwelling common spaces should be possible to provide for alternate age requirements.
7. The location of children's and parents' bedroom should allow alternatives to satisfy diverse life-style patterns.

REFERENCES

Alexander Christopher. "The City as a Mechanism for Sustaining Human Contact." In *Environment for Man the Next Fifty Years,* edited by W. R. Ewald, Jr. Indiana University Press, Bloomington, 1967.

Anderson, L., et al. "Convenience versus Privacy." *Building Research and Practice* (Jan./Feb. 1973):30–31.

Bowlby, J. *Attachment and Loss.* Vol. 1 *Attachment.* New York: Basic Books, 1969.

Cooper, Clare, and Hackett, Phyllis. "Analysis of the Design Process of Two Moderate Income Housing Developments." Working Paper #80, June 1968, Institute of Urban and Regional Development, University of California, Berkeley.

"Flexible Dwellings have many Advantages." *Build International* (April 1969).

Gesell, A. (ed.). *The First Five Years of Life: A Guide to the Study of the Pre-School Child.* New York: Harper, 1940.

Great Britain, Ministry of Housing and Local Government, Sociological Research Station. *Children's Observations on Six High-Density Estates.* London: Her Majesty's Stationery Office, 1969.

Great Britain, Ministry of Housing and Local Government. *Homes for Today and Tomorrow.* London: Her Majesty's Stationery Office, 1961.

Great Britain, Department of the Environment. *Children at Play.* London: Her Majesty's Stationery Office, 1973.

Hart, R. A. "Review of Theory and Research on Children's Relationship to the Physical Environment." In *Children in the Residential Setting* edited by A. M. Pollowy. Université de Montréal, Centre de Recherches et d'Innovation Urbaines, 1973.

Hart, R. A., and Moore, G. T. "The Development of Spatial Cognition: A Review." In *Image and Environment,* edited by R. M. Downs and D. Stea. Chicago: Aldine-Atherton, 1973.

Jephcott, P. *Homes in High Flats.* Edinburgh: Oliver & Boyd, 1971.

Kira, Alexander. *The Bathroom Criteria for Design.* Center for Housing and Environmental Studies, Cornell University, Ithaca, N.Y., 1966.

Kurtz, Stephen A. "And Now a Word from the Users . . ." *Des. & Env.* 2, 1 (Spring 1971):41–on.

"The Low Income Family as a 'Client', Who's Going to Live Here Anyhow?" *Progressive Architecture* 142 (Sept. 1967).

Millar, Susanna. *The Psychology of Play.* Penguin Books, 1968.

Newman, Oscar. *Architectural Design for Crime Prevention.* U.S. Department of Justice, March 1973.

Nicholson, C., and Marsh, H. *Children's Outdoor Activities on Three Medium Density Estates.* Ministry of Housing and Local Government, Sociological Research Station, Great Britain, August 1968.

Perin, Constance. "Concepts and Methods for Studying Environments in Use." In *Proceedings of Environmental Design Research Association Conference,* UCLA, Los Angeles, California, 1972.

Piaget, J., and Inhelder, B. *The Child's Conception of Space.* New York: W. W. Norton, 1967.

Piaget, J., and Inhelder, B. *The Psychology of the Child.* New York: Basic Books, 1969.

Pollowy, Anne-Marie. *Children in the Residential Setting.* Université de Montréal, Centre de Recherches et d'Innovation Urbaines, 1973.

Raven, John. "Sociological Evidence on Housing, 1. Space in the Home; 2. The Home Environment." *Arch. Review* 142 (Sept. 1967).

Rothblatt, Donald W. "Housing and Human Needs." *Town Planning Review,* No. 42 (1971):130–144.

Sauer, L., and Marshall, D. "An Architectural Survey of How Six Families Use Space in Their Existing Houses." In *Proceedings of Environmental Design Research Association Conference,* UCLA, Los Angeles, California, 1972.

Weiner, Irving B., and Elkind, David. *Child Development; A Core Approach.* New York: Wiley, 1972.

12

Predictors of Residents' Satisfaction in High-Rise and Low-Rise Housing

Guido Francescato
Sue Weidemann
James Anderson
Richard Chenoweth
University of Illinois, Urbana-Champaign

INTRODUCTION AND OBJECTIVES

In the architectural ethos that had its roots in le Corbusier's visions of *La Ville Radieuse*[1] the tall building was uncritically accepted as the generalized solution for urban housing. Thus both in Europe and in the United States much publicly assisted housing built after World War II was high-rise, particularly in high-density situations and in the case of programs of massive slum clearance, such as urban renewal. It is important to remember that in le Corbusier's proposal the main advantage of the tall building was that of permitting the reintroduction of greenery, open space, air circulation, and sunlight in the overcrowded situation typified by Paris *Ilôt Insalubre*. Additional advantages ranged from better automobile circulation (by means of elevated freeways) to the presumed smaller target tall buildings offered to enemy bombers. Preoccupied as they were with the mechanics of making cities work, of quickly reconstructing war damage, or of providing shelter for the masses of suddenly demobilized armies, designers paid scant, if any, attention to the social effects of the particular type of building.

By the mid-fifties, however, it was apparent that many developments based on high-rise solutions were having problems. With this realization a number of residents' satisfaction surveys were launched in Great Britain and Sweden in an effort to provide policymakers and designers with more reliable information than that available through journalistic and impressionistic accounts. In the United States it was not until the mid-sixties that similar studies were begun. While these studies exhibit great variety of approach and cannot be uniformly regarded as rigorous in their overall methodology, one conclusion appears fairly inescapable. As Adams and Conway point out "the success of tall buildings is largely determined by the type of household living in them. It seems that high-rise dwellings are suitable only for certain types of people at certain stages of their life-cycle."[2]

A discussion of tall buildings as residential environments requires a definition of what constitutes a tall building. For the purpose of this chapter any building higher than a three-story walk-up will be considered tall. While there is some evidence that considerable variation exists in residents' satisfaction as a function of increase in height, the present chapter is concerned primarily with the examination of differences between the walk-up situation and buildings serviced by elevators. Such differences have been shown by previous research to be meaningful in identifying a threshold above which residents generally perceive their housing unit as being "off the ground." Also, buildings requiring elevator service usually impose greater design constraints than walk-ups due to the more stringent demands for lining up structural and mechanical elements in the vertical plane. These constraints often result in buildings which are perceived as "institutional" (and thus less satisfying) by their occupants, especially when located in low-rise neighborhoods,[3] more prone to crime and vandalism,[4] and quite unsatisfactory for the social activities of children and teenagers.[5,6,7,8]

In spite of these considerations, it is not clear, however, that high-rise housing is an unsatisfactory building type. In the body of existing research it is extremely difficult to isolate factors that are ordinarily, but not necessarily, associated with high-rise design, such as dislike for large and monotonous buildings, difficulty of establishing territoriality, undesirable location, etc. All the studies mentioned above support the conclusion that for relatively higher income groups, for single adults, for elderly households, and in cases where the trade-offs with desirable conditions (such as proximity to jobs, etc.) can be obtained only with tall buildings, this type of residential environment can be highly satisfactory.

It is also important to note that in many instances land costs, high urban densities, and of late the pressures of energy and land conservation all tend to increase the likelihood that high-rise solutions will not be massively abandoned. For instance the New York State Urban Development Corporation has recently built quite a number of developments of this type, and more are on the drawing boards both in the United States and in Europe.

Continuing study of the conditions that make for a successful housing environment appears therefore to be in order. As part of this effort we have carried out an investigation entitled: "User Needs: Evaluating Housing for Low and Moderate Income Families." The major objectives of this study are:

1. to develop reliable and valid measures for the assessment of residents' satisfaction with their housing;
2. to identify and reliably measure design, managerial, social, and psychological factors that influence the degree of residents' satisfaction; and
3. to make both the measurement procedures and the substantive findings available—in a form understandable to nonresearchers—to government agencies, legislators, planning and architectural offices, management firms, and others involved in making policies and decisions about multifamily housing.

STUDY DESIGN AND METHODOLOGY

The universe of information impinging on these research questions is rather large and complex. Table 12-1 shows the four major categories of variables that were hypothesized to be relevant to housing satisfaction. The table also shows the available sources of information. The approach to data collecting and analysis is analogous to that proposed by Campbell and Fiske in their "Multitrait-Multimethod Matrix."[9] In this approach the intercorrelations resulting from measuring each variable (or each group of variables) by means of a number of different methods are examined. Thus it becomes possible to determine how adequately any method fulfills the basic prerequisites of a measuring instrument, i.e., reliability, convergent validity, and discriminant validity. In addition, the likelihood of accurate interpretation of research findings is enhanced because this approach allows the assessment of method vari-

TABLE 12–1
Sources of Information

*Methods** / *Variables*	*Occupants*	*Managers*	*Researchers*	*Architects*	*Community*
Physical Characteristics – Site – Units					
Occupants – Characteristics – Perceptions – Behavior					
Management – Policies – Perceptions					
Community – Access – Perceptions					

*Methods in each source of information could include questionnaires, interviews, observations, archival records, etc.

ance, i.e., the variation in test scores that is due to bias inherent in a particular measurement method.

Thirty-seven housing developments located in ten states were selected for study, mainly on the criterion of diversity. The dimensions along which the developments varied were location, age of occupancy, population, overall design, building types, and assistance programs. Fifteen sites were located in "central city" zones of major metropolitan areas; the rest were either suburban, outlying areas, or smaller cities. Length of occupancy varied between thirty-three years and three months. All projects were designed for general occupancy except one which was for elderly occupants. Racial composition of the population varied between totally white and totally black. Two projects had substantial Spanish-speaking population and one had American Indian population. Twenty-eight sites were low-rise (one to three stories), five were high-rise (with some low-rise mixture), and four were rehabilitated medium size structures (three to five stories). Eleven projects were Public Housing; the other twenty-six were built under Titles 221(d)3, 221(d)4, and 236 of the National Housing Act. Of these, eleven were built through state housing development agencies, two by a municipal city housing development corporation, and the rest by private, limited-profit, or nonprofit developers.

No attempt was made at selecting a representative sample of publicly assisted housing. The great variety exhibited by housing projects made it impossible within the resources available for this study.

The data collecting procedures used were self-reports, direct observations, photographic and cinematographic observations, and archival records. These have been reported elsewhere.[10] Data analysis is now in progress and a complete research report will be made available.

The results reported here are obtained from analysis of data collected by means of only one of these instruments: the Occupant Satisfaction and Perception Survey (OSAPS). This instrument consisted of a questionnaire mailed out to residents of the thirty-seven developments in our sample. Since the large number of potentially important variables would have resulted in an excessively long questionnaire, three separate questionnaires were developed. Demographic questions, questions about prior housing, and questions about satisfaction with specific features of the housing environment were the same within all three questionnaires; other items differed. This arrangement produced three questionnaires of different length and of partly different variable content. The three questionnaires were named OSAPS I, II, and III and they contained 121, 120, and 187 items respectively. For the following analyses nineteen items common to the three forms were used.

The questionnaires were mailed to a sample of at least one-third of the adult population in each development. Within this sample, each potential respondent was randomly assigned to receive either OSAPS I, II, or III. Consequently, it was possible to study the influence of questionnaire differences upon rate of return, willingness of respondents to answer all questions, and inter-item consistency. A total of 1,906 questionnaires were returned, resulting in an overall return rate of 32%.

FINDINGS

For the purposes of this chapter, a reduced sample was selected from the total sample. This reduction was necessary to avoid comparing responses from urban areas (where all high-rise buildings were located) with those from suburban and rural areas. The reduced sample was then subdivided into two subgroups: those living in high-rise buildings (n = 135) and those living in low-rise buildings (n = 192) The high-rise developments were located in the state of New York; two were in New York City, one in Yonkers, and one in Utica. The low-rise sites were in the following locations: Chicago, Illinois; Yonkers, New York; Ithaca, New York; Minneapolis, Minnesota; and Knoxville, Tennessee.

Table 12-2 contains the mean values of some demographic variables describing these two population subgroups. There are significant differences between these two groups on four of these variables: age, education, length of residence in town, and length of residence on site. High-rise residents were somewhat older, less educated, and lived in the community longer than the low-rise residents.

In order to examine the relationship between specific features of the housing environment and residents' satisfaction with their place of residence for each of these samples (high- and low-rise residents), fourteen variables were obtained from items common to all three OSAPS forms. Respondents were asked to state their level of satisfaction with each of the items making up these variables. Table 12-3 presents the means and standard deviations for these variables and indicates where significant differences between low-rise and high-rise residents occurred.

While it was not the purpose of this analysis to

TABLE 12-2
High and Low Rise Residents: Means on Descriptive Variables

Variables	*High-Rise Residents*	*Low-Rise Residents*
Age of respondents	38.14	32.37**
Number living in home	2.74	2.87
Education of respondent*	3.00	3.75**
Years lived in town	18.76	14.65**
Months lived on site	11.18	15.80**

*Level of education: 1 = some high school, 2 = high school degree, 3 = some college, 4 = college degree.
**Means significantly different, $p < .01$.

TABLE 12-3
Means and Standard Deviations[1] for High- vs. Low-Rise Residents

Variables	High-Rise Residents		Low-Rise Residents	
	Mean	*Stand. Dev.*	*Mean*	*Stand. Dev.*
Other residents in this development	3.21	1.06	3.10	0.97
People living 2–3 blocks outside development	2.97	1.05	3.11	0.80
Recreation facilities	3.02	1.17	2.54**	1.02
Parking arrangements	3.17	1.16	2.88*	1.24
Laundry facilities	2.76	1.37	2.93	1.22
Protection from crime and vandals	2.70	1.44	2.59	1.28
Access to the community	3.57	1.03	3.47	0.97
Privacy from neighbors	3.63	1.13	3.30*	1.24
Privacy from others in family	3.80	0.98	3.72	0.74
Management factors[2]	3.11	1.01	3.13	1.01
Comparison to last place[3]	2.59	0.62	2.38	0.67
Freedom to make changes to home[4]	3.06	0.99	3.05	0.89
Appearance factors[5]	3.58	0.96	3.27	0.98
Satisfaction with "living here"	3.55	1.25	3.33	1.17

1. Fourteen variables obtained from common OSAPS items.
2. Index of 2 OSAPS items: management, management rules.
3. Index of OSAPS items: last residence's appearance, satisfaction with last residence.
4. Index of 2 OSAPS items: changes to inside of home, changes to outside of home.
5. Index of 3 OSAPS items: appearance of this development, the outside of my home, the grounds of this development.
* Means significantly different, $p < .05$.
**Means significantly different, $p < .01$.

compare the levels of satisfaction in the two groups, it is commonly thought that there are differences in levels of satisfaction between high-rise and low-rise housing residents. The information in Table 12-3 indicates that for satisfaction with "living here" there was no significant difference between high-rise and low-rise residents. Only with respect to satisfaction with "recreation facilities," "parking arrangements," and "privacy from neighbors" does there appear to be a difference between low-rise and high-rise residents.

The next level of inquiry concerns the examination of each of the thirteen variables from OSAPS to determine whether, and to what extent, their power of predicting overall satisfaction varies between the two residents' subgroups. Previous analysis of OSAPS data has shown that for samples of people differing in terms of age, education, and sex there are significant variations. In other words, different housing factors are related to residents' satisfaction for populations of different demographic characteristics.[11,12]

Data analysis concerning possible variations in the thirteen variables was accomplished using the multivariate statistical technique of multiple regression analysis. This technique is based on developing a linear equation that predicts the value of a criterion variable from information about several predictor variables. Thus for each of the two samples (high-rise residents and low-rise residents) a multiple regression equation was computed to determine which of the thirteen aspects of the housing environment (listed in Table 12-3) best predicted residents' satisfaction with "living here." While this approach involves a number of complex issues for which there are few single agreed upon solutions,[13,14,15] it nevertheless is a frequently

TABLE 12-4
Predictors of "Satisfaction with Living Here"[1]

Predictors	*Beta*	*St. Error*	R^2 *Change*[2]
	High-Rise Respondents		
Management index	0.19	0.12	0.46
Comparison to last place index	0.34	0.15	0.15
Privacy from neighbors	0.20	0.09	0.04
People in the 2-3 block area	0.18	0.09	0.03
Safety and security	0.18	0.08	0.02
$R = 0.828$	$R^2 = 0.685$	$N = 81$	
	Low-Rise Respondents		
Management index	0.45	0.08	0.46
Comparison to last place index	0.42	0.13	0.12
$R = 0.767$	$R^2 = 0.588$	$N = 111$	

1. These results are from the final significant step of the stepwise multiple regression procedure.
2. R^2 change is the increase in the proportion of total variance accounted for by the inclusion of each predictor variable to the stepwise procedure.

utilized and helpful procedure for obtaining estimates of the relative influence of the predictor variables upon the criterion variable.

Before discussing the particular results from these analyses two features useful in interpreting such analyses will be considered briefly. One type of information that is obtained through multiple regression is the proportion of variance of the criterion variable that is accounted for by the predictor variables. R^2 is an estimate of that proportion; the higher the percentage the better one is able to predict the criterion variable. Additional information is obtained by examining the regression coefficients (or beta weights, if the data have been standardized) of the predictors. In general, an approximation of the relative importance of a variable in predicting the criterion is indicated by the relative size of its beta weight.*

*There is no absolute way to interpret beta weights. One must consider additional factors such as (1) the degree of correlation between the predictor variables, (2) the number

Table 12-4 contains the sum
from the two multiple regressi
from the high-rise sample appe
of the table while the low-ris
percentage of variance acc
significant predictor vari
each case. Sixty-nine p
a set of five variable
59 percent was acc
ables in the low-ri
iables are useful
with "living he
the compositi
the two gro
residents
the mar
dence

of p
lik
f

appearance of three additional predictors for the high-rise sample makes it clear that there are differences in the perceptions of these two groups.

For the residents of high-rise housing, "satisfaction with privacy from neighbors," "the people in the 2 - 3 blocks around the development," and "safety and security" were aspects that accounted for additional variance. Together, these three predictors increased the variance accounted for by 9 percent over what was explained by the first two predictors. In contrast these same three aspects of the housing environment were not able to account for any significant variance in satisfaction with place of residence for the low-rise residents.

IMPLICATIONS

It is important to note that the sample chosen for the analysis reported here consisted of developments of recent design and construction. While this characteristic may not be very significant in the ow-rise sample, it is possible that it influenced to a nsiderable degree the responses obtained in the gh-rise group. In other words these high-rise build- s were located, designed, and built with far greater than that evidenced by the typical public housing k tower. This situation may account for the lack nificant difference in satisfaction levels between gh and low-rise residents. The results presented e 12-3 suggest that for an urban situation, and type of population in this sample, carefully high-rise developments can be at least as ry to residents as low-rise developments.

2-4 presents results which tend to confirm ance ascribed to management factors by dies. For both building types the quality ent is seen as a very high predictor of isfaction. For the high-rise group, the privacy variables also confirms findings dies, notably those by Cooper[16] and ady cited. It is important to notice that in both subgroups people relate th satisfaction to perceptions of living in a bet than their previous residence. This result c the view that satisfaction cannot be assessed in lute terms but is, in part, a function of resid expectations and of comparisons with previ experiences.

A comparison of Table 12-3 and Table 12-4 show which of the measured variables were of little importance in predicting the satisfaction of the two respondent groups—these are variables listed in Table 12-3 but not found in Table 12-4.

For example, while "recreation facilities" has the lowest mean for the low-rise group, indicating that it is the aspect with which respondents were least satisfied, it does not appear to be related to satisfaction with "living here." One explanation for this might be that the residents did not expect recreation facilities to be supplied with their dwelling; another might be the recreation facilities were regarded as unimportant.

Table 12-4 suggests implications for both designers and managers. For designers, these findings suggest that when dealing with a high-rise situation greater attention should be paid to providing privacy between units. Locational factors, especially those related to the character of the immediate surroundings, should also be considered very carefully. While these factors are often beyond the control of the designer, the location having been selected by the developer, housing authority, or others, the way in which the site plan is handled will frequently influence the visual and physical interaction between a development and the area immediately adjacent to it. The provision of safety and security is of interest both for architects and for managers as it is generally thought to be related to design features such as entrances, corridors, and the like as well as to supervision by guards and other management staff.

Finally, the residents' perception of the important relationship between satisfaction with management and satisfaction with their current housing suggests

that—to a large extent—a carefully designed development may succeed or fail on the strength of its management regardless of whether high or low rise.

NOTES

1. Le Corbusier (Jeanneret-Gris, C. E.), *The Radiant City*, New York: Orion Press, 1967.
2. B. Adams and J. Conway, "The Social Effects of Living Off the Ground," Occasional Paper No. 1/75, London: Department of the Environment, Housing Development Directorate, 1975.
3. C. Cooper, N. Day, and B. Levine, "Resident Dissatisfaction in Multifamily Housing," Working Paper No. 160, University of California, Berkeley, 1972.
4. O. Newman, *Architectural Design for Crime Protection*, Washington: U.S. Dept. of Justice, Law Enforcement Assistance Administration, 1971.
5. G. L. A. Downing and J. P. T. Calway, "Living in Flats—Problems of Tenants and Management," *Journal of the Royal Society of Health*, No. 83 (1963).
6. J. Morville, *Two to Five in High Flats*, London: Housing Centre, 1961.
7. Cooper et al., "Resident Dissatisfaction in Multifamily Housing."
8. I. Reynolds and C. Nicholson, *The Estate Outside the Dwelling*, London: Department of the Environment, 1972.
9. Donald T. Campbell and Donald W. Fiske, "Convergent and Discriminant Validation by the Multitrait-Multimethod Matrix," in Fishbein and Martin (eds.), *Readings in Attitude Theory and Measurement*, New York: Wiley, 1967.
10. G. Francescato, S. Weidemann, J. Anderson, and R. Chenoweth, "Evaluating Residents' Satisfaction in Housing for Low and Moderate Income Families: A Multimethod Approach," in D. H. Carson (general ed.), *Man-Environment Interactions: Evaluations and Applications*, Vol. 5, (Methods and Measures), Environmental Design Research Association, Inc., 1974, pp. 285–296.
11. J. Anderson, S. Weidemann, R. Chenoweth, and G. Francescato, "Residents' Satisfaction: Criteria for the Evaluation of Housing for Low and Moderate Income Families, Paper No. 1, in *Papers of the National Conference of American Institute of Planners* (Confer-In 74), Washington, D.C., 1974.
12. G. Francescato, S. Weidemann, J. Anderson, and R. Chenoweth, "A Systematic Method of Evaluating Multifamily Housing," *DMG-DRS Journal* 9, 2 (unknown):153–58.
13. R. B. Darlington, "Multiple Regression in Psychological Research and Practice," *Psychological Bulletin* 69, 3 (1968):161–82.
14. F. N. Kerlinger, *Foundations of Behavioral Research*, New York: Holt, Rinehart & Winston, 1973.
15. M. M. Tatsuoka, *Validation Studies: The Use of Multiple Regression Equations,* Champaign, Ill.: The Institute for Personality and Ability Testing, 1969.
16. Cooper et al., "Resident Dissatisfaction in Multifamily Housing."
17. Newman, *Architectural Design.*

13

A Survey of Residential Responses to High-Rise Living

Jerald Greenberg
Carl I. Greenberg
Wayne State University

INTRODUCTION AND OBJECTIVES

Within the last decade, architects as well as social scientists have widely studied the effects of residential environments on human behavior.[1] These investigations have primarily focused on institutional environments,[2] dormitories,[3] and private homes.[4] Specific research efforts focusing on user perceptions of tall buildings have typically examined the office building. These studies have found complex interrelationships to exist between design parameters and user preferences and responses.[5] Yet, despite the widespread prevalence of high-rise apartment living, little is known about the ways apartment residents perceive their environments. The present investigation was designed to explore this issue.

The investigation focused specifically on three major variables. The first was floor of residence. If there is some unique aspect of high-rise living, then it would be important to look for differences in environmental perception as a function of this variable. One factor likely to mediate the relationship between floor of residence and environmental perception may be street noise. Previous research has shown that street noise detracted from residents' satisfaction with their dwellings.[6] As a result, it was hypothesized that residents of higher floors would experience lower levels of street noise and would consequently report greater satisfaction with their quarters than residents of lower floors.

A second variable studied was the effect of apartment density. Research on the effects of high density and crowding has consistently demonstrated the adverse nature of these conditions. Studies have shown that individuals who are crowded together display greater negative interpersonal affect,[7] increased physical withdrawal from others,[8] and less altruistic behavior.[9] In general, recent studies have demonstrated that a person's satisfaction with his environment is inversely related to the density of the environment.[10] Thus, it was hypothesized that residents of more densely populated apartments would show more dissatisfaction with various aspects of

TABLE 13-1
Correlations Between Bipolar Rating Dimensions of the Apartment and the Building and Measures of Floor of Residence, Density and Expected Length of Occupancy

	Floor of residence		*Apartment density*		*Expt'd length of occupancy*	
Rating dimension	*Apt*	*Bld*	*Apt*	*Bld*	*Apt*	*Bld*
adequate size–inadequate size			14	14	-24	
quiet–noisy	-23			23		-16
small–large			-15	-19		
private–public		-18	14	16	-29	
warm atmosphere–cold atmosphere						-16
expensive–cheap						-16
empty–full					-18	
efficient–inefficient	-22					-15
cheerful–gloomy					-18	-17
satisfied–not satisfied	-13				-21	-15
secure–insecure	-24	-32	35	28	-21	
friendly–hostile			19		-21	-19
colorful–drab					-24	-20
crowded–spacious				-17		
conducive/entertain.–not cond./entertain.					-19	-18
cond./studying–not cond./studying	-17		25	20	-25	
comfortable–uncomfortable			15		-18	-15
convenient–inconvenient	-25	-18				
functional–non-functional	-22	-16	14			
good acoustics–bad acoustics				18	-22	-21
roomy–cramped				17		-22
wide–narrow				14		-17

Note: All decimal points are omitted. Tabled values are significant at or beyond the 0.10 level. The second adjective in each pair was scored higher.

their environment than residents of less densely populated apartments.

A final variable expected to affect environmental perception was expected length of apartment occupancy. It was hypothesized that occupants who planned a longer term of residence would report greater positive feelings toward their environment, presumably as a result of their greater need to justify this decision. These residents must psychologically prepare themselves for a longer stay and cognitively adjust their beliefs to conform to the external realities of the situation. In other words, residents who anticipate a shorter length of occupancy would have less need to distort in a positive direction their environmental perceptions than residents who anticipate longer tenancy. Thus, satisfaction with apartments is expected to vary in direct relation to expected length of occupancy.

STUDY DESIGN AND METHODOLOGY

Survey description

Following from the comments of Goodrich[11] and Lowenthal[12] on survey methodology, the decision was made to use a mail questionnaire of residential environments. The questionnaire covered information about the respondents' personal background in addition to questions on their perceptions of their residential environment. The apartment and the building were rated on twenty-two separate dimensions with seven-point bipolar semantic differential scales. The rating dimensions were selected on the basis of their potential significance to the three major variables. Many of the scale items were taken from Canter's[13] connotative dimensions in architecture and Kasmar's[14] lexicon of environmental descriptors. The actual adjective pairs used are shown in Table 13-1. Also included was a seven-point unipolar rating scale of satisfaction with twenty different features of the apartment and the building. These items are shown in Table 13-2.

Building description

The apartment building was a newly opened fifteen-story residential building located off a heavily traveled thoroughfare on the campus of Wayne State University in Detroit, Michigan. All floors except the first, which was excluded from the survey, had identical floor plans. Equal numbers of efficiency, one-bedroom and two-bedroom apartments were located on each floor.

Sample

One hundred and two residents of the building responded to the survey. This constituted a return rate of approximately one-third. The average length of occupancy at the time of survey completion was one month. About one-third of the respondents (38.9%) lived on the lower floors; i.e., floors 2 through 8. Approximately half the respondents were female (48.5%). About two-thirds were graduate students (66.7%). The average age was twenty-five.

Procedure

The questionnaire was mailed to each occupant of the building. Accompanying the questionnaire was a letter explaining the purpose of the survey and instructions to return the completed form to a box located at the reception desk. Tenants were given three weeks to complete the survey.

FINDINGS

Each respondents ratings on each response scale were correlated with the three major variables: (a) floor of residence, (b) apartment density, and (c) expected length of occupancy. Table 13-1 shows the significant Pearson correlations between each variable and each rating dimension with respect to ratings of the apartment and ratings of the building. Table

TABLE 13-2
Correlations Between Satisfaction with Various Apartment or Building Features and Measures of Floor of Residence, Apartment Density and Expected Length of Occupancy

Apartment or building feature	*Floor of residence*	*Apartment density*	*Expt'd length of occupancy*
kitchen appliances		14	14
kitchen space			
closet space			-15
lighting			-14
university furniture			28
number of windows		20	
size of windows	-13	18	-17
placement of windows		18	
number of elec. outlets		19	
placement of outlets		18	
room placement		14	
elevators	25		
stairwells	15		
parking	15		
maintenance/public areas		18	
maintenance/apartment		17	
security	17	22	
space within apartment		13	
space within building		13	-20
laundry facilities	19	14	

Note: All decimal points are omitted. Tabled values are significant at or beyond the 0.10 level. Positive correlations indicate greater dissatisfaction.

13-2 shows the significant Pearson correlations between measures of satisfaction with various features of the apartment and the building and measures of the three major variables. Because of the exploratory nature of many of the measures and the variables, significant correlations were accepted at or beyond the 0.10 level.

Floor of residence

As shown in Table 13-1, the higher the floor of residence, the more residents perceived their apartments as being quiet, efficient, secure, conducive to studying, convenient, and functional. The higher the floor of residence of the responding tenants, the more they tended to see their building as private, secure, convenient and functional. In addition, the higher the floor of residence, the less tenants indicated satisfaction with elevators, stairwells, parking, and laundry facilities. Individual t tests were performed to compare the responses of tenants in floors 2 through 8 (the lower floors) to those in floors 9 through 15 (the upper floors). Analyses disclosed that residents of upper floors perceived their apartments as significantly quieter ($t[63]=2.21, p < .04$), more efficient ($t[63]= 1.97, p < .06$), more insecure ($t[63]=2.30, p < .03$) and more functional ($t[63]=1.87, p < .07$) than residents of lower floors.

Taken together, these findings suggest that there is a direct relationship between floor of residence and overall satisfaction. In fact, specific ratings of satisfaction were found to be positively correlated with floor of residence ($r=.13$).

Apartment density

A density measure for each apartment was derived from the ratio of the number of people living in the apartment to the number of possible bedrooms in the apartment. Thus, an efficiency apartment was given a denominator of one; a one-bedroom apartment was given a denominator of two (bedroom and living room); and a two-bedroom apartment was given a denominator of three (two bedrooms and living room).

As indicated in Table 13-1, the greater the density of the apartment, the more residents perceived them to be inadequate in size, small, public, insecure, hostile, not conducive to studying, uncomfortable and non-functional. In addition, as density increased, tenants tended to perceive their building as more inadequate in size, small, public, insecure, crowded, not conducive to studying, cramped, narrow and having bad acoustics.

Table 13-2 shows that as apartment density increased, tenants were more dissatisfied with kitchen appliances, the number, size, and placement of windows, the number and placement of electrical outlets, room placement, maintenance of public areas and the apartment, security, space within the building and the apartment, as well as laundry facilities.

These data suggest that occupants of more densely populated apartments find their apartment and their building to be uncomfortable places to live. Density also creates dissatisfaction with various features of the building, presumably as a result of increased competition for these features.

Expected length of occupancy

As shown in Table 13-1, the less time tenants expect to live in the building, the more they perceive the apartment as inadequate in size, public, full, gloomy, insecure, hostile, drab, not conducive to entertaining or studying, uncomfortable, having bad acoustics, and not satisfying. Similarly, those anticipating shorter tenancy perceived their building as noisy, cheap, having a cold atmosphere, inefficient, gloomy, hostile, drab, not conducive to entertaining, uncomfortable, having bad acoustics, cramped, narrow, and generally not satisfying.

Table 13-2 shows that tenants expecting shorter terms of residency were more dissatisfied with the kitchen appliances and the university furniture, but also more satisfied with the closet space, lighting, size of windows, and space within the building.

Taken together, these findings suggest that tenants who anticipate longer terms of occupancy generally report more satisfaction with their environments than tenants who expect to move sooner. It may be speculated that this finding reflects the long-term tenant's need to psychologically justify his long-term occupancy decision.

IMPLICATIONS FOR ENVIRONMENTAL DESIGN

In general, the data support the proposition that a resident's perception of his apartment and his building are affected by the floor on which he lives, the density of his apartment, and the length of time he expects to live in the building.

The general implications are that architects and designers need to exercise caution in assessing residents' satisfaction with high-rise residences. Buildings or apartments should not be judged without consideration of the living habits and expectations of the residents. Just as designers of institutional buildings, dormitories, and private homes have already realized, the need to consider man's needs and behavior is also of critical importance in the design of high-rise apartment buildings.

The finding that persons anticipating longer stays in apartments see their living environment as more positive has specific implications for designers. Designers should be aware of some potential considerations which would maximize satisfaction for either long-term or short-term residents. Preparatory to this stage, additional research needs to be conducted in order to determine the variables which moderate the relationship between anticipated term of residence and environmental perception. Such investigations may eventually lead designers to consider different design strategies for residences designed to house long-term or short-term tenants. One design may be used for the less satisfied short-term tenant and another for the more readily satisfiable long-term tenant. Designers should be aware of the potential for cutting costs by capitalizing on the long-term residents' greater willingness to be pleased with their environment. Short-term residents may be less easily satisfied and may warrant additional expenditures in order to make them feel more positive toward their environment. However, one must use caution and not cut costs so much that potential long-term tenants would change their minds and become short-term tenants. It is assumed that long-term residents perceive their environment more positively in order to justify their decision of long-term occupancy. Thus, a resident may more readily distort his perception of the environment than actually leave the environment. Leaving may be seen as a very extreme reaction to dissatisfaction and reserve its use as a last resort. But, if an environment is seen as too objectionable, residents may find it impossible to justify a decision to stay there and take the more extreme measure of moving.

The present research reinforces the need for architects and designers to join in a collaborative relationship with psychologists in order to solve design problems from a man-environment systems viewpoint.

REFERENCES

1. See, e.g.: R. B. Bechtel, "The Public Housing Environment: A Few Surprises," in W. J. Mitchell (ed.), *Proceedings of the EDRA 3/AR 8 Conference* (University of California at Los Angeles, 1972). D. M. Fanning, "Families in Flats," *British Medical Journal* 4 (1967):382–86. R. Gutman (ed.), *People and Buildings* (New York: Basic Books, 1972). J. Lang, C. Burnette, W. Moleski, and D. Vachon (eds.), *Designing for Human Behavior: Architecture and Behavioral Sciences* (Stroudsburg, Pa.: Dowden, Hutchinson & Ross, 1974). H. Sanoff, "The Social Implications of Residential Environments," *International Journal of Environmental Studies* 2 (1971): 13–19.
2. See, e.g.: W. H. Ittleson, H. M. Proshansky, and L. G. Rivlin, "The Environmental Psychology of the Research Ward," in H. M. Proshansky, W. H. Ittleson, and L. G. Rivlin (eds.), *Environmental Psychology: Man and His Physical Setting* (New York: Holt, Rinehart and Winston, 1970). M. P. Lawton, "The Human Being and the Institutional Building," in J. Lang et al., *op. cit.*, pp. 60–71. L. A. Pastalan and D. H. Carson (eds.), *Spatial Behavior of Older People* (Ann Arbor, Michigan: Institute of Gerontology, 1970). W. R. Rosengren and S. DeVault, "The Sociology of Time and Space in an Obstetrical Hospital," in E. Friedson (ed.), *The Hospital in Modern Society* (New York: Macmillan, 1963).
3. See, e.g.: M. Heilweil (ed.), "Student Housing, Architecture and Social Behavior" (Special Issue) *Environment and Behavior* 5 (1973). M. M. Gerst and R. H. Moos, "The Psychological Environment of University Student Residences," in W. J. Mitchell, *op. cit.*, pp. 13-3-1 to 13-3-9. L. Wheller, "Student Reactions to Campus Planning Options: A Regional Comparison," in W. J. Mitchell, *op. cit.*, pp. 12-8-1 to 12-8-9.
4. D. Canter and R. Thorne, "Attitudes to Housing: A Cross-cultural Comparison, *Environment and Behavior* 4 (1972): 3–32. H. Sanoff and M. Sawhney, "Residential Livability: A Study of User Attitudes towards Their Residential Environment," in W. J. Mitchell, *op. cit.*, pp. 13-8-1 to 13-8-10.
5. R. Gutman and B. Westergaard, "Building Evaluation, User Satisfaction and Design," in J. Lang et al., *op. cit.*, pp. 320–29. P. Manning, *Office Design: A Study of Environment* (Liverpool, England: The Pilkington Research Unit, 1965).
6. D. Appleyard and M. Lintell, "The Environmental Quality of the City Streets: The Resident's Viewpoint," *Journal of the American Institute of Planners* 38 (1972):84–101.
7. W. Griffit and R. Veitch, "Hot and Crowded: Influences of Population Density and Temperature on Interpersonal Behavior," *Journal of Personality and Social Psychology* 17 (1971):92–98.
8. S. Valins and A. Baum, "Residential Group Size, Social Interaction and Crowding," *Environment and Behavior* 5 (1973):421–39.
9. L. Bickman, A. Teger, T. Gabriele, C. McLaughlin, M. Berger, and E. Sunday, "Dormitory Density and Helping Behavior," *Environment and Behavior* 5 (1973):465–90.
10. C. K. Eoyang, "Effects of Group Size and Privacy in Re-

sidential Crowding," *Journal of Personality and Social Psychology* 30 (1974):389–92.

11. R. Sommer and F. D. Becker, "Room Density and User Satisfaction," *Environment and Behavior* 3 (1971):412–417; R. J. Goodrich, "Surveys, Questionnaires and Interviews," in J. Lang et al., *op cit.*, pp. 234–43.
12. D. Lowenthal, "Research in Environmental Perception and Behavior: Perspectives on Current Problems," *Environment and Behavior* 4 (1972):333–42.
13. D. Canter, "An Intergroup Comparison of Connotative Dimensions in Architecture," *Environment and Behavior* 1 (1966):37–48.
14. J. V. Kasmar, "The Development of a Usable Lexicon of Environmental Descriptors," *Environment and Behavior* 2 (1970):153-69.

14

Elderly People in Tall Buildings: A Nationwide Study

Lucille Nahemow
M. Powell Lawton
Sandra C. Howell
Philadelphia Geriatric Center

Should we build tall buildings to house the elderly? This question has been debated for several years with little clarity concerning the relevant issues involved.

1. What elderly? i.e., farm people or city folk?
2. Where? Site selection is a critical factor for residential buildings.
3. What are the correlates of high-rise housing? i.e., tall buildings are frequently found in large projects but this need not necessarily be the case; tall buildings can be built on scattered sites. Howell (1975) argues that "a high-rise structure which houses 50-75 family units belongs, for evaluation purposes, in a different class from a building which houses 150-200 units" (p. 20).
4. What will the associated problems be and how can we deal with them?

Despite the fact that a great many subsidized elderly units are multi-story, there has been almost no research on the psychological impact of building height. Gelwicks (1971) studied preference for floor expressed by elderly and younger persons when shown sketches of buildings, and found that older people favored lower floors. Newman (1972) investigated height and size of family public housing and found a tendency for big buildings to be associated with higher crime rates. However, the findings regarding building height alone was equivocal, in part because the study was limited to New York City.

DESCRIPTION OF THE STUDY

The present research was designed to investigate the relation between the physical characteristics of the housing environment and tenant well-being. A national probability sample of elderly housing in the United States was obtained. In 1971, 3,654 tenants from coast to coast were interviewed, and 662 were

This research was supported by Grant #93-P-75064/AoA, U.S. Dept. Health, Education and Welfare.

re-interviewed in 1974. These tenants resided in housing projects sponsored under the HUD low-rent public housing program. The buildings were all at least three years old in 1971. This probability sample of 154 sites were drawn simultaneously from the universe of public housing projects with elderly-designated units throughout the country. The twelve geographic areas from which sites were drawn themselves represented a probability sample of all geographic areas in proportion to the distribution of elderly-designated units throughout the United States.

Environmental data gathered from all 154 sites included census information on each community, neighborhood characteristics, proximity to resources, site and building characteristics, organizational characteristics of the housing, on-site services offered, administrator attitudes and preferences, and aggregate social characteristics of all tenants living in each site. Individual tenant data were gathered through interviews with approximately twenty tenants from each site. Interviews were conducted in tenants' apartments by trained interviewers in the summer of 1971. The interviewer spent about a week in each site gathering the environmental and tenant data. All sites solicited cooperated, and the tenant interview completion rate was 89 percent. In 1974, approximately half of the public housing sites were revisited. Photographs of buildings and neighborhoods and information on nearby land usage were obtained.

Indices of Tenant Well-being

The study focused upon the prediction of tenant well-being. Six measures of the well-being of the tenants were developed, abbreviated from longer scales that had "worked," and were pre-tested extensively. The indexes of well-being follow:

Housing Satisfaction

1. How much do you like living in this neighborhood?
2. If you could live anywhere you wanted, where would you like to live?
3. How much do you like living here?

Motility

1. How often do you go out of this building in warm weather?
2. How often do you leave the neighborhood?

Morale

1. Do you have a lot to be sad about?
2. Do things keep getting worse as you get older?

Friendship

1. How many people at this housing do you consider very good friends?
2. In the past week how many friends (not relatives) did you visit in their apartments, or visited you in yours?

Kinship

1. How often do you see (the relative that you see most frequently)?

Participation in Activities

1. The number of on-site activities engaged in during the past year.

The intercorrelations between these indices range from +0.42 (between self-reported health and motility) and –0.08 (between housing satisfaction and contact with relatives) with a median of +0.08. Since these indices obviously measure different aspects of well-being, they were not combined. Each one was used separately as a criterion measure. These indices differ from one another in the degree to which they would seem to reflect intensely personal concerns. For example, the answer to the morale question, "Do you have a lot to be sad about?" would be expected to be more related to the person's health and the health, or possible recent death, of friends and relatives, than to any question of building design. We intend to discover whether any combination of physical characteristics of housing and neighborhood can affect basic morale. However, we must recognize at the outset that it is unrealistic to expect that any single design property will greatly affect people's basic outlook on life.

BUILDING SIZE AND HEIGHT AND TENANT WELL-BEING

In a previous paper, Lawton et al. (1975) reported the results of six regression analysis which were performed to uncover the relationship between building size and height on each of the above aspects of tenant well-being. Regression analysis is a complex statistical procedure which permits us to discover the amount of variance which is predicted by each of a succession of factors.* In order to ascertain the amount of *unique* variance contributed by building height and size on tenant well-being, the following personal variables entered into the multiple regression equation first: age, sex, race, marital status, length of residence in the building, whether or not the person was receiving welfare benefits, and self-reported health. Following the personal variables, two environmental control variables were entered into the equation. These were (a) whether the housing was public or private and (b) size of community. Only then were building size and height entered into the regression equation.

Our major finding was that after the variance due to age, sex, race, marital status, health, welfare status, length of residence, public vs. private management, and size of community was partialled out, height of building had an independent relation to two of the indices of well-being:

1. Motility—the extent to which people left the building and traveled out of the neighborhood, (0.7% of variance, $p < .001$) and,
2. Housing Satisfaction†—People in low buildings liked their housing and their neighborhoods better (1.2% of variance, $p < .001$).

Size of project (the total number of apartment units) had a negligible relationship to all aspects of tenant well-being. Similarly building height had a negligible impact upon morale, friendship, family contact, and participation in activities.

Thus, we found that elderly tenants seemed relatively unaffected by whether they lived in a high-rise or a garden apartment. They engaged in the same number of activities, had as many friends, saw relatives as often and were equal in general morale. However, some of them (enough to make a statistical difference) persistently were more satisfied and more likely to traverse their neighborhoods when living close to the ground.

BUILDING HEIGHT IN PUBLIC AND 202 HOUSING FOR THE ELDERLY

First, we examined the distribution of building height. Elderly designated units in publicly supported housing have a wide range of building heights, from one to twenty-two stories. While one-quarter of the buildings were single story structures, more than half of the elderly tenants resided in buildings over six stories high.** The median number of floors was over six stories high. Since this was one of the definitions of high-rise suggested for this conference, we may conclude that a good many tall buildings are being built in the United States to house elderly people.

*See Lawton and Cohen (1974) for a discussion of the procedure employed and Kerlinger and Pedhazur (1973) for a general explanation of regression analysis.

†Actually, the level of housing satisfaction was high for all people in elderly housing, both high-rise and low-rise dwellings. If we had simply asked, "Do you like it here?" the answer would have been "yes." Elderly people are particularly likely to say that they like their current situation no matter what it is. This was even found to be the case in one of the most notoriously poor nursing homes in New York City, which has subsequently been closed down for malpractice, and in the back ward of a state mental hospital (Nahemow 1973). We used a *scale* of housing satisfaction and when people who resided in high- and low-rise buildings were contrasted on that scale, we found those in low buildings more contented.

**In the selection of sites for this study, a probability sample of tenants was obtained. In order to simultaneously sample sites, differential weighting of sites according to the national distribution of tenants across sites was performed.

CORRELATES OF HIGH-RISE BUILDINGS

Tall buildings do not occur at random. We know that there are more high-rise buildings in New York City than there are in Toccoa, Georgia. Tenants might be affected by related factors rather than building height per se. In other words, there are other differences between living in New York City and Toccoa than height of residence building. Size of community was found to be strongly correlated with height of building ($r = .61$). Twice as many high-rise as garden apartments (14:7) were considered by the interviewers to be in slums. In high-rise projects significantly more precautions to protect tenant security were reported. This was true for both the building as a whole and the individual apartment units ($X^2 = 66.9$, df = 6, $p < .001$). Despite these precautions, the managers reported more fearfulness and crime in the high-rise units (see Table 14-1). This complex of factors seems to be strongly related to site selection for high-rise buildings: The usual location results in another cluster of variables correlated with high-rise buildings that might help to explain tenant satisfaction.

High-rise buildings are more likely to have an elderly tenants' organization and a variety of activities on the site. The neighborhood of medium-tall buildings had more of what we called "life enriching" services, such as libraries, theaters, churches, etc., within ten blocks than did one and two story units. They also had a greater variety of medical services in the neighborhood.* (This may be one reason why people who reside in low buildings go outside their neighborhoods more frequently.) It was interesting that no difference was found in the availability of what we called "life supporting" services, such as groceries, butcher shops, cleaners, banks, etc. There were the same number of tenant rules on the average for residents of high-rise and low-rise buildings, and equal job satisfaction among the managers of both.

*Presence or absence of neighborhood medical facilities formed a Guttman Scale with a coefficient of reproducibility of 0.926. The correlation between building height and neighborhood facilities was 0.31 ($p < .001$).

TABLE 14-1
Guttman Scale of Fear of Crime*

1. How safe is the neighborhood for older people to walk about during the day?
2. How safe is the neighborhood for older people to walk about in the night?
3. Are crime, gangs, holdups, drunks or drug addicts hazardous for elderly tenants?
4. Do your elderly tenants seem to feel uneasy about their personal safety on the grounds?
5. Do they feel uneasy in the buildings?
6. Do they feel uneasy in their apartments?

Correlation between building height and fear of crime: $r = .48, p < .001$.
*Coefficient of reproducibility = .898.

In brief, it seems clear that high-rise buildings are more common in urban than rural locations and many of the key correlates of high-rise buildings are related to this fact.

RELATIONSHIP BETWEEN MAINTENANCE AND ATTRACTIVENESS OF PROJECT AND BUILDING HEIGHT

Two more regression analyses were performed in the same manner and with the same variables described earlier. Interviewers and local HUD staff members, selected for their familiarity with the buildings, both made a series of ratings of each building. For the interviewers the ratings were factor analyzed —a procedure which shows which of an array of variables cluster together. For the interviewers' ratings, six items grouped together. These all related to the attractiveness and maintenance of buildings and grounds. The resultant factor was called "building quality," and was used as the dependent variable for the regression equation. The regression analysis again forced personal variables into the equation first, then public vs. private management, and size of community before entering building size and height.

Building height was found to be unrelated to building quality as judged by interviewers. On the other hand, size of total housing project was significantly related. Large projects were often poorly maintained and considered unattractive (3.7% of variance, $p < .001$). The same pattern emerged when HUD ratings were used instead of interviewers' ratings, despite the fact that the correlation between HUD and interviewer ratings was only 0.41 (2.6% variance, $p < .001$). Thus it would seem that to outside observers building size seems more critical than building height, suggesting poor building and ground maintenance.

Nonetheless, tenants had been less satisfied in tall buildings independent of building size. We are still left with the key question. What about tall buildings turns people off?

USER'S COMMENTS

In 1974, when interviewers returned to visit some of the original sample, they made a great effort to record the spontaneous comments of tenants. We did not ask, "Do you like living in a high-rise (or a garden apartment)?" but rather let people talk about their concerns relating to their buildings. Their spontaneous comments were then punched on IBM cards, and statements revealed a fair number of negative comments regarding high-rise buildings. There were general statements such as: "I wouldn't live in a high-rise"; "They build projects too high"; "The building is too high"; "Building shouldn't be so high," from residents of Omaha, Nebraska, and Charlotte, North Carolina. There was only one spontaneous positive comment from a woman in Augusta, Georgia, who said, "We have a great view of the downtown, especially at Christmas time."

The specific comments were more revealing. From places as far removed as Lorain, Ohio, and Dinuba, California, people expressed concern about fire and fire safety (this was in 1974 *before* "Towering Inferno"). In Charlotte, North Carolina, people said: "You should not make buildings over eight stories for fire safety"; "Fire Department's hook and ladder only go up to eight stories." In Benson, Minnesota, a person said, "In case of power failure or fire there is no way to get the elderly out." In Dinuba, California, "I was afraid that in case of fire, I would have to climb out the bedroom window" and in New York City, "I would like a fire escape."

Clearly people are afraid of becoming trapped in their apartments in case of fire. Many seem to find the argument that the building is completely fireproofed and consequently there is no need for fire-escapes or other precautions unconvincing. There may be an element of reality in their disbelief. First, a front-page article in the *New York Times,* July 12, 1975, shows 400 people trapped in a ninety minute blaze in a fully "fireproofed" building. They had saved their lives, the article explained, by bashing out the huge glass windows. Elderly people might not have the strength to do that and are very much aware of their incapacity. Generally, older people cannot smell or hear or see quite as well as they used to and they sense that this might make them sitting ducks in case of disaster. They need a feeling of security. The theme of wanting egress both from the apartment and from the building runs through the comments.

In Wilmington, North Carolina, Charlotte, North Carolina, Augusta, Georgia, and New York City, people all say that they would like a second way to get out of their apartment: "another door," "a back door," or at the very least, "a fire escape." With regard to egress from the building, the focus was upon the elevators. "Elevators keep breaking down (Brooklyn, New York)" "Electric storms stop elevators," "Elevator breaks down about once a month (Augusta, Georgia)," "Elevator breaks down and I have to walk up with a bad heart (NYC)."

There seems to be one other problem that afflicts the residents of high-rise buildings, and that is confusion brought about by lack of orienting codes and personalization of floor or doors. In Cincinnati, Ohio, a resident of a nine story building complained, "I have trouble recognizing my floor from the elevator and have trouble recognizing my own door." In a fifteen story building in Cleveland, a resident said, "It was difficult to find my apartment when I first moved in." In Richmond, California, in a six story building with single-loaded corridors* a tenant found that, "All floors look alike. I have mistakenly tried to open the wrong door."

It is our impression that residents seem more negative about high-rise living when the units are placed in suburban settings. In these areas tenants may be cut off from their neighbors by the visibly different life style that high-rise living implies. Moreover, many of these people have lived all their lives in private residences close to the ground. Fifty-five percent of our sample previously resided in single family dwellings. As Hogue and Marcus have noted, many people feel that living in one's own one or two story home is the ideal (1975). We can not address the question of building height in a vacuum, nor can we write off the effect of living for sixty-five years in a house with a yard and a back door. Although a few may have grown accustomed to apartment living, many elderly people must adjust to a radically different way of life.

SUMMARY

In conclusion we have found from a national study of housing for the elderly that when we control for other correlated but basically irrelevant factors, i.e., race and public versus private management, the effect of high-rise living on elderly people does not appear to be very great. In this we concur with Schumacher and Cranz who found that "in itself high rise formation has little impact" (1975). It was not found to affect an individual's morale, the extent of his or her social contacts either in or out of the building or the extent of participation in activities. In addition, it seems to be unrelated to interviewers' or HUD employees' ratings of building quality and is unrelated to the manager's satisfaction with his job.

There is a complex of interrelated factors that goes along with high-rise or low-rise buildings. High-rise projects are likely to be large projects as well. They are frequently, but not necessarily, built in urban places, and all too often are found in center-city slums. They are likely to have a variety of security measures but leave tenants feeling unsafe nonetheless. The neighborhoods are seen as rich in resources and in services.

Even when all other correlates are partialled out, there seem to be some elderly tenants who dislike high-rise living. These people are likely to have moved in from private houses. They are afraid of fire, uneasy that the elevator will leave them stranded, and anxious about having only one entry point to their apartments.

RECOMMENDATIONS

There does not seem to be any reason why we cannot continue to build some high-rise units for elderly people. There is a good deal of evidence that many can adjust happily to them and that they do not have a deleterious impact on the life style of most elderly people. After all, we do live in a crowded world and we have other evidence that amenities such as transportation and accessible medical service and closeness to relatives is of critical importance to elderly people (Nahemow and Kogan 1971). It may be unrealistic to think that we can always build garden apartments on appropriate sites. However when we do build high-rise units, care should be taken to provide good emergency elevator service. Consideration should be given to a viable substitute to the back door. Fire precautions should be discussed with all tenants to give them a feeling of understanding and personal control over their own fate (in addition to greater safety in case of actual fire). There should be a greater attempt made

*It is sometimes thought that double-loaded corridors produce such confusion.

on the part of housing authorities to match tenants to apartments. An elderly person with a fear of height should not be placed on the seventh to the twentieth floor. In addition, we urge caution to builders contemplating putting up high-rise units in rural and suburban places. In *Architecture for a Crowded World,* Lyonel Brett (1970) says that buildings have three uses: functional, environmental and symbolic. A twenty story building placed in a neighborhood with nothing but two story row housing contains different symbolic meaning than the same building would have in Chicago. Particularly if it is segregated elderly housing, as many buildings are, it stands out like a beacon announcing, "We are a bunch of old people who have been dropped into your neighborhood." To evaluate the building in terms of its functional and environmental features only is to disregard the fact that man is primarily a symbolic animal. While the construction of some high-rise units for the elderly will and should continue, there are many places in which a tall building would be an affront to both common sense and good taste.

REFERENCES

Brett, L. *Architecture for a Crowded World.* New York: Schocken Books, 1970.

Gelwicks, L. "Master Plan, Methodist Retirement Center." Gelwicks, Walls & Associates, Santa Monica, 1971.

Howell, S. C. "Taxonomies of the Built Environment." In *Methodology for the Evaluation of Residential Environments for the Functionally Handicapped,* edited by L. Nahemow. Washington, D.C.: Gerontological Society, 1975, pp. 18-22.

Kerlinger, F. N. and Pedhazur, E. J. *Multiple Regression in Behavioral Research.* New York: Holt Rinehart & Winston, 1973.

Lawton, M. P., and Cohen, J. "The Generality of Housing Impact on the Well-being of Older People." *J. Geront.* 29 (1974):194-204.

Lawton, M. P.; Nahemow, L.; and Teaff, J. "Environmental Characteristics and the Well-being of Elderly Tenants in Federally Assisted Housing." *J. Geront.* 29 (1975).

Nahemow, L. "Environmental Adaptation of the Aged." Paper presented at annual meeting of the Gerontological Society, Miami, 1973.

Nahemow, L., and Kogan, L. S. *Reduced Fare for the Elderly. Final Report.* New York City Office for the Aging, 1971.

Newman, O. *Defensible Space.* New York: Macmillan, 1972.

Schumacher, T., and Cranz, G. *Housing for the Elderly, A Planning and Design Study.* Princeton: Princeton University School of Architecture, 1975.

15

Perceptions of Building Height: An Approach to Research and Some Preliminary Findings

Sandra J. Newman
Institute for Social Research
University of Michigan

INTRODUCTION

There are many indications that the attention of researchers in a variety of disciplines has turned toward understanding the relationship of people to the physical environment, both natural and built. Increasingly, the mutuality of interdisciplinary interest has generated collaborative efforts across fields, and areas of study that have remained determinedly "pure" are beginning to accommodate and even encourage multidisciplinary or interdisciplinary involvement[1]. Architecture is one of those fields whose scope is expanding, in part, at least, because of interest in studying people-environment relations.

To date, studies of people's relationship to the physical environment have had a number of different orientations. One approach, which has become more clearly defined over the last decade, emphasizes people's *responses* and *reactions* either to the physical environment, in general, or to a more specifically defined set of environmental conditions or physical phenomena. Even within this more narrowly defined area, however, further specification is possible. On the one hand, our concern may be with reactions that are primarily biological or physiological in nature. Finding oneself in a threatening or hazardous environment, for example, may be associated with certain measurable physical effects on pulse rate, body temperature and overall equilibrium. On the other hand, we may be interested in responses that are more clearly perceptual, attitudinal, or behavioral. In this instance, the relevant questions are: Under what conditions are particular environments perceived as dangerous? By whom? For what reasons? How unsatisfactory are these environments? And what kinds of adjustments in behavior(s) do these perceptions and attitudes engender?

In this chapter, we will focus on this second class of responses which, to be distinguished from the biological variety, will be called social-psychological and behavioral responses. The aim will be to examine reactions people may have to a particular phenomenon in the built environment, namely, high-rise residential buildings. These reactions include the way people perceive and evaluate various features of their dwellings in high-rise structures, the satisfaction or dissatisfaction they derive from residing in them, and their behavioral responses to them.

Before turning to this specific issue, however, it is necessary to summarize the background and rationale of this research approach. This is addressed in the next section of the chapter. Following this summary, a general conceptual framework applicable to the study of social-psychological and behavioral reactions to many different features of the physical environment will be presented. The framework will then be applied to the specific feature of high-rise residential buildings in the fourth section of the chapter in which we will discuss some recent empirical research on responses to residing in high-rise buildings. A summary of the issues presented in the chapter, and the implications of the research approach for future study, will be covered in the fifth, and final, section.

RATIONALE FOR THE STUDY OF SOCIAL-PSYCHOLOGICAL AND BEHAVIORAL RESPONSES TO THE PHYSICAL ENVIRONMENT

There is considerable agreement on the importance of studying the relationship between aspects of the built environment and the users of that environment. Designers, social scientists and users each hope to improve the quality of the designed environment and concomitantly, increase the satisfaction derived from the environment[2].

In recent years, the concern with trying to maximize the satisfaction people derive both from components of their physical and social environments—for example, their housing, neighborhood, family life or health—and from their life as a whole, has been the impetus for the formation of an interdisciplinary area of investigation, alternately known as quality of life research or social indicator research[3,4,5,6,7,8]. The rationale for these studies lies in the belief that there is a need for more and better "social" reporting, and that the collection and study of social and subjective indicators of the quality of life can parallel, and more importantly, supplement economic indicators which have been widely used to gauge the state of the economy. Thus, it is envisioned that attitudinal measures of such concepts as satisfaction are potentially useful inputs to policy decisions in both the public and private sectors. In short, the argument for the collection and analysis of subjective measures of attitudes, perceptions, and assessments appears to be a clear and persuasive one: an individual's feeling of well-being is best understood when information about both the objective characteristics of his/her situation and his/her perceptions of these characteristics are examined.

If we are studying residential location decisions of households in terms of the choice between single family versus high-rise apartment living, for example, it would be important to know the objective characteristics of the two types of residences, such as their respective prices, floor areas and accessibility to open space. A better understanding of the decision process would be achieved, however, if we also determined how the individual views the different prices of the two alternatives relative to what he/she would actually receive in terms of housing service, whether he/she perceives the space available in the two units to be widely divergent, or whether accessibility to open space makes any difference to him/her at all.

A growing number of studies have found striking discrepancies between objective characteristics and the perceptions of these characteristics[3,4,5,6,9,10]. Rather poor correlations, for example, have been found between an objective measure of density (defined here as number of households per acre) and a subjective measure of crowding[11], physical measures of air quality and residents' perceptions of air quality[12], and objective and perceptual measures of water quality[13].

Methodological research has focused on the conceptual and motivational origins of the perceptions and assessments that people make of the different domains in their lives. Some have suggested that subjective assessments connote a standard against which one judges one's own situation[4,14]. Comparisons between what one now possesses and what one expects or aspires to, as well as what one thinks is just or equitable, have also been set forth as possible interpretations of subjective evaluations[6].

The implication of the foregoing discussion is not that we should restrict our attention exclusively to subjective indicators; as Marans and Rodgers have noted, subjective indicators are necessary but are not sufficient because, ". . . they might be used to justify the preservation of the status quo, because the population being questioned is unaware of alternatives to what may be considered intolerable conditions by outside observers"[6]. On the contrary, it is argued that both types of variables need to be considered and that the discrepancies between them are themselves worthy areas for further investigation.

How, then, can we summarize the implications for research on human responses to a particular feature of the physical environment, such as building height, that are suggested by these varied methodological considerations? First, a strong case appears to exist for collecting and analyzing information about both the objective nature of the phenomenon being investigated, but also about the subjective, attitudinal responses to that phenomenon—perceptions, assessments, preferences, satisfactions, and behaviors.* The importance of including both types of measures is primarily based on the hypothesis that discrepant findings may result from using just one or the other of these variables alone. This hypothesis further implies, however, that even when both variables are taken into consideration, the subjective measures may alter or mediate the effects of the objective variables. As we begin to discuss the conceptual model and then present some recent empirical results on perceptions of building height, this particular issue will become clearer.

*This, in turn, raises questions about the methods for collecting information of this kind and about the differences between these various subjective variables. These issues will be considered after the conceptual framework is presented in the next section.

Second, because of the persuasive case for looking at subjective responses, we obviously need to obtain and analyze information about the source(s) of these subjective responses, namely, the perceivers themselves. The work of Gans[15], Rainwater[16], Fried[17], Berger[18], and others documents the diverse orientations of different socioeconomic groups toward particular aspects of their physical (and social) environments. More recently, the range of variables potentially useful in characterizing and distinguishing the responses of different subgroups within the population has been expanded to include not only individual demographic variables such as age, sex, income and education, but more general sociological and psychological concepts such as life style, stage in the life cycle, value orientation, and needs and preferences[2].

THE CONCEPTUAL FRAMEWORK

Each of the substantive considerations just discussed can be incorporated into a conceptual framework for research. The framework can accommodate studies of people's responses either to the physical environment generally defined (e.g., the "community," the "city," the "region"), or to some particular feature of that environment, for example, building height.**

The basic components of the framework are a number of different variables which constitute social-psychological and behavioral responses and the manner in which those responses may be exhibited. Six primary classes of variables are accounted for: (a) characteristics of the individual whose responses are

**A good deal of work has been done by researchers at the Institute for Social Research on building conceptual models for the exploration of people's responses to residential environments, generally, and specific features of those environments. This section draws heavily on this past work. Interested readers are referred to citations 3, 4, 5, 6, 10, and 19.

being studied; (b) objective features of the environment to which the individual is responding or reacting; (c) the individual's perceptions of the environment; (d) and (e) the individual's assessments of and satisfaction with the environment; and (f) the individual's behavior with respect to the environment.

As noted earlier, the first two variable groups are viewed as the basic *inputs* to the model. The characteristics of the individual may include demographic factors, socioeconomic background, life style, or any number of other characteristics that are potentially important for the particular issue under study. When applied to data on large population groups, the inclusion of variables in this category enables the researcher to describe the differing responses of specifically identified subgroups within the population.

The second category of variables includes features of the environment that are measured in a systematic manner by someone other than the individual whose responses are being studied. Often these objective features or indicators are definitional in nature and little, if any, disagreement would exist between two or more different measurements of the same feature. These features include such things as number of rooms and floor area per dwelling unit, number of stories in the structure, and so on.

The four remaining groups of variables—perceptions, assessments, satisfactions, and behaviors—constitute measures of response or reaction to the environment and, as such, are viewed as the model's *outputs.* Perceptions are measures of the way the individual "reads" the environment and are based, to a greater or lesser degree, on past experience and observation. This past experience provides some standard of comparison for the individual perceiver. Implicit is the notion that variations in past experiences and, therefore, standards of comparison between individuals may result in markedly different perceptions of the same environmental feature. Standards of comparison also play a role in the way an individual assesses his/her environment and the amount of satisfaction he/she derives from it. In an assessment measure, for example, we might ask people to judge the upkeep of dwelling units in their neighborhood; in a satisfaction measure we would ask them how satisfied they are with the upkeep of dwelling units in their neighborhood.

The final type of variable records the actual behavior(s) of the individual. Behaviors are the most obvious manifestation of response to the physical environment and perhaps for that reason have been most often measured in the past. (Mobility rates, for example, have been collected by the U.S. Census Bureau since 1860.) Included in this category are a large variety of coping or adapting behaviors. These coping behaviors range from intermediate adjustments, such as changing the pattern of use of existing housing spaces or changing the existing structure to provide more or better space, to much stronger manifestations of the need to alter one's environment, such as moving from one residence to another. In the former, the individual attempts to fashion a more satisfactory and supportive environment[2] out of the current setting; in the latter, the current setting is exchanged for a new and hopefully more satisfactory and supportive, environment. This model applies to voluntary changes or shifts only, although it is recognized that some changes are made involuntarily.

The question of how these various categories of variables are linked or related still remains unanswered. This issue is best addressed graphically, and in Figure 15-1 the multiple linkages between the measures are presented. The personal characteristics of the individual are viewed as logically prior to and possible determinants of the environmental features, and the individual's perceptions, assessments, satisfactions and behaviors. The way an individual perceives a particular feature of the physical environment depends, in part, upon the characteristics of that feature but may also be based upon his/her standard of comparison. The evaluations he/she makes of the environmental feature, and the satisfaction he/she derives from it, may follow from his/her perceptions. Any action taken vis-à-vis the environment is shown as a result of the individual's effort to cope with the environment as he/she perceives and evaluates it, and

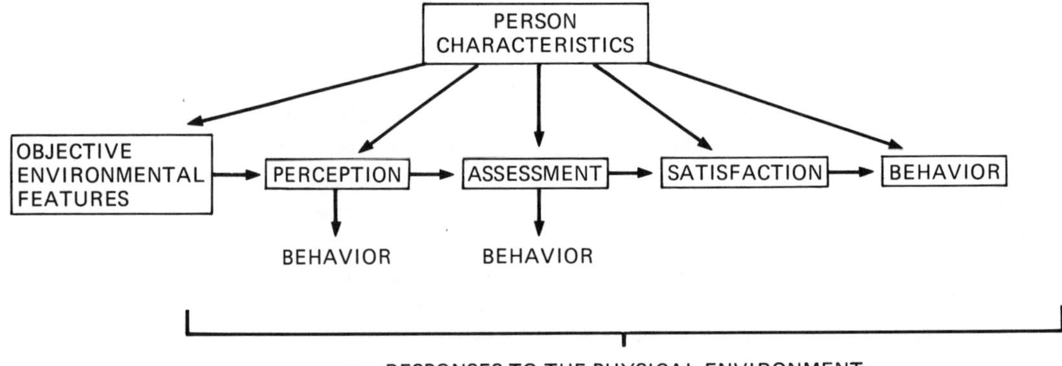

Figure 15-1
Conceptual framework for studying social-psychological and behavioral responses to the physical environment.

as a reflection of his/her satisfaction or dissatisfaction with it. Intermediate coping behaviors are also accommodated by the model and are seen as results of each intermediate stage of the response sequence. Finally, the direct effect of basic personal characteristics (and, concomitantly, frames of reference, experience, values, etc.) on each of the responses is included. In this manner, the possibility that differences in perception of the same objective environmental features by individuals with different personal characteristics, for example, is explicitly taken into account.

Before discussing the application of the framework to the study of people's responses to high-rise residential buildings, a few words should be said about potential sources of data for each component of the model. Because the major goal of the research to be undertaken within this framework is an analysis of people's attitudes toward and evaluations of the environment, it seems clear that the preferred source of this information is the people themselves. This suggests the collection of survey data, whether administered through personal interview, over the telephone or through mail-back or self-administered questionnaires. Surveys can also provide information for the three remaining components of the model, namely, person characteristics, objective environmental features, and behaviors. This is accomplished with additional questions asked of the respondents directly or by training interviewers to observe environmental attributes of the house, neighborhood or community settings in which respondents live.

SOME RECENT EMPIRICAL FINDINGS

Data from the 1971 national survey study, the *Quality of Life in America,* allows us to apply the conceptual framework to the study of people's responses to high-rise residential buildings[4]. Although all components of the model are not measured, a sufficient number and variety are included in this data base for a useful application of the framework. The specific objective of this analysis is to study the satisfaction high-rise apartment dwellers derive from their housing.* To do this we compare residents of high-

*A behavioral measure was not chosen as the variable to be explained for three primary reasons. First, the *Quality of Life* data contain only one measure of behavior vis-à-vis the residential environment, namely, whether the respondent desires to move, and includes no measures of intermediate behaviors. In addition, an application of the percentage of the sample rise structures to see whether the housing satisfaction of the first group differs significantly from that of either of the latter two groups. Within the context of the conceptual framework, a more precise statement of the question to be answered is: does the objective environmental feature of the height of a building in which a person lives significantly affect the housing satisfaction he/she enjoys, once characteristics of the person and his/her perceptions and assessments of relevant environmental features are taken into account?*

Housing satisfaction, the factor to be explained, is measured by the following question asked of all 2,164 respondents (after a series of other questions concerning their dwelling unit): "Considering all the things we have talked about, how satisfied or dissatisfied are you with this (house/apartment)?"

The respondent answered this question in terms of a seven-point satisfaction scale previously explained to him or her. The scale ranged from "completely satisfied" (the first point) to "completely dissatisfied" (the seventh point).

As shown in Figure 15-2 a graphic plot of the average housing satisfaction scores for respondents living in each of the three types of structures, namely, single family, low-rise and high-rise buildings, indicates that satisfaction drops as we move from residents of single family houses to those in high-rise units. The largest drop, however, takes place between single family and low-rise with a much smaller decline between low-rise and high-rise. This simple association between the type of structure in which people live and the extent to which they are satisfied with their housing, however, does not account for a large number of additional factors which may have relatively more important effects on housing satisfaction than just dwelling unit type alone. As indicated in the preceding discussion on the conceptual framework, personal characteristics, other objective environmental features besides housing type, and subjective evaluations and perceptions of the environment may each, or may all, play a significant role. The observed significant difference in satisfaction scores may result because residents of the different housing types differ in their distribution across these other, more important, variables. If, for example, high-rise dwellers are younger than residents of the other building types and age has a fundamental relationship to satisfaction, then it is age and not housing type that explains the satisfaction scores. We need to assess the satisfaction which people derive from their house or apartment after the effects of these other variables have been taken into account. Multivariate analysis, such as regression, can provide this information and is the technique used to fit the model.

Table 15-1 shows a listing of the specific measures included in the multivariate analysis. Four variables measuring characteristics of the respondents are included: income, education, race, and stage in the life cycle. The inclusion of these variables is important for at least two reasons. First, as noted earlier, these characteristics may have direct effects on the satisfaction scores. Their inclusion allows us to see whether different demographic subgroups of the population, for example, manifest different responses to the environment. Second, their inclusion prevents spurious

---

reporting the desire to move (i.e., 27.6 percent) to the approximately 4 percent of the sample living in buildings with more than four stories resulted in too few observations for useful analysis if further specification of subgroups desiring to move or satisfied to stay was to be undertaken. Third, there are problems associated with the use of a multivariate technique, such as regression, when the dependent variable is dichotomously scaled, as is the case for the "desire to move" variable (i.e., desire to move = 1, satisfied to stay = 0). Housing satisfaction, however, is scaled intervally and hence, no such problems arise.

*For the purposes of the present analysis, "low-rise" is defined as three stories or less, and "high-rise" is defined as four stories or more. Unfortunately, a sample of adults which is designed to be representative of the national adult population, such as the sample in the *Quality of Life Survey,* does not include a large proportion of people living in very tall buildings. As shown in Appendix 15A the estimated proportion of the population living in structures with four stories or more across the nation varies between 2.9 and 5.7. These estimates are based on five different nationally representative sample surveys undertaken by researchers at the Institute for Social Research since 1971.

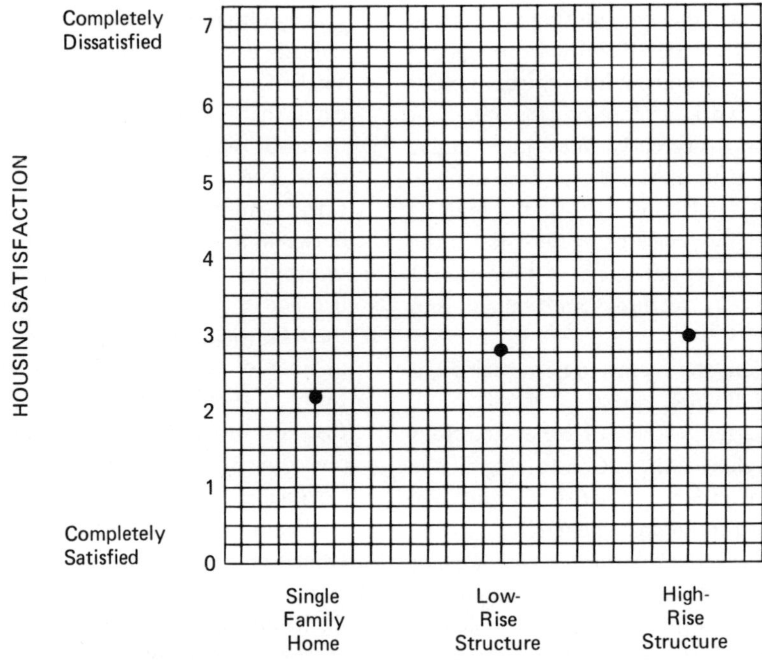

Figure 15-2
Mean satisfaction score by type of dwelling unit.

TABLE 15-1
Matrix of Explanatory Variables—Dependent Variable: Housing Satisfaction

I. *Person Characteristics*	II. *Objective Environmental Features*	III. *Perceptions and Assessments*
		A. *Of Residence*
Income	Dwelling unit (DU) type: whether high-rise	Perception of room size
Life cycle	Whether public housing	Assessment of well-built
Education	Age of structure	Assessment of heating in winter
Race	Upkeep of structure	Assessment of housing costs
	Measure of crowding (actual number of rooms—number of rooms required according to family size and composition)	B. *Of Neighborhood Setting*
	Rent/income ratio	Perception of safety of neighborhood
	Urbanicity (type and size of city or town)	Assessment of neighbors
		Assessment of upkeep of neighborhood houses

correlations between housing satisfaction and other variables that may result merely because of important relationships between background characteristics and satisfaction.

Eight objective environmental features are also listed in the matrix. All of these measures are based on either the interviewer's observation or observations in combination with data elicited from the respondents. While the variable measuring dwelling unit type indicates whether the respondent lives in a high-rise structure, it should be noted that is does not differentiate between these stories. To the extent that the latter has an effect on housing satisfaction, this effect will, unfortunately, not be measured.

The urbanicity variable is constructed from data on the size and location of the city or town in which the respondent lives. Table 15-2 shows the proportion of people living in single family, low-rise and high-rise structures by categories of urbanicity. Not surprisingly, almost three-fourths (74.4 percent) of all high-rise apartment dwellers are situated in central cities. The inclusion of this urbanicity variable allows us to control for any effects which living in central citites may have on housing satisfaction.

Probably the most "subjective" of these objective indicators are the age and upkeep of the structure in which the respondent lives. Both are based on the observations of the interviewer, and were recorded when the interview was administered.

The final groups of variables are the respondents' perceptions and assessments of four features of his/her dwelling unit and of three facets of the neighborhood area. Although our primary interest is the determinants of satisfaction with housing, it seems clear that features of the neighborhood area, such as safety or upkeep, might contribute to this response, as well. The conceptual model allows us to test the importance of this linkage between the housing environment and the neighborhood environment.

To estimate the influence of living in a tall residential structure (relative to that of a number of other environmental variables or indicators, both objective and subjective, as well as characteristics of the person) on overall satisfaction with housing, four regression equations were estimated. In each equation, a dichotomous variable was included which had a score of one if the respondent lived in a high-rise building and a score of zero if he/she lived in either a single family or low-rise residence. In addition, the base set of person characteristics—life cycle, education, race and a measure of family income—were included in the four equations. The first equation included only these

TABLE 15-2
Proportion of Respondents Living in Different Types of Dwelling Units by Geographic Location

	Single Family Home	*Low-Rise Structure*	*High-Rise Structure*
Central cities (cities in the 12 largest SMSAs)	2.8%	24.1%	74.4%
Large cities (other cities over 100,000 population)	23.7	19.5	5.1
Suburbs (places with population over 100,000 located in 12 largest SMSAs or rural areas with less than 2,500 population in all SMSAs)	8.3	19.1	19.2
Small towns and cities (places with population between 2500 and 100,000 not in 12 largest SMSAs)	33.8	31.0	0.0
Rural areas (places with population at less than 2,500 and not in an SMSA)	31.4	6.2	1.3
Total	100.0%	100.0%	100.0%
(Number of observations)	(1,475)	(481)	(78)

five variables. In each subsequent equation, the variable groups listed in Table 15-3 representing objective environmental features, perceptions and assessments of the residence and of the neighborhood setting were added one at a time to observe both the relative contribution of each set of variables to the prediction of housing satisfaction, and the effect of the addition of each set on the importance of living in a tall residential building.

Table 15-3 shows the results of adding each of the three groups of measures to the base set of predictors and dwelling unit type variable. In the equation predicting housing satisfaction using only the base set of variables plus dwelling unit type, only 4 percent of the total variation in housing satisfaction is explained. Once objective characteristics of the environment are added, such as the degree of crowding in the apartment, the age of the structure, and the upkeep of the structure, this percentage increases markedly to 20 percent. A second dramatic increase occurs when the respondents' perceptions and assessments of their own residences are taken into account, such as how well-built the structure is or whether the rooms in the apartment are too large or too small. At this stage, the proportion of variance explained increases to 38 percent. The addition of three neighborhood evaluations—safety, upkeep of neighborhood houses and the people who live nearby—does not add appreciably to our understanding of housing satisfaction. The overall explanatory power, however, does increase slightly from 38 percent in equation III to 40 percent in equation IV, even though the variables added relate to an environmental setting which is, to a large extent, separable from the house itself.

Most simply stated, these empirical findings suggest that objective data on the environmental features of the residential environment, and perceptual and attitudinal data elicited from people about the residential environment, particularly their housing, are helpful in accounting for their satisfaction with their housing.

What is more salient to the specific purpose of this chapter is the relative importance of living in a high-rise structure to overall satisfaction with housing. As is clearly demonstrated in Table 15-3, the dwelling unit type variable is significantly associated with housing satisfaction in the first equation only, where it is also the single environmental measure included. Once we take into account other features of the environment and the way people respond to these features in terms of their perceptions and assessments (equa-

TABLE 15-3
Rank Order of Overall Explanatory Power of Determinants of Housing Satisfaction, by Variable Group[a, b]

I. *Base Set and Whether High-Rise*

Race
Education
DU type: whether high-rise
* * * * * * * *
Life cycle
Income

$R^2 = .04$

II. *Base Set and Whether High-Rise and Objective Environmental Features*

Upkeep of structure
Measure of crowding
Education
Urbanicity
Race
Age of structure
Rent/income ratio
* * * * * * * *
Life cycle
Whether public housing
DU type: whether high-rise

$R^2 = .20$

III. *Base Set and Whether High-Rise and Objective Environmental Features and Perceptions and Assessments of the Residence*

Assessment of well-built
Assessment of heating in winter
Perception of room size
Upkeep of structure
Measure of crowding
Education
Assessment of housing costs
Urbanicity

TABLE 15-3 (continued)

III. (continued)

Age of structure
Rent/income ratio
* * * * * * * *
Race
Whether public housing
DU type: whether high-rise
Life cycle

$R^2 = .38$

IV. *Base Set and Whether High-Rise and Objective Environmental Features and Perceptions and Assessments of the Residence and of the Neighborhood Setting*

Assessment of well-built
Assessment of heating in winter
Perception of room size
Education
Measure of crowding
Assessment of housing costs
Assessment of upkeep of neighborhood houses
Upkeep of structure
Assessment of neighbors
Age of structure
Urbanicity
Rent/income ratio
* * * * * * * *
Race
Whether public housing
DU type: whether high-rise
Perception of safety of neighborhood
Life cycle

$R^2 = .40$

a. The mean value of the dependent variable is 2.418
b. Variables listed above the asterisked line are significant at the 0.05 level; those below are not.

tions II-IV), however, the fact that people may live in high-rise housing appears to have little effect on the satisfaction they derive from it.

SUMMARY AND IMPLICATIONS

In this chapter we have considered a specific set of human responses both to the physical environment generally, and to particular features of that environment, such as high-rise residential buildings. These responses include the way people perceive the environment, their evaluation or assessment of it, the satisfaction they derive from it and their behaviors directed at coping with it. The basic rationale for studying this set of responses centers on the premise that people's subjective judgments and evaluations, and not only the objective characteristics of their situation, are inextricably related to their feelings of well-being and satisfaction.

This discussion was followed by the development of a conceptual framework for the study of these responses to both objective and subjective indicators of the physical environment. This framework was then applied to an investigation of responses to living in high-rise residential buildings. It was found that when just the simple relationship between housing satisfaction and dwelling unit type was examined alone, people living in single family homes had the greatest satisfaction while those living in high-rise structures had the least. However, once a large number of additional, important factors were taken into account, including the personal characteristics of the respondents, the objective features of their respective residential environments, and their perceptions and assessments of these environmental features, residing in a high-rise structure had little effect on satisfaction with the dwelling unit. In other words, once it is known whether a person lives in a large city or a small town, is at an early stage in the life cycle in which there are small children at home or at a later stage with no children living at home, perceives the rooms in the dwelling unit to be too small or too large, and evaluates the costs of the unit as either too high or too low, and so on, also knowing that this person lives in a high-rise structure does not add very much to an understanding of why he/she is either satisfied or dissatisfied with his/her dwelling unit. On the one hand, a representative sample (such as the one upon which the analysis in this chapter is based) does not include many people who live in very tall buildings. Thus, the possibility that these residents experience great dissatisfaction with their housing, specifically because they are tall, has not really been tested. On the other hand, for those respondents we have been able to study, these results may imply that living in a high-rise building, per se, has few, if any, properties which are uniquely associated with housing satisfaction or dissatisfaction. In other words, it is essentially perceptions of and attitudes toward features of the housing environment, rather than building height, which make a difference.

How can this finding be reconciled with some past research which generally seems to indicate that most people are negatively disposed toward living in high-rise buildings [21,22,23,24]? Two answers to this question seem most plausible. First, much of this past research has relied on measures of simple association, i.e., the distribution of categories in one variable across categories of another variable. Essentially, this is the type of analysis represented by the graph in Figure 15-2, which shows the relationship between dwelling unit type and housing satisfaction alone. However, as we have seen, results from this bivariate analysis were quite misleading: when we simultaneously considered a variety of other relevant variables, the results of the simple association were not sustained. It seems reasonable, therefore, that the analysis methods used contribute to the inconsistency.

Second, and probably more importantly, this

APPENDIX 15A
Proportion of the Population Living in Different Types of Dwelling Units, as Reported by 1971 Quality of Life in America Study and Survey Research Center Omnibus Studies, 1973–1974

Type of Structure	*Quality of Life*	*Omnibus Studies*			
		Spring '73	*Fall '73*	*Spring '74*	*Fall '74*
Trailer	4.3% (93)	3.6% (52)	4.6% (66)	4.9% (75)	5.5% (83)
Detached single family	68.4 (1,475)	69.8 (999)	71.1 (1,024)	67.0 (1,024)	70.2 (1,064)
2 Family, side by side	3.6 (78)	3.4 (49)	4.2 (60)	3.7 (56)	2.6 (39)
2 Family, one above the other	4.5 (97)	3.9 (56)	2.1 (30)	2.8 (43)	1.8 (28)
Detached 3-4 family	4.0 (86)	2.2 (31)	3.1 (44)	3.1 (48)	2.4 (37)
Rowhouse	3.2 (69)	3.6 (52)	2.2 (32)	5.2 (80)	2.3 (35)
Apartment (5 or more apartments, 3 stories or less)	6.9 (148)	7.9 (113)	7.0 (101)	8.1 (124)	8.0 (121)
Apartment (5 or more apartments, 4 or more stories)	3.6 (78)	2.9 (42)	3.5 (50)	4.2 (64)	5.7 (86)
Apartment (in partly commercial structure)	1.2 (26)	1.4 (20)	1.0 (14)	0.7 (10)	0.5 (7)
Other	0.3 (7)	1.3 (18)	1.4 (20)	0.3 (5)	1.1 (16)
Total	100.0% (2,157)	100.0% (1,432)	100.0% (1,441)	100.0% (1,529)	100.0% (1,516)

analysis has been directed at understanding what accounts for the *satisfaction* which people derive from their housing. However, the research of Michelson[21,22], Foote et al.[23], and Meyerson et al.[24] has uniformly focused on *preferences* rather than satisfactions. In particular, respondents were asked about the type of dwelling unit in which they would most like to live and not how satisfied they were with the dwelling unit in which they currently live. Needless to say, it is not surprising that results obtained from analyzing a preference question differ from results of an analysis of satisfaction. For example, it is clear that a preference for a single family home could result as much from the desire for ownership as a preference for living in a split-level structure.

In any case, it would be interesting to see whether a similar type of multivariate analysis directed at understanding preferences for different types of dwelling units would result in findings that differ from those obtained in the analysis of housing satisfaction. Divergent results might indicate that people adjust to their present housing situations and, in fact, may even indicate that they are relatively satisfied with them; nevertheless, if given a choice, they might prefer some alternative type of housing. Additionally, such divergent findings would raise an important policy question, namely, is it more important to fulfill people's preferences or to facilitate their satisfaction? Hopefully, future research will help to provide some answers.

REFERENCES

1. University of Michigan, Division of Research Development and Administration. "Architecture revisited." *Research News* 25 (Sept.-Oct. 1974).
2. Association of Landscape Architects. "Task Force Report on Post Construction Evaluation" (mimeo), 1975.
3. Campbell, A., and Converse, P. *The Human Meaning of Social Change.* New York: Russell Sage, 1972.
4. Campbell, A.; Converse, P.; and Rodgers, W. *The Quality of Life in America.* New York: Russell Sage, 1976.
5. Andrews, F., and Withey, S. "Developing Measures of Perceived Life Quality: Results from Several National Surveys." *Social Indicators Research* 1 (1974):1-26.
6. Marans, R., and Rodgers, W. "Toward an Understanding of Community Satisfaction." In *Urbanization–The State of Knowledge,* edited by A. Hawley and V. Rock. Washington, D.C.: National Academy of Sciences, 1974.
7. Office of Management and Budget, Statistical Policy Division. *Social Indicators 1973.* Washington, D.C.: U.S. Dept. of Commerce, 1973.
8. Flax, M. *A Study in Comparative Urban Indicators.* Washington, D.C.: The Urban Institute, 1972.
9. Campbell, A. *White Attitudes toward Black People.* Ann Arbor: Institute for Social Research, University of Michigan, 1971.
10. Newman, S. "Objective and Subjective Determinants of Prospective Residential Mobility." *Social Indicators Research* 2 (1) (June 1975):53-65.
11. Marans, R., and Mandell, L. "The Relative Effectiveness of Density-Related Measures for Predicting Attitudes and Behavioral Variables." *Proceedings of the American Statistical Association* (1972):360-363.
12. Jacoby, L. *Perception of Air, Noise and Water Pollution in Detroit.* Ann Arbor: Department of Geography, University of Michigan, 1972.
13. Marans, R.; Newman, S.; Wellman, J. D.; and Kruse, J. *Living Patterns and Attitudes of Water-oriented Residents.* Ann Arbor: Institute for Social Research, University of Michigan, 1975.
14. Withey, S. "Values and Social Change." In *Subjective Elements of Well-being,* edited by B. Strumpel. Paris: OECD, 1975.
15. Gans, H. *Urban Villagers.* New York: Free Press, 1962.
16. Rainwater, Lee. "Fear and the House-as-Haven in the Lower Class." *Journal of the American Institute of Planners* 32 (Jan. 1966):23-31.
17. Fried, M., and Gleicher, P. "Grieving for a Lost Home." In *The Urban Condition,* edited by L. Duhl. New York: Free Press, 1963.
18. Berger, B. *Working Class Suburb.* Berkeley: University of Calif. Press, 1960.
19. French, J., et al. "Adjustment as Person-Environment Fit." In *Coping and Adaptation,* edited by G. Cohelo et al. 1974. New York: Basic Books, Inc., 1974.
20. Morgan, J., et al. (eds.). *Five Thousand American Families: Patterns of Economic Progress,* Vol. I, Appendix A. Ann Arbor: Institute for Social Research, University of Michigan, 1974, pp. 341-344.
21. Michelson, W. "Most People Don't Want What Architects Want." *Transaction* 5 (July-Aug. 1968):31-37.
22. Michelson, W. "Potential Candidates for the Designer's Paradise." *Social Forces* 46 (1967):190-196.
23. Foote, N., et al. (eds.). *Housing Choices and Housing Constraints.* New York: McGraw-Hill, 1960.
24. Meyerson, M., et al. *Housing, People and Cities.* New York: McGraw-Hill, 1962.

16

The Impact of High-Rise Housing on Older Residents

Galen Cranz
University of California

Thomas L. Schumacher
Princeton University

INTRODUCTION

One of the major justifications for high-rise building* has been economy of minimized per-unit land costs. One of the major criticisms has been that it is socially too costly for housing in that family life is hard to maintain and crime is difficult to curtail. A great practical concern shared by policymakers in urban affairs is whether we should continue to build high-rise housing.

In order to answer this question we need to refine it: Are there any residential populations for whom this form may provide an adequate or even a desirable living environment? This chapter discusses the possibility that high-rise housing may be appropriate to serve the needs of the elderly. Their residential requirements may be different from those of families; specifically, variations in the relationship of dwelling unit to the ground plane, and the manner by which friendships are formed, may require other kinds of environmental supports.

METHOD

The method of investigation of the impact of high-rise housing on older residents was to compare responses of residents in low-rise and garden units with those in high-rise units. Consistent differences between the two groups would indicate that the building type had an impact which could be interpreted as negative or positive depending on the type of responses observed. If there were no differences between the two types we would have to conclude that high- or low-rise formation by itself has no impact on residential satisfaction.

A version of this chapter was prepared for, but not presented at, conference on "Human Response to Tall Buildings," sponsored by the American Institute of Architects, held in Chicago, July 17–19, 1975.

*In this chapter, "high-rise building" is taken to mean any building with an elevator. The average height of the buildings used in this survey was ten to twelve stories.

The data for this comparison came from a study conducted for the state of New Jersey Office of Community Affairs, Division on Aging, to evaluate and generate housing standards for the elderly. In the spring of 1974, 280 forty-five-minute questionnaires were administered to residents of eight government-supported, low-, moderate-, and middle-income independent living projects. According to our overall methodological tactic of comparing high- and low-rise in order to understand high-rise environments, these data were marshalled into a series of contrasts and comparisons on several different variables which could be imagined as relevant to residential satisfaction. The variables were not selected on the basis of a systematic theory; rather the data were examined for a wide range of social, behavioral, and psychological variables for which a relationship to building type could be argued.

FINDINGS

Preference for Urban, Suburban or Rural Location

In keeping with the common psychological practice of liking what one has, the data from Table 16-1 shows that residents prefer their present urban, suburban or rural locations in which they already find themselves. Most of those from high-rise buildings prefer urban locations, but the majority of these

TABLE 16-1
Preference for Urban, Suburban, or Rural Setting by High-Rise or Garden Apartment Building Type
("Ideally, where would you feel most comfortable living—in an urban, suburban or rural setting?")

	Urban		*Suburban*		*Rural*		*Total*	
	No.	*%*	*No.*	*%*	*No.*	*%*	*No.*	*%*
High-Rise								
Columbus Homes	23	65	6	17	6	17	35	100
Hanson Homes	24	69	8	23	3	9	35	101*
Bethany Manor	2	6	33	94	0	0	35	100
Trent Center	24	69	7	20	4	11	35	100
Josephson Homes	25	76	8	24	0	0	33	100
Subtotal	98	57	62	36	13	8	173	101*
Garden								
Camiano Homes	15	43	19	54	1	3	35	100
Oakhurst Homes	2	6	31	89	2	6	35	100
Tarklin Acres	16	44	14	39	6	17	36	100
Subtotal	33	31	64	60	9	8	106	99**
Grand Total	131	47	126	45	22	8	279	100

*Percentages add up to more than 100% due to rounding.
**Percentages add up to less than 100% due to rounding.

buildings are located in high-density urban areas. In the only tower where people prefer suburban settings (Bethany), the context is a low-density one. Thus, the high-rise formation per se probably does not account for the relationship between high-rise and urban preference. Rather, current location may account for such preference.

This conclusion is reinforced when one examines the preferences of those in garden apartments. Two complexes are in medium-density contexts (Camiano and Oakhurst) and their tenants tend to prefer suburban settings (although not strongly in the case of Camiano). In the most nearly rural setting (Tarklin Acres) residents tend to prefer neither rural nor suburban contexts, but urban. The isolation of these apartments from community services probably accounts for this implied dissatisfaction. Urban (high-density) preferences are not necessarily linked to high-rise living.

Use of Communal Spaces

One of the presumed advantages of garden apartments over high-rise buildings is a more direct relationship to the ground, making it easier for people to use the outdoors. Table 16-2 shows a tendency toward greater use of the outdoor seating areas by garden apartment tenants (90%) than by high-rise tenants (77%). The difference is less than expected; for buildings with elevators the effect of real distance from an individual unit to the ground is apparently minimized. The attenuated relationship between the individual unit and outdoors is not as disruptive to the social life of older people as it is for young mothers who have to supervise their children's play.

From the frequency of outdoor use in Table 16-3, the absence of striking differences between high-rise and garden dwellers is apparent. Some 54% of the garden apartment dwellers and only 40% of the high-rise

TABLE 16-2
Sitting Outdoors in Summer by Building Type
("Do you ever sit outside in the summertime?")

	Yes		*No*		*Total*	
	No.	*%*	*No.*	*%*	*No.*	*%*
High-Rise						
Columbus	31	89	4	11	35	100
Hanson	27	77	8	23	35	100
Bethany	29	83	6	17	35	100
Trent Center	24	69	11	31	35	100
Josephson	22	69	10	31	32	100
Subtotal	133	77	39	33	172	100
Garden						
Camiano	33	94	2	6	35	100
Oakhurst	29	85	5	15	34	100
Tarklin	33	92	3	8	36	100
Subtotal	95	90.4	10	9.6	105	100
Grand Total	228	87.3	49	17.7	277	100

TABLE 16-3
Frequency of Use of Outdoors by Building Type
("How often do you sit outdoors?")

	Daily	*Nearly Always*	*Occasionally*	*Never*	*Total*
High-Rise					
Columbus	10	5	14	2	31
Hanson	12	9	2	0	23
Bethany	1	17	10	0	28
Trent Center	13	7	1	0	21
Josephson	13	4	2	1	20
Subtotal	49 = 40%	42 = 34%	29 = 24%	3 = 2%	123 = 100%
Garden					
Camiano	15	0	18	0	33
Oakhurst	16	4	9	2	31
Tarklin	23	11	2	0	36
Subtotal	54 = 54%	15 = 15%	29 = 29%	2 = 2%	100 = 100%
Grand Total	103 = 46%	57 = 26%	58 = 26%	5 = 2%	223 = 100%

tenants use the outdoors daily. But these people say they use the outdoors "nearly always." When combined, the two categories "daily" and "nearly always" show high-rise residents as equally consistent users of the outdoors (74% compared to 69%). The percentage of those who "never" sit outside is equally low (2% for both groups). This reinforces the fact that sheer distance between unit and ground does not have as strong an impact as might be expected.

Building formation has a fundamental impact on the use of the lobby; most garden apartments do not have lobbies. Table 16-4 shows that towers tend to have high lobby use; however, not every high-rise has a frequently used lobby. In two cases (Bethany and Josephson), management policy discourages lobby use. The sheer presence or absence of a lobby will obviously affect its use, but other factors can intervene between the availability of this space in high-rise buildings and its widespread use.

Table 16-5 also testifies to the impact of availability of a facility. Most of the community facilities listed show marked differences in frequency of use between high-rise and garden tenants, but in most cases these variations serve only to indicate which facilities are absent from the low, dispersed housing pattern. In a few instances, however, contrasts are meaningful: community rooms, game or bingo rooms, flower gardens, outdoor seating, indoor seating, and laundry rooms are present in most of the projects of both types. The percentage of users is roughly similar for towers and garden apartments. The percentage of community room use is lower for the average high-rise than garden because there is no such space in one of the towers, Columbus Homes. Surprisingly, flower garden use looks lower in garden apartments than in high-rise apartments, but this result is an artificial one, probably reflecting ambiguity about the meaning of flower garden in this context. Garden apartments have individual, not community, flower gardens, so tenants do not say they use them. No reliable difference between high-rise and garden types can be assigned to use of community spaces.

TABLE 16-4
Use of Lobby by Building Type
("Do people ever congregate or socialize in the lobby?")

	Yes	*No*	*Total*
High-Rise			
Columbus	27	7	34
Hanson	25	9	34
Bethany	6	28	34
Trent Center	33	2	35
Josephson	9	21	30
Subtotal	100 = 60%	67 = 40%	167 = 100%
Garden			
Camiano	8	27	35
Oakhurst	0	1	1
Tarklin	0	36	36
Subtotal	8 = 11%	64 = 89%	72 = 100%
Grand Total	108 = 45%	131 = 55%	239 = 100%

TABLE 16-5
Building Type by Percentage Who Report Using Selected Community Spaces

	High-Rise		*Garden*		
*Community Space**	*No.*	*%*	*No.*	*%*	*Total*
Community room	98	56.6	84	79.2	182
Game or bingo room	61	35.1	36	34.0	97
Pool room	38	21.8	2	1.9	40
Lounge area	52	30.0	7	6.6	59
Coffee, cigarette vending area	49	28.2	3	2.8	52
Craft room	41	23.6	14	13.2	55
Community kitchen	50	28.7	16	15.1	66
Mail area	131	75.3	8	7.5	139
TV room	49	28.2	1	1.9	50
Visitor lounge	47	27.0	3	2.8	50
Flower garden	60	34.5	11	10.4	71
Outdoor recreation area	42	24.1	19	17.9	61
Other recreation (Ping-Pong, etc.)	34	19.5	6	5.7	40
Library or reading room	62	35.6	5	4.7	67
Outdoor seating area	108	62.1	47	44.3	155
Laundry room	111	63.8	61	57.5	172
Chapel facilities	47	27.0	13	12.3	60
Telephone	44	25.3	3	2.8	47
Piano or music area	40	23.0	2	1.9	42
Movie area	60	34.5	3	2.8	63
Beauty parlor	14	8.1	2	1.9	16

*Totals vary because not all sites have all facilities, and not all respondents were aware of these facilities.

View from Apartment

Table 16-6 shows that more respondents in garden apartments (79%) than in high-rise buildings (50%) find the view from their apartment attractive. This could mean that panoramas are not as popular as views of the ground which would give the lower formation an "aesthetic advantage." However, a project-by-project examination of this table shows that tenants in a high-rise, Bethany Manor, rate their view the most attractive of all the projects. In large part this must be attributed to the ocean view, but intricate landscaping and care in maintenance of the grounds may claim an effect as well. At the other extreme, the highest number of "ugly" ratings comes from another high-rise, Columbus Homes, where the landscaping is the least well maintained. Not until garden and tower configurations are compared with well elaborated and maintained grounds can it be concluded that height alone has an impact on older people's aesthetic judgments about their view. (Even then there might be a bipolar split, some liking panoramas with beautiful grounds, others liking direct street-level views.)

Garden apartments tend to be more complex in their landscaping and better maintained. These virtues should be applied to projects regardless of building height.

Sexual Segregation

Thinking that the concentrated organization of the high-rise might produce more social interaction, hence differentiation, the relationship between sexual segregation and building type was examined (Table 16-7). In only two of the eight projects do residents share the conviction that there is a place which belongs to the men, so no generalizations can be made. The two are high-rise projects where the designation of a space as "men's" was formally introduced by the previous management. Social programming can prob-

TABLE 16-6
Quality of View by Building Type
("Do you find the view from your window attractive, ordinary or ugly?")

	Attractive	*Ordinary*	*Ugly*	*Don't Know*	*Total*
High-Rise					
Columbus	7	19	8	1	35
Hanson	11	19	3	2	35
Bethany	34	1	0	0	35
Trent Center	17	13	4	0	34
Josephson	18	15	1	0	34
Subtotal	87 = 50.3%	67 = 38.7%	16 = 9.2%	3 = 1.7%	173 = 99.9%*
Garden					
Camiano	26	9	0	0	35
Oakhurst	28	4	3	0	35
Tarklin	30	6	0	0	36
Subtotal	84 = 79.2%	19 = 17.9%	3 = 2.8%	0 = 0.0%	106 = 99.9%*
Grand Total	171	86	19	3	279

*Percentages add up to less than 100% due to roundings.

TABLE 16–7
Extent of Sexual Segregation by Building Type
("Is there a place in the buiding which seems to 'belong' to the men?")

	Yes	*No*	*Total*
High-Rise			
Columbus	1	34	35
Hanson	0	35	35
Bethany	6	26	32
Trent Center	34	1	35
Josephson	27	1	28
Subtotal	68 = 41.2%	97 = 58.8%	165 = 100%
Garden			
Camiano	0	35	35
Oakhurst	1	34	35
Tarklin	0	36	36
Subtotal	1 = 0.9%	105 = 99.1%	106 = 100%
Grand Total	69	202	271

ably overcome whatever architectural tendency might exist that either promotes or hinders sexual segregation.

Security

Since security is a vital issue for older people, it is important to consider the possibility that it can be improved through architectural configuration. The centrality of the high-rise might make access easier to control, thus safer; or the direct relationship between each unit and its own entry might make surveillance more effective in creating a sense of safety. The average difference between positive responses in towers (34.1%) and garden configurations (7.7%) to the question of perceived safety (Table 16–8) hints that the latter interpretation may be the case.

On closer inspection, however, neither conclusion can be defended. The security problem is restricted to two buildings. Columbus Homes is located in an area of Newark noted for crime and other indices of deviance and disorganization. The neighborhood, not the building alone, would seem to be responsible for security problems. In Trent Center a murder had occurred in the building during the interview period. Although residents who were in the lobby the following morning concluded regretfully that the victim had not been wise in letting strangers into her apartment, the cry for improved security was everywhere. In neither Columbus nor Trent Center can the blame be pinned on the building as a physical entity or on its relationship to its surroundings. Tarklin Acres in Vineland has the next highest complaint vote (six out of thirty-five), but that may reflect residents' anxiety about the adjacent public housing project for families with children and teenagers rather than the difficulty of imposing control on a site with many points of access. Our conclusion is that the surrounding neighborhood seems to be the most significant factor in affecting residents' feelings of security.

Table 16–9 shows the ways residents proposed to

TABLE 16–8
Adequacy of Security by Building Types
("Do you think security is a problem in this building?")

	Yes	*No*	*Total*
High-Rise			
Columbus	25	10	35
Hanson	5	30	35
Bethany	0	35	35
Trent Center	24	11	35
Josephson	5	28	33
Subtotal	59 = 34.1%	114 = 65.9%	173 = 100%
Garden			
Camiano	1	34	35
Oakhurst	1	33	34
Tarklin	6	29	35
Subtotal	8 = 7.7%	96 = 92.3%	104 = 100%
Grand Total	67	210	277

improve security and bears out the importance of the surrounding neighborhood inferred from the preceding table. Of nine recommendations, "improving the neighborhood" was second only to having more police. The high-rise and garden sites do not differ significantly from one another in the frequency in which residents suggest these two improvements. Neither housing type generates solutions which rely more than the other on mechanical physical versus social managerial modes.

Privacy and Community

Another possible way in which the two types of configurations might differ is the amount of privacy they offer the individual tenant. Thin walls, being passed by other tenants on their way down long corridors, or the knowledge that one's apartment is but a cubicle suspended within a much larger structure might make high-rise residents feel they lack privacy. In garden apartments, residents might find that ground floor windows limit visual privacy, or that the smaller clusters of units might set up a social expectation that one be neighborly whether or not one was so inclined.

Table 16–10 shows a slight tendency for building type to affect feelings of privacy, but the relationship is not statistically significant. Further research might show that the high-rise formation tends to make some people judge that their unit lacks adequate privacy, while the garden formation tends to make some feel that their units are too isolated. The overwhelming majority (93.7% and 93.4%) for both types felt that the degree of privacy was satisfactory. It appears that building type per se has no significant impact on feelings of privacy.

There is equal need for privacy and contact. One indicator of a minimal amount of contact among people is whether or not they recognize each other by sight. Table 16–11 shows that this variable is strongly affected by building type. Over four-fifths (86.7%) of the garden apartment dwellers know each other by sight compared with less than half (47.1%)

TABLE 16–9
Ways to Improve Security by Building Type
("What do you think is the best way to improve security?")

	Better Locks	*Make Watch Committee*	*More Police*	*Better Lighting*	*Improve Visibility*	*Improve Neighbor-hood*	*Exclude Outsiders*	*Isolate Elderly*	*Other*	*Total Responses*
High-Rise										
Columbus	10	2	3	1	2	5	0	5	1	29
Hanson	4	0	7	0	0	8	9	1	5	34
Bethany	2	3	9	3	5	3	0	0	2	27
Trent Center	1	3	7	1	0	4	2	0	12	30
Josephson	0	1	16	0	1	1	2	0	2	23
Subtotal	17 = 11.9%	9 = 6.3%	42 = 29.4%	5 = 3.5%	8 = 5.6%	21 = 14.6%	13 = 9.1%	6 = 9.1%	22 = 15.4%	143 = 100%
Garden										
Camiano	1	1	4	5	4	13	1	6	0	35
Oakhurst	2	3	9	1	2	0	1	0	0	18
Tarklin	1	1	18	4	0	0	6	3	2	35
Subtotal	4 = 4.5%	5 = 5.7%	31 = 35.2%	10 = 11.4%	6 = 6.8%	13 = 14.8%	8 = 9.1%	9 = 10.2%	2 = 2.3%	88 = 100%
Grand Total	21	14	73	15	14	34	21	15	24	231 = 100%

TABLE 16-10
Adequacy of Privacy by Building Type
("Do you think your living arrangement offers adequate privacy?")

	Too Private (Isolated)	*Just Right*	*Not Private*	*Total*
High-Rise				
Columbus	0	30	5	35
Hanson	1	34	0	35
Bethany	0	35	0	35
Trent Center	0	30	5	35
Josephson	0	34	0	34
Subtotal	1 = 0.6%	163 = 93.7%	10 = 5.7%	174 = 100%
Garden				
Camiano	1	33	1	35
Oakhurst	0	35	0	35
Tarklin	3	31	2	36
Subtotal	4 = 3.8%	99 = 93.4%	3 = 2.8%	106 = 100%
Grand Total	5	262	13	280

TABLE 16-11
Recognition of People by Housing Type
("Do you know the folks here by sight?")

	Total Number of Units in Project	*Yes*	*No*	*Total Sample Size*
High-Rise				
Columbus	1500	17	18	35
Hanson	100	16	19	35
Bethany	230	27	8	35
Trent Center	158	11	24	35
Josephson	152	11	23	34
Subtotal		82 = 47.1%	91 = 52.9%	174 = 100%
Garden				
Camiano	40	33	2	35
Oakhurst	90	23	12	35
Tarklin	150	35	0	35
Subtotal		91 = 86.7%	14 = 13.3%	105 = 100%
Grand Total		173 = 62%	106 = 38%	279 = 100%

of the high-rise dwellers. This difference, to some extent, is a function of population size. The high-rise buildings tend to have more people in the total project than do the garden complexes, so it is easier to recognize others. The configuration of high-rise buildings could mean that apartment dwellers do not see others going to and from their apartments because the elevator is enclosed and often at a distance from one's unit. But according to our data, sheer size is most important in this respect.

The relationship between feelings of boredom and building type (Table 16-12) shows a similar pattern. Slightly less than half (47.1%) of the high-rise residents say that they are never bored, whereas three-fifths (62.3%) of the garden dwellers make this claim. This relationship may be a function of the smaller population in garden complexes, better social programming, or some psychological consequence of the garden-style environment. Insofar as boredom is related to the absence of social contact, the most likely explanation is that the smaller population size of the garden projects permits a greater sense of involvement among residents and between residents and their building manager.

Another variable which shows the same pattern is reported in Table 16-13. When asked if their activity had increased, decreased, or stayed about the same since moving into their building, more garden apartment dwellers reported an increase (40.1%) than did high-rise tenants (29.3%). Conversely, reports of a decrease were greater in high-rises than in the low buildings. Boredom, not knowing people by sight, and a decrease in activity show the same direct relationship to the high-rise building type, indicating the possibility that the three are linked. Bored people may be those who do less and know fewer people. Whether this constellation is linked to the total number of people in one's residential environment or to the organization of people into one type of spatial configuration or another has important policy implications for the use of high-rise buildings for housing the elderly.

At this point it is impossible to conclude either way. On the one hand, a "critical mass" of residents

TABLE 16-12
Feelings of Boredom by Building Type
("Are you ever bored here?")

	Combined (Seldom, Often, Sometimes)	*Never*	*Total*
High-Rise			
Columbus	18	17	35
Hanson	28	7	35
Bethany	16	19	35
Trent Center	16	19	35
Josephson	14	20	34
Subtotal	92 = 52.90%	82 = 47.1%	174 = 100%
Garden			
Camiano	20	15	35
Oakhurst	4	31	35
Tarklin	16	20	36
Subtotal	40 = 37.7%	66 = 62.3%	106 = 100%
Grand Total	132 = 47%	148 = 53%	280 = 100%

TABLE 16–13
Level of Activity by Building Type
("Since you moved here has your activity increased, decreased, or stayed the same?")

	Increased a Lot or Increased a Little	*Stayed the same*	*Decreased*	*Total*
High-Rise				
Columbus	1	22	12	35
Hanson	15	6	14	35
Bethany	7	17	11	35
Trent Center	11	14	10	35
Josephson	17	9	8	34
Subtotal	51 = 29.3%	68 = 39.1%	55 = 31.6%	174 = 100%
Garden				
Camiano	11	23	1	35
Oakhurst	14	16	5	35
Tarklin	18	9	9	36
Subtotal	43 = 40.1%	48 = 15.3%	15 = 14.2%	106 = 100%
Grand Total	94 = 34%	116 = 35%	70 = 30%	280 = 100%

seems necessary for a variety of potential friendships. On the other hand, intimate groupings are more conducive to interaction. High-rise buildings must, as an economic necessity, provide the "critical mass," but physical designs and special organization can create small subgroupings of three to five units and then bind them together to create a sense of community, that is, shared destiny and shared interests.

SUMMARY AND CONCLUSIONS

1. Residents prefer the urban, suburban, or rural locations in which they already find themselves; building height does not affect these preferences.

2. Garden apartment dwellers use outdoor seating areas slightly (90%) more than tower residents (77%). However, the difference is less than expected given the greater physical distance between unit and ground in high-rise buildings. Furthermore, difference in building form does not significantly affect the frequency of use of the outdoors.

It can be concluded that for the elderly, elevators can compensate for the increase in physical distance because they do not need a direct visual or kinesthetic relationship between the apartment interior and the ground plane.

3. High-rise buildings often have features such as lobbies which garden apartments lack. One might speculate that in the garden apartments opportunities for informal socializing would be less; therefore, the rates of knowing people by sight would be lower. This proved to be untrue, but possibly because garden developments are smaller than high-rise projects. If population were held constant, perhaps the presence or absence of a lobby would affect the social life of the group. As the evidence stands now, the lobby is used, although to varying degrees. If there is a more attractive gathering area, or a policy against hanging around in the lobby, it is used less frequently than average. Thus, lobby use is variable and its effect on social life uncertain. This contradicts assumptions about the significance of the lobby as a locus of activity. Under some circumstances, the outdoor

entry and its approach might be far more important areas for casual social life and its benefits.

4. No reliable differences between high-rise and garden types can be assigned to use of community spaces: community rooms, game or bingo rooms, flower gardens, outdoor seating, and laundry.

5. The view from one's apartment is more frequently rated attractive in garden than in high-rise projects. The garden developments tend to have more complex and better maintained landscaping, a difference resulting from environmental management and not necessarily dependent on low- or high-rise architecture.

6. No generalizations can be made about the relationships between sexual segregation and building type because in only two projects did residents acknowledge any. These are the only two of the eight projects in which areas for men and women were formally designated, attesting to the power of deliberate policy rather than informal norms.

7. The surrounding neighborhood seems to be far more significant than any other factor in affecting the residents' feelings of security. Of the ways suggested by respondents to improve security, "increasing the number of police" and "improving the neighborhood" were the top two of nine choices, and residents of tower and garden apartments made these recommendations in equal proportions. Neither type of building form elicited security solutions which were more socially based or more mechanically/physically based than the other.

The two favored solutions say, essentially, "Let's not have the problem" (improve neighborhood) or "Let's hire someone else to solve it" (increase policing). Both express the desire to escape the problem altogether. Jane Jacobs has argued convincingly that hired surveillants can never replace informal surveillance performed by the users of a neighborhood, yet the idea of forming such a tenants' committee was not a popular choice. More education about the importance of each person watching out for others is needed. People who now watch the comings and goings of others are usually called "busybodies." Management should explain the important function of these people.

8. Although the relationship is not statistically significant, high-rise formation tends to be correlated with the judgment that the individual's apartment lacks adequate privacy. The overwhelming majority (over 90%), however, felt that the apartment had neither too much nor too little privacy, so it appears that building type has no significant impact on feelings of privacy.

9. Whether or not tenants recognize each other by sight is strongly related to building type. The larger population size and the circulation system of towers combine to produce a lower recognition level than in garden complexes.

Boredom, not knowing people by sight, and a decrease in activity show the same direct relationship to the high-rise building type, leading to speculation that the three are linked. Whether provoked by sheer population size alone or size in combination with the circulation patterns inherent in the tower, these indicators of social satisfaction point to one implication: the smaller the population the better. The greater the population size (once over 100 units), the more compensatory money and thought must be invested in the initial design of community spaces and in the social activities and services which take place within them. Yet further research is needed to determine which variable dominates, if indeed one can be shown to consistently take precedence.

GENERAL POLICY

From a wide range of social, behavioral, and psychological variables, in only one area did the high-rise building type have an unequivocal impact. Three indices of social satisfaction—knowing other people, degree of boredom, and amount of activity—appear to be negatively affected by the high-rise configuration, specifically its size.

For the other variables, there is either no difference between tower and garden configurations or the high-rise masks other variables, such as neighborhood or landscaping, which have a greater impact on the dependent variables than the facts of tallness, bigness, or circulation per se.

For housing older citizens, then, the high-rise building may be suitable in most ways. Because social life is extremely important to a person who no longer has work and its routine contacts, the high-rise form can best be used when all the planning parties involved are assured that the initial physical design and the follow-up social services will be elaborate and rich in the communal areas.

17

The Influence of Familiarity and Age Factors on Responses to Residential Structures

Brenda Egolf
Roy C. Herrenkohl
Center for Social Research
Lehigh University

An interest in comparing people's reactions to different types of buildings is met with considerable methodological difficulty. One reason is that to obtain responses one generally has had to conduct a survey of persons who occupy the different buildings in which there is interest. The rationale is that only those who live in a building can say what it is like to live there. However, the survey method poses a variety of difficulties. One is the cost in time and money of surveying large numbers of people. Another is the difficulty in having respondents react to more than the building in which they live. When one can trust only the responses of those who live in a particular building, comparing reactions to different buildings is out of the question.

The survey method in actuality limits information on responses to a single building, although researchers sometimes show little hesitancy to generalize such information to the general building type. Furthermore, when results from studies of the desirability of different types of residences are interpreted, there is a tendency to assume a simple, one-to-one relationship between building type and desirability.

A further inadequacy of previous studies is the tendency to believe that there is a "typical" or average response to each building type. Anyone reasonably well versed in statistics knows that while there is in fact a statistical average, this average may no more reflect the feelings of actual persons than the average of 2.25 children per family reflects the exact number of children in any family. Too little attention is given to the individual variation which the "average" response only summarizes.

The present study was designed to study two issues which are believed to account for some of the variability in people's responses to a type of residential setting. One issue is the age of the person; the other is his familiarity with a type of residential structure.

The perspective taken here is that of a person considering a place to live and examining alternative types of setting. The hypothesis is that people find residential settings which are familiar more desirable than those which are unfamiliar. The issue of familiarity refers both to having lived in a building and to accumulated experience over a person's lifetime in ways other than living in a type of building. The rational for this hypothesis is that moving into and adjusting to residential settings which are familiar involves less change in patterns of living than moving into settings which are unfamiliar. Prior to the move there would be less anticipation of the change and the associated stress that such changes entail. The psychological significance is that there is more assurance that the many needs to be satisfied in a residential setting can actually be satisfied in a familiar setting where the person "knows his way around" than in an unfamiliar setting where he does not. Consequently, less stress due to adjustment is anticipated.

An additional consideration in understanding the desirability of a residential setting as a place to live is the life span developmental stage of the individual. The hypothesis is that persons of different ages find certain types of structures more desirable than other types.

Again the needs of the person are at issue. Some types of residences may provide for or be perceived as providing for the needs of certain age groups and not for others. An additional question is whether age and familiarity operate independently of each other or interact, that is, are influential on desirability in some coordinated way.

The present study employs the method of presenting respondents with pictures of different residential buildings. There are several advantages to this method. One is that respondents can view a number of pictures representing different types of buildings. Second, the pictures of the buildings can be selected or evaluated with reference to specific qualities of the buildings. Third, several illustrations of the same type of building can be shown, thus making it possible to obtain an indication of a response to a building type in contrast to a response to a single building. Fourth, with pictures one can select the sample of respondents to meet certain theoretically relevant spcifications.

This method has recently been used by Danford and Willems (1974), who demonstrated that subjects' responses to actually viewing a building corresponded to a high degree to the responses of subjects viewing pictures of the same building, a result that provided what they referred to as "convergent" validity for the responses, that is the two types of responses were similar where one would expect them to be so. However, these authors expressed concern over the lack of what they referred to as "divergent" validity in their data. That is where one would expect no relationships, there were in fact relationships.

In summary, the present study is both an examination of a methodology which offers potential for the study of human responses to the built environment and also an examination on a preliminary basis of potentially important influences on human responses.

METHOD

Overview

The method of the study was to present to respondents a series of seventy-six projected slide pictures depicting different residential settings such as high-rise buildings, low-rise buildings, row-type buildings, twin or semi-detached houses, garden apartments, single family dwellings, mobile homes, tents and trailers, the latter being referred to as "temporary shelters." Respondents were first asked to rate each dwelling pictured in a slide on degree of crowding. (The crowding issue will not be discussed in the present chapter.) Each slide was presented a second time and was rated by the respondent on his degree of familiarity with that type of structure. The slides were presented a third time and each was rated for desirability of the structure as a place to live. Respondents then completed a questionnaire providing background information. Finally, the study was explained and all questions answered.

Respondents

The number of respondents was 339. This total was comprised of the following:

N	*Description*
38	Two-year business school students
170	Four-year college students
95	Adults (post-college to retirement age)
36	Elderly (senior citizen groups)
339	

All of the respondents were from an urban area of eastern Pennsylvania having a population of approximately 200,000. All respondents were residents of the area, excepting some of the four-year college students who were from a wider geographical area. Approximately one-half of the elderly group were residents of high-rise (eight story) buildings.

Selection of photographs

In a preliminary pilot study eighty color slides had been used. These depicted a variety of housing styles in a variety of neighborhood settings. Respondents rated how crowded each type of residence would be and these ratings were factor analyzed. Results indicated three factors involving (a) tenement-like and row homes, (b) high-rise buildings and (c) single family dwellings. Pictures with ratings not clearly related to one of these factors were dropped and new pictures depicting mobile homes, garden apartments and temporary shelters (e.g., tents and trailers) were added. The new set of seventy-six pictures was then used in the present study. The assumption was that eight types of residential structures were depicted: high-rise, low-rise, row, twins, garden, mobile homes, temporary shelters (tents and trailers), and single family dwellings.

Questionnaires

In the rating of the pictures respondents were asked to rate a picture for their familiarity with the type of residence depicted. The scale ranged as follows: 1=unfamiliar, 2=slightly familiar, 3=moderately familiar, and 4=very familiar. The building's desirability as a place to live was rated on a scale which ranged as follows: 1=definitely, yes; 2=maybe, yes; 3=maybe, no; 4=definitely, no. In addition to providing the ratings, background information, including the respondents age, was also provided.

Procedure

Respondents were assessed in groups ranging from five to fifty in number. The slides were presented with a carousel-type projector with a timing device, which made it possible to control the time for presenting each slide. Presentation times for the crowding and familiarity issues were eight seconds for each slide. For the third presentation of the slides the time of presentation was reduced to five seconds.

Statistical analyses

Factor analyses of the rating were done. These were principal components analyses with unity in the diagonals. A varimax rotation procedure was performed as a second step. A score was derived by summing the ratings of pictures determined by means of the factor analysis to represent structures of a particular dwelling type. Zero-order correlations were then computed between the different "scores" of crowding, familiarity and desirability and between these scores and selected background information. A multiple correlation analysis was done to assess the relationship between the dependent variable, the desirability rating score for each factor and three independent variables, the familiarity score on that factor, the respondent's age, and an interaction of age and familiarity score. The interaction was a cross-product of age and familiarity score.

RESULTS

Factor analytic results

A separate factor analysis was done on the set of familiarity ratings and on the set of desirability ratings. The results indicated strikingly similar factors associated with each set of ratings when seven factors were rotated. Specifically, when only those ratings with the highest factor loadings were considered, the factors are essentially the same regardless of which of the two issues was considered. The seven factors were one less than the anticipated eight since twin homes and row homes combined as one factor. Description of the content of the factors is as follows:

Factor A High-rise apartments (ten pictures). The picture ratings with the highest loadings are those which tend to accentuate the height of the buildings. With one exception all the buildings are greater than twenty stories. Desirability ratings of pictures on this factor had loadings which ranged from a high of 0.80 to a low of 0.60 and familiarity ratings had loadings which ranged from 0.82 to 0.49.

Factor B Mobile homes (eight pictures). The picture ratings with the highest loadings are mobile homes from various angles. Possibly because of the singularity of design, ratings of all pictures included tended to have very high loadings. Desirability ratings had loadings which ranged from a high of 0.84 to a low of 0.71 and familiarity ratings had loadings ranging from 0.85 to 0.78.

Factor C Low-rise apartments (ten pictures). The picture ratings with the highest loading were five story buildings which also appeared to be rather old. Desirability ratings of pictures on this factor had loadings which ranged from a high of 0.73 to a low of 0.47 and familiarity ratings had loadings which ranged from 0.80 to 0.57.

Factor D Twin or row homes (nine pictures). The picture ratings with the highest loadings were row houses and twin houses. Desirability ratings had loadings as high as 0.77 and as low as 0.45 while familiarity ratings had loadings which ranged from 0.80 to 0.50.

Factor E Temporary shelters (five pictures). The picture ratings with the highest loadings were a pop-up, tent-trailer in the woods, a green tent in the woods and a blue tent. Desirability ratings ranged from a high of 0.89 to a low of 0.72 and familiarity ratings had loadings which ranged from 0.89 to 0.59.

Factor F Garden apartments (seven pictures). The picture ratings with the highest loadings were different views of two garden apartment complexes. Desirability ratings of pictures has loadings which ranged from a high of 0.81 to a low of 0.67 and familiarity ratings had loadings which ranged from 0.81 to 0.70.

Factor G Single family homes (eight pictures). The picture ratings with the highest loadings are single family, two story, and ranch-type dwellings. Desirability ratings of pictures had loadings which ranged from a high of 0.73 to a low of 0.30 and familiarity ratings had loadings which ranged from 0.77 to 0.43.

Descriptive statistics on "scores"

For the purpose of further study each respondent's ratings of the pictures selected for each factor were summed to provide scores respectively for familiarity and for desirability. These scores can be taken as an index of a respondent's familiarity with a type of building or the desirability of living in the type of building or structure represented by the pictures included on a factor.

Tables 17-1 and 17-2 present descriptive statistics for the familiarity "scores" and desirability "scores" respectively. It is notable that with very few exceptions these cover the full range of possible scores, indicating that there is considerable variability between persons in their responses to the type of buildings depicted in the pictures. Tables 17-1 and 17-2 also present the average rating on each factor. Single family homes and twin or row homes are ranked first and second on familiarity—the former between points marked "moderately familiar" and "very familiar"; the latter between points marked "slightly familiar" and "moderately familiar." Garden apartments and temporary shelters also fell between those same points. The low-rise apartments were rated as least familiar, between points marked "unfamiliar" and "slightly familiar." Low-rise apartments and high-rise apartments were also rated in this interval although closer to the "slightly familiar" rating point.

Average ratings of desirability of a residential setting as a place to live led to somewhat the same ordering. Single family dwellings were rated first in desirability between the rating points marked "definitely, yes" and "maybe, yes." This was the only type rated in that interval. Garden apartments and twin or row homes were second and third respectively, rated between the points designated "maybe, yes" and "maybe, no." The remainder fell between the points designated "maybe, no" and "definitely, no." Of this group temporary shelters were rated more desirable, followed in order by high-rise buildings, mobile homes, and low-rise apartments.

These results also reflect the relationship between familiarity and desirability. The familiarity rank of a type of residential setting is essentially the same as the desirability rank of that type. The exception is a reversal of the second and third rankings of twin or row homes and garden apartments.

Correlational analyses

Table 17-3 presents correlations between respondent's familiarity scores and desirability scores for each of the seven housing types. The hypothesis that familiarity and desirability are associated is supported by these results.

Relationships between scores on familiarity and on desirability are such that the more familiar are the more desirable. The relationships are all statistically significant but range from a high of $r = -0.58$ for Factor E: temporary shelters, to a low of $r = -0.26$ to -0.27 for low-rise apartments, twin and row homes, and garden apartments. High-rise buildings are second only to temporary shelters in the association between

TABLE 17-1
Familiarity with the Type of Residence Pictured: Descriptive Statistics

Housing Dimension	*No. of Pictures*	*Mean**	*S.D.*	*Minimum** Score*	*Maximum** Score*	*Average Rating*	*Rank*
A: High-Rise Apts.	10	18.04	7.42	10	40	1.80	5
B: Mobile Homes	8	13.62	6.35	8	32	1.70	6
C: Low-Rise Apts.	10	16.33	7.43	10	40	1.63	7
D: Twin or Row Homes	9	21.61	6.56	9	36	2.40	2
E: Temporary Shelters	5	11.07	4.94	5	20	2.20	4
F: Garden Apts.	7	16.52	5.58	7	28	2.35	3
G: Single Family Homes	8	25.17	5.27	8	32	3.14	1

*Lo scores = "unfamiliar" and hi scores = "familiar."

**The lowest possible score is indicated by the number of pictures on a factor; the highest possible score is the number of pictures multiplied by 4.

TABLE 17-2
Desirability of Type of Residence as a Place to Live: Descriptive Statistics

Housing Dimension	*No. of Pictures*	*Mean**	*S.D.*	*Minimum** Score*	*Maximum** Score*	*Average Rating*	*Rank*
A: High-Rise Apts.	10	31.43	7.02	10	40	3.14	5
B: Mobile Homes	8	27.77	5.32	10	32	3.47	6
C: Low-Rise Apts.	10	38.46	2.93	22	40	3.84	7
D: Twin or Row Homes	9	26.50	5.42	9	36	2.94	3
E: Temporary Shelter	5	15.08	4.88	5	20	3.01	4
F: Garden Apts.	7	14.88	4.89	7	28	2.12	2
G: Single Family Homes	8	13.37	3.85	8	31	1.67	1

*Lo scores = "desirable" and hi scores = "undesirable."
**The lowest possible score is indicated by the number of pictures on a factor; the highest possible score is the number of pictures multiplied by 4.

familiarity and desirability (r = -0.37, and shared variability is 13%).

Table 17-4 presents correlations between a respondent's age and desirability scores and between familiarity scores and desirability scores for each type of residence. The largest correlations are between age and familiarity. The relationship between age and familiarity scores for high-rise (A), mobile homes (B), low-rise (C), and twins and rows (D) is such that the older the people, the more familiar they are with the type of dwelling. However, for temporary shelters and single homes the relationship is reversed, that is, the older the people, the more unfamiliar they are with the type of residence.

Relationships between age and desirability scores are much weaker. Only desirability ratings for temporary shelters and for single homes are significantly related to age. The relationship is such that the older the person the less desirable each of these types of residential setting is to the individual.

Table 17-5 presents multiple regression results

TABLE 17-3
Correlations Between Scores on Familiarity and Desirability for Each Residential Type

Factor: Housing Dimension	*Correlation of Familiarity with Desirability*
A. High-Rise Apartments	-.37**
B. Mobile Homes	-.32**
C. Low-Rise Apartments	-.26**
D. Twin or Row Homes	-.26**
E. Temporary Shelters	-.58**
F. Garden Apartments	-.27**
G. Single Homes	-.34**

*$p \leqslant .05$. Lo Scores = unfamiliar. Lo scores = desirable.
**$p \leqslant .01$. Hi scores = familiar Hi scores = undesirable.

TABLE 17-4
Correlation Between Respondent's Age and Ratings of Familiarity and Desirability for Each Type of Residence

	Age-Familiarity	*Age-Desirability*
A. High-Rise Apartments	.18**	.03
B. Mobile Homes	.12*	-.02
C. Low-Rise Apartments	.17**	.02
D. Twins or Row Homes	.23**	.00
E. Temporary Shelters	-.23**	.28**
F. Garden Apartments	.01	.05
G. Single Homes	-.33**	.22**

*$p \leqslant .05$. Lo scores = unfamiliar. Lo scores = desirable.
**$p \leqslant .01$. Hi scores = familiar. Hi scores = undesirable.

when the respondent's familiarity rating, age and the interaction of the familiarity rating and age are correlated with the desirability rating score associated with each factor. These results indicate that the familiarity rating is consistently the best predictor of desirability. Indeed, little is added when age and the interaction of age and familiarity are added.

DISCUSSION

Relationship between familiarity and desirability

There are several possible alternative explanations for the results reported above beside the hypothesized relationship. The importance of such alternatives is to make interpretation of the results equivocal. Several possible explanations will be considered.

One question is whether the familiarity ratings in fact represent the experience of living in the type of building represented by the factor. This can be examined by relating the familiarity rating for a factor of a respondent's actual previous residence(s). Table 17-6 indicates these results. For all but one factor the highest correlation is between previous residence in that type of building and the respondent's indication of familiarity with that same type. In other words having lived in a particular type of residence is associated with a rating of greater familiarity with that type of residence than with other types of residence. The one exception is the correlation between living in a low-rise building and the familiarity rating of factor D, twin or row homes. This correlation is greater than the rating of low-rise apartments by only 0.01. Thus, generally these data support the validity of the familiarity rating.

Another question is whether respondents are rating the quality of the exterior appearance of the residence rather than the type of residence. This is an alternative for which no relevant data was gathered. While most of the buildings pictured seem well maintained there are some, particularly the low-rise buildings, where deterioration is evident. This fact may explain the relatively low desirability rating and is an issue requiring control in any further study using the present method.

A third alternative explanation is that since the rating of familiarity preceded the rating of desirability, the latter is simply a repetition of the former. There is no empirical evidence on this point. Logically, however, it is hard to see why familiarity should be

TABLE 17-5
Multiple Correlations of Familiarity, Age, and the Interaction of the Two with the Desirability Rating Associated with Each Type of Residential Structure

			t values		
Dependent Variable: Desirability Rating	*R*	R^2	*Familiarity*	*Age*	*Age × Fam Interaction*
(16) A: High-Rise Apts.	.38	.14	-3.96**	.54	.22
(17) B: Mobile Homes	.34	.11	-4.89**	-1.90	2.22*
(18) C: Low-Rise Apts.	.27	.07	-2.53*	.65	-.02
(19) D: Twin or Row Homes	.28	.08	-4.01**	-1.14	1.61
(20) E: Temporary Shelters	.60	.36	-6.46**	.97	.64
(21) F: Garden Apts.	.28	.07	-1.91	.99	-.67
(22) G: Single Family	.36	.13	-1.29	2.11*	-1.55

*$p \leq .05$.
**$p \leq .01$.
df = 1 and 335.

TABLE 17-6
Correlations Between Ratings of Familiarity with Each Type of Residence and Whether or Not the Respondent Has Ever Lived in Each Type of Building

	Familiarity Rating of Residential Type						
Actual Previous Residence	*A High-Rise*	*B Mobile*	*C Low-Rise*	*D Twins/Rows*	*E Temporary Shelter*	*F Garden*	*G Single*
High-Rise	*-.37***	.00	-.10	-.01	.10	-.11*	.11*
Low-Rise	-.16**	-.11*	*-.17***	-.18**	-.07	-.12*	-.04
Garden	-.25**	-.10	-.16**	-.07	-.02	*-.28***	-.01
Row	-.00	-.06	-.16**	*-.29***	.16**	.11*	.25**
Twin	-.12*	-.07	-.05	*-.17***	.05	-.09	.05
Single	-.06	-.01	.00	.19**	-.15**	-.10	*-.35***
Mobile	-.03	*-.29***	-.02	.06	.01	.01	.05
Temporary Shelter	-.06	-.20**	-.05	-.01	*-.49***	-.06	-.04

*$p \leqslant .05$. Actual previous residence: hi score = lived there.
**$p \leqslant .01$. Familiarity rating: high score = low familiarity.

associated with desirability unless the familiar is more desirable. Again, this issue should be controlled in any further study.

Another alternative explanation is that for the particular group of respondents in the study, a relationship exists between familiarity and desirability but does not exist for the population in general. The present sample of respondents was not random and does not represent the full range of residential experience that might be desired. However, care was taken to obtain a full age range among respondents. What is lacking is a full range of high-density urban to rural residents which would provide the maximum distribution on familiarity. Thus, this alternative explanation cannot with the present data be excluded. In general, while there is some equivocation in the present results they are also sufficiently consistent to merit further study.

The import of a respondent's age

Alternative explanations for the identified relationships between age and familiarity are essentially those listed above, that is, the photographs used have qualities other than housing type to which respondents may be reacting. There are also technical research design issues such as the ordering of response ratings which might explain the results. Also, the selection of respondents may be responsible for the relationship between age and familiarity. Little can be added to what has been said above on the first two points. However, the latter issue bears further consideration particularly in view of the relatively small associations between the respondent's age and rating of desirability across residential types.

The relationship between age and familiarity indicates that the older respondents are more familiar with high-rise apartments, mobile homes, low-rise apartments, and twins or rows than younger respondents. By contrast the younger respondents are more familiar with temporary shelters and single family dwellings. There are probably at least two factors at work. One is socioeconomic status; the younger (college student) respondents are on the average more affluent that the older respondents, some of whom are in public (high-rise) housing. Consequently, the younger respondents are more often familiar with single family homes. However, the relationship between the independent variables, age and familiarity, with the dependent variable, desirability of temporary shelters, is most likely purely a function of age differences, that is, the younger are more likely to have used tents and/or trailers than older respondents, although one cannot rule out altogether the possibility that this result is also due in some way to socioeconomic differences.

The overall weakness of the relationships between age and desirability is striking. In two statistically significant relationships the older the respondent the less desirably both temporary shelters and single family homes are perceived. In the multiple correlation analysis the relationship between age and desirability is removed; however, the one for single family dwellings remains. This latter is such that the older the respondent the less desirable a single home. There are several possible reasons for this result. Among them is the statement made by one respondent who lived in a high-rise building for the elderly to the effect that she would be lonely living in a single family home. This may suggest that in some way or another the pictures of single family homes depict social isolation which makes the setting undesirable.

The lack of statistically significant relationships between age and desirability of living in the other types of residence may be due to other factors. For example, the range of experience at each age level may not be sufficiently diverse to reveal the relationship.

Psychological significance of familiarity

There are two broad considerations regarding familiarity with one's residential setting. One is the psychological significance of anticipating taking up residence in either a familiar or an unfamiliar residential setting. The other is the psychological significance of adapting to a familiar or to an unfamiliar residential setting after one has moved in. These two circumstances will be considered briefly below.

Several authors have described the effect of moving from one's home to a new home, particularly when the move is forced by an urban relocation program. For example, Fried (1963) has referred to the psychological impact of such a move as "grieving for a lost home." However, losing a home may be only a part of the problem. The other part may be the difficulty of moving to an unfamiliar residential setting. There are several possible situations which can occur when a family moves from one home to another. These can be described in a conventional psychological conflict paradigm. This paradigm characterizes conflict in terms of a person's response to different goals or outcomes. Specifically there are those goals or outcomes which are sought or *approached* because they are desirable and there are those that are not sought, in fact are actively *avoided* because they are not desirable. A family's move from one home to another can be considered in these terms.

1. *Avoidance-approach.* When a family is moving from one home which they find undesirable to a new residence which they find desirable.
2. *Approach-approach.* When a family is moving from one home which they find desirable to a new residence which they also find desirable.
3. *Approach-avoidance.* When a family is moving from a home they find desirable to a home they do not find desirable.
4. *Avoidance-avoidance.* When a family is moving from a home they find undesirable to a home they also find undesirable.

Two questions can only be raised here; however, they merit further study. One is: (1) What is the social psychological impact on the people involved of each of the four circumstances listed above? (2) What can be done to minimize detrimental effects which may occur in one or another of these circumstances? The import of the results presented above is that if the residential setting is familiar, the prospect of the move will be attractive. However, if the setting were to be unfamiliar, the prospect would be unattractive and thus to be avoided. While the familiar setting may pose relatively few problems for a family when they move, the unfamiliar will pose difficulties.

The second issue, adapting to a new residential environment, is a second stage in the process of moving from one home to another.

After coping with the conflict that may be associated with the prospect of leaving one home and moving into another, the next difficulty is actually adapting to the new home. This is particularly difficult if the type of residential setting is unfamiliar. That people can adapt is commonly accepted. Such a change is suggested by results from a study of high rise buildings (Stevenson et al. 1967) were the percentage of those finding their high-rise residence unsatisfactory dropped from 20% early in their residence to 8% after several months.

While such a process of adaptation or familiarization often occurs, there are also cases where for one reason or another the process is only partially completed. More information is needed regarding both the characteristics of persons who do not adapt readily to unfamiliar circumstances and the characteristics of residential settings, such as high-density residential environments, which pose difficulties for those who are unfamiliar with them. Furthermore, given such information, strategies are needed for making the familiarization process easier.

Suggestions for Further Research

There are a variety of methodological issues requiring examination in further research. Because the present study is correlational in nature, certain controls are lacking. Furthermore, consideration is needed of the specific characteristic of the pictures to which a person is responding. In this vein consideration could be given to manipulating these stimuli in a systematic fashion.

A strength of the method is the capability to present the pictures to a variety of persons. However, to optimize this feature random selection of respondents from defined populations would provide more generality to the results. Furthermore, more information is needed on background of the individual to verify that past experience is in fact what the respondent was reflecting in rating familiarity. Similarly, more information is needed to determine specifically what desirability means to respondents.

In summary, the method used in the present study has a potential for use in the study of people's responses to various aspects of architectural design. The capability to select or even create pictures which contain the desired content and to compare them to pictures which lack that content or have it to a different degree is important. While the method is in some ways artificial, this may be offset by the potential for experimental control which the method offers.

REFERENCES

Danford, G. Scott, and Edwin P. Willems. "Reliability and Validity of Subjective Responses to an Architectural Display." In *9: Multivariate Methods, Man-Environment Interactions: Evaluations and Applications*, edited by D. Carson. Milwaukee: Environmental Design Research Association, 1974.

Fried, Marc. "Grieving for a Lost Home." In *The Urban Condition*, edited by L. Duhl. New York: Simon and Schuster, 1963.

Stevenson, A.; Martin, E.; and O'Neill, J. *High Living: A Study of Family Life*. London: Melbourne University Press, 1967.

18

Colony Square: An After-Occupancy User-Needs Evaluation

Robert J. Young
Georgia Institute of Technology

INTRODUCTION AND OBJECTIVES

Colony Square is the second contemporary mixed-use complex after Peachtree Center in Atlanta and is unique in that it includes 264 permanent residential units in high-rise towers and projects 18 low-rise townhouse units.

The inclusion of permanent residential occupancy is expected to generate "continuous activity" and this facet of Colony Square continues to distinguish it from a series of other mixed-use developments which will come onto the Atlantic market in the next year or two.

The complex is now essentially complete after first occupancy in 1969 save for the townhouses and consists of approximately 3,000,000 sq. ft. (gross) of high-rise office/residential/hotel/commercial space on a twelve-acre site. The site is about two and one-half miles to the north of the central business district and to the immediate south of one of the city's most exclusive close-in residential areas, Ansley Park, and to the immediate north of a sagging retail/commercial/residential counterculture.

Space allocation is as follows:

High-Rise Office: 811,000 sq. ft. (gross) in two towers of 22 and 24 stories.

High-Rise Permanent Residential: 460,500 sq. ft. (gross) in three towers of 14 and 16 stories consisting of 97 apartments with rent to $1,200/month and 167 condominiums to $100,000+.

Low-Rise Townhouses: 18 units yet to be built in the $200,000+ range.

High-Rise Hotel: 489,000 sq. ft. (gross) in a single 26 story tower with 500 guest rooms and support facilities.

Plaza, Mall, Retail: 507,000 sq. ft. (gross) in two levels of shopping and circulation. Leasing of space incomplete.

Parking: 690,000 sq. ft. (gross) on three underground levels for approximately 2,000 automobiles. Separate parking area for permanent residential occupants.

Colony Square by architects Jova/Daniels/Busby,

and developer Cushman Corporation purports to advance the theme "cities are livable and urban life can, should, and must be good." A stated objective of this $100,000,000+ complex is "to build a development that will attack the problems of the city on both the technological and human fronts; a place that offers all the *excitement* and *convenience* of the city—with special emphasis on the human dimensions to make the convenience and excitement enjoyable."

Research objectives and benefits are:

1. To measure the achievement of Colony Square in terms of its design objectives,
   a. "cities are livable and urban life can, should, and must be good,"
   b. "to build a development that supports and enhances the positive characteristics of urban life and eliminates or reduces the negative ones."
2. To do so by comparing the solution advanced by the architect and developer to the end result as experienced by the USER, from the perspective of those who,
   a. live in the complex,
   b. work in the complex,
   c. shop in the complex,
   d. visit the complex.
3. To provide a vehicle by which those directly affected (THE USERS) may be heard.
4. To establish guidelines by which the physical development of future urban complexes may be enhanced with regard to human needs. These guidelines being of value to,
   a. the architect,
   b. the planner,
   c. the developer,
   d. the owner,
   e. the manager,
   f. and, in the final analysis, *THE USER*.

STUDY DESIGN AND METHODOLOGY

The study presently consists of three tiers, the first of which has been completed and the second of which is in progress.

Tier one

Tier one is an abbreviated evaluation by visitors (transient-users) to the Colony Square complex during the November 11, 1974, Atlanta Chapter American Institute of Architects sponsored "Architecture in Atlanta" open house. It consisted of an eighteen-question survey in five response categories:

1. Respondent Statistical Data
2. Concept
3. City Impact
4. Reactions/Evaluation
5. Suggestions.

The survey was distributed to the first 700 of what eventually turned out to be an overflow crowd of 2,000+ visitors. Some 9% of the questionnaires were returned—most that afternoon but a few later by mail, with several including page-long addenda in which the respondent expanded upon the survey format and included a response at length to the day's experience. A crowd some four times larger than was expected was a welcome indication of the public's interest in architecture in general, and this complex specifically, but contributed to the resulting turmoil and low response as did distribution of several other pieces of descriptive literature along with the survey.

Tier two

Tier two consists of an in-depth evaluation by those who live (apartments and condominiums) and work (office and retail) in Colony Square. The residential portion of the evaluation, the results of which are just now being received, consists of nine response categories:

1. Respondent Statistical Data
2. Respondent Background Data
   - Work/Residence Experience
   - Housing Type Experience
   - Housing Location Preference
   - Education
   - Employment

3. Mixed-Use Concept
4. City/Neighborhood Impact
5. Designer/Developer Objectives
6. Colony Square—General

Circulation	Noise
Construction	Size
Landscape	Privacy
Materials	Public Spaces
Parking	Management
Access	Shopping
Layout	Satisfaction
Facilities	Convenience

7. Colony Square—Residences

Circulation	Parking
Security/Safety	Privacy
Height	Service
Children	Comfort
Neighborliness/Soc.	Lobby
Management	Unit Layout
Convenience	Value
Storage	Special

8. Semantic Differential Rating
9. A.I.A. Comparative Section

In addition to providing extensive user generated data three specific comparisons will be possible.

1. User (permanent) to user (transient) as tier two results are compared to tier one results.
2. The rating scale for Colony Square as used for the evaluations of those attending the "Spaces for the Species" A.I.A. National Convention in Atlanta in May 1975 is included. This will afford a more reliable comparison between "user" evaluation and "architect" evaluation than the small user sample made for convention purposes.
3. Architect/Developer objectives can be compared to user perception of the completed development.

Surveys containing special sections on "office" and "retail" will also be a part of tier two with those special sections replacing "Colony Square—Residences" in the previously described response categories.

Tier three

Tier three will build upon the data gathered in phases one and two and primarily involve participant observation techniques; follow up surveys to provide an evaluation and response over time by a constant survey population; personal interviews with users, architects, building management, etc.; photographic studies; movement studies; and area-use studies.

FINDINGS

It is realized that results thus far represent only tier one data and responses from the transient user. They will take on increased value when meshed with the remaining portions of the study. Tier one results by response category followed by tier one questionnaire data are given below:

Respondent statistical data

Over 90% ranged in age from 20 to 65 with 3% younger and 5% older. The largest group (40%) was in the 50 to 65 category. About two-thirds of those responding were female and of the total about 40% had taken part in previous "Architecture in Atlanta" tours. In assessing familiarity with Colony Square none lived or worked there, 40% were there for the first time, and the remainder had visited previously. Twenty-three employment designations were listed covering a wide range of job types with essentially all being "white-collar" but with no single group standing out as dominant.

Concept

An overwhelming 94% felt the mix of office/residential/shopping such as exists at Colony Square was a good idea, although about a quarter would have preferred a suburban office park/condominium development.

City impact

Only 15% thought developments like Colony Square take away from the interest and/or viability of the downtown area and roughly 80% felt the effect of Colony Square on the surrounding areas to both the north and south of 14th Street was positive.

Reactions/evaluation

Almost 90% felt that Colony Square is "people oriented" and found the architecture (visual appearance) of the complex successful and 86% felt the complex to be generally successful. Four out of five of the visitors said there were features of the complex which would cause them to return again with most of these making reference to restaurants, entertainment (Fairmont Hotel), and ice skating. Several reserved judgment until after the retail shopping areas had been completed.

Suggestions

The three questions asked in this area were:

1. If you could make a *single change* in anything connected with Colony Square, what would it be?
2. What do you find to be the *most desirable* feature, characteristic, aspect, etc., of Colony Square?
3. What do you find to be the *least desirable* feature, characteristic, aspect, etc., of Colony Square?

Responses to the first four categories indicate a highly favorable response to the complex; however, it is in these last three open-ended questions that some of the most meaningful information was gathered as well as some of the most difficult to deal with.

The attention of architects, planners, owners, and managers to user input such as this may well make the difference in dealing with what could otherwise be largely unvoiced but present feelings—and as a result enhance a generally good building or improve a not so good building.

It is interesting to note that the single desired change or least desired feature by far the most frequently mentioned was to alter the decor of the Fairmont Hotel—this feeling expressed by over 20% of the respondents. It is all too easy as designers to say that the "public" does not know what it wants, but here a clear statement was made of what was not wanted—with frequently blunt adjectives!

Single change

The single changes mentioned most frequently after the Fairmont Hotel interior included in descending order of frequency: add more planting, revise color scheme to add warmth, introduce more directional signs, paint the rough concrete surfaces, reduce prices, add a grocery store to the complex, nothing, add wind screens, clean up the surrounding area, increase living unit privacy, build over less of the site, add medical facilities, make it cozier, add water fountains, add seating, improve the transition to Ansley Park, and improve the lighting effects.

Most desirable

Those features viewed as being most desirable in descending order of frequency mentioned included: an "all in one" development, convenience, visual impact of the exteriors, compactness, openness, location, mall areas, diversity, ice rink, amenities, total atmosphere, parking newness, stores, changes in level, covered shopping, pedestrian scale, uniqueness, and good traffic patterns.

Least desirable

After the hotel decor the features considered least desirable in descending order of frequency mentioned were: the expense of everything, excessive use of concrete, the expense of parking, lack of directional signs, none, lack of a grocery store, it is too big, the lack of colors, cold feeling, automobile traffic, few provisions for the elderly, lack of a drug store, accessibility, poor living location, no local flavor and not Atlanta oriented, does not represent Atlanta as a whole, too formal, not people oriented, the parking entrance, lack of green elements, and a poor transition to Ansley Park.

The summary above to the last three questions of the survey is obviously incomplete but can begin to convey to the designer the view of the public and the user. In expanded form as will be the case in the remainder of the Colony Square study such information can begin to serve as the basis for design and development guidelines.

Questions asked in the tier one survey with tabulated responses are given in Table 18-1.

CAMPBELL-STONE AND WHEAT STREET TOWERS

User needs both actual and "as perceived" can be of help to the design professional as he undertakes to mold the physical man-built environment if he will avail himself of them.

The responses of the permanent Colony Square users are as yet unavailable. They as well as results from other studies will help the designer better understand high-rise urban living. As a "Paper within a Paper" the author provides a brief background of research conducted on two Atlanta high-rise residences during the summer of 1974, and results to selected questions of interest. Of special interest is the fact that census data show the two buildings to be in census tracts which are almost diametrically opposed to one another.

Campbell-Stone

Campbell-Stone is a predominately white high-rise residential building for the elderly located in suburban Atlanta between a retail area and a middle to upper income single family residential area. It is an air conditioned structure mellowed with age, consisting of two connected towers of 9 and 15 stories in an open setting. It has a long waiting list for prospective residents and a management judged by the author as competent and concerned about the residents' welfare. Campbell-Stone has 393 units with survey results based on responses from slightly over 5% of its residents. It has many buildings sponsored and/or provided activities including mandatory meal service.

Wheat Street Towers

Wheat Street Towers is a primarily black high-rise residential building for the elderly located near downtown Atlanta in a low income primarily retail and commercial area. It is an air conditioned structure (except hallways) of 14 floors and 210 units, although not all were occupied at the time of the study. Survey results represent approximately 25% of its residents. It is located adjacent to the Wheat Street Baptist Church which sponsored construction of this recently completed building which is essentially the only one of recent vintage in the area. It has few building sponsored and/or provided activities and no meal service.

Findings

"Typical resident" profile—Campbell-Stone

The "typical" Campbell-Stone resident is a retired widow over 75 years in age living by herself who has lived at Campbell-Stone for four years or more. She has previously lived in other than high-rise housing and associates either more or the same with neighbors in the building than she did at her previous residence. She enjoys high-rise living more now than originally and considers the building pleasant to come home to, comfortable, safe, pretty, very well maintained,

TABLE 18-1
Survey Questions with Tabulated Responses

Section	Question	Response	%
STATISTICAL DATA	Sex of Respondent	Male	19
		Female	39
		NR	42
	Age of Respondent	Under 20	3
		20 to 34	24
		35 to 49	28
		50 to 65	40
		66 to 80	5
		Over 80	0
	Have you taken part in previous "Arch. in Atlanta" tours?	Yes	39
		No	60
		NR	1
	What is your general employment category?	______	
	What is your familiarity with Colony Square?	Live in Colony Square	0
		Work in Colony Square	0
		Have visited previously	57
		This is first contact	40
		NR	3
CONCEPT	Is the mix of office/residential/shopping such as exists at Colony Square a good idea to you?	Yes	94
		No	3
		NR	3
	Would you prefer developments similar to Colony Square or suburban office park/condominium developments?	Colony Square	68
		Suburban	21
		NR	11

TABLE 18-1 (continued)

Section	Question / Response	%
CITY IMPACT	Do developments like Colony Square take away from the interest and/or viability of the downtown area?	
	Yes	15
	No	81
	NR	4
	Effect of Colony Square development on the surrounding areas *North of 14th Street*?	
	Positive	86
	Negative	6
	NR	8
	Effect of Colony Square development on the surrounding areas *South of 14th Street*?	
	Positive	79
	Negative	3
	NR	18
REACTIONS/EVALUATION	Do you feel that Colony Square is "people oriented"?	
	Yes	89
	No	5
	NR	6
	Do you find the architecture (visual appearance) of Colony Square to be . . .	
	Successful	89
	Unsuccessful	8
	NR	3
	Overall do you feel Colony Square is generally . . .	
	Successful	86
	Unsuccessful	3
	NR	11
	Are there features (shops, etc.) of Colony Square which would cause you to return again on your own?	
	Yes	81
	No	11
	NR	0
	If yes, please state what . . .	
	______	
	Suggestions	
	The three questions in this section have been covered earlier in this chapter.	

enjoys the view the building height affords, and is not disturbed by its height. She has close friends in the building and enjoys living in the proximity of a large number of others, is not disturbed by tenant noise, and can almost always find someone to talk to.

"Typical resident" profile—Wheat Street Towers

The "typical" Wheat Street resident is a retired widow of about 60 years in age living by herself who has lived at Wheat Street for a year or less. She has previously lived in other than high-rise housing and associates either more or the same with neighbors in the building than she did at her previous residence. She enjoys high-rise living more now than originally and considers the building pleasant to come home to, comfortable (although she wishes the hallways had been air conditioned), reasonably safe, pretty, but maintenance to be only fair to good, enjoys the view the building height affords and is not disturbed by its height. She has close friends living in the building and enjoys living in the proximity of a large number of others, is usually not disturbed by tenant noise and can almost always find someone to talk to.

The Best and Worst of High-Rise Living

Campbell-Stone—best

In descending order of frequency mentioned the Campbell-Stone resident liked the security/safety, convenience, companionship, independence, and privacy.

Wheat Street Towers—best

In descending order of frequency mentioned the Wheat Street resident liked the security/safety, fellowship, convenience, privacy, quiet, independence, and view.

Campbell-Stone—worst

In descending order of frequency mentioned the Campbell-Stone resident disliked the threat of fire, and missed "home."

Wheat Street Towers—worst

In descending order of frquency mentioned the Wheat Street resident disliked the dark hallways, lack of security, lack of activities, danger of fire, lack of privacy, the building height, and being "away from her family."

The selected survey results shown in Table 18-2 will give some qualification to the general comments made above. However, it should become clear that the two populations studied had much more in common than might initially have been suspected.

TABLE 18-2
Campbell-Stone and Wheat Street Towers: Selected Survey Results

	Campbell-Stone %	*Wheat Street*
Sex of Respondent		
Male	10	17
Female	76	68
NR	14	15
Employment Status		
Working	10	19
Retired	76	62
Unemployed	10	9
Looking	0	2
NR	4	8
Marital Status		
Married	5	11
Single	10	26
Widow	75	45
Widower	10	6
NR	0	12

TABLE 18-2 (continued)

	Campbell-Stone	*Wheat Street*
	%	
Respondent Age Group		
Under 30	0	6
30–45	0	13
46–55	0	11
56–65	0	28
66–74	38	26
Over 75	48	15
NR	14	1
Other Residents Ages		
Same	33	21
Younger	14	4
Older	5	15
Spread	43	36
NR	5	24
Time in this Bld.		
6 Mo. or Less	5	21
6–12 months	0	21
1 year	0	40
2 years	14	0
3 years	10	0
4 years	24	0
5 years	10	0
Other	19	0
NR	18	18
How Tall Is H.R.		
Two Stories	0	0
Three	5	0
Four	0	0
Five	5	0
Six	5	0
Seven	0	0
Eight	5	2
Nine	5	0
Ten	10	0
11–15	24	66
Other	10	2
NR	31	30
Previous HR Experience		
Lived	5	4
Worked	0	2
Both	10	0
NR	85	94

TABLE 18-2 (continued)

	Campbell-Stone	*Wheat Street*
	%	
Previous Residence		
HR Apt.	24	4
LR Apt.	24	36
SF Residence	38	55
NR	14	5
Apartment Shared		
Yes	5	15
No	95	83
NR	0	2
# Children Sharing Apartment		
None	48	47
One	0	0
Two	0	0
Three	0	0
Four	0	0
Other	0	0
NR	52	53
Automobile Owned		
Yes	38	9
No	62	70
NR	0	21
Parking Convenience		
Yes	48	15
No	0	9
NR	52	74
Feeling of Safety in Various Locations		
Apartment		
Yes	86	72
No	0	2
NR	14	26
Hallways		
Yes	67	45
No	0	11
NR	33	44
Elevators		
Yes	67	55
No	0	11
NR	33	34
Stairwells		
Yes	48	23
No	4	17
NR	48	60

TABLE 18-2 (continued)

		Campbell-Stone	*Wheat Street*
		%	
Feeling of Safety in Various Location (continued)			
Bld. Grounds			
	Yes	52	47
	No	0	6
	NR	48	47
Sur. Neigh.			
	Yes	42	15
	No	10	26
	NR	48	59
Personal Theft in Apt. Experienced			
	Yes	0	0
	No	81	66
	NR	19	34
Knowledge of Theft from Others			
	Yes	38	4
	No	19	51
	NR	43	45
Possibility of Theft Bothers You			
	Yes	5	28
	No	62	36
	NR	33	36
Greatest Theft Possibility in			
	Low-Rise	43	40
	High-Rise	0	9
	NR	57	51
Are Security Provisions Adequate			
	Yes	57	43
	No	10	15
	NR	33	42
Proper Fire Action Known			
	Yes	86	60
	No	0	23
	NR	14	17
Building Conveniently Located *to* (yes)			
	Recreation	38	19
	Social Activities	38	26
	Business	48	26
	Entertainment	52	30
	Church	71	66
	Drug Store	67	17
	Auto Ser. Station	48	26

TABLE 18-2 (continued)

		Campbell-Stone	*Wheat Street*
		%	
Building Conveniently Located to (yes) (continued)			
	Dept. Store	48	11
	Library	43	4
	Schools	24	23
	Cultural Act.	38	11
	Medical Facility	38	47
Dense Living Enjoyed			
	Yes	86	70
	No	5	6
	NR	9	24
Tenant Noise is Disturbing			
	Yes	5	17
	No	86	64
	NR	9	19
Bld/Apt. Provisions for Old/Physically Handicapped			
	Yes	33	43
	No	24	26
	NR	43	31
Someone Usually Avail. to Talk to			
	Yes	95	85
	No	5	2
	NR	0	13
Elevator Delay			
	Yes	14	28
	No	71	64
	NR	15	8
Stair Use Necessary			
	Yes	5	9
	No	71	64
	NR	24	27
Stair Use by Choice			
	Yes	29	15
	No	33	40
	NR	38	45
Existence of Open Space Around Building			
	Yes	95	40
	No	0	45
	NR	5	15

TABLE 18-2 (continued)

	Campbell-Stone	*Wheat Street*
	%	
Adequate Storage in Apartment		
Yes	86	55
No	10	26
NR	4	19
Additional Storage in Building Available		
Yes	67	6
No	10	51
NR	23	43
Active in Affairs of Neighborhood		
Yes	19	23
No	57	49
NR	24	28
Neighborhood Activity Now vs. Previous		
More	25	23
Less	15	26
Same	20	26
NR	40	25
Assoc. with Neighbors this Bld. vs. Previous		
More	24	19
Less	0	13
Same	33	43
NR	43	25
Contact with Others in Building		
Great Deal	29	19
Some	48	47
Little	0	17
NR	23	17
Known Residents in Bld. Live on Your Fl.		
Yes	14	28
No	48	28
NR	38	4

TABLE 18-2 (continued)

	Campbell-Stone	*Wheat Street*
	%	
Apt. Large Enough for Comfort		
Yes	76	77
No	10	2
NR	14	21
HR Living Enjoyed *More Now* than Originally		
Yes	90	79
No	5	17
NR	5	4
View Bld. Height Gives Is Enjoyed		
Yes	90	89
No	0	6
NR	10	5
Building Height Is Disturbing		
Yes	0	9
No	86	87
NR	14	4
Degree of Privacy		
Enough	90	74
Too Much	0	4
Too Little	0	13
NR	10	9
Quality of Building Maintenance		
Excellent	33	9
Very Good	33	23
Good	10	23
Fair	10	21
Poor	10	11
Very Poor	0	11
NR	4	2
Building Is Pleasant Place to Live		
Yes	95	89
No	0	2
NR	5	9

TABLE 18-2 (continued)

		Campbell-Stone	*Wheat Street*	
		%		
Bld. Appearance Is				
	Pretty	90	77	
	Ugly	0	0	
	Nondescript	0	2	
	NR	10	21	
Apt. Is Warm Enough in Winter				
	Yes	100	74	
	No	0	6	
	NR	0	20	
Apt. Is Cool Enough in Summer				
	Yes	90	77	
	No	0	11	
	NR	10	12	
Adequate Sunlight in Apartment				
	Yes	86	79	
	No	5	4	
	NR	9	17	

TABLE 18-2 (continued)

			Campbell-Stone	*Wheat Street*	
			%		
Pleasant and Adequate Lighting Levels in					
	Main Lobby				
		Yes	90	66	
		No	0	26	
		NR	10	8	
	Elevator Lobby				
		Yes	90	74	
		No	0	9	
		NR	10	17	
	Hallways				
		Yes	95	47	
		No	0	34	
		NR	5	19	
	Apartments				
		Yes	90	77	
		No	0	0	
		NR	10	23	

19

Residential Choice and Housing Satisfaction in a Singles High-Rise Complex

Gerda R. Wekerle
York University

INTRODUCTION AND OBJECTIVES

We cannot infer from data collected by different researchers using varying conceptual frameworks and methods based on life in particular public housing developments in Philadelphia, New York City, Galsgow, or Melbourne that all high-rise residents regardless of social class, stage of the life cycle, or life style will suffer immeasurable harm by living in high-rise buildings. Pruitt Igoe is no more representative than is the John Hancock Center of high-rise living. In order to begin to understand the implications of high-rise residential environments for urban social change it is necessary to study the widest possible range of high-rise environments and populations in order to specify more precisely the spatial, symbolic, and social organizational factors involved in any given population's response to living in high-rise buildings. In cities such as San Francisco, Minneapolis, and Toronto, the future of high-rise buildings is hotly debated on the grounds that they are destructive to the quality of urban life and are harmful both to residents who live in them and the larger community. Despite the controversy surrounding high-rise apartments and the demands in some communities that further construction be prohibited on social welfare grounds (Toronto, Minneapolis), there has been little research to guide planners in making decisions about the suitability of high-rise apartments for specific urban subpopulations.

It is the studies detailing incidents of crime, delinquency, and vandalism in public housing developments that have received the most media attention and are often cited as "typical" of all high-rise developments.[1] Yet these studies tell us more about the problems created by concentrating multiproblem families in housing stigmatized by the rest of society

The author wishes to acknowledge the helpful comments offered by Janet Abu-Lughod, Sheldon Goldenberg, Edward T. Hall, and William Michelson as well as John Zeisel's editorial assistance.

than they tell us about the high-rise form of residential development.

Interest in the social consequences of high-rise living has been recent and studies have not built on one another. They have either been case studies of specific high-rise environments (often public housing)[2] or surveys of particular types of households (e.g., elderly or family households) all living in high-rise buildings, but in different cities.[3] Studies focusing solely on the experiences of families with children find a high level of dissatisfaction, lack of self-esteem, etc., when residents perceive they have little housing choice and are unlikely to ever attain their ideal of a single family house. The population I studied is satisfied with high-rise living since it represents the "ideal" for some households, while others still view it as only a short-term commitment. The solution to the "problem of high-rise apartments" is not to stop building them altogether, as has happened in Toronto and Denmark, since they are filling a need for some people at some points in their lives, but to encourage alternative forms of housing and increase the amount of choice available to all.

In 1969, I was living in Chicago and wanted to do a study of high-rise living as it is experienced by residents. Since most of the high-rise buildings under construction were aimed at moderate to upper income groups, I was primarily interested in why people with a choice of alternative housing chose high-rise living and how they fared. In particular, I wanted to study life in a large multibuilding apartment which combined residential, commercial, and recreational facilities and purportedly offered residents a total life style package. I chose to study single persons because they have been left out of most family housing studies, despite sharp increases in the number of single person households in the sixties.[4] Young adult and elderly non-family households represent an important user group whose housing needs and satisfactions must be taken into account when planning for residential accommodation in the city, since they represent a large segment of the demand for inner city apartments.

STUDY DESIGN AND METHODOLOGY

This chapter is based on a study[5] conducted during 1969 to 1971 at Chicago's Carl Sandburg Village, a high-rise complex housing approximately 6,000 residents in nine buildings ranging from 27 to 43 stories and 82 townhouses. Located on Chicago's Near North Side, Carl Sandburg Village is within one and one-half miles of Chicago's Loop and within easy walking distance of the Rush Street night club district, exclusive Michigan Avenue shops, the Gold Coast, and Lake Michigan. Because there was little available research on high-rise apartment living when I began this study, the research design was kept fairly flexible and a multimethod approach was chosen. The research was designed as an exploratory case study to discover the most important problems and concerns as defined by the key actors involved in one multibuilding, center city, high-rise development. Although residents' experiences were the major focus of the study, in-depth interviews were also conducted with architects, owners, managers, rental agents, clerks, secretaries, building engineers, and security guards. Extensive field notes were kept of all visits to the site and during the six-week period I lived in one of the Sandburg buildings.

With the permission of Carl Sandburg Village's management, a random sample of apartment units stratified by apartment size was drawn from four representative buildings out of seven in the complex. (Two buildings not yet fully occupied were excluded from the study.) Seventy-five apartment units were sampled and interviews were conducted with forty-two tenants between February 1970 and August 1971. Interviews lasted between 45 minutes and three and a half hours. In addition, all the residents of the smallest Sandburg building, which had only studio and one-bedroom apartments and a relatively high proportion of young single tenants, were canvassed. An eight-page questionnaire was mailed to all apartments in the building and was followed up with a telephone call or letter to nonrespondents. Ninety-four questionnaires (45%) were returned.

FINDINGS

Use of the physical environment is shaped by users' values and the symbolic meanings they attach to physical spaces and is modified by the characteristics of residents, their expectations, and social organization. In studying the "fit" of the environment of Carl Sandburg Village to its particular user population, I looked at why people chose this particular housing environment over others and their behavioral expectations of what life would be like in that environment; secondly, what was the environment-as-experienced by residents and to what extent were the expectations of the social and physical environments met; and lastly, satisfaction was related to the place of current housing environment in resident's projected family mobility cycle.

Resident Self-Selection and Reputation of the Housing Complex

The symbolic and social aspects of the residential environment were of prime importance in attracting residents to Carl Sandburg Village. Residents who moved there were predominatly drawn from the Chicago Metropolitan area (83% of the interview sample and 82% of the questionnaire sample) and one-third of the residents in each sample moved there from other apartments on the Near North Side, the area in which Carl Sandburg Village is located. They were attracted to this area because it has traditionally served as a "reception area," which attracts a high proportion of singles, childless couples and Bohemians.[6] Since 1963, when the first building opened for occupancy, Sandburg has attracted a very homogeneous population of upper middle class, well-educated, and single young adults. The population I studied shared these characteristics.*

It is the extreme homogeneity of Sandburg's tenant population and the promise of a "swinging" life style that initially attracted many residents to Carl Sandburg Village.

Approximately one-third of the tenants interviewed were disenchanted with other neighborhoods which lacked the social life and the kind of people with whom they wanted to associate. They felt dissatisfied because neighbors were "too old and too quiet" and because "there was not much activity and not very many young people." Those who lived in suburbs felt that they were "marginal" in a neighborhood with a predominantly familistic orientation and the move to Sandburg was to be with others more like themselves. The "social environment" was cited by 57% of the interview sample and 45% of the respondents to the questionnaire as a reason for choosing this particular housing environment.

> I was attracted by the social life. Some friends live here; the girl I'm dating. The type of housing guarantees a certain type of person: the same age, same interests, majority are young singles. It's like a small town and the management can provide many facilities [lawyer, male, single, age 25].

Neighboring Patterns at Sandburg

Previous studies[7] have characterized young adults living in city neighborhoods as disinterested in neighbors or involvement in a local community. Yet a major attraction of Sandburg was precisely the social environment of status similars. At Sandburg, three major factors found in previous research to encourage interaction among neighbors were present: residents were highly homogeneous in terms of age, class, and stage of the life cycle;[8] there was a social psychological selectivity of residents who wanted to interact;[9] and

*Of the forty-two residents interviewed for this study, 74% were under forty and 71% were unmarried; in the questionnaire sample, 85% were under 40 and 86% unmarried. Men were concentrated in higher paying professional and managerial positions and 81% earned more than $12,500 yearly. Women tended to work at lower level management, clerical, and secretarial jobs and 68% earned less than $12,500 per year.

finally, there was a high residential concentration of individuals who occupied a deviant social status.

Sandburg's image as a friendly place created high expectations among residents that they would be involved in an active social life. For some, these expectations were fulfilled and even surpassed, while other residents were deeply disappointed. By providing a large pool of "marriage eligibles" in a small area,[10] Sandburg fills the expectations of some residents to meet dates and mates. Half the respondents I interviewed and 60% of the questionnaire sample had dated someone living at Sandburg; they dated an average of six residents. Four people I interviewed had met their spouse while living in Sandburg. Respondents in the interview sample knew an average of nine other people living at Sandburg; those in the questionnaire sample knew an average of seven neighbors. Fifty-five percent of the people I interviewed had at least one friend in the complex; while in the questionnaire sample, 84% had a friend at Sandburg.

Despite the relatively high levels of neighboring found at Sandburg, tenants' satisfactions with the social environment varied considerably. Most occupants found that living at Sandburg did not automatically guarantee participation in on-going social networks and activities. The small minority of older and married tenants at Sandburg complained of being left out at Sandburg. However, each of these groups tended to associate primarily with neighbors that shared its own age and marital status. Residents most successful in making new acquaintances tended to be outgoing and even aggressive and used a wide range of channels to meet neighbors. Although most initial contacts were made in the hall and elevators, residents also became acquainted at the pool, at the tennis courts, at the ski club, at various Sandburg functions, at the supermarket, at the bus stop. Between 36% and 50% of all contacts with neighbors were made initially through friends outside the complex, through local groups, through coworkers, through bars in the area. These relationships were reinforced by seeing one another as neighbors.

Although recreational facilities such as the pool, tennis courts, and various clubs at Sandburg are an important sales feature for this housing development, less than half the residents I interviewed had ever used any of these facilities. However, this finding does not imply that such facilities are unnecessary frills and can be left out of high-rise apartment developments altogether. Residents were very specific about their reasons for not using Sandburg facilities more. The major complaint of half the residents I interviewed was that Sandburg's pool and tennis courts were too expensive and too crowded. Annual membership fees of $75 for use of an outdoor pool open only two months of the year and $40 for outdoor tennis courts were considered prohibitive by tenants who had ready access to free public facilities. Residents criticized the owners for treating the facilities and clubs as purely a money-making venture and would like to see a much wider range of activities than are presently available: an indoor swimming pool, sauna, and gymnasium, more activities and spaces that bring people together. Tenants expressed the need for semi-public spaces to which all residents have access, such as lounges or coffee shops, where involvement can be minimal or great. Present clubs have a relatively low attendance because they demand a regular commitment of time. Most tenants prefer not to be tied down in this way and desire activities where they can drop in at will.

Satisfaction with the Physical Environment

When respondents to the questionnaire ranked the three most important factors influencing their decision to move to Carl Sandburg Village, closeness to work was most important; closeness to entertainment was second most important; "best housing for the money" was third in importance; and "high percentage of singles" ranked fourth. However, location is less important in choosing Sandburg than may be supposed since one-third of the residents already lived on the Near North Side prior to moving to Sandburg and many other residents did not consider living anywhere but on the Near North Side. It was the combination of "extras" Sandburg had to offer over other housing in the area that tipped the scales in its favor—the high percentage of singles who lived there, the good maintenance and security, rents lower than those on the adjacent "Gold Coast." This combination in a residential complex in a desirable location explains why people chose Carl Sandburg Village.

Previous studies of residential satisfaction have treated a household's complaints about its current residence as a measure of lack of congruence between that household's needs and its living space[11] and plans to move have been used as a further indicator of dissatisfaction.[12] However, findings of this study and Michelson's recent research in Toronto[13] suggest that response to current housing environments must be interpreted in light of a household's projected housing career. Few people today choose one type of housing or one neighborhood for a lifetime. The availability of age-specific and even life-style-specific environments means that housing consumers may be satisfied with one type of housing for a particular stage of the life cycle, while aspiring to other types of housing in the longer term. Similarly, expressed satisfaction with a particular housing environment may be more a reflection of a houshold's mobility cycle (a subjective factor) than related to objective conditions of the environment. For example, households who prefer high-rise living at Sandburg for some time, and intend to live there in the foreseeable future, tend to be *less satisfied* with the physical aspects of the housing development than residents who have only a short-term commitment to downtown high-rise living and anticipate that they will move to a suburban house in the long term. Thus, it is necessary to examine complaints about a housing environment in the context of residents' behavioral expectations and longer-term housing goals.

Although Sandburg residents are generally satisfied with their own apartments, they tended to be less satisfied with communal facilities. These are aspects of the physical environment over which they have least control. Younger residents tended to be more concerned about increased recreational and social facilities than the upkeep of communal areas. But older residents, who had lived at Sandburg for some time, considered it their home, and expected a high quality of upkeep, complained of garbage on the malls, overgrown and weedy lawns, dirty elevators, and broken machines in the laundry rooms. The different standards that each group applied to the environment may in part be attributable to the fact that they were at different stages of the housing cycle.[14] For older residents, Sandburg living closely approximates their housing ideal and they are quick to perceive management lapses. For many of the younger residents, high-rise apartment living is not their ideal housing but only a combination of temporary tradeoffs for the next few years. At present, their highest priority is not a home so much as a congenial social environment or a convenient base of operations.

Despite a widespread concern that high-rise apartments are encouraging greater passivity and may be discouraging certain life styles,[15] none of the Sandburg residents interviewed felt that living in an apartment prevented him/her from engaging in desired activities or forced him/her to make adaptations in life styles. According to residents, good soundproofing between apartments allowed for entertaining and other hobbies and prevented the loss of privacy and conflict with neighbors documented by other studies of multiple dwellings.[16]

More than 90% of the respondents expressed a very high level of overall satisfaction with the physical environment at Sandburg with the emphasis on the internal aspects of the individual dwelling. This tends to reinforce previous research,[17] which found that the internal aspects of the dwelling are more important to residents of multiple dwellings than are external characteristics, while for residents of single family houses, the converse is true.[18]

Although other studies have found that the ability to modify and adapt a given housing unit to a household's own needs is closely related to housing satisfaction, and high-rise residents often chafe under restrictions which prevent them from doing so,[19] residents at Sandburg seemed to be largely accepting of the environment as given. When residents were asked "If there is any aspect of your apartment that you could change, where would it be?" most changes concerned the kitchen: more and better appliances, such as dishwashers and garbage disposals, more cabinet space. Although one out of four residents interviewed had made at least one physical modification to the apartment, most were cosmetic and temporary measures such as wallpapering, painting, or installing bookcases. A few residents installed parquet flooring, bars, or better quality fixtures.

This suggests that a demand for greater flexibility in the design of high-rise buildings must be interpreted in the light of residents' overall housing choice and projected length of residence. More flexible environments should be a high priority for those households who have the least amount of housing choice, are forced into high-rise living as a last resort, and see no chance of ever attaining alternative forms of housing. For people who freely choose high-rise living, often as only a short-term solution,* the ability to modify may not be a high priority.

Maintenance is a major concern to high-rise residents.[20] Because tenants feel that maintenance is a service they are paying for and some move to apartments expressly to avoid the maintenance involved in homeownership, this is an area in which conflicts between management and tenants can most easily occur. But at Sandburg, tenants are highly satisfied with day-to-day maintenance particularly as it affects their own dwelling unit.

> They are very prompt with repairs, often come the same day and then they leave a card to say that they've been here. We have had good response each time that we've called down to the office. In general, the service is good. A few times, when something went wrong on the weekends, for example, a drain was plugged up, I got prompt service [secretary, female, single, age 56].
>
> We call up the janitorial staff any time. There's so many little conveniences, especially for single girls, that they [girls] don't want to bother with. In brownstones, there are too many problems with repairs or maintenance [teacher, female, single, age 27].

*About 30% of Sandburg residents move yearly and residents live there an average of three years.

Residents' satisfaction was largely due to Sandburg's organization of the maintenance function. Complaints were handled through a central office and were not the individual responsiblity of each janitor, as is the case with many other high-rise buildings. The assistant manager of the development was in charge of a stafff which included his assistant, nine chief engineers (one for each building), janitor's assistant, twenty-five painters and their apprentices, carpenters, security men, and doormen who met daily to allocate maintenance assignments.

Management-Tenant Relationships

Residents' satisfaction with the management of high-rise buildings plays a significant role in their overall satisfaction with the housing development, yet this dimension is often overlooked by evaluation studies focusing solely on the physical aspects of environment. At Sandburg, residents were highly satisfied with management's responsiveness in handling routine repairs and maintenance when these occurred in individual apartment units. At the same time, there was a general perception that tenants were powerless in dealing with a large corporation landlord who is the more powerful partner in the relationship and in a strong position to take full advantage of lease agreements favoring landlords.

A recurring theme among Sandburg tenants was that management had consistently "broken faith" with them. Because the development was built on urban renewal lands and was often described as a "moderate income project" residents felt that their rents were unnecessarily high even though they were below HUD guidelines for federal mortgage insurance. Tenants charged that management had changed policies when it was financially to its advantage even when the tenant was protected by the lease (e.g., changes in subleasing policies). When promised facilities such as a shopping center, theater, and recreation center did not materialize, some tenants were disappointed and became more skeptical of management.

Another area of contention were the fees tenants paid over and above their rents: payment for a credit check when they moved in; a month's security deposit; garage parking ($32 monthly); sublease fee $50; changing roommates $25; master T.V. antenna hookup $20; airconditioners $5 each per month; pool $75; tennis courts $40.

Like tenants elsewhere,[21] Sanburg residents felt exploited by their landlord and mistrustful of the owners' policies and motives regarding rent levels, security deposits, and the payment of other miscellaneous fees. The large scale of the development and bureaucratic organization of management contributed to residents' feeling that they were powerless in dealing with an uncaring landlord. Residents' respond by engaging in "crimes against bureaucracy"—crimes of low visibility against the buildings and facilities committed by people who consider it fair retribution against an impersonal and rich organization.[22]

Management, in turn, comes to *expect* destructive and antisocial acts from its tenants, and feels justified in initiating preventive measures and formal control mechanisms. These very actions designed to avoid *projected* exploitation reinforces tenants' lack of trust in management.[23]

Residents' attitudes were summed up by one tenant:

> The practices—although not illegal, are questionable. Promises are made to the tenants and are not fulfilled. There is a public relations glossing off of the management shortcomings, which are not illegal. For instance, they say they are planting so and so many trees, and they are not. Now they are not committing something that is illegal. They are breaking faith. Almost in every instance that applies to the building, the faith is broken in one way or another. In little ways I think I'm being shortchanged. I do not think that the management is doing anything illegal against me or against any other person. But they are cutting corners on an awful lot of things which should be part of a tenant's right.

Landlord-tenant relations at Sandburg are typical of the adversary relationship existing between tenants in mass housing and a bureaucratically organized powerful landlord. Each party mistrusts the other. Tenants are quick to charge that the management is cheating them. Management, on the other hand, by making arbitrary changes which are not explained, and by running everything which has to do with the complex as a strictly money-making venture, contributes to tenants' distrust.

Future Residential Mobility

It is possible for residents to be satisfied with their current housing in the short run (anticipating that it will be temporary), while still aspiring to another housing type that more closely approximates their long-term housing ideal. Furthermore, people may find one type of housing ideal for one particular stage of the life cycle but not for another. Despite the extremely high level of satisfaction with residence at Sandburg, almost three-quarters of the respondents in my study planned to move within five years. Michelson[24] also found that the majority of families in high-rises are satisfied with their housing, yet 75% of them expected to move within five years and a large proportion had originally moved to a high-rise with such a move in mind. This suggests that mobility of high-rise residents cannot be used as an indicator that the environment is not meeting residents' housing needs. Rather, mobility must be examined within the context of a household's mobility cycle[25] and take into account past and future moves and the meaning they have for people.

At Sandburg, two types of residents anticipated a future move: confirmed urbanites who were frequently older, but also included some younger residents, and temporary urban dwellers who planned to live in the center city only during the pre-family state of the life cycle. For confirmed urbanites, center city residence provided convenient access to work, entertainment, and friends. They tended to be career-oriented rather than family-centered and suburbia conjured up visions of physical and social isolation. Although they may move away from Carl Sandburg Village, a high proportion will remain on the Near North Side, often in another high-rise building.

The young, pre-family households who were only temporary urban residents aspired ultimately to a single family house in the suburbs[26] or a townhouse in the city which they viewed as the best environment for raising a family. While still single, many (40% in the questionnaire sample and 64% in the interview sample) preferred to live on the Near North Side. Those moving to another high-rise building may seek a cheaper apartment or one with higher status; an apartment with more recreational facilities or none at all. Although the attainment of their ideal housing goal lies in the future, this group is satisfied with current housing as long as there is sufficient variety of housing choice within its means. Mobility becomes blocked when vacancy levels in rental buildings are low, condominium conversions take place, and house prices are high. Under these circumstances, households whose aspirations for a house in a low density neighborhood cannot be met, and who find that high-rise living is no longer temporary, but more or less permanent may become highly dissatisfied with high-rise apartment living.

IMPLICATIONS AND CONCLUSIONS

This research has important implications for architects and planners. It suggests the necessity for conducting research across a broad range of user groups before condemning a particular housing form such as high-rise apartments as inappropriate for all households. Further, it highlights the important role played by symbolic and social organizational factors in residential satisfaction. While current planning practice and theory is emphasizing the need for socially mixed residential communities, one finding of the study is that age and style of life are emerging variables that differentiate American cities. Age-segregated residential communities for young adults are merely an extension of a trend started by retirement communities and housing for the aged and they are flourishing for some of the same reasons: residents feel marginal to other housing environments, the physical environment provides recreational facilities geared to active adults, an age concentration of persons with similar social characteristics provides opportunities to meet people.

Surveys showing a high level of resident satisfaction with high-rise buildings[27] do not reflect a fundamental value change in consumer preference for a detached single family house.[28] High-rise apartment living is viewed by the majority of households as suitable for only certain life cycle stages—pre-family, post-family, childless couples, and never-married households. Thus, the demand for high-rise apartments, especially in center city neighborhoods, is not constantly expanding but may remain relatively stable as households marry, have children, and search for a house. Demand may actually contract once the postwar baby boom population has passed into child-rearing stages or if a depressed economy slows down the formation of single person households. Viewing residential satisfaction with high-rise buildings in the context of a housholds' housing career aspirations helps explain some of the apparent contradictions in the findings of different research on high-rise residents.

NOTES

1. Oscar Newman, *Defensible Space: Crime Prevention Through Urban Design* (New York: The Macmillan Company, 1972).
2. William L. Yancey, "Architecture, Interaction, and Social Control: The Case of a Large-Scale Public Housing Project," *Environment and Behavior* 3 (March 1971): 13–21; Pearl Jephcott, *Homes in High Flats* (Edinburgh: Oliver and Boyd, 1972); Anne Stevenson, Elaine Martin, and Judith O'Neill, *High Living: A Study of Family Life in Flats* (Melbourne: Melborne University Press, 1967); William Moore, Jr., *The Vertical Ghetto* (New York: Random House, 1969); Anthony Wallace, "Housing and

Social Structure: A Preliminary Survey with Particular Reference to Multi-Storey, Low-rent Public Housing Projects," Philadelphia, Philadelphia Housing Authority, 1952. (mimeo)

3. Irving Rosow, *Social Integration of the Aged* (New York: Free Press, 1967); William Michelson, *Environmental Change* (Toronto: Centre for Urban and Community Studies, 1973).
4. During the decade 1962-1972, the proportion of household heads who were primary individuals increased from 6.6% to 9.3% for men and from 54.7% to 58.7% for women (U.S. Dept. of Commerce, "Marital Status and Living Arrangements: March 1972." Current Population Reports. Series P-20 No. 242, November). In 1969, about 1.7 million persons 20 to 34 years of age were living in their own apartments compared with 926,000 in the first half of the decade (U.S. Department of Commerce, "Marital Status and Family Status, March 1969." Current Population Reports. Series P-20 No. 198, March 15). For men under the age of 35 this represented an increase from 5.2% in 1962 to 10.7% in 1972 of households living alone (U.S. Department of Commerce, CPR Series P-20, #242, Nov. 1972).
5. Gerda R. Wekerle and Edward Hall, "Highrise Living: Can the Same Design Serve Both Young and Old?" *Ekistics* 33 (March 1972):186-191; Gerda R. Werkle, "Vertical Village: The Social World of a Highrise Complex," Ph.D. dissertation, Northwestern University, 1974; "Vertical Village: Social Contacts in a Singles Highrise Complex," paper presented at the American Sociological Meetings, San Francisco, 1975.
6. Harvey W. Zorbaugh, *The Gold Coast and the Slum* (Chicago: University of Chicago Press, 1929); Anselm Strauss, *Images of the American City* (New York: The Free Press of Glencoe, 1961).
7. Zorbaugh, *Gold Coast*; Arnold Rose, "Living Arrangements of Unattached Persons," *American Sociological Review* 12 (August 1947):429-434; "Interest in the Living Arrangements of the Urban Unattached," *American Journal of Sociology* 53 (May 1948):483-493; Joyce Starr and Donald Carns, "Singles in the City," *Society* 19 (February 1972):43-48.
8. Leon Festinger, Stanley Schachter, and Kurt Back, *Social Pressures in Informal Groups: A Study of Human Factors in Housing* (Stanford, California: Stanford University Press, 1950); Sylvia Fleis Fava, "Contrast in Neighboring: New York City and a Suburban County," in *The Suburban Community*, edited by William Dobriner (New York: G. P. Putnam, Sons, 1958), pp. 122-130; Herbert J. Gans, "Planning and Social Life: An Evaluation of Friendship and Neighbor Relations in Suburban Communities," *Journal of the American Institute of Planners* 27 (May 1961):134-140.
9. Fava, "Contrast in Neighboring"; "The City, the Suburb, and a Theory of Social Choice," in *The New Urbanization*, edited by Scott Greer, Dennis McElrath, David Minar, and Peter Orleans (New York: St. Martin's Press, 1968), pp. 132-168.
10. Alvin Katz and Reuben Hill, "Residential Propinquity and Marital Selection: A Review of Theory, Methods and Fact," *Marriage and Family Living* 20 (February 1958): 27-35; James Beshers, *Urban Social Structure* (New York: The Free Press of Glencoe, 1962).
11. William Michelson, "Analytical Sampling for Design Information: A Survey of Housing Experience," EDRA 1, Chapel Hill, N.C., 1969.
12. Peter Rossi, *Why Families Move* (New York: The Free Press of Glencoe, 1955).
13. Michelson, *Environmental Change*.
14. Ibid.
15. Wallace, "Housing and Social Structure"; "Mental Health in the High-Rise," *Canadian Journal of Public Health* 62 (September-October 1971):426-431; Social Planning of Metropolitan Toronto, *Families in High Rise Apartments* (Toronto, 1973).
16. Leo Kuper (ed.), *Living in Towns* (London: Cresset Press, 1953); John Raven, "Sociological Evidence on Housing (2: The Home Environment)," *The Architectural Review* 142 (1967), p.236+; Michelson, "Analytic Sampling."
17. Michelson, "Analytic Sampling"; Michelson, *Environmental Change*.
18. Rossi, *Why Families Move*, p. 84.
19. Franklin D. Becker, *Design for Living: The Residents View of Multi-Family Housing* (Thaca, N.Y.: Center for Urban Development Research, Cornell University, 1974).
20. Hubert Leo Campfens, "Landlord and Tenant Relations in Apartment Developments: Examination of Interests and Behaviour," Ph.D. dissertation, University of Toronto, 1971; Becker, *Design for Living*.
21. Ted R. Vaughan, "The Landlord-Tenant Relation in a Low-income Area," *Social Problems* 16 (Fall 1968):208-218; Becker, *Design for Living*.
22. Erwin Smigel and H. Laurence Ross, *Crimes Against Bureaucracy* (New York: Van Nostrand Reinhold, 1970).
23. This is no more than the operation of the factors of selective perception (Tamotsu Shibutani and Kian Kwan, *Ethnic Stratification: A Comparative Approach* [New York: Macmillan, 1965]) and self-fulfilling prophecy (Robert K. Merton, *Social Theory and Social Structure* [New York: The Free Press of Glencoe, 1957], pp. 179-195).
24. Michelson, *Environmental Change*.

25. Ibid. Michelson suggests three stages: a baseline stage common to newly formed households or those new to the city; a stage of incremental changes where people make short-term tradeoffs for housing that does not yet approximate their ideal; and third, approximation of their ideal residential environment.
26. Surprisingly, more men than women prefer a suburban house (22% vs. 10%). This difference has also been found by Michelson (*Environmental Change*), who reports that men stand to gain more from suburban living than women, who bear most of the social costs of isolation, lack of services, and poor transportation.
27. Michelson, *Environmental Change*; Social Planning Council of Metropolitan Toronto, *Families in High Rise Apartments*.
28. Nelson Foote, Janet Abu-Lughod, Mary Mix Foley, and Louis Winnick, *Housing Choices and Housing Constraints* (New York: McGraw-Hill, 1960); John B. Lansing and Eva Mueller, with Nancy Barth, *Residential Location and Urban Mobility* (Ann Arbor, Michigan: Institute for Social Research, University of Michigan, 1964); Michelson, "Analytic Sampling"; Michelson, *Environmental Change.*

20

Design Guidelines for High-Rise Family Housing

Clare Cooper Marcus
Lindsay Hogue
University of California, Berkeley

This chapter is concerned with the social implications of high-rise family housing and attempts to translate some of the burgeoning social science findings regarding high-rise living into usable design guidelines. After reviewing the literature on high-rise housing, we have concluded that, for those who are dissatisfied, it does not provide an appropriate living environment because too few of the attributes of a single family house have been accounted for in the design of the building. This chapter analyzes what those attributes are, why their absence creates problems for some with high-rise living, and suggests some design and management solutions.

Many high-rise buildings unsuited to residents' needs continue to be built, despite repeated indications of their lack of suitability, especially for families with young children. It is our contention in this chapter that the basic difficulty with high-rise for families is, very simply, that many people carry with them a conscious or unconscious memory of, or aspiration for, a traditional single family home (Adams and Conway 1974; Michelson 1973; Homenuck 1973). We are assuming this as a "given" since the desire for a single family house over all other forms of housing is repeated in study after study. For the purposes of this chapter, we are not concerned with the unconscious or covert reasons for this preference, suggested by some to symbolize the need for a separate and distinguishable "symbol of self" (Cooper Marcus 1974); by others, to represent an attempt by an essentially male-dominated society to keep women captive as "janitors of the home" (Wright 1974); or by others, to represent a desire to avoid conflict with people unlike themselves (Perin 1974). What we *are* concerned with is how the single family house facilitates certain mundane, day-to-day activities and behaviors associated with family life, and by comparison, how these same behaviors are facilitated or impeded in the high-rise apartment. If

The authors wish to acknowledge a grant from the Beatrix Farrand Fund, Department of Landscape Architecture, University of California, Berkeley, which supported the preparation of this chapter.

Figure 20-1
Paradise lost?

the reader *disagrees* with this, our basic assumption—i.e., that most people, and especially families, carry with them a conscious or unconscious memory of or aspiration towards the single family house—then he or she may well have difficulty accepting what follows! It was not our intention to do yet another qualified, empirical case study of a high-rise building; our intention was and is to try and make some sense out of the considerable literature available and to make the major findings available to designers and policymakers in a format that is logical, jargon free, and hopefully provocative of further thought. The guidelines might also prove useful to students of design, social scientists, and environmental managers, for the purpose of education, phrasing hypotheses for further study, and the development of good management policies.

Before embarking on the main part of this chapter, there are a number of general assumptions about high-rise housing which we wish to make clear.

It is clearly apparent from the literature that certain groups are more suited to high-rise living than others. In particular, families with children under five are frequently the least satisfied; those with older children, slightly more satisfied; adult families and the elderly the most satisfied. A British study illustrates this point well (Dept. of the Environment 1972):*

*The sample comprised 874 housewives interviewed in five high-rise developments in London and Sheffield in 1967. The study was designed to find out how different household types reacted to various building form and site plans, and was carried out by Ingrid Reynolds and Charles Nicholson of the Sociological Research Section of the Department of the Environment.

Households Living off the Ground	*% Unhappy*	*(N)*
Households with all children under 5	39	(49)
Households with some children under 5 and some over 5	31	(134)
Households with all children over 5	14	(165)
Adult households	12	(321)
Elderly households	10	(205)
Total		(874)

Similarly, data from a Canadian survey of high-rise and single family dwellers in Toronto indicates the following (Homenuck 1973):†

Life Cycle Stage	*% Preferring Detached, Semi-Detached, or Townhouse*	*(N)*	*% Preferring High-Rise*	*(N)*	*Total (N)*
Single parents with children at home	54	(6)	46	(5)	11
Single parents with no children at home	61	(28)	39	(18)	46
Married, over 35, no children at home	69	(96)	31	(43)	139
Single under 35	72	(41)	28	(16)	57
Single over 35	83	(10)	17	(2)	12
Married with 1 child	89	(91)	11	(11)	102
Married, under 35, no children	90	(66)	10	(7)	73
Married, with 2 or more children	96	(125)	4	(5)	130
					570

In this chapter we are concerned primarily with the needs of families with children; although certain changes might improve high-rise environments for adult households and the elderly, we have not specifically combed the literature pertaining to these groups and mention them only when there may be conflicts with families with children in the same setting.

Our contention is, then, that high-rise housing is most unsuited to families with one or more children under five (Homenuck 1973; Adams and Conway 1974), largely because the behavioral needs of these families have been ignored (Grégoire 1971), or because the environment was initially designed for childless adults and later inhabited by families (Cooper 1969). We do not believe that a high-rise is inherently and at all times *wrong* for families, only that as *presently designed,* most high-rise buildings are unsuitable for such groups. We recognize that in certain situations (economic, cultural, topographic, etc.) high-rise housing may be the only alternative available. Our hope is that this chapter will point the way to such buildings being designed and managed in a more humane way, assuming that every effort has been made on the part of the developer, designer, client, etc., to provide a low-rise or single family alternative.

Our process in this chapter was to review all the empirical studies we could find on the responses of families with children to high-rise living. Typically these involved interview-surveys with random samples of residents; in a few cases, where children's out-

†The sample comprised 572 randomly selected residents in the borough of Etobicoke and N. York in Toronto. The sample was drawn from five different areas and complexes in the following proportions: High-rise, private, rental complex (16%); high-rise, private condominium complex (34%); a second high-rise private rental complex (16%); middle class neighborhood of detached homes close to high-rise development (17%); middle to upper class neighborhood of detached homes (16%). 49% of the interviewees were male, 51% were females.

door play was of particular interest, interviews were supplemented with systematic behavioral observation studies. Since we found very similar findings cross-culturally, especially as regards problems with children in high-rise settings, we included studies from Canada, Britain, Denmark, and Australia, as well as from the United States.

Our procedure, once having located the studies, was to categorize what seemed to be frequently cited problems (and advantages) of high-rise living. As we did this, and categories began to emerge which had to do with "parking," "entering the site," "children's play," etc., it became apparent that most problems in a high-rise were *not* problems in a single family house because of the different building form, density, ownership pattern, etc. After many false starts trying to organize the myriad of data in this area, we finally felt most comfortable in outlining typical daily behavior patterns and needs of families with children, and then reviewing how well they are accommodated, first by a single family house, and second, by a high-rise dwelling unit. Based on the comparison, guidelines for the design of improved high-rise environments for families were developed. This approach may seem somewhat simplistic, but after considering various ways of approaching the relevant information, we found this to be the most revealing of the problems experienced by high-rise families, and most suggestive of potential solutions.

For the most part, the reader will find the statement headed "Need," and that headed "Single family house," not footnoted. These statements are, in most cases, such obvious "truths" about people's responses to, or use of, their home environment, that we did not feel they need empirical evidence to back them up. They emerged out of both authors' many years of housing research, and considerable familiarity with the housing-evaluation literature.

In most cases, the longer statements under the heading "High-rise" are footnoted. When a problem-area emerged again and again in the literature, we tried to word it into a simple statement, and referenced only those studies where major pieces of research supported the statement being made. With the limited time at our disposal (we were working on a six-month, $2,800 budget) we found it impossible to cite every study that supported every statement we made. Suffice to say, there could be many more footnote references than there are; however, our literature search was exhaustive, and we doubt if there are many more significant high-rise studies than those we have listed in the bibliography.

Finally, the statements headed "Suggestions" are purely informed hunches on our part. We make no apology for this; one of us is a designer trained partially in social science, one a social scientist trained partially in design. We felt it quite within our capabilities to make that often frowned-upon leap from social science data to possible design or managerial solutions. In fact for us, it seemed less a leap and more an exciting, creative, and logical step from one field to another.

The behaviors have been organized in what seemed to us to be a logical sequence, but the numerical order in no way indicates priorities.

1. Owning a home.
2. Feeling that one's home is individual and supportive of a positive self-image.
3. Entering the home environment.
4. Controlling entry of nonresidents.
5. A visitor approaching the dwelling.
6. Transferring people or objects from the parked car to the dwelling.
7. Individualizing and beautifying the entry.
8. Meeting (and avoiding) neighbors.
9. Having space to live flexibly.
10. Changing the size of the home.
11. Preschoolers playing.
12. School-age children playing.
13. Teenagers meeting and hanging out.
14. Doing things at home that need visual privacy from the outside.
15. Doing things at home that create noise.
16. Engaging in outdoor recreation requiring privacy.

17. Performing utilitarian chores and hobbies requiring space outside the dwelling.
18. Using the windows.
19. Doing the laundry.
20. Taking out the garbage.
21. Storing things.

BEHAVIOR–OWNING A HOME

Need

Many people in Western societies need to feel a dwelling unit is their own before they feel they have "made it," before they put down roots and are willing to take time and spend money to maintain or improve it.

Single family house

Most single family homes in the United States are owned or are being purchased by the families who live in them. This tends to give residents of single family homes a certain status, a sense of "having made it" in the eyes of society. Not only do the improvements they are willing to make increase the house value, but they benefit those living there by enabling them to make creative modifications to their environment, thus hopefully providing a living environment more suited to their needs. A home of one's own also fulfills many needs for "being in control"; with few exceptions, no one can tell you what to do in your own house.

High-rise

Most high-rise units are rental apartments and are not individually owned, although recently some have been converted into or built as condominium units which can be purchased. Except in very high-rent, high-class buildings, apartment residents tend to be thought of as "transient," somehow not as "stable" or "committed" as homeowners are. Added proof of this fact is the way our present tax structure "rewards" people who do buy homes, through tax incentives and rebates (Becker 1974).

Suggestions

1. In cases where high-rise living is a semi-permanent rather than a transition stage in the life cycle, allow residents to purchase their units through a co-op or condominium arrangement. If residents feel they will benefit financially by changing the unit and keeping it well maintained, they will be more financially willing to improve it and contribute to its upkeep.

2. Ensure that the equity in a co-op or condominium apartment is as easily transferable as that in a single family house should a resident wish to move.

3. Ensure that, within reason, there are as few rules and regulations as possible—for example, about owning pets, having children, painting the apartment, putting up pictures; the fewer the rules about what a resident may or may not do, the more likely he or she is to feel in control of the environment, and "at home." In a study of seven New York multifamily developments, Becker concluded that privacy, which was highly valued, was basic to the notion of territoriality and control and was affected more by management policy and attitudes than by design consideration. This further suggests that if high-rise housing is to fulfill some of the needs which are met by the single family house, particularly privacy and control, then management must be especially efficient and sensitive (Becker 1974).

4. Encourage residents to select their own colors for their apartment and do their own painting, if they so desire. Studies indicate that many multifamily residents *wish* to do this, and the very act of person-

alization positively effects residents' pride in their environment and their willingness to assume responsibility for maintenance (Becker 1974).

5. Ensure that residents have real decision-making powers regarding the social and physical environment of the building or development as a whole, just as they would have control over the exterior maintenance of their home, and (possibly) the overall environment of the neighborhood in a single family residential area.

6. One of the basic differences between single family and multifamily living is that in the latter there are many semi-public areas or facilities which are maintained by the management, not the individual householder. One study indicates a positive correlation between a management that is efficient, considerate and polite, and a general satisfaction with living in a particular development (Becker 1974). Every effort should be made to ensure that: (a) an on-site manager is available; (b) it is clear to residents exactly how they should report vandalism, damage or malfunctions, and these are seen to quickly and courteously; (c) management does not intrude into residents' personal lives or dwelling units without their permission; (d) rules set by management for the behavior of residents and their children should be clearly publicized via a Residents' Manual, along with the rationale behind such rules (Becker 1974).

BEHAVIOR—FEELING THAT ONE'S HOME IS INDIVIDUAL AND SUPPORTIVE OF A POSITIVE SELF-IMAGE

Need

Many people identify strongly with their home environment and feel satisfied if its appearance to self and friends supports the image they want to create of who they are. Conversely, an environment viewed negatively by residents and outsiders has a debilitating effect on the self-images of those who live there.

Single family house

Not only is the single family house the "ideal" for most people in this society, but the variety of types, facades, etc., enable buyers to select one that most closely reflects their self-image. In addition, the single family home dweller—since he is also generally an owner—can change or modify the dwelling to suit his needs, thus creating a more self-supporting environment.

High-rise

Although in the popular literature, the high-rise apartment is typified as lacking in individuality, supportive of anonymity, there is little evidence to suggest that residents want or expect a facade treatment that supports the individuality of each household. They do want the ability to control and individualize the *interior,* however. "We seem to take a kind of schizophrenic attitude toward multifamily housing: we encourage people socially and economically to "improve" single family homes by landscaping them, painting interiors, adding storage space and building patios (and the value of the property *increases* because of these modifications), and yet we actively discourage the same activities in apartment residents. The assumption that each new occupant of an apartment wants it returned to its original condition may be false. People want to find a new residence clean and well-maintained, but that it should look exactly like all other apartments is not clear. Residents may want to personalize or improve an unmodified apartment as much or more than one that has been modified and is beginning to develop some character of its own" (Becker 1974:20).

The overall *size* of a development is another factor which is reported in the popular literature as likely to be a hardship for residents. However, a number of studies indicate that overall size per se matters less than: (a) the actual layout of buildings on the site; (b) what can be viewed from any particular dwelling; (c) the degree of variety and color in the facade design or landscaping (Department of the Environment 1972; Norcross 1973; Becker 1974). Thus, a small development may be viewed more negatively than a large one if its overall features are monotonous, monochromatic, rectilinear, with little relief from landscaping, and if a large number of similar units can be seen from within the dwelling.

Suggestions

1. Whatever the size of the development, every effort should be made to vary the building heights, facade treatments, size and character of spaces between buildings.

2. Since a number of studies indicate a positive correlation between high-quality landscaping, and

Figure 20–2
People respond positively to variety in building height, landscaping, size of open spaces, and so forth.

overall satisfaction, a considerable portion of the initial design effort (in time and money) should go into the exterior spaces and the overall site-plan and landscaping (Department of the Environment 1972; Cooper 1969; Becker 1974). However, it should be remembered that the positive effects of such non-institutional designs can easily be reduced by subsequent poor maintenance.

3. Care should be taken that no dwelling has a view of numerous other similar dwellings, without some relief through landscaping, facade differentiation, etc.

4. There seems to be no particular size of development considered ideal by *managers.* In one study where managers of seven New York developments were interviewed, some reported a preference for managing 200 units or less because of increased personal contact; others preferred 300 or more because of the greater economy in providing services and personnel (Becker 1974).

5. Allow residents to paint the interior of their apartment, and allow subsequent residents to modify further or to return to original condition if it is not to their taste.

BEHAVIOR—ENTERING THE HOME ENVIRONMENT

Need

There seems to be a universal but rarely articulated pleasure derived from approaching one's home, anticipating a reunion with one's family, or a meal, or a chance to be alone and relax after a busy day. This feeling heightens with the first sight of the neighborhood and home environment, which increases as car is parked, or footsteps bring one nearer, and the resident finally passes through the semi-private spaces around the dwelling and so to the doorway.

Single family house

The house can generally be seen and recognized at a distance as "home"; at each approach the residents may consciously or unconsciously recognize the decisions they made about the house exterior (the paint they chose, the facade treatment they may have selected in a tract house, etc.), or conversely, see things they dislike and plan to change them. Once having parked, or set foot on the "site," (1) the passage from street to door is generally brief; (2) it is through areas (garage or from yard) totally maintained by the homeowner; and (3) it is private in that neighbors or strangers are unlikely to be present.

High-rise

The building may be perceived much further away than the single family house can be, and for some the anticipation of arriving home may be pleasurably lengthened. It is possible, too, that for many people, the pleasure of viewing one's own identifiable house on approaching it is replaced among high-rise dwellers by the pleasures of viewing the building or collection of buildings, and the community they house and personify. Once having entered the "site," however, the high-rise dweller will have a much longer transition-passage through semi-private spaces. The nature of high-rise buildings, causing wind to rush down them, can make the entry a windy and unpleasant place to be. The resident then moves through the lobby, elevator, corridor, etc., where he or she may (1) resent having to cope with face-to-face encounters in these spaces; in some moods and at some times, a resident may wish for the quicker and more private transition from the privacy of the car to the privacy of the home afforded by a single family house; (2) be irritated by the institutional and un-homelike qualities of the materials and design at eye level; (3) be annoyed at less-than-perfect maintenance and upkeep of semi-public areas; (4) feel fearful of encountering someone who is not supposed to be in the building or who may have criminal intentions; (5) be annoyed at elevator delays or breakdowns, especially at night—"the time when . . . some deep-seated need, a primitive anxiety to reach shelter and safety, inflames us all with an instinctive urge to hurry home" (Jephcott 1971). Complaints about the inadequacy in the number and frequency of elevators is frequently mentioned in low and moderate income high-rise studies (Cooper 1969; Jephcott 1971; Becker 1974). The necessity to use an elevator may have subtle, but cumulatively serious, repercussions on apartment life in high-rises: the elderly person alone taking an evening walk around the block, the teenager taking off on his bicycle for a spin when things get "heavy" at home, the mother stepping out in the garden to get a breath of fresh air while her children nap—all these are made more difficult, if not impossible. ". . . That the lift may even dictate the pattern of the tenant's day was shown in the case of the mother who never went out in the afternoon because of the risks of the early evening queues which meant she could not be sure of getting back in time. She was also liable to incur blank looks if her pram stopped others from squeezing onto the lift. . ." (Jephcott 1971:56).

Suggestions

The long transition space from car or sidewalk to dwelling cannot be altered—but the nature of the experience in that space can be improved by:

1. Ensuring that the facade design and landscape-screening at the building entry (a) reflect a homelike and noninstitutional quality; and (b) prevents the wind-tunnel effect at ground level, so often experienced on approaching high-rise buildings. This is especially important in buildings for the elderly who are less strong physically (Jephcott 1971).

2. Having a locked foyer with possible addition of a twenty-four-hour doorman to prevent access by strangers. If this is financially infeasible, then the manager's or superintendent's office should be located adjacent to, and looking out onto, the main lobby so that there is surveillance at least during working hours. Entry lobbies should be oriented to the street or parking areas, since the natural surveillance from these areas increases the safety of the entrance (Newman 1972; Becker 1974).

3. Providing attractive, comfortable, and well-maintained lobbies and corridors (with seating to encourage resident use) so that residents and visitors alike can feel that they have walked into a home, not an impersonal office building.

4. Ensuring that all maintenance is done by the management—maintenance of portions of semi-public interior space by the residents themselves does not seem to work. Residents view these areas as extensions of their dwelling units; consequently poor maintenance reflects on their satisfaction with their housing.

5. Avoiding long corridors which have connotations of institutional, nonresidential buildings. If at all possible, corridors should be carpeted to reduce noise problems, to facilitate a homelike effect, and, by use of different colors on different floors, to individualize each level in the building. There should always be high lighting levels in corridors, lobbies and other shared access ways.

6. Creating an access arrangement so that a maximum of only six or seven households share each floor —people will soon recognize their neighbors and feel a greater sense of safety and responsibility towards their own floor.

7. Having a frequent and reliable elevator service with especially high-quality hardware where children are housed who may use elevators as play objects. It is essential, too, that one larger-than-normal, service elevator be provided for people moving furniture in and out, for stretchers, etc. Ensure, too, that all elevators (a) are adequate in size, especially for families with children who may want to take down toys and bicycles, people with shopping carts, etc.; (b) are well maintained and made of vandal-proof materials; (c) are operable by children aged six and over, if children are housed in the building; (d) have

an alarm button within reach of children, for emergency breakdowns.

BEHAVIOR—CONTROLLING ENTRY OF NONRESIDENTS

Need

At a time of rising crime rates, people increasingly feel the need to make their homes free from illegal entry and their neighborhoods safe to walk in. Residents want to feel secure in their home environment and to know that possessions left in semi-public areas will be protected (e.g., their cars). They want control over who enters the site, who uses facilities on the site, and what behavior occurs there.

Single family house

Traditionally, people of all times and many cultures have felt "the house" to be the one inviolably safe retreat from the pressures—both physical and social—of the outside world. The form of the house—basically a box set on the ground and separate from others—has come to symbolize all that is implied regarding privacy, security and intimacy in the home.

There is a clearly defined edge to the lot of a single family house. The edge may be boldly defined by a fence, hedge, etc., or may be more subtly defined by a change in level of material. The semi-private yard is clearly the property of the residents living in the house it surrounds, a fact that discourages people who do not belong from entering. Anyone entering who is not recognized can be rightfully questioned.

High-rise

The boundary between the site of a high-rise development and adjacent public or semi-public areas is often poorly indicated. With perhaps one to several hundred people living there, entering from different directions, the transition space—from street to building entrance—is generally seen as semi-public. And yet numerous studies indicate that residents of multifamily housing (both high- and low-rise) strongly object to nonresident "outsiders" using those facilities which are often located in those semi-public transition spaces—such as parking, strolling, and sitting areas, play spaces, etc. (Becker 1974; Byrom 1972). Objections usually include the fact that nonresidents have not "paid for it," will not take care of the property, and do not belong there. But since particularly high-rise sites are often shared by so many residents, recognizing who does and does not belong can be very difficult, and challenging those who are known "not to belong" may be even more difficult (Becker 1974).

Potentially a more serious problem than nonresidents using facilities is that of crime in semi-public areas of high-rise buildings. Recent studies (Newman 1972; Day et al. 1971; Yancey 1971; Becker 1974) have indicated that security in high-rises in potentially moderate or high-crime areas, tends to be worse where there are multiple entries to the building and no control over who comes in or out. Crimes in such cases tend to occur most frequently in those semi-public areas (e.g., firestairs, corridors, and elevators) over which there is little or no casual surveillance, and which form the territory of no particular person or group of people. A recent study which looked at high- and low-rise New York development, concluded: "The high-rise developments clearly presented a greater number of areas in which the resident felt unsafe" (Becker 1974). One of the most satisfactory solutions to this problem is to restrict entry to one or a few entrances which are mechanically controlled, either by a doorman or by residents. Becker concluded that since one of the "largest, single items of the operating budget is for guards' salaries . . . money spent initially on good territorial definition and security design in the long run should result in lower operating costs" (Becker 1974:119).

Suggestions

1. Clearly define the site edge from the surrounding spaces by fencing, planting, a gate, a pavement and/or elevation change, a name, etc. Any design means by which a newcomer clearly feels that he or she has entered a different kind of space will tend to discourage those who do not belong from entering.

2. Restrict entry to the site to only a few places around the site. Of course, in the case of a very large development of many high-rises, approach roads, etc., this will be more difficult.

3. Place the buildings close to the edge of the site so that transition spaces visible from the surrounding streets are relatively narrow, and so that the buildings themselves define and protect *inner* court spaces where play, strolling, and sitting areas are clearly the territories of the adjacent buildings.

4. If the decision is consciously made to provide on-site facilities to meet both resident and community

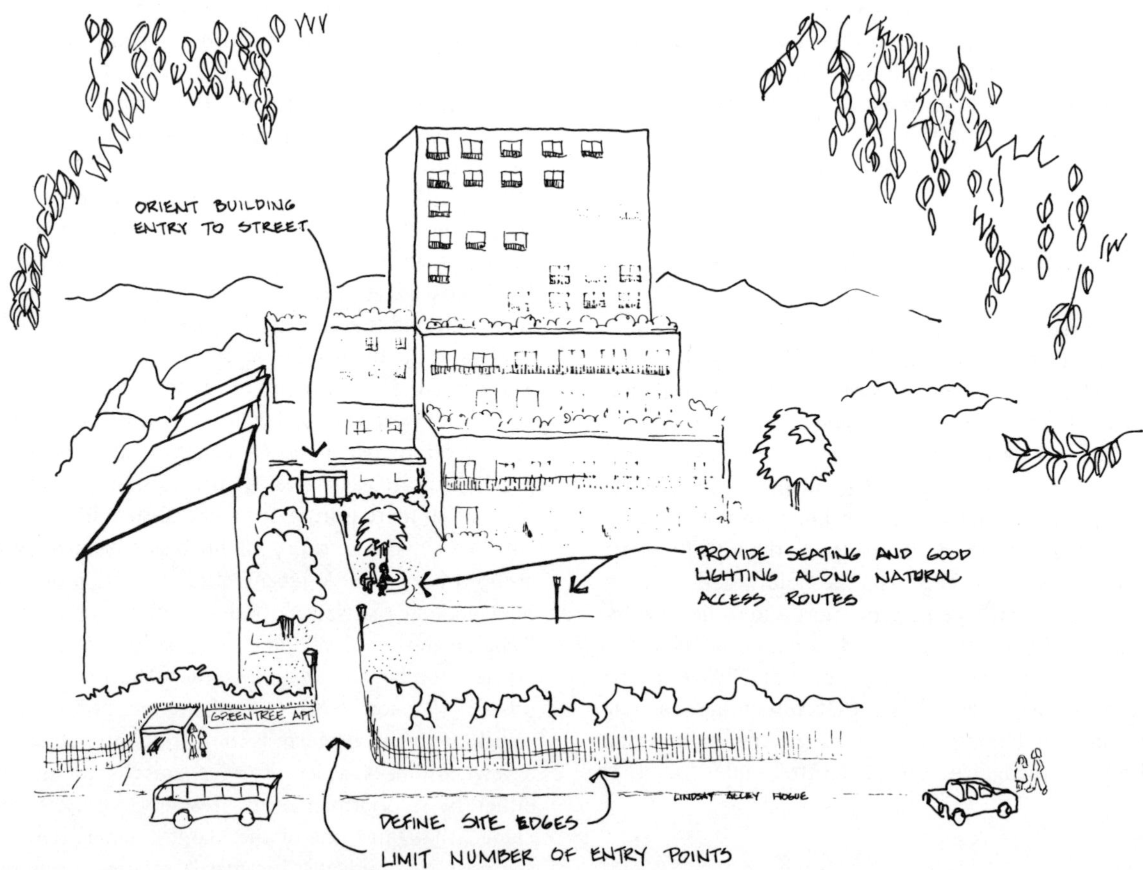

Figure 20-3
Restrict entry to the site and clearly define the site edges.

needs, they should be (a) located on the boundaries of the site with equal access to residents and nonresidents; (b) their size, operating budget, staffing, etc., should be scaled to meet the joint use demands of both development and surrounding community (Becker 1974).

5. Multiple building entries should be avoided; lobbies should all be locked with entry controlled by a doorman or by the residents via an intercom.

6. Locate and design building entries so that the approaches to each are well lighted, are potentially under casual surveillance from neighboring units, and are fairly close to a public street or sidewalk. Approaches to buildings via large, anonymous open spaces between buildings should be avoided.

7. There is some evidence to indicate that the higher lighting levels and greater degree of casual surveillance in single-loaded or against double-loaded corridors, may result in lower levels of vandalism and crime in the former, when the building is located in

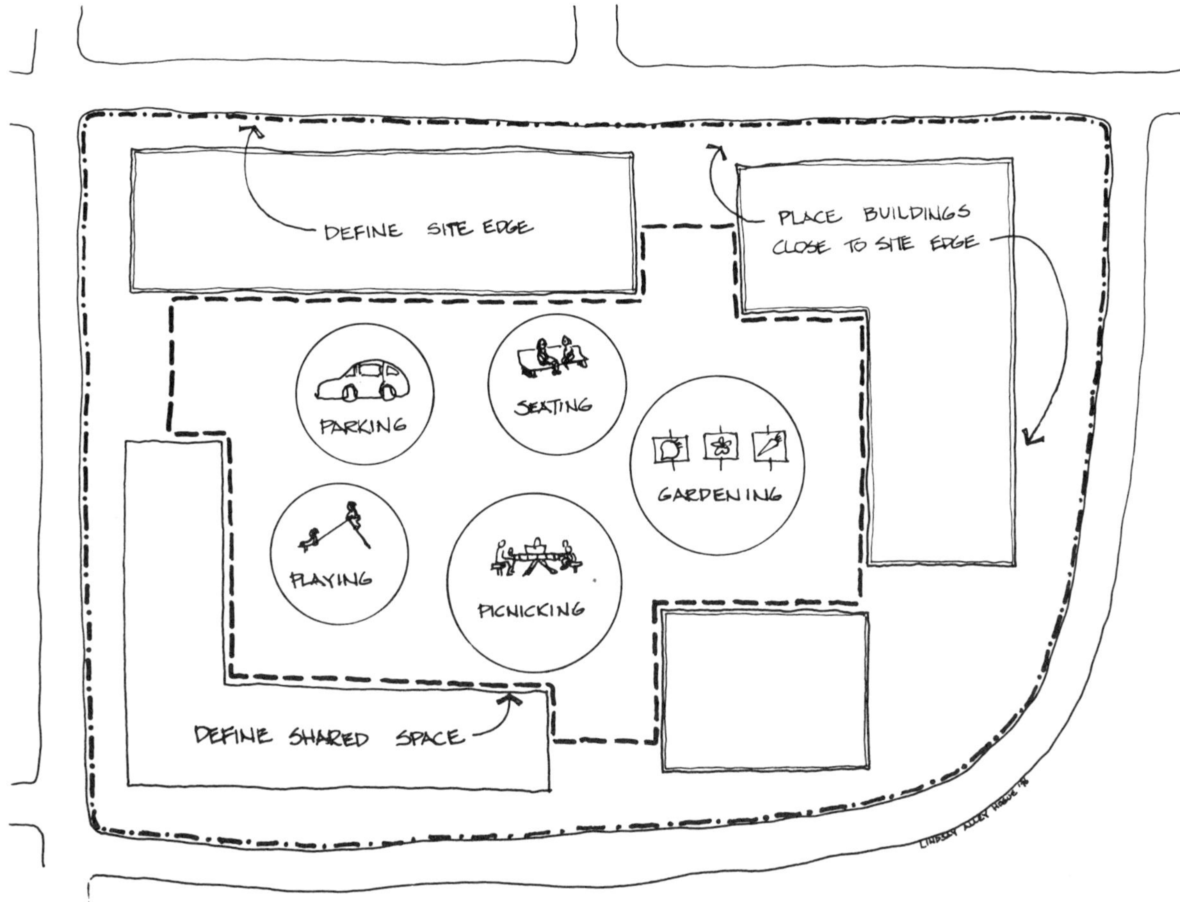

Figure 20–4
Use the building to define the space.

an area where these behaviors might be expected (Newman 1972; Becker 1974).

BEHAVIOR—A VISITOR APPROACHING THE DWELLING

Need

Visitors, delivery people, mailmen, doctors, and maintenance workers need to be able to find those whom they are looking for, especially in emergencies.

Single family house

Callers are used to finding a house on a street and usually have little difficulty locating the street name and house number.

High-rise

Since there are so many units in a high-rise building and since several buildings are often contained on the same site and have similar appearances, callers, visitors, etc., often have difficulty finding the particular building they are looking for (Jephcott 1971). Lack of a directory of residents' names may also make finding the unit once inside the building a difficult procedure.

Suggestions

1. Provide clear signing in parking areas and on adjacent roadways to indicate the building name(s) and location before visitors and callers start their search for a parking space and then a specific building.

2. Provide information panels with unit numbers (or names, but not both) alongside an intercom and buzzers at the building entries so callers can notify residents they are wanting to enter the building and can identify themselves.

3. If it can be afforded, a doorman can provide some of the services normally performed by neighbors in a single family house situation, such as taking in parcels or deliveries for someone not at home and insuring that those people coming in have good reason for entering.

BEHAVIOR—TRANSFERRING PEOPLE AND OBJECTS FROM THE PARKED CAR TO THE DWELLING

Need

People like to park close to their homes so that: (a) carrying shopping, etc., from car to dwelling is as easy as possible; (b) guiding small children or elderly people from car to dwelling requires few physical difficulties; (c) they feel secure in the car-to-home transition at night.

Single family house

Parking is generally adjacent to the unit in a garage, carport, or driveway with additional close parking on the street. In newer homes, the passage from car to home is completely inside, with a connecting door from garage to kitchen or utility room.

High-rise

Complaints about parking frequently cited by high-rise dwellers include: distance from the car to the dwelling unit, inability to see one's car from the dwelling unit for surveillance purposes, difficulties in maneuvering in the parking lot, annoyance at having to search for a parking space (Becker 1974). The worst possible parking arrangement is under the building, in an underground garage which is not kept locked or its entry not controlled by a guard. Then residents can rely neither on mechanical control nor personal surveillance to protect their vehicles.

Parking in high-rise units is, of necessity, some distance vertically and horizontally from the units. This makes the passage from car to home particularly cumbersome when residents are carrying several bags of groceries, and/or small children and their toys, when elevators are unreliable, and when the waiting area in an underground parking area is cold and unpleasant. The physical impossibility of one person carrying more than, say, two full bags of groceries at a time may result in several journeys from parking garage to dwelling, or in more frequent, smaller shopping trips—thus leading to more gas consumption and air pollution. A typical single family home dweller may, on the other hand, make one large shopping trip a week, since the transferring of, say, six bags of groceries from car to adjacent kitchen is not a great problem.

At the age between beginning to walk (at about one year) and being able to move around in public places in a fairly controlled and predictable way (at about three years), children have to be constantly watched. This can make the passage from car-to-elevator-to-corridor-to-dwelling a particularly wearing experience for parents, especially when they may also be carrying things, talking to other children or adults, etc. The problem this raises may even result in a parent leaving a small child at home alone for a brief time rather than go through this hassle.

In reverse, when leaving the home for, say, a family outing, the proximity of car to home in the single family house means that picnic equipment, etc., can be brought out and loaded by degrees, that forgotten items can be quickly retrieved from the house, etc. A similar outing for a high-rise family means infinitely more preplanning, and more frayed nerves when a critical item is remembered just as the car is about to leave.

Suggestions

1. Where financially feasible, parking should be in a locked garage at the base of the building, since this combines a minimum distance between car and dwelling, and a form of mechanical security to compensate for lack of casual visual surveillance.

2. Parking places should be numbered and designated, and each should have a sizable locker adjacent to it for sports or recreation items and bicycles which residents may not want to carry back and forth to the dwelling.

3. The elevator waiting area should be in a glass-enclosed lobby which is pleasantly decorated, carpeted, heated—i.e., it is really a transition-entrance to the home environment rather than just a part of the cold concrete garage setting. There should be convenient shelves or tables close to the elevator door for resting parcels on. A communal notice board for want ads, for sale notices, etc., might alleviate the boredom of waiting. The fact that the lobby is enclosed means that small children do not have to be constantly watched to protect them from moving cars.

4. The horizontal distance from elevator to dwelling entrance should be as short as possible. According to one study, the ideal total horizontal distance from dwelling to car should be no more than 100–200 feet (Becker 1974).

BEHAVIOR—INDIVIDUALIZING AND BEAUTIFYING THE ENTRY

Need

One of the primary attributes of a private dwelling is an entry which is individual and clearly belongs to one family only. In addition to this, many residents like to have an area forming part of the entry on the public side of the dwelling (i.e., where their efforts

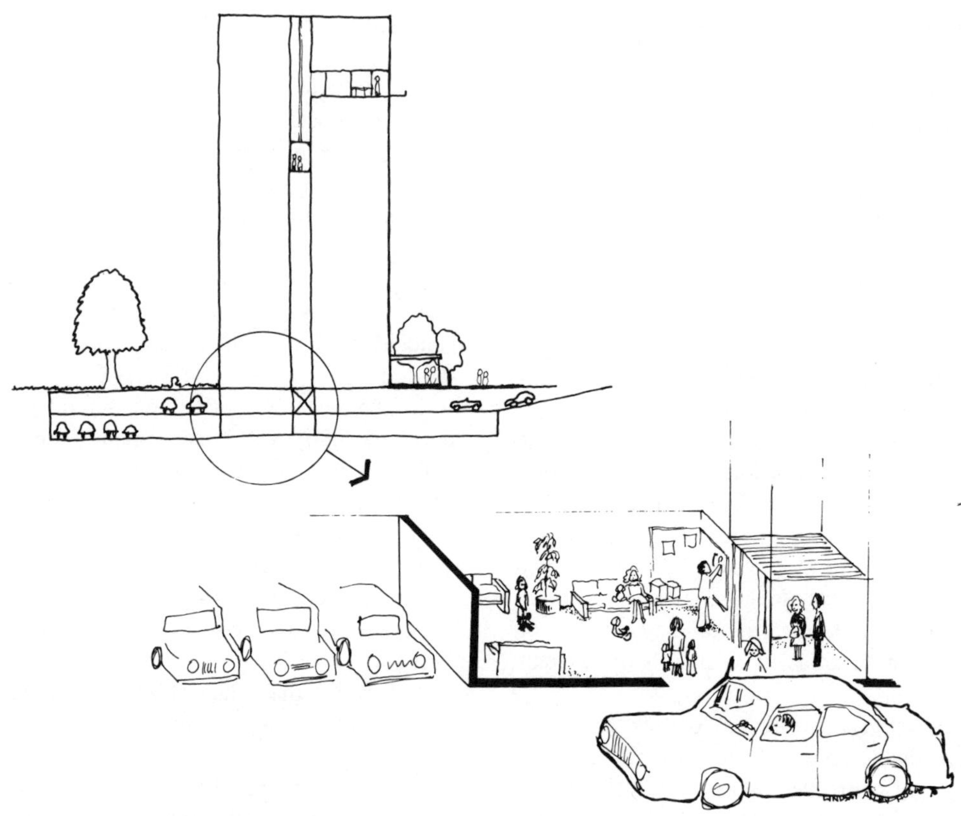

Figure 20-5
Waiting for the elevator should be a pleasant experience.

are visible to callers and passersby) where they can further individualize the approaches to the home by planting, entry decorations, lights, etc. This area gives pleasure both to the occupants and to passersby and provides a pleasant, semi-private space in which visitors can wait when calling on residents.

Single family house

The front yard, porch, or garden space between the front of the unit and the public street provides residents of single family houses with this kind of visible display space. In a study which inquired what made different multifamily housing designs more or less "homelike," the primary factors contributing to a "homelike" feeling were those usually associated with single family housing: private entrances and no one living above or below (Friedberg 1974).

High-rise

In high-rise units there can, of course, be no private entries. Nor is there generally any semi-private transition or display space between the public access area (foyer or corridor) and the unit itself. Residents thus lack an area to individualize and beautify, a space where they can show others that "this is mine and I care about how it looks." "Personalization reinforces the occupants' own sense of identity as well as expressing it to others, and is important in demonstrating control over a bounded spatial area. It is a way of demonstrating to others that the space is occupied by someone *in particular.* . . . We found almost no sign of any type of personalization of exterior areas at the high-rise buildings. Door mats were the only sign of personal ownership outside the apartment" (Becker 1974:143-144).

Suggestions

Provide some kind of physical transition between public access way and door—perhaps by means of an indentation, recess, overhang, level change, etc. Care should be taken that the entry is not so separate and recessed that it becomes a safety-hazard; and the micro-design of this space should facilitate its decoration—for example, shelves for ornaments or plants (if there is enough light), areas for personally-selected doormats or porch lights, etc. The greater the number of residents sharing the access way, the greater the need for this "personal" entry way; where only four or five, for example, share a common foyer on each floor, that may become a satisfactory *communal* entry—decorated and personalized by all those who use it.

BEHAVIOR—MEETING (AND AVOIDING) NEIGHBORS

Need

For many people, privacy is construed as the ability to avoid unwanted social interaction with neighbors. But at the same time many people need to be able to make friends or acquaintances in their neighborhood, so they do not feel isolated or cut off, to give them a feeling of belonging, and to enable them to call for help in emergencies.

Single family house

Due to the physical separation of adjacent units set back from the street and use of the entry by only one household, unwanted neighbor-encounters can generally be avoided. Desired contact with neighbors frequently occurs when one or both are doing something utilitarian in adjacent yards (e.g., gardening, cleaning the car, etc.). Friendly exchanges also often take place while one person is working in the front yard or sweeping the porch and another passes by on the sidewalk. Walking with dogs and kids provides a good reason for initial communication.

High-rise

The large number of residents sharing common entrance facilities—such as elevators, corridors or hallways in high-rises—enormously increases the *potential* possible social encounters. Yet the evidence suggests that for comparable income groups and family types, there tends to be more social contact between residents of walk-up buildings than in high-rises served by elevators (Cooper 1969; Stevenson 1967; Becker 1974).

Residents in high-rise buildings seem to greet each other less, or have difficulty in making contact, or have contacts of shorter duration (Becker 1974; Stevenson et al. 1967; Ministry of Housing 1970; Department of the Environment 1972). Unlike the house dweller, high-rise residents do not have semi-private transition spaces (yard, porch, driveway) in which they might feel comfortably enough "at home" to make an initial contact with an adjacent or passing neighbor (Willson 1968). They seldom see each other doing utilitarian tasks, or have any "excuse" to say hello, such as making contact via an accompanying dog or child (both of which are fre-

WINDOWS ARE HIGH AND SEPARATED FROM ACCESS BALCONY BY PLANTER INSURING ADEQUATE PRIVACY
PROVIDE WINDOWS IN BALCONY, LOW DOWN SO TOTS CAN SEE OUT
DEFINE UNIT ENTRY TO ENCOURAGE RESIDENTS TO INDIVIDUALIZE THE AREA AROUND IT
PLAY AREA CLOSE TO UNIT ENTRIES, VISIBLE FROM UNIT PROVIDES SAFE, USABLE TINY TOT PLAY AREA
LINDSAY ALLEY HOGUE

Figure 20-6
Access ways can be designed to enhance personalization of units and child care.

quently banned in apartments). As a result, many residents feel very isolated and lonely, especially the elderly and young housewives (Adams and Conway 1974; Department of the Environment 1972; Willson 1968; Becker 1974). Interior access areas do not provide areas conducive to neighborly contact, except of a very brief nature. Studies comparing neighboring behavior in interior as opposed to exterior access areas found that more contact occurs on exterior, balcony access ways, perhaps because this more nearly approximates a public sidewalk (Stewart 1970; Rothblatt 1971).

Evidence also suggests that the fewer the people sharing an entrance way or corridor, the more likely they are to be able to recognize and greet one another, and the less likely they are to perceive their environment as anonymous and un-neighborly. Comparing some low- and high-rise developments, Becker concluded: "More frequent and extended contact between neighbors was possible at the low-rise development by virtue of the semi-private outdoor activity spaces—back and front yards, front entrances facing common pathways and courtyards. Contacts in high-rise buildings more often occurred in public or semi-public spaces such as lobbies and elevators, and were of shorter duration" (Becker 1974:180).

Suggestions

1. Since some residents need contact with their neighbors more than others, provide units on exterior access ways for those who need it and interior access for those who prefer more privacy. Elderly residents and young parents who are housebound, who are the ones most often complaining of being isolated or lonely, should be housed in gallery or balcony access units (Stewart 1970; Department of the Environment 1972). Young and middle-aged working people tend to prefer privacy and like living in a building with interior access corridors. Provide them with this option (Byrom 1970).

2. For those who are looking for some neighborly contacts, minimize the number of units sharing an entrance-way or corridor; for those who have chosen a high-rise to fulfill a need for privacy and anonymity, access ways shared by many are preferable. A development providing for both groups, and explaining the possible behavioral responses in different access-forms, should accommodate the range of needs on the neighborliness-to-anonymity continuum.

3. Provide some kind of shared space for each group of units where utilitarian tasks could be done; this may enable residents to meet others sharing their floors, if they so desire (Rothblatt 1971). In one Australian development, the laundry room served as the primary place of contact among tenants (Stevenson et al. 1967).

4. A meeting space for a tenants' or co-op organization to convene will facilitate contacts through this kind of semi-formal meeting (National Council of Women in Britain 1970). Depending on the size of the development, this space need not necessarily be larger than the equivalent of one apartment. Large annual general meetings, etc., at which more than a basic core of involved residents might be expected, can always be accommodated in a nearby school or community meeting space.

5. Adult recreation facilities which are often called for and which *may* facilitate neighbor-contacts (though there is no proof for this) are tennis and a swimming pool (Cooper 1969; Kubas 1973; Norcross 1973; Michelson 1973). There is no evidence to indicate that a multi-purpose recreation room is needed or used for adult recreation activities.

BEHAVIOR–HAVING SPACE TO LIVE FLEXIBLY

Need

Most families like to have enough space in the home (1) to provide some private space for each family member; (2) for play; (3) for storage; (4) for carrying on conflicting activities in separate areas; (5) for guests to sleep over; (6) for formal and informal dining; (7) for normal day-to-day activities of cooking, bathing, cleaning, etc.; and (8) for hobbies, crafts or do-it-yourself activities (Becker 1974; Adams and Conway 1974).

Single family house

The single family house generally does very well at providing for most of the above needs; in addition to the normal functional spaces of bathrooms, kitchens, living rooms, bedrooms, etc., there is often useful extra space in the form of an attic or basement, a garage, storeroom, utility room, back porch, etc. The significance of these spaces is that the home is flexible enough to accommodate many kinds of periodic or unplanned for activities—such as having relatives to stay, taking up a space-consuming hobby, creating a job-office in the home, storing toys for younger children, doing "dirty" jobs such as cleaning a bicycle or painting a table, etc. Most importantly, too, a single family house often has a separate living and dining room, or a separate family room and formal living room. Teenagers can be entertaining friends in one of these rooms, while parents are reading in another; a babysitter can be watching the children in one area while the mother is studying in another. This flexibility of use is crucial to stable family relations and to changing demands on space over time.

In a study of 761 incipient movers in Toronto, Michelson (1973) found that of those moving from an apartment to a house, more than three-fourths (76.4%) cited "size or amount of floorspace" or "layout of unit" as their reason for choice of the new dwelling type. Of those moving from apartment to apartment, only 31.5% cited these factors as important in their choice; of those moving from house to apartment, only 33.9% noted these factors. The primary reason advanced by those moving to the suburbs related to the size and layout of the dwelling unit mostly readily available there (i.e., single-family houses), especially number of bedrooms, number of bathrooms, and storage—and *not* any perceived advantage of a suburban location.

High-rise

Units in a high-rise generally do not have as much overall floor space as a single family unit and often use an open rather than a closed plan. This means the kitchen, dining, and living areas are only marginally separate from each other. There is rarely provision for screening, or a means of separating activities. There is no attic, basement, porch, garage, etc., and consequently little room for storage or space for carrying on potentially conflicting activities and hobbies, except in the bedrooms. How much spatial division is required will depend on the individual family and their preference as well as their stage in the life cycle, but in most families there is need for some. In one study of seven New York multifamily developments, a third of all the residents mentioned conflicts in internal space-use, especially where children were concerned, and particularly involving the use of television. Three ways of dealing with these conflicts were mentioned: (a) time territory—people use different rooms for different purposes at different times; (b) space territory—people transferred their activities to a different room; (c) cooperation-capitulation—everyone engages in the one activity determined by the dominant person or group. This kind of resolution usually works in the parents' favor. In the same study, one-third to one-half reported problems with hobbies, especially those which were too "messy," or which could not be completed at one time and had to be left out (Becker 1974).

Suggestions

1. Provide one room for each family member. In cases where bedrooms accommodate more than one child, design for the placement of bunkbeds in minimally-sized sleeping alcoves, with the rest of the room used as a play area.

2. Provide a means of screening or separating the dining and living areas so it is possible to have two separate "living areas" when activities in the two areas are in conflict (the screen should have some soundproofing qualities).

3. Provide a small "extra room" in the unit which can be used for play, for families with young children. These children do not play outside as much as their counterparts in low buildings and therefore the indoor space will be highly used. Later in the life of the family, such a room might be used for guests, for a study, a hobby room, a dark-room, an office, etc. (Maizels 1961; Department of the Environment 1972; Wharton 1970; Morville 1969; Stewart 1970).

4. Provide adequate storage areas to compensate for the space a garage, attic or basement normally provides. Bulk storage is needed at ground level for bicycles, prams, etc. A dead storage locker in a basement or elsewhere should be provided for each family to keep extra furniture, luggage, etc., which they use

occasionally (Becker 1974; Adams and Conway 1974).

5. The most radical solution might be to provide each household with an open area within the building, say 12,000 cubic feet, which they then could subdivide—and change—according to their needs, much as a business can subdivide an open office floor. Although often debated in architectural circles, we could find no example of this actually having been carried out and evaluated.

6. Most families with small children prefer a large eat-in kitchen plus a multipurpose room which can be used alternatively for play or for formal dining. "In high-rise buildings where there is greater pressure for young children to remain in the apartment . . . the added flexibility of this arrangement may be especially important (Becker 1974). In one East Coast study, the *least* preferred arrangements were a living/dining combination, or a large eat-in kitchen with no alternative eating space (Becker 1974).

BEHAVIOR—CHANGING THE SIZE OF THE HOME

Need

As families change in size or composition, they often need the opportunity to physically expand or modify their home environment, as an alternate to moving. Such changes might include the addition of a child to the family; the divorce of the parents and the need to rent out one or more rooms for added income; the accommodation of an elderly relative who comes to live with the family, etc.

Single family house

Attics and basements in single family homes provide a family with temporary or permanent space to expand into. Since such homes are usually owned by their residents, structured additions can be made without the consent of anyone else. Since a single family house stands on a separate lot with space around it, there is the physical opportunity to add a room over a garage, for example, or turn a sun porch into an extra room. That is, there are few limitations —other than money and building regulations—to expansion of the house. Such additions can usually be made less expensively than buying a larger home.

High-rise

A high-rise unit never has the "extra" space of an attic, basement, or such to modify into living space. If a family increases in size, there is rarely any means of expanding or modifying the unit, since there is physically no way to expand "out," and since it is not often owned by the family living in it. Instead, a family must make do by using space for more than one purpose or it must move.

Suggestions

1. Make allowances for residents to take down or put up nonstructural walls, under managerial supervision.

2. Provide a number of unit sizes in the building at varying prices, so as the family size increases and as income increases the family can change its accommodation but still stay within the old neighborhood if it so chooses.

BEHAVIOR—PRESCHOOLERS PLAYING

Need

Preschoolers need to play close to parent or supervising adults and yet have contact with other children their own age. They need to be able to manipulate and explore the environment, to play with a wide range of toys, to run and make noise, to use up energy, stretch their muscles, etc. (Gëhl 1971).

Single family house

A preschooler can easily play outside his home within supervisory distance of a parent inside. He often has contact with other neighborhood children his own age who live close by, who he meets by bicycling on the sidewalk or hearing them in an adjacent yard. He can dig, hammer, and play in the yard, which provides a very manipulable environment. He can usually run, ride a tricycle, and make noise freely because he is making it outside, where it is less of a problem in that it is absorbed by plants and soft materials.

High-rise

Parents of preschoolers often report having to curb their children's play in the apartment because of the annoyance their noise may cause to neighbors (Jephcott 1971; Department of the Environment 1972). Several studies report children in high-rise buildings playing outdoors less frequently than children in low-rise buildings. (Maizels 1961; Morville 1969; Department of the Environment 1972).

Young children in a high-rise building cannot play outside adjacent to their home except on the private balcony or adjacent access corridor or balcony. These are generally unsuitable because: (1) the parents fear the child may climb up to look out—and fall off a balcony (Willis 1957); (2) neighbors—and especially those without children—react negatively to children playing in the access corridors, foyer or stairways and the noise that they cause (Reynolds and Nicholson 1969; Becker 1974); (3) noise from children playing in groups in access ways, or toys left out in these areas, may cause annoyance to neighbors and this may in turn cause strained adult relations (Morville 1969); (4) neither balcony nor corridor allows children sufficient space or freedom to do what pleases them most—climb, run, play with wheeled vehicles, dig, and manipulate the environment. However, these are the only semi-private areas that are close enough to the unit for a parent doing other chores inside to supervise. Occasionally, in a few cases where a wider than normal access deck has been provided in a high-rise, it has successfully served a number of functions, including children's play (Demers and Aldhouse 1966; Darke and Darke 1972; Department of the Environment 1972). In order for such areas to be successfully used for children's play, however, it is essential that only families with children be housed on the same floor, or their noise will still bother other residents (Ministry of Housing 1970; Adams and Conway 1974).

Children between the ages of approximately one and five years like to play with or parallel to other children their own age and this social contact is extremely important in their psychological development. Many children above the first or second floor in a high-rise are deprived of this opportunity because it is too much of a chore for parents to take them down to ground-level communal play areas, and because the children are too young to make this trip by themselves (Stevenson et al. 1967; Morville 1969; Jephcott 1971; Adams and Conway 1974). In a single family house, much casual outdoor/indoor play takes place as parents are partially involved in other chores—preparing a meal, washing up, gardening, etc. Children of this age do not usually want continued parental supervision or contact, but do need to be able to check back for approval, assistance, reassurance, etc., very often (Morville 1969). A high-rise parent can, of course, take his or her child to a ground-level play area or adjacent park, but cannot usually, at the same time, involve himself or herself in necessary household tasks. Hence these visits, if they occur, are likely to be much more abbreviated than the casual in-and-out play of a house-dwelling child (Morville 1969).

For all these reasons, it is not surprising that study

after study reports that of all groups surveyed in high-rise housing, those families with preschool children are invariably the least satisfied (Cooper 1969; Jephcott 1971; Homenuck 1973; Becker 1974; Adams and Conway 1974). Writing of the high-rise building as an essentially anti-child environment, Van der Eyken (1967) points out that it requires a type of behavior which is acquiescent, silent, restrained—the antithesis of childhood.

Suggestions

1. Preferably house families with small children only on the lowest three floors of a high-rise or in townhouses or low-rise apartments on a site where childless couples, elderly or students are housed in the high-rise units (Stevenson et al. 1967; Reynolds and Nicholson 1969; Stewart 1970; Ministry of Housing 1970; Adams and Conway 1974).

2. Where it is inevitable—because of land costs, etc. —to house families with small children above the first three floors of a high-rise, consider: (1) housing families in duplex or "maisonette" units, where the two floors make apartment living more "home-like" and relieve some tensions over keeping small children quiet (Becker 1974); (b) providing at least one multipurpose room or bedroom which is larger than minimum-standard size, since children will be indoors more and make greater demands on interior space for play and activities than would be true if they had easy access to the outdoors; (c) providing a communal terrace or widened access deck where a small play area for children is within sight of most of the units. Equip it with a variety of small scaled play equipment and of surfaces such as sand, tan bark, etc. (which can be manipulated) with seating and a paved bicycle path suited to young children's play (Maizels 1961; Stewart 1970; Rothblatt 1971; Department of the Environment 1972).

3. On individual, private balconies that will be used for play, ensure that the railings are high enough so that children will not accidentally fall off. Provide a "window" in the balcony so a child can see out. Make sure there are no gaps at the bottom of the balcony railing or spaces where toys can fall or be pushed through.

4. Provide play areas at ground level, close to the building entry in a safe location, with small-scaled climbers and swings so preschoolers and young children up to seven or eight can use them. Surfacing should be soft and manipulable. Provide comfortable seating with attractive views for supervising adults. This play area for small children should be bounded in some way by planting or by sinking it slightly so that the boundary itself is a play facility; this will greatly facilitate the supervision of small children who tend to wander off and who have little sense of danger (Becker 1974; Hogue 1974; Zeisel and Griffin 1973).

5. Provide a supervised "drop-off" play area with challenging, interesting equipment where parents can leave their child for, say, up to two-hour stretches. This facility should be in addition to, or part of, a regular child-care facility for working parents. A "drop-off" facility would give the at-home parent a needed few hours each day to do chores or have time to relax (Jephcott 1971; Reynolds and Nicholson 1969).

6. Ensure adequate soundproofing, especially on floors where children are to be housed. Studies of apartment living where sound insulation *is* adequate report very few worries concerning children annoying neighbors (Morville 1969).

7. If families with children are to be housed in the development, it is especially crucial to spend time and money on ensuring the environment is safe and attractive for the children and their parents, since there is a highly significant and positive correlation between residents feeling that their development is a good place to raise children and their overall satisfaction (Becker 1974).

8. Design the whole site as a potential play area, being aware that children will play anywhere and everywhere they can. Studies in England, the United States, and Denmark indicate that children use the

Figure 20–7
Providing for supervised play is crucial in high-rise settings.

whole site for play more than they do designated play areas (Morville 1969; Bussard 1974; Becker 1974; Department of the Environment 1972; Cooper Marcus 1974).

BEHAVIOR–SCHOOL-AGE CHILDREN PLAYING

Need

It is essential for their psycho-social development that school-age children have opportunities close to home for large motor development (climbing, running, swinging, etc.), for social play, ball games, fantasy, bicycling, etc. Most of these need space and the freedom to make noise. Although school-recess times allow for some of this behavior, there are still times before and after school, during weekends and vacations, when school-age children need to be able to play casually and without inhibition, close to home.

Single family house

Children are remarkably adaptable and will use whatever space is available for their needs. Children will find places to hide and fantasize in the backyard or basement, spaces for ball games or bicycling on the sidewalk or on the street (where traffic is infrequent), etc. Since there is usually easy visual access from home to street, children can check if their friends are out playing and go out to join them if they are. Parents can easily call a child in for a meal; children can easily return to the house for a brief snack, visit to the toilet, etc.

High-rise

Although children of this age can—unlike preschoolers—manipulate the elevator and are generally felt to be responsible enough to play out of sight of their parents for short periods, there are still serious problems occasioned by the horizontal and vertical separation of home from casual outdoor play space (Morville 1969; Becker 1974). For example: (1) parents cannot easily call to a child to remind him or her of a chore or to tell the child that dinner is ready; (2) the child cannot easily and casually bring a friend in, or come back for a forgotten toy, or for a visit to the toilet; (3) from several floors up, a child may not be able to recognize whether or not his friends are out playing; (4) if a child is injured or involved in a fight, he cannot easily call to his parents for help; (5) the child's casual contacts with adults other than his own family are lessened. "No one leans on a sill or pops out to look at a pram, no couples have a half-hour's blether [chat] at the gate, no father mends a fence, no gran sits on the step minding a toddler. . . . A five-minute count at Red Road on a summer evening showed seventeen or so adults about the place compared with 120 children. Most of the grown-ups were rapidly making their way into a building or going off in a car. . ." (Jephcott 1971:87); (6) since boys are frequently given greater territorial freedom at an earlier age than girls, and since the landscaping around high-rises (flat, open spaces for ball play) are often more appealing to boys than girls, girl residents are potentially more severely limited by high-rise living than their brothers (Bussard 1974).

There are also problems stemming from the very density of children on the land, which are not necessarily peculiar to high-rise buildings but are true of all high *density* developments: (1) The great variety and number of children that may be playing together in a high-density play area may give the parent some cause for concern at not having "control" over who their children play with. In a single-family situation, people generally have an idea of who their neighbors might be before they move in (Becker 1974). (2) In order to accommodate large numbers of children with minimum maintenance, the landscape architect may have eliminated bushes, shrubs, hidden places, climbing trees, etc.—just those natural features which children in a single family house are most likely to find in their backyard or on the block. The high-rise child is usually faced with some combination of hard surfaces, grass and ground cover ("keep off") which often limit his activities to ball games, running, use of equipment, and perhaps bicycling. More introspective (requiring privacy) or manipulative (requiring malleable environments) activities are often expressly discouraged.

Describing the situation in a Syracuse, New York high-rise development, Becker writes: "In the absence of anything else to do in the immediate area, it seems likely that the excitement of playing with elevators or just hanging around and climbing over cars is an improvement over whatever else could be found in the area. This behavior does not seem particularly conducive to children's growth and development, but it seems to be a natural adaptation to the existing circumstances. Children need to engage in challenging and interesting behaviors, and they will find ways of doing this whether or not they are socially desired or approved" (Becker 1974:137). In a very different geographical situation, in the Scottish city of Glasgow, Jephcott describes similar problems—regardless of culture, children's play needs at different ages seem to be very much the same. "In multi-storey housing their play is hedged in by negatives—you mustn't play in the hall, chalk on the pavement, make a see-saw on that well, cycle on this path. . . . The places where the child plays are becoming more exposed to public view. . . . The open, tidy estate makes a most inferior setting for play compared with the variety of the street, its passages, old wells, derelict buildings, culs-de-sac, stairways, unexpected corners. Children are natural foragers but where, on a multi-story estate, is the flotsam and jetsam which is treasure-trove to the child—an old door, a cardboard carton, a plank, a bucket, a length of rope?" (Jephcott 1971:83–84).

(3) The open space on a high-rise site frequently "spills out" onto the surrounding streets, i.e., is not enclosed by building or fencing. In addition, the streets are usually much busier than in a lower-density setting. Hence, parents may have the double worry of a child being out of sight and calling distance *and* being able to wander or run into adjacent busy streets (Morville 1969; Ministry of Housing 1970; Department of the Environment 1972). The result may be that even school-age children are kept in for a larger proportion of the day than was true in previous low-rise homes (Jephcott 1971). In one study (of Scottish low and moderate income family high-rises) it was reported that "children get no door-step play with all the chances of other children's company that this normally affords. Tenants fairly often referred by name to a child in their block who was exceedingly shy or the one who would not stay with anyone but his mum. . . . Teachers from a school with many high-flats' children noted them as reluctant talkers and oddly incurious about each other. . . . Mothers criticised themselves as being so tetchy with the children, and teachers at a school which had many pupils from high flats noted that they talked a good deal about their mother being cross. . . . Sheer shortage of space means the child is liable to be nagged at for precisely what, at that age, he should be doing" (Jephcott 1971:94, 96, 97–98).

Suggestions

1. To cope with the problem of parental separation from children playing, one or more parent-substitutes in the form of popular play leaders may need to be provided. In a moderately large development, a very small addition to each household's rent would be sufficient to pay the salaries of such leaders; or, conversely, the necessity of such personnel where children are to be housed in high-rises should be recognized from the start, and an adequate amount budgeted for the running costs of the buildings (Adams and Conway 1974; Jephcott 1971; Reynolds and Nicholson 1969).

2. To facilitate the task of such play leaders, the outdoor areas used for play should: (a) be bounded on the outer edges of the site by fencing or thick planting to prevent children running into the street; (b) have access to indoor toilets and washing facilities so that children do not have to return to their apartments if they don't want to. The complaints of children urinating in fire stairs or elevators generally come from developments where there is no ground-level toilet and children cannot be bothered to go back up ten floors, or cannot get there in time (Becker 1974; National Council of Women in Britain 1970); (c) have access to a small equipment store and office for the convenience of the play leaders; (d) be provided with a great variety of play equipment for climbing on, swinging, sliding, balancing, jumping from, etc. Children tend to play much more frequently and for longer periods on equipment which incorporates the "old favorites" (swings, slides, etc.) in new and unusual ways, than on expensive architect-designed sculptures (Hole and Miller 1966; Department of the Environment 1972).

3. Where budgets do not allow for play leaders, negotiations should be made with the local Recreation and Parks Department to provide a visiting playmobile at times of peak need (generally, 4–6 p.m. on school days; longer in school vacations).

4. Play areas for older children need not be as frequent as those for preschoolers since older children have an increased range of movement and like to play together in large social groups. However, since children of this age group are noisier than preschoolers, the location should ensure that adjacent families are not annoyed.

5. Since older children often have to supervise

younger siblings, place a tot-lot within close visual range of the older children's play area. The two age groups should be separate, however, for safety.

6. Designer or management should not assume that community facilities, several blocks away, will form an adequate substitute for on-site facilities; these will not provide for incidental or short-time play periods when a child is cautioned not to go far away.

7. Since this age group is very involved with movement and mobility, provide an interesting and challenging bicycle circuit round and through the development. If this is *not* provided, children will be sure to ride bicycles anyway, and will tend to damage landscaping, etc., in the process (Cooper Marcus 1974; Becker 1974).

8. Since more outdoor play of children takes place on hard surfaces than on grass, provide hard-surface areas outside building entrances, around play equipment areas, and in small enclaves off the main pedestrian walkways (Cooper Marcus 1974; Department of the Environment 1972).

9. If provided play areas are ignored or vandalized, management and designer should immediately meet with those involved to try and understand their grievances and provide better for their needs. In a study of seven New York multifamily developments, all of which reported problems with children's play, Becker concluded: ". . . people do not accept dysfunctional environments passively. They will act on them to either make them more functional for their purposes, not use them at all, or destroy them. These behaviors are one means of clearly communicating their dissatisfaction and the dysfunction. Much less damage would occur if these first symptoms were used to diagnose problems and initiate a series of creative problem solving sessions with those persons directly involved: the children" (Becker 1974:139).

10. It is especially important that play areas for this age group in a high-rise setting be challenging, with a great variety of things to do, physical skills to test and accomplish, since there is a clear tendency for children in high-rise developments potentially to engage in a much higher proportion of passive activities (sitting, standing, watching, talking) than is true in low-rise or single family neighborhoods (Becker 1974; Cooper Marcus 1974; Department of the Environment 1972). In addition to the tendency outdoors (often because of the lack of anything challenging to do), one U.S. multifamily study indicated that inside the apartment, also, ". . . parents were restricting their children's activities . . . to passive ones such as watching TV of playing with puzzles" (Becker 1974: 150).

11. The clear attraction of a place where children can meet their peers and find interesting things to do is even more important in a high-rise than a low-rise development since: (a) high-rise children tend to spend less time playing outdoors than low-rise children (Morville 1969; Cooper Marcus 1974; Becker 1974), and when they *are* outdoors, need a central gathering place; and (b) because there seems to be a tendency for high-rise children to less often have friends come to their home to play than is true in low-rise developments (Becker 1974).

12. It is especially important that high-rise children be offered the opportunity to play, dig, build, etc., in an adventure playground (Cooper 1970), since: (a) there is limited room for constructive and creative play in the dwelling; (b) the landscaping around high-rises is generally neat, ordered, and created for adults' visual pleasure and ease of maintenance, rather than children's needs for exploration and creativity; (c) no one has a backyard where he can build a tree house, or have his own garden; (d) it is most unlikely that the building is close to open country where such behavior is naturally accommodated.

13. If the site or the budget (for play leaders) precludes an adventure playground, consideration should be given to planting robust, low-branching trees whch can sustain climbing; shrubbery (such as rhododendron) which makes a good exploring and hiding environment; a left-over, wild area which the maintenance staff leaves alone, which as Jephcott puts it, ". . . would give the children the chance to burn the

discarded couch, have three shots to break the bottle, dig to Australia, etc." (Jephcott 1971).

14. Where there is a long cold or wet season, provide a semi-enclosed, heated shelter which children can gravitate to at those times when, in a single family housing situation, they would return indoors for a brief time.

15. The whole site should be designed as a potential play area, for it will undoubtedly be used that way. The worst possible solution—too often provided in contemporary high-rises—is a site designed primarily for adults to look at (from above) and walk through, to which play areas have been tacked on.

BEHAVIOR—TEENAGERS MEETING AND HANGING OUT

Need

Teenagers need to be able to hang out and meet their friends in semi-public areas close to home where there is activity to watch and where they can be seen (Cooper Marcus 1974; Ertel 1974). They need to be able to play basketball, repair their cars, go to movies and inexpensive coffee shops where they can meet others away from parental restriction. They need to have easy and cheap access to such areas from their homes, as well as a private space *in* the home where they can socialize with friends.

The "problem" of teenagers hanging out in public or semi-public places which tends to be seen as a lower or working class phenomenon, is in fact a facet of teenage culture in general. "Middle class teenagers engage in the same activities, but greater access to cars or larger homes with more complete separation of activities from parents provide a series of private settings that low and moderate income persons, particularly in the urban environment, do not have available. . . . Teenagers use public spaces like we (middle class) use our private space. We then apply middle class standards to those settings to determine appropriate behavior . . . and find those activities which we do in private but which they do in public unacceptable" (Becker 1974:160).

Single family house

The single family house often has sufficient space for teenagers to meet with friends in reasonable privacy. In addition, in older residential areas of moderate density where teenagers can easily walk or bicycle to school, where shops are never far away and bus services are reasonably frequent, the teenager is at an advantage. He or she can easily get to a friend's house or go shopping or go to the movies without being dependent on being driven there by parents, or owning (and being able to drive) a car. In new suburban subdivisions, the teenager may be one of the most disadvantaged family members, since public transport is rarely provided, commercial facilities are not intermingled with housing, distances to friends are greater because of the low densities. Dependence on parents driving the teenage children everywhere may lead to resentments on both sides.

High-rise

A teenager in a high-rise unit has certain advantages and disadvantages when compared to one living in a single family house. The disadvantages include: (a) less interior space than in a house, which may mean a minimally-sized bedroom, no separate family room, den or other space in which to get together away from the family. With minimal interior space, teenagers may be forced to get together in semi-public areas within the building, such as the lobby, and adults may strongly disapprove of this (Becker 1974); (b) more restrictions on making noise, playing stereos loudly, playing musical instruments, etc. (Becker 1974); (c) less space for storage of sports equipment, bicycles, "collections," etc. (Becker 1974; Adams and Conway 1974); (d) more restrictions on decorating his or her private space—hanging up posters, painting walls, putting up shelves, etc. (Becker 1974; Martini 1974).

Among the advantages are: (a) many potential friends living within a short distance (assuming there is an average spread of families at different stages in the life cycle within the development; (b) probable walking access to shops, restaurants and other commercial facilities; (c) access to public transportation (unless the high-rise is located uncharacteristically in a suburban low-density area); (d) places on site for active sports, hanging out, showing off, etc.—a few minutes from everyone's dwelling and often within sight of many of them.

Suggestions

Some solutions to the disadvantages of high-rise living for teenagers might include the provision of:

1. a sound-insulated teen center on the site, with a recreation room and TV, record-playing, parties, etc.; facilities for pool or Ping-Pong; a quiet study area; and a place just to "hang out." This facility should be supervised by a paid staff person selected by the teenagers in consultation with the management, and it should be out of sight and hearing of possibly-disapproving adults (Becker 1974; Homenuck 1973);

2. outdoor spaces and commercial facilities where teenagers can fool around, show off, be noisy without disturbing the parents or other adults (Cooper Marcus 1974; Becker 1974; Ertel 1974; Wood 1961);

3. dwelling units that may house children or teens, *not* located adjacent to or above units for elderly families, who are especially sensitive to noise;

4. good sound-proofing between units, bearing in mind that sounds travel down and sideways more easily than up; that sounds made by people are more disturbing than those made by equipment (washing machines, mixer, etc.); and that noise is more disturbing if heard in the bedroom than in the living room or kitchen. There have been cases in Germany where residents have sued the builder for not providing adequate sound insulation, and where tenants have demanded a reduction in rent to compensate for the disturbance caused by inadequate sound insulation (Homenuck 1973);

5. wall areas of corkboard in teenager's bedroom, for ease of decoration and for sound-proofing;

6. built-in shelves for storage of books, hobby-equipment, etc.;

7. a possible second entrance close to the teenager's bedroom so that he or she may come or go in privacy; after the children have left home, this arrangement might allow the family to rent the room for extra income.

BEHAVIOR—DOING THINGS AT HOME THAT NEED VISUAL PRIVACY FROM THE OUTSIDE

Need

Residents need adequate visual privacy in the home from passersby and neighbors. The degree of privacy required varies with different people and with different stages in the life cycle; however, most people agree that privacy is most needed while sleeping, bathing, dressing, etc., and less so while doing utilitarian tasks such as cleaning, cooking, etc.

Single family houses

Residents have sufficient space between houses, especially in the front and back, that passersby do not usually come too close to the unit. However, sometimes the side of a house is so close to the next house that people keep drapes drawn over the side windows, or resort to erecting a fence, or planting a hedge.

High-rise

Where internal access corridors are used, units have complete visual privacy from passersby. This kind of access arrangement tends to be preferred by families without children, i.e., young and older adults, working people, because it is usually carpeted and appears luxurious, is private and draft-free. In fact, often the chief complaint is not too little privacy but too much, resulting in residents feeling isolated and withdrawn from normal activity and day-to-day life (especially parents who do not work and have young children or older residents) (Adams and Conway 1974). Since most units are off the ground, passersby cannot look into the windows, except from an adjacent high-rise unit. In balcony access units, there generally are windows overlooking the access way and residents in the units do complain of people seeing in if window sills are too low (Department of the Environment 1972). In many cases, families prefer this arrangement though, since it allows parents to supervise their child playing on the access balcony from inside (Department of the Environment 1972; Hole and Miller 1966; Stewart 1970). It also alleviates some of the feeling of being isolated experienced by young mothers, etc., because they have some visual contact with adjacent activity, and because it is used for informal chatting with neighbors (Adams and Conway 1974; Department of the Environment 1972). Ground floor units in a high-rise suffer severely from overlooking if they are adjacent to public paths, parking, etc., and there is no privacy barrier such as planting or a patio fence (Department of the Environment 1972; Ministry of Housing 1970).

Suggestions

1. House families who demand a great deal of privacy in units off the ground in building with internal access corridors.

2. Locate families who require less privacy in the units, and who appreciate seeing out onto the access balcony from their units, in buildings with exterior access balconies. Use cleristory or high windows and orient balcony to kitchen side of unit, not living or bedroom side (Department of the Environment 1972).

3. Provide screening between ground floor units and public areas outside the building to insure these units have sufficient visual privacy from activity close to the units.

BEHAVIOR—DOING THINGS AT HOME THAT CREATE NOISE

Need

One of the freedoms which being "at home" allows is being able to make noise if you want to—whether it be playing the stereo, having a party, running a power saw, allowing your children to run and scream, or having a fight. At times, most people need to let off steam in some way which creates noise.

Single family houses

The separation of houses from one another ensures that only the loudest noises can be heard in adjacent dwellings; closing of windows and doors can further control noise transference.

High-rise

In apartments, whether high- or low-rise, a dwelling unit can be adjacent to as many as four others. Although many studies indicate that residents *expect* to hear a certain level of sound from adjacent units in apartment buildings (Cooper 1971; Becker 1974), there are indications that many resent having to curb what would be considered acceptable noise-producing activities in a single family home, such as stereos, parties, children, etc. (Becker 1974).

In one Toronto study, it was found that over time people with a need for privacy (and not everyone demands it to the same extent) seemed to be able to adjust to mechanical noise (traffic, appliances, etc.), but continued to find "people" noises bothersome (parties, conversations, children playing, etc.) (Baine et al. 1972).

Families with children probably suffer the most from poor soundproofing in that children's normal behavior must often be curbed in order not to upset neighbors (Shankland, Cox & Associates 1967; Stevenson et al. 1967; Stewart 1970; Cappon 1972). This restriction is doubly frustrating to parents and children alike since the alternative of allowing the child to run outside and let off steam is often not available (Wharton 1970; Stewart 1970).

Suggestions

1. Soundproofing should be a very high priority concern at the design and construction stage.
2. If at all possible, units above the ground floor and all internal corridors, should be carpeted.
3. Families with children should be housed on or close to the ground so that they have easy and immediate access to outdoor play areas and do not create problems by making noise playing in the apartment, the corridors, etc.
4. Where families with children must be housed on higher floors, ensure that they are all together on one floor or floors since parents will be more tolerant of other children's noise and less restrictive of their own children (Stevenson et al. 1967; Stewart 1970; Department of the Environment 1972; Adams and Conway 1974).
5. Plan units so that quiet areas (bedrooms) in one unit are adjacent to those in the next unit; problems arise when bedrooms are located above, below or next to the living room of an adjacent unit.
6. A communal workshop should be provided for using power tools.
7. A teen center should be provided where loud music and parties will not disturb residents.

BEHAVIOR–ENGAGING IN OUTDOOR RECREATION REQUIRING PRIVACY

Need

There is a need, particularly among adults in areas of the country with warm to hot weather during some or all of the year, for a private area adjacent to the home which can be used for outdoor eating, drinking, entertaining friends, sunbathing, meditating, etc.

Single family house

Backyards, patios, decks, etc., in a single family house typically provide an area for the above activities. They can be made as private as needed by the addition of fencing, planting, etc.

High-rise

Eating, sunbathing, drinking, and entertaining friends can be accommodated to a limited extent on a high-rise balcony, providing it is large enough, oriented to the sun, and partially recessed or with semisolid side walls for privacy from adjacent units. Barbecuing can be accommodated just as well on a balcony as in a yard or patio (as long as there are not management rules against it), but it is generally difficult to seat more than the family at an outdoor meal.

Suggestions

1. Provide each unit with an adequately sized individual, private balcony adjacent to the living and/or dining areas, conveniently accessible from the kitchen.

Recessed balconies are generally cheaper to build and provide more privacy than cantilevered balconies.

2. Where balconies are cantilevered and located fairly close to each other, consider providing storage cabinets as privacy and sound screens between them.

3. Orient the balcony so it gets sun during part of the day so residents can sunbathe there if they wish.

4. Provide a private room with kitchen facilities and some adjacent outdoor space, which residents can rent in order to entertain large groups of friends. When the occasional but very important gatherings take place—such as birthday parties, weddings, anniversaries, etc.—the apartment dweller may be hard-pressed for space to do this in the home.

BEHAVIOR—PERFORMING UTILITARIAN CHORES AND HOBBIES REQUIRING SPACE OUTSIDE THE DWELLING

Need

There are many leisure-time and/or money-saving activities which people like to do outdoors, close to the home—such as gardening, fixing or painting furniture, fixing or cleaning cars, bicycles or motorcycles, doing small carpentry jobs, etc. These not only bring pleasure to the person doing them, but some (such as gardening, furniture maintenance, carpentry, etc.) may add immeasurably to a resident's sense of "fit" with his or her environment.

Single family house

There is generally space for such activities in a yard, patio, garage, or driveway, and there is generally no limitation on what can be done beyond the normal ones of respect for one's neighbors, and municipal codes. There is generally sufficient storage space that tools or equipment associated with these activities can also be safely housed (e.g., in garage, basement, garden shed, back porch, etc.).

High-rise

Several sets of limitations preclude these activities in high-rises (Demers and Aldhouse 1966; Stevenson et al. 1967; Rothblatt 1971; Adams and Conway 1974). (1) Lack of ground-level private open space precludes gardening—though growing plants in pots or planters can certainly take place on a balcony. (2) Proximity to neighbors may inhibit one from activities involving noise (e.g., sawing, hammering, using power tools). (3) Lack of storage space may inhibit the acquisition of tools or equipment. (4) Lack of any flexible interior space generally precludes the setting up of a hobby or workroom where messy projects can be undertaken, left half-done until another day, etc. (5) Separation of the dwelling from the parked car may make it more difficult to spend time working on the car—for example, the person working may like to do so within sight or sound of the family, may want to be close to the phone, may also be watching their children, etc. Proximity to the dwelling also means easy access to water and detergent, a vacuum cleaner, tools, etc.

Suggestions

1. On balconies, provide built-in planter boxes, or shelves for plant pots, or hooks for hanging baskets. Provide a seat with a built-in storage area beneath for such things as bags of potting mixture, fertilizer, empty flower pots, etc. (Willis 1957).

2. Provide balconies only on west, east or south facing facades since balconies will be virtually unused on the north side (Thiberg and Misra 1966).

3. Provide a balcony large enough (minimum of 10′ × 5′) so that small repair jobs or painting can be done there and laundry can be dried.

4. Provide a shared communal workshop where power tools can be used without disturbing neighbors, where dirty jobs can be done, and where neighbors might meet over these tasks (Becker 1974; Rothblatt 1971; Byrom 1970).

5. Provide a space at grade for vegetable gardens

that residents can use if they wish. One study of a New York family high-rise without balconies found almost three-fourths of the residents desiring a place to garden (Becker 1974). If residents are elderly, plots 6′ X 8′ are probably all that are needed, and they should preferably be in raised planters (Cook 1972).

6. Provide a communal area on site for cleaning and maintaining vehicles. Ideally this would include hoses for washing, locked storage areas for tools, and maintenance pits for repairs. These spaces become especially important where residents cannot afford the expense of commercial car washes or tune-ups. There should be a seating area close by so others can watch or "kibbitz," and there should perhaps be some kind of intercom system between this facility and the apartments.

BEHAVIOR—USING THE WINDOWS

Need

The windows of a dwelling fulfill a number of needs, the most obvious being to let sufficient daylight into interior rooms; other, less obvious needs are to allow those inside views in different directions and to allow people, if they wish, to personalize their dwelling by use of drapes, display of objects on the window sill, etc.

Single family house

A house generally provides views in all four directions; the street orientation is generally toward activity and the back view towards green and private areas. In addition, there are side views which may take in the driveway and activity there, or other, private secluded views similar to the back. Near views can be enhanced by the owner through changing the landscaping, erecting fences to increase privacy, adding flowers and plants, etc. Distant views—obtainable if the house is located on a hill or sloping site—are especially sought after, as evidenced by the increasing house prices and rents experienced in any urban area that extends from flatland to hillsides.

Since the single family house is generally no more than two floors in height, residents can easily use its windows for adding personal touches to the overall exterior decor through choice of window curtains, shades, shutters, etc., and by use of window sills to display ornaments, trophies, toys, plants—all of which are displayed (albeit perhaps unconsciously) to say to the passerby, someone *in particular* lives here. In addition, windows are often used to display notices, discernible to passersby, which convey a direct message about the residents' community or political views—"Vote for Dimaggio," "Block Parent," "Boycott Grapes," "Neighborhood meeting to discuss. . . ."

High-rise

Having a distant view is one of the positive attributes of living in a high-rise which virtually all high-rise dwellers agree upon, regardless of income or stage in the life cycle (Adams and Conway 1974; Department of the Environment 1972; Ministry of Housing 1970; Becker 1974; Thiberg and Misra 1966). Generally, there is a view in one direction only; therefore orientation of the building to provide good views to as many residents as possible is very important. Providing each unit with a usable balcony is especially important in that it provides a locale for the creation of a near-view of the residents' own creation (flower boxes, planters, ornaments, etc.) and increases the apparent size of the room adjacent to it. High-rise dwellers, except those on the lower two or three floors, cannot, however, use their windows to add personal touches to their dwelling, since they would not be visible from outside, nor would they display political posters, notices, etc. Many high-rise buildings provide carpets and drapes, which are all of a standard color so as to not—in the architect's eye—distract from the exterior aesthetics. An alternative aesthetic value is that observed in buildings administered by the Greater London Council, where householders can hang any curtains they wish and the kaleidoscopic exterior effect adds immeasurably to the standard concrete-and-glass facade.

Suggestions

1. Having a view from their dwelling unit is related to residents' overall satisfaction with their living environment (Department of the Environment 1972). In orienting the building, give serious consideration to what the residents will be looking at, especially from the living room. There is evidence that the view *out*—for many nondesigners—is far more significant than the facade appearance of their own building (Ministry of Housing 1970).

2. Make sure that the balcony design does not obstruct the view outside for persons *seated* in the dwelling (Adams and Conway 1974).

3. If the above is unavoidable, try to provide an additional low window in the living room so that an elderly or isolated person who receives much consolation from a view of outside activity can be seated and still see out. Perhaps this particular window should be unopenable to avoid the fear of those with children that they would learn to open it and fall out.

BEHAVIOR—DOING THE LAUNDRY

Need

Residents need to be able to do their laundry in or very close to the home.

Single family house

Most houses have space in them for a washer and dryer; doing the laundry is easily facilitated in that it must be carried up and down only one set of stairs and can be done at the same time as other household activities. If the family has no washer and dryer, laundry has to be done in a laundromat, which may entail more difficulty with coming and going, childcare, etc. For families with a lot of laundry, however, going to a laundromat may be more convenient, in that a number of machines can be used simultaneously, thus minimizing the overall time taken to do the laundry.

High-rise

Generally a laundry is provided, convenient to the unit, and is shared by all residents on each floor or on several floors. In several studies of high-rises, the convenience of doing washing close to the unit has been cited as among the chief *assets* of high-rise apartment living. Many smaller or older apartment buildings do not provide communal machines. Generally, residents appreciate having laundry facilities on each floor, and prefer to use the dryer rather than a communal drying yard (especially in the United States) for drying laundry. A balcony provides sufficient space for the drying of smaller articles (Becker 1974).

Suggestions

1. Provide laundry facilities on each floor, or at least on every second floor. According to one study, moderate levels of satisfaction will be achieved when one machine is provided for every fifteen people; for very high levels of satisfaction, less than ten persons should share each machine (Becker 1974).

2. Laundries should be open during a wide range of hours (say, 8:00 A.M. to 10 P.M.) so that working people can do their washing early or late in the day.

3. Machines should be serviced by a company that is very close by so that repairs and maintenance can be effected expeditiously (Becker 1974).

4. Residents care a good deal about the attractiveness, maintenance and security of a communal laundry

and are likely to complain if these are below the standards of nearby commercial laundromats, especially if they are paying as much if not more than at these laundries (Becker 1974).

5. Management should not set rules against the drying of small clothes on balconies; if necessary, they might restrict the display of washing to below the level of the balcony rail, in case other residents are bothered by this.

BEHAVIOR–TAKING OUT THE GARBAGE

Need

Residents need to store and dispose of trash and garbage in a safe, sanitary, and convenient way.

Single family house

Residents usually have sufficiently large storage areas for garbage inside the kitchen for immediate disposal and an area close by outside for storing garbage cans before collection. Garbage disposal units in the sink help to decrease the amount of waste requiring disposal in many modern homes. If added protection outside is required to keep dogs, racoons, etc., from getting into garbage prior to collection, residents can build fences with gates around the can storage area and alter the storage area to suit his needs. With growing interest in home food growing and composting, wet garbage may increasingly be used in the vegetable garden, thus reducing garbage storage needs.

High-rise

To some degree, garbage disposal in these units is similar to that in a single family home in that: (a) the sink is usually equipped with a disposal unit, and (b) there is sufficient room in the kitchen for immediate garbage storage.

Disposal of garbage outside the unit is obviously different—each family's garbage is disposed into a common disposal facility shared with other families, i.e., chute, garbage shed, etc. The opening is generally small, therefore not accommodating just any size of garbage. Disposal of large-sized parcels and trash can be very inconvenient (Adams and Conway 1974; Department of the Environment 1972). Many times the chute is placed adjacent to a dwelling unit, causing noise disturbance which is especially bothersome if the chute is used at night (Becker 1974; National Council of Women in Britain 1970; Adams and Conway 1974). Residents complain that children often have difficulty using garbage chutes and can get their fingers caught in the opening. Many parents feel they are unsafe for children to use, as they may play with them or crawl in (Becker 1974; Adams and Conway 1974). If they are poorly designed, with too many jogs, garbage can get caught or lodged in them and inconvenience a great many residents and the building manager (Becker 1974; Adams and Conway 1974; National Council of Women in Britain 1970). A chute opening which is poorly sealed can be a problem in that flies and odors from it can be a bother to those living nearby, especially if it is not enclosed in a separate room. The greater the number of families sharing such a facility, the less anyone will feel responsible for its upkeep and cleanliness (Becker 1974; Adams and Conway 1974; National Council of Women in Britain 1970).

Suggestions

1. Provide adequate space in the kitchen for the temporary storage of garbage, preferably below the sink.

2. Provide each sink with a garbage-disposal unit which can be easily maintained or repaired by maintenance personnel or by a servicing company located

close to the development. Clear instructions on its use should be included in a tenants' manual.

3. Provide a garbage disposal chute opening on each floor, conveniently located to all units on the floor. Minimize the number of units sharing the chute to decrease problems of maintenance (Department of the Environment 1972).

4. Insure that the chute is large enough for the disposal of large shopping bags full of garbage as well as medium-sized boxes. Provide a convenient means of disposing of larger items safety elsewhere (Department of the Environment 1972).

5. Locate the chute in a separate room off the access way to minimize problems of odors and flies in the access area (Department of the Environment 1972). Provide a tight seal on the chute opening.

6. Soundproof the chute from adjacent units so that noise of garbage dropping in it is not a problem (Becker 1974).

7. Design openings safe for children's use, so they do not get their fingers caught and so they cannot accidentally fall in or crawl in. Parents frequently ask their children to take out the garbage, so disposal areas should be designed with them in mind (Becker 1974).

8. Sharp angles should be avoided in chute design to minimize problems with clogging (Becker 1974).

BEHAVIOR–STORING BULKY POSSESSIONS IN OR NEAR THE DWELLING

Need

Householders need to store bulky items such as sports equipment, luggage, unused furniture, tools, etc., in places where they are available but not where they will get in the way of day-to-day storage activities.

Single family house

Most detached houses have some kind of discretionary storage space such as a garage, garden shed, attic, basement, back porch, etc., which is under the control of the householder and easy to get at.

High-rise

Storage is one of the most frequently mentioned problems in multifamily housing, both in terms of overall quantity and the ability to store certain large items (Committee on Housing Research and Development 1972; Norcross 1973; Adams and Conway 1974; National Council of Women in Britain 1970). Sometimes the actual square footage provided may meet some kind of minimum standard, but it is broken up into pieces too small for storing large pieces of equipment. Since some of these–such as bicycles, large toys, sports equipment–are only needed outside, there is the added chore of carrying them up to the apartment.

Suggestions

1. There should be a walk-in storage room within the dwelling; it need not be expensively finished and can be an interior room. A rod for hanging clothes not currently in use is especially important in regions with large seasonal changes in temperature.

2. A bulk-storage locker for infrequently used items (luggage, extra furniture, out-of-season sports equipment, etc.) should be provided for each dwelling in the basement of the building. The storage area, as well as each locker or storage-cage, should be securely locked (National Council of Women in Britain 1970; Becker 1974; Adams and Conway 1974).

3. There should be a lockable storage area adjacent to each designated parking space so auto and picnic equipment need not be carried upstairs.

4. A locked storage room under the supervision of the manager, near the lobby, might optionally be used by residents for leaving baby-buggies, shopping carts, bicycles, children's wagons, etc., which a single family house dweller would normally leave on the porch, in the garage, or in the backyard.

REFERENCES

Adams, Barbara, and Jean Conway. "The Social Effects of Living Off the Ground." IABSE (British Group) Tall Buildings and People, St. Catherine's College, Oxford, September 1974, pp. 150–157. Session 6.

Becker, Franklin D., and Lawrence P. Friedburg. *Design for Living: The Residents' View of Multifamily Housing.* Center for Urban Development Research, Cornell University, Ithaca, New York, May 1974.

Berry, F. J. "Living High." *Housing and Planning Review,* January-February 1967.

Bor, Walter. "High Buildings: A Blessing or a Curse?" *Architectural Design,* September 1974.

Bor, W. G., and J. B. Cullingworth. "Residential Development Densities." *Town Planning Institute* 47 (January 1967).

Bussard, Ellen. "Children's Spatial Behavior in and around a Moderate Density Housing Development: An Exploratory Study of Patterns and Influences." M.Sc. thesis, Cornell University, Ithaca, New York 1974.

Byrom, Connie. "How High?" *Town and Country Planning,* September 1970.

Byrom, John. "Shared Open Space in Scottish Private Enterprise Housing." Edinburgh: Architectural Research Unit, University of Edinburgh, 1972.

Cappon, D. "Mental Health in the Hi-Rise." *Ekistics* 196 (March 1972).

Carpenter, E. K. "Space Scale and Sickness: The Effects of Human Crowding." *Progressive Architecture* 47 (December 1966).

Committee on Housing Research and Development. *Families in Public Housing: An Evaluation of Three Residential Environments in Rockford, Illinois.* Champaign-Urbana, Ill.: University of Illinois, 1972.

Cook, Barbara. *Survey Evaluation of Low-Cost, Low-Rent Public Housing for the Elderly, Pleasanton, California.* (Mimeo.) Berkeley, California: Sanford Hirshen & Partners, Architects, 1972.

Cooper, Clare C. "Interview-Survey Data on Resident-Attitudes at Geneva Towers." (Mimeo.) 1969.

Cooper, Clare C. "Adventure Playgrounds." *Landscape Architecture,* October 1970.

Cooper, Clare C., and Stephen Marcus. "Observations at Three San Francisco Redevelopment Agency Housing Developments." (Mimeo.) San Francisco: San Francisco Redevelopment Agency, June 1971.

Cooper, Clare C. "The House as Symbol of Self." In *Design for Human Behavior,* edited by J. Lang et al. Stroudsburg, Pa.: Dowden, Hutchinson & Ross, 1976.

Cooper, Clare C. "St. Francis Square: Attitudes of Its Residents." *American Institute of Architects' Journal,* December 1971.

Cooper Marcus, Clare C. "Children's Play Behavior in a Low-Rise, Inner-City Housing Development." *Proceedings of the Fifth Annual Conference of Environmental Design Research Association.* Stroudsburg, Pa.: Dowden, Hutchinson & Ross, 1974.

Darke, Roy, and Jane Darke. "Sheffield Revisited." *Built Environment,* November 1972.

Davies, E. P. "The Problems of Multi-Storey Housing Development." *Housing* 5, 5 (January 1970).

Day, Noel, et al. "San Francisco Public Housing—Research and Development Modernization Project: Phase 1: Tentative Modernization Plan and Research Plan for Phase 2. Report to H.U.D." (Mimeo.) San Francisco, 1971.

Demers and Aldhouse. "Park Hill: Occupier Reaction Study." *Official Architecture and Planning* 29 (February 1966).

Department of the Environment. *The Estate Outside the Dwelling: Reactions of Residents to Aspects of Housing Layout.* London: H.M.S.O., 1972.

Ertel, Michael. "Programming and Evaluating Teenage Hanging Places." Environmental Design Research Association. *Proceedings of Fifth Annual Conference,* Milwaukee, 1974.

Fanning, P. M. "Families in Flats." *British Medical Journal* 18 (1967).

Friedberg, M. L. "Comparative Perceptions of Residential Environment and Home Image." Master's thesis, Cornell University, Ithaca, New York, 1974.

Frommes, Bob. "Living in Flats." *Housing and Planning Review,* July-August 1969.

Gëhl, Ingrid. *Living Environment.* (English Summary.) Copenhagen: Statens Byggesorsknings Institut. Report #71, 1971.

Grégoire, Ménie. "The Child in the High-Rise." *Ekistics* 186 (May 1971).

Hogue, Lindsay, "New Recommendations for the Design of Low and Moderate Income Low-Rise Housing Based on a

Comparative Analysis of Housing Regulations and Consumer Preferences." Master's thesis, Cornell University, Ithaca, New York, 1974.

Hole and Miller. "Children's Play on Housing Estates: A Summary of Two BRS Studies (Building Research Station Current Papers Design Series 46)." *Architects' Journal,* June 1966.

Homenuck, Peter. *A Study of High Rise: Effect, Preferences and Perceptions.* Toronto: Institute of Environmental Research, Inc., December 1973.

Jensen, Rolf. *High Density Living.* New York: Praeger.

Jephcott, Pearl. "Social Factors in Housing Design." *Housing Review* 18, 1 (January-February 1969).

Jephcott, Pearl. *Homes in High Flats.* Edinburgh: Oliver & Boyd, 1971.

Kubas, James J. *A Report on Research into Patterns of Recreation and Leisure in the Borough of North York.* North York, Ontario, Canada: Department of Planning and Development, Borough of North York, 1971.

Lansing, J. B., and R. W. Marans. "Evaluation of Neighborhood Quality." *Journal of the American Institute of Planners,* May 1967.

Maizels, J. *Two to Five in High Flats.* London: The Housing Center, 1961.

Martini, Sten. *New Suburban Housing.* (English Summary.) Copenhagen: Socialforsknings-instituttets Publication No. 61, 1974.

McCall, Colin. "Nae Use for the Bairns." *Architect,* January 1972.

Michelson, William. "Residential Mobility as a Deficit Compensating Process." Paper presented to Canadian Sociology and Anthropology Association, Kingston, Ontario, May 29, 1973.

Michelson, William. *Environmental Change: An Interim Report on Results From the Project "The Physical Environment as Attraction and Determinant: Social Effects in Housing."* Toronto: Department of Sociology and Centre for Urban Community Studies, University of Toronto, October 1973, Research Paper #60.

Michelson, William, and Kevin Garland. *The Differential Role of Crowded Homes and Dense Residential Areas in the Incidence of Selected Symptoms of Human Pathology.* Toronto: Center for Urban and Community Studies: University of Toronto, December 1974, Research Paper #67.

Ministry of Housing. *Families Living at High Density: A Study of Estates in Liverpool, Leeds and London.* London: H.M.S.O., 1970.

Ministry of Housing and Local Government. *Homes for Today and Tomorrow.* London: H.M.S.O., 1961.

Morville, Jeanne. *Children's Play on Flatted Estates.* (English Summary.) Copenhagen: Statens Byggesorsknings Institut, Report #10, 1969.

National Council of Women in Britain. "Guidelines for Happier Living in High Blocks." *Housing* 6, 3 (September 1970).

Newman, Oscar. *Defensible Space.* New York: Macmillan, 1972.

Norcross, Carl. *Townhouses and Condominiums: Residents' Likes and Dislikes.* Washington, D.C.: Urban Land Institute, 1973.

Perin, Constance. "Social Governance and Environmental Design." In *Responding to Social Change,* edited by B. Honikman. Stroudsburg, Pa.: Dowden, Hutchinson & Ross, 1974.

Raven, John. "Sociological Evidence on Housing 1. Space in the Home." *The Architectural Review* 142, 1 (July 1969).

Raven, John. "Sociological Evidence on Housing 2. The Home Environment." *The Architectural Review* 142, 1 (September 1969).

Reynolds, Ingrid and Charles Nicholson. "Living Off the Ground." *The Architects' Journal* 150, 34 (August 20, 1969).

RIBA. "Family Life in High Density Housing." (Summary of RIBA Symposium.) *The Architects' Journal* 125 (May 30, 1967).

Rothblatt, Donald N. "Housing and Human Needs." *Town Planning Review* 42, 2 (April 1971).

Schmitt. *Multistorey Housing.* New York: Frederick A. Praeger, 1966.

Shankland, Cox and Associates, "Front and Back: Problem of the Threshhold." *The Architects' Journal* 22 (November 1967).

Sheppard, D. *Access Arrangements in High Blocks of Flats.* Survey by Building Research Station, Department of Scientific and Industrial Research, December 1962.

Sillitoe, Helen Ruth. "Living in Flats: A Study of Some Aspects of Living Conditions in Flats in West Germany." *Housing* 5, 3 (September 1969).

Stevenson, A., E. Martin, and J. O'Neill. *High Living: A Study of Family Life in Flats.* Melbourne: University Press, 1967.

Stewart, W. F. R. *Children in Flats: A Family Study.* London: National Society for the Prevention of Cruelty to Children, 1970.

Thiberg and Misra. *Orientation and Floor Level: A Study of Preferences of Dwellers in Point-Blocks.* National Swedish Institute for Building Research. Report #35, 1966.

Van der Eyken. *The Preschool Years.* London: Penguin Books, 1967.

Weterle, Gerda, and Edward Hall. "High Rise Living: Can the Same Design Serve Young and Old?" *Ekistics* 196 (March 1972).

Wharton, Kate. "Sad Storeys for Children." *The Architect and Building News* 7, 3 (October 1, 1970).

Willis, Margaret. "Private Balconies in Flats and Maisonettes." *Architects' Journal* 125 (March 7, 1957).

Willson, Norman. "High-rise Is Inevitable." *The Architect and Building News* 1, 7 (December 4, 1968).

Wood, E. "Housing Design: A Social Theory." *Ekistics* 12 (December 1961).

Wright, Gwendolyn. "A Woman's Place is in the Home: Women and American Domestic Architecture from 1965 to the Present." M.Arch. thesis, University of California, 1974.

Yancey, William L. "Architecture, Interaction, and Social Control: The Case of a Large-Scale Public Housing Project." *Environment and Behavior* 3, 1 (March 1971).

Zeisel, John, and Mary Griffin. "Feedback Childview: A Diagnostic Evaluation of Childview Housing, Allston, Massachusetts." (Mimeo.) Cambridge, Mass., 1973.

Part IV

The Response to Emergency

21

Movement of People in Building Evacuations

J. L. Pauls
National Research Council of Canada

INTRODUCTION AND OBJECTIVES

Facilities for the movement of people are a major concern in building and fire codes, particularly in situations where rapid egress is required for occupant safety in emergencies. Fire is usually considered the most probable reason for rapid evacuation of all or part of a building; however, other emergency conditions, such as bomb threats, tornadoes, or loss of electric power might lead to evacuation in certain types of buildings.

The problem of fire in high-rise buildings has received much attention recently in the popular and technical literature, including building and fire codes [1-9]. Although difficulties in evacuation in high-rise fires are frequently mentioned (along with problems of smoke movement and fire department access), little original research has been done on this subject [10-15]. The limited recorded rationale for present-day exit requirements in codes is often based on a few, very limited and dated studies of movement in buildings[16-22].

The literature on evacuation is largely based on studies of the movement of people in contexts not perceived as genuine fire emergencies. Information, especially quantitative information, about how people move in buildings during actual fires is difficult to obtain. A few researchers have examined in detail the behavior of persons in fires; a much larger research effort, however, has been on their behavior in large-scale emergency situations, e.g., natural disasters [23-27]. (A paper in press reviews these areas in slightly more detail[28].) Such studies indicate that, contrary to popular belief, panic is relatively rare in these situations; in general, people cope remarkably well not only with fire emergencies but also with a wide variety of disaster situations.

Research on behavior in a range of circumstances should assist greatly in the transition from findings about movement in nonemergency or drill situations

This chapter is a contribution of the Division of Building Research, National Research Council of Canada, and is published with the approval of the director of the division.

to hypotheses about evacuation in cases of actual fire in buildings. It should be noted that communication systems, increasingly being provided in high-rise buildings for use in fire emergencies, have a considerable influence on how people perceive an emergency or a drill situation. This is one of the factors that may influence people to construe a drill situation as an actual emergency or conversely an actual emergency as a drill[14]. Therefore it seems reasonable to assume that the findings reported below, although based on observations of drills and normal egress, are generally applicable to many evacuation situations.

These introductory comments indicate not only the need for more detailed information about occupant movement in high-rise building fires but also the potential validity of developing such information in nonfire situations, such as drills. Studies of crowd egress in high-rise office buildings and in buildings with public assembly occupancies have been conducted during the last six years in Canada. The objective of these studies of movement of people was to develop largely empirical information which would contribute to improved design and operation of buildings, both through direct communication with designers and others in practice and through the medium of building codes[14,29].

STUDY METHODS

In 1969 the author was invited to take part in observations of a test evacuation of Vancouver's twenty-two story B. C. Hydro office building. Working with a team of seventeen observers, an attempt was made to record key events and conditions during the phased evacuation of about 1,000 people (with a fire floor and lower floors cleared first). The report[12] based on these observations describes the building and its occupancy; evacuation planning, organization, and procedure; key events during the drill (shown on a time scale); the speeds, flows, and densities of people on the exit stairs; environmental conditions in the stairs; and some findings of a questionnaire given to evacuation-control personnel in the building.

As a result of this study the author was invited by Canada's Dominion Fire Commissioner to conduct observations of a variety of evacuation exercises usually held in buildings occupied by the federal government in Ottawa. Between 1970 and 1974 some forty test evacuations were observed in office buildings ranging between eight and twenty-nine stories in height.

The majority of these evacuations were total evacuations (in which all occupants attempt to leave the building more or less simultaneously by way of exit stairs). The chief goal in observations of such total evacuations was the collection of data describing crowd movement down exit stairs.

Other observed evacuations in the larger buildings used more selective procedures in which particular floors of buildings were cleared in a predetermined sequence (floors in the assumed fire areas, then the top floors, and then perhaps the other floors in descending order). In addition to documenting crowd movement down stairs, observations were made of the use of communication systems and the supervision of evacuation by fire wardens.

Observation techniques included equipping between two and fifteen observers with portable cassette recorders operating continuously to register all observations and background sounds. These observations, plus tape recordings of communication systems used in the evacuations, supplemented by visual records provided by slide photography and video tape recording, could all be played back in the correct time scale. For example, the time at which each photograph was taken was readily recorded by attaching a cassette recorder microphone directly to each camera so that the shutter operation, the camera operator's comments, and the background soundtrack were recorded automatically.

Using these techniques, each evacuation drill could be rerun for detailed analysis. Such a large amount of raw data was produced in some drill observations that the processing is not yet complete. A good example of how extensive such observations could be occurred in a twenty-one-story office building from which over 2,000 people were evacuated without prior warning according to a phased procedure requiring nearly thirty minutes to complete. Nearly twenty channels of audio recording were made at both fixed and moving observation positions. As in other drills, observers moving with the evacuees from floor areas to the building exterior were able to record information about many behavioral variables, often without attracting the attention of people only a few feet away.

Questionnaires were distributed to about 10 percent of the population of two buildings immediately following evacuation drills. Results revealed that some evacuees interpreted these surprise evacuation drills as genuine emergencies. Other results described the evacuees' normal use of exit stairs, their capability with stairs, their perceived speeds and densities during the evacuation, etc. The questionnaire included nearly forty items, many of which provided insights not otherwise quickly obtainable.

Aside from the challenges of recording human behavior under field conditions, it is difficult to manipulate and display data so as to provide useful information about the complex phenomena being studied. These difficulties are made more acute by the almost total lack of precedents for movement studies, either in high-rise office buildings or in public-assembly buildings. For this reason, charts such as shown in Figures 21-1 and 21-2 require more than a quick glance to appreciate their meaning and potential usefulness. (Similar charts have been used by Predtetschenski and Milinski[20].)

Figures 21-1 and 21-2 show, in graphical form, two basic procedures that can be used to evacuate some or all occupants from a high-rise building in case of fire. In both charts the vertical scale is a spatial dimension, effectively the egress path provided by the exit stairs serving each story of a building. The horizontal scale is time, measured from the initiation of a fire alarm which begins the evacuation. Each line on the chart is a movement trace indicating where a particular evacuee is in the exit stair at a particular time. Such traces usually record the observers' movement down the stairs with evacuees. The slopes of the lines indicate speeds of movement.

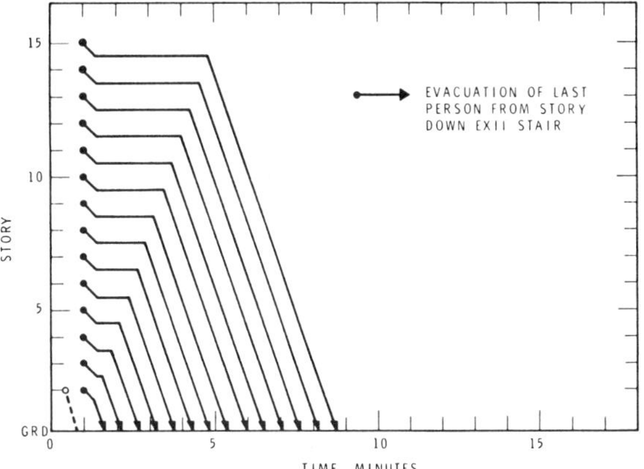

Figure 21-1
Total evacuation of fifteen-story office building.

Figure 21-1 displays movement traces characteristic of total evacuations, the conventional procedure where all building occupants attempt to leave the building at the same time. Illustrated is the total evacuation of a fifteen-story office building with with two 44-in. (1.12 m) wide exit stairs. Each story is assumed to contain seventy persons at the time the evacuation begins. Applying somewhat optimistic but still realistic evacuation-initiation and flow asssump-

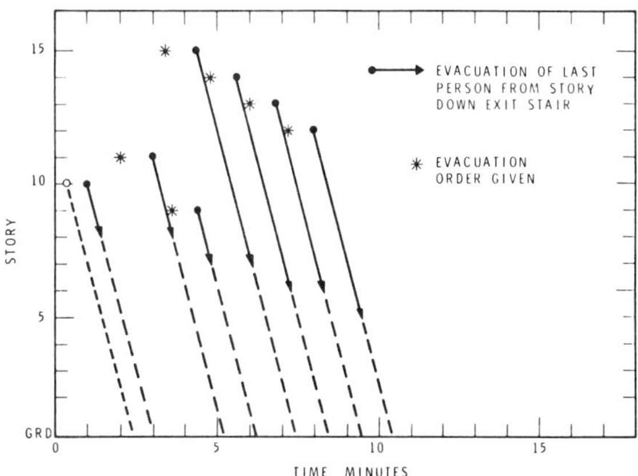

Figure 21-2
Phased, partial evacuation of fifteen-story office building.

tions, it can be predicted that such a building will be cleared of all people, by means of the stairs, in just under nine minutes.

Figure 21-2 shows movement traces characteristic of phased, partial evacuations in which both the need to evacuate particular floors and the priority of such evacuations are determined by trained staff in the building or by fire department personnel. Communication systems are used to help make decisions and give directions regarding such an evacuation. In Figure 21-2 the fifteen-story building is assumed to have a fire on the tenth story. Only the top half of the building is evacuated and people from the upper floors may be directed to seek refuge on certain lower floors or they may be moved to the building exterior at ground level. In any event, because of the time required to control an evacuation using a phased procedure, nearly nine minutes are required merely to move half the building population to below the fire area.

Charts such as shown in Figures 21-1 and 21-2 can be used to illustrate a variety of procedures as well as particular events (e.g., movement up stairs by fire department personnel, and smoke contamination of portions of exits). Graphical simulations using such formats are also very useful. Rather than describing this in detail, a report will be given of some study findings that must be understood to give such charts proper dimensions and make reasonable quantitative predictions about crowd movement on stairs.

FINDINGS PERTAINING TO TOTAL EVACUATIONS

Observations of thirty total evacuation drills dealt almost entirely with movement of crowds down exit stairs. The observations were made in office buldings ranging between eight and twenty stories in height with evacuation populations ranging between 130 and 1,500 persons. Elevators and voice communication systems were not used in these evacuations. Important variables and factors such as density, personal space, crowd configuration, speed, flow, and evacuation time are described below with a brief report of preliminary findings.

Density and personal space

Density, or number of persons occupying a certain space, is influenced not only by the number of persons who must use the stairs during an evacuation but also by individual psychological desire for space and interpersonal separation. In the total evacuation drills most evacuees chose to occupy a space requiring an average of about two stair treads of a typical 44-in. (1.12-m) wide exit stair (Figure 21-3). In terms of density, the inverse of unit area, the average density in total evacuations was about 0.14 persons per square foot (1.5 persons per square meter). Further discussion of density and movement, not necessarily in evacuation situations, is given by Fruin in his book on pedestrian planning[21]).

The space that evacuees regard as acceptable while they are in the exit depends on many factors including speed of movement, type of clothing worn, relationship to people sharing the exit space, and individual emotional state. The limited information about the space a person tries to maintain around himself suggests that in situations perceived as real emergencies a larger personal space is desired[30]. This could lead to lower densities in exits or, alternatively, if more space were not available, to increased discomfort, perhaps even extreme anxiety regarding personal safety.

Crowd configurations

Evacuees did not walk in a highly regimented fashion, shoulder to shoulder, or even in regular staggered files. Side-to-side body sway, individual concern for interpersonal separation, varying needs for handrail support, and concern about not rubbing against sometimes rough walls, all influence the configuration of evacuees on exit stairs. Thus the traditional assump-

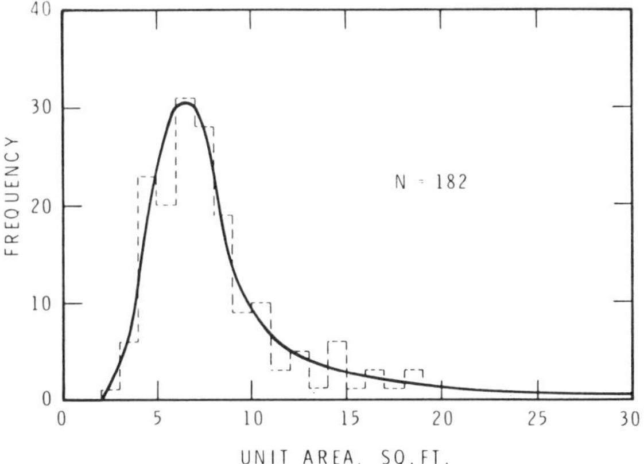

Figure 21-3
Frequency distribution of unit area (stairway area per person) in seventeen stairways during evacuations of high office buildings.

tion about units of exit width or regular lanes of egress movement[16,22] is to be questioned. Further discussion of the questionable validity of the traditional unit of exit width concept is given below in discussing flow rates.

Speed of descent

Speeds of descent on exit stairs varied according to density (Figure 21-4). Widely separated individuals could move at speeds up to about eight stories per minute. At the apparently comfortable density of about one evacuee on every two treads of a typical 44-in. (1.12-m) wide stair, the descent speed was about four stories per minute, the equivalent of about 100 ft. per minute (30 m per minute) along the slope of the stairs. With three evacuees on every two treads, the descent speed approached zero.

Flow

Flow on stairs, or number of people per minute passing a fixed point, also depends on density. Figure

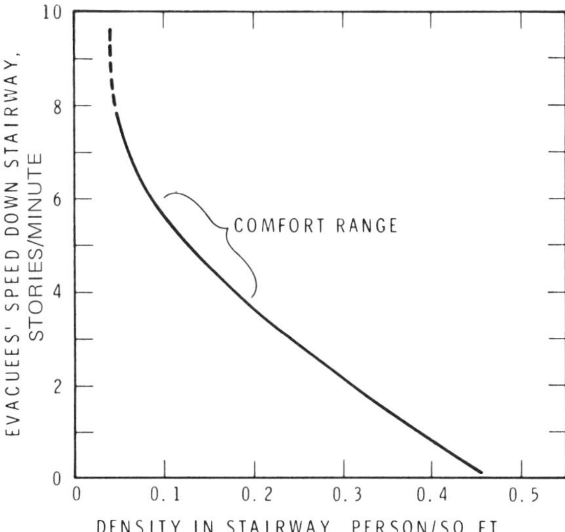

Figure 21-4
Effect of density on speed down exit stairways in evacuations of high office buildings.

21-5 shows this relation, calculated using the equation for flow as the product of density, speed, and stair width.

Several things should be noted in Figure 21-5. First, the mean flow is stated in terms of 22 in. (0.56 m) of stairway width simply to make the graph more easily understood by designers and officials who normally work with this unit of exit width concept. Second, the mean flows actually measured in total evacuation drills almost invariably fell below the curve plotted in this figure. Thus, this curve should be used only to make the most optimistic predictions of mean flows to be expected in total evacuations. It can be reported that, in general, the mean flows for all observed total evacuations averaged only twenty-four persons per minute per 22 in. (0.56 m) of stair width. During a total evacuation in mid-winter, when evacuees wore bulky clothing, mean flows were only about twenty persons per minute per 22 in. (0.56 m) of stair width. Third, the peak mean flow occurs when the density of evacuees on the exit stairs is

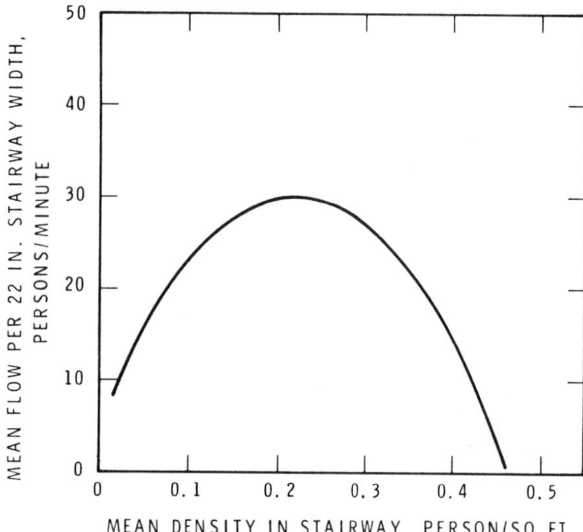

Figure 21-5
Effect of density on flow down exit stairways in evacuations of high office buildings.

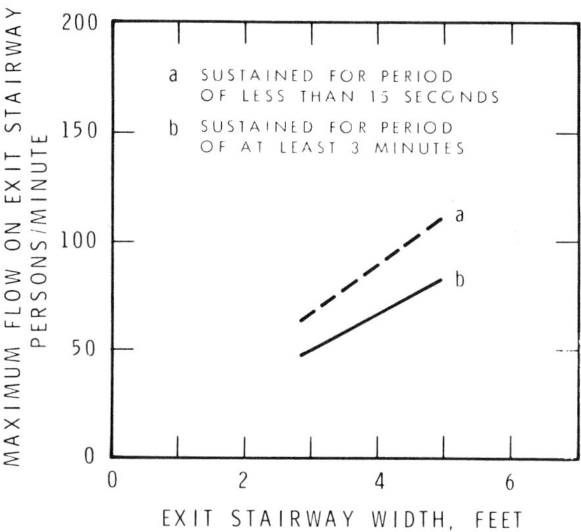

Figure 21-6
Effect of exit stairway width on flows in evacuations of high office buildings.

somewhat greater than the density that evacuees may regard as most acceptable in terms of comfort.

Possibly the most striking feature of such flows is that they are much lower than the conventionally assumed flow figure of forty-five persons per minute per 22 in. (0.56 m) of stair width. This figure is often assumed in exit design regulations[22]. An examination of highly influential reports such as that published in 1935[16] suggests that a figure of forty-five persons per minute is based on somewhat artificial test results that are not good indicators of what can be achieved by typical building occupants in a total evacuation. Tests performed by the author as well as other earlier tests reported in the literature[17] confirm that very high flows down stairs can be achieved only in very contrived situations involving specially motivated groups of individuals who temporarily disregard the normal need for personal space. Figure 21-6 shows that higher flows, even in total evacuations, are only sustained for very brief periods of time and should not be used in predicting mean flows in total evacuations.

Figure 21-6 also shows that, when other factors affecting flow are controlled, flows on stairs are proportional to stair width, at least in the range of stair widths observed. Counts of flows on stairs having widths of 36, 42, 44, 45, 47, 48, 56 and 60 in. (0.91 m to 1.52 m) suggest that the conventional unit of exit width concept, which recognizes only 22-in. and 12-in. (0.56-m and 0.31-m) increments in crediting exit width, is unreasonable. In other words, flow plotted against stair width is a ramp function rather than a step function, as assumed in building codes [22]. With increasing use of performance requirements and also with the impending conversion to metric, use of an exit-design formula based on a mean flow of about four to five persons per minute per 0.10 m (4 in.) of stair width appears more realistic and flexible than the traditional 22-in. (0.56-m) unit of exit width formula.

A minor constriction in the width of the egress path does not significantly reduce egress flow. For example, a crowd descending a stair 48 in. (1.22 m) wide can move through a 36-in. (0.91-m) doorway without reducing the flow below the fifty to sixty persons per minute sustained on the stair alone. Ob-

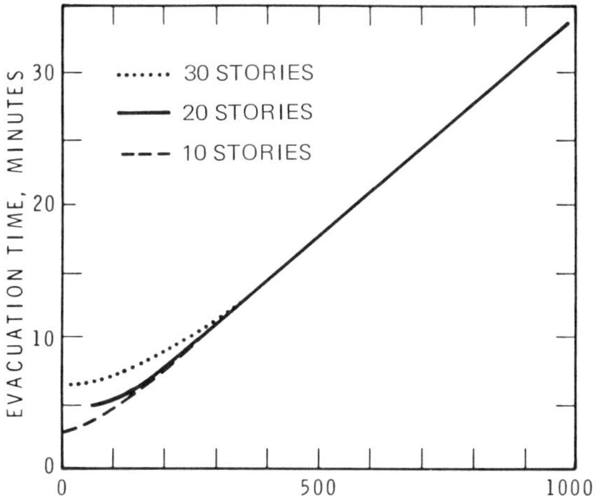

Figure 21-7
Predicted total evacuation times of tall office buildings using exit stairways.

servations also indicate that crowd flow is not greatly affected by minor constrictions caused by an occasional person stopping at one side on the stair nor by having a few fire fighters walk up the stairs against the descending flow of evacuees.

Evacuation time

Based on empirically derived density, speed, and flow relations and partially validated by observed total evacuation times, Figure 21-7 shows that the time required to complete the total evacuation of an office building is mainly dependent on actual building population and available stair width. Buildings with small populations will have reduced densities and flows in the exit stairs, and thus the graph is nonlinear at the left. At the extreme left side of Figure 21-7 the predicted evacuation time is the time taken by a single individual to react to an alarm and descend the stairs. Thus, for this condition, evacuation time is almost entirely determined by building height.

In predicting evacuation times in office buildings with a variety of occupancy conditions, one should be aware that some simplifying assumptions have been made in developing Figure 21-7. For example, it is assumed that evacuees take with them only the clothing normally worn at their work place. If clothing intended for protection from rain or moderately cool outdoor conditions is worn or carried, evacuation time will probably be increased by roughly 15 percent. If, for mid-winter cold weather conditions, evacuees prepare for more than a few minutes of outdoor exposure by putting on or carrying bulky outdoor clothing, the evacuation time will be increased by roughly 25 percent.

The information in Figure 21-7 is based on the following assumptions: (1) the evacuees are typical office workers with some previous experience of total evacuation drills in high-rise office buildings, (2) the evacuees will not be aware of the reason for evacuation, although most may believe that the alarm has not been activated by a serious emergency, (3) there is some trained supervision on each office floor, i.e., evacuation of confused or reluctant occupants will begin within a minute or two of the alarm's being sounded.

Even in situations where these assumptions are true, there will be a range of actual evacuation times. For the particular conditions described, perhaps 90 percent of the actual evacuation times will be within ± 20 percent of the times predicted. During those evacuation drills in office buildings in Ottawa, which were held under fair weather conditions (i.e., no special outdoor clothing requirements), the actual evacuation times for thirty-eight exit stairs were, overall, only about 3 percent longer than the time predicted in Figure 21-7. (Almost all these buildings had fewer than 200 evacuees per 22 in. of exit stair width.)

The total evacuation times predicted in Figure 21-7 are about 50 percent longer than the times suggested in previously published predictions[11]. Total evacuations in mid-winter could take twice the time suggested in previously published predictions.

Typical populations of general-purpose office buildings appear to be about half as great as is often assumed in building codes (i.e., one person for every 100 sq. ft. of gross rentable area). Thus, errors caused by previous optimistic predictions of evacuation flows and times may fortunately be offset by the use of very conservative population assumptions. Now that a better appreciation of evacuation flow is available, it is important that factors, in addition to population, be more carefully examined so that evacuation time predictions and other expectations will have greater validity. Such factors include normal stair use, evacuee experience with previous drills, the management aspects of high-rise evacuations, and evacuees' physical abilities (discussed below).

An improved ability to predict total evacuation times is somewhat academic unless the factors that affect the acceptability of the times are considered. For example, when a serious fire occurs, how much time is available before floor areas become smoke logged[1,5] and for what period of time can exit stairs be used by crowds of evacuees before smoke becomes psychologically or physiologically unacceptable [25,31]? Will the use of an exit stair for fire department access and firefighting operations rule out the use by evacuees of one or more exit stairs after five, ten, or fifteen minutes? Traditionally, seven to ten minutes has been considered acceptable as a workable total evacuation time, but this criterion, like many others, is now in need of reexamination. At some set of building and occupancy conditions (height, number of stories, construction, population, occupant characteristics, etc.) other approaches to coping with life safety in high-rise fires become more appropriate. Figures 21-1 and 21-2 give some indication of the limiting conditions that might be considered in choosing between the total evacuations already described and the selective, phased, partial evacuations now to be described.

FINDINGS PERTAINING TO SELECTIVE EVACUATIONS

In phased evacuations, exit stairs are generally reserved during initial stages of evacuation for people on the fire floor and adjacent floors (Figure 21-2). The ten-phased evacuation drills observed in high-rise buildings in Ottawa included sequential evacuation of occupants on some or all of the other floors, starting from the top. The upper floors could become untenable before most of the lower floors because of smoke movement due to stack effect during cold weather[1,5]. In buildings having zoned air-handling systems for groups of floors, th priority with which floors are to be evacuated could differ.

Movement characteristics

In the drills observed in Ottawa the phasing or sequencing of evacuation usually resulted in much lower overall evacuee densities and flows but higher descent speeds than was the case with total evacuations. The following example illustrates these and other features of the observed nontraditional, evacuation procedures.

In a phased, partial evacuation of a twenty-two-story office building 195 people from floors 14, 15, 13, and 22 walked, in that sequence to the ground floor, following instructions communicated on the building's public address system. The average flows on the two 38-in. (0.97-m) exit stairs, from the time the first evacuee reached the ground to some nine minutes later when the last evacuee reached the ground, were about twelve persons per minute or about seven persons per minute per 22 in. (0.56 m) of stair width. Flows were somewhat intermittent; peak flows, sustained for periods of at least 15 seconds, reached forty-eight persons per minute or twenty-eight persons per minute per 22 in. (0.56 m) of stair width. This compares with average peak flows of thirty-two persons per minute per 22 in. (0.56 m) of stair width in total evacuations. Even during peak flows the density on the stairs only reached 0.17 person per square foot (1.8 persons per square meter) or approximately two stair treads per evacuee. On the average, each evacuee occupied nearly four stair treads of area. Speeds of descent ranged from 3-1/2 to 6 stories per minute.

This example is typical of phased, partial evacuation drills observed in Ottawa office buildings. By comparison, the hypothetical phased, partial evacuation of 490 people illustrated in Figure 21-2 assumes similar density and speed conditions; however the flow is assumed to be less intermittent (with the mean flow assumed to be twice as great as described in the example above).

Time required

Optimistic, perhaps unrealistic, assumptions are made in Figure 21-2 regarding the time required for the building's fire-emergency personnel to ascertain the fire location and severity, make decisions about needed evacuation, and direct occupants with appropriate public address announcements. In the above example of the phased evacuation of a twenty-two-story building, about five minutes of the twelve minutes elapsing between the initial alarm and the arrival of the last evacuee at the ground floor was taken up with such management aspects of the selective evacuation procedure. In other words, the efficient use of exit facilities is not only dependent on the evacuee's movement down stairs but is also greatly influenced by management of the evacuation, either by building fire-emergency personnel or by fire department personnel.

Communications

Selective evacuation procedures require that public address and telephone systems be provided and maintained, and that trained, experienced persons are present to supervise the evacuation. The training of personnel to operate fire emergency communication systems before fire department personnel arrive or, under fire department supervision, after their arrival is a major concern of the Dominion fire commissioner in Canada. In has been found, for example, that many people selected from among those working in a building cannot cope with the stress and responsibility of operating communication systems even in a training and practice context where a variety of emergencies are merely simulated[32,33].

Preprogrammed, recorded public address announcements, although they have some advantages over live announcements[2,34], may cause difficulties when activated by false alarms or by legitimate alarms registered on a floor above or below the fire floor. There is thus still a need for competent personnel to operate communication equipment to override, on occasion, automatic systems.

Refuge behavior

Selective approaches to high-rise evacuation are made possible by the provision and proper operation of systems for fire and smoke control and for communication. Aside from the problems of making such systems work, there are a number of other difficulties, including occupant-behavior, that are not yet resolved. For example, it is not clear whether people who are aware of a fire in a high-rise building will tolerate remaining in probably safe refuge areas, located perhaps above the fire floor. In addition to asking the question "Are refuge areas safe?" one must also ask "Are refuge areas perceived to be safe by those who have to use them?"

Information on the behavior of people in fires is extremely limited. What information we do have indicates that people cope remarkably well in fire emergencies[25]. Behavior that may appear to be excited and disorganized is often quite reasonable. Unfortunately, the information that does exist on this subject pertains almost entirely to situations where people have the opportunity of evacuating or escaping to the perceived safety of the outdoors relatively easily (in contrast to what might be the case in a large high-rise building). To accomplish this, people will even move considerable distances through smoke-contaminated spaces[25]. What is needed now is information on such factors as how people will behave in a perceived refuge situation, what messages should be directed to them, what supervision should be provided, and what activities they should undertake to reduce anxiety and the desire to escape.

It is not surprising, therefore, that many large high-rise buildings are being designed and operated in a far more sophisticated manner than was the case even a decade ago. If these measures prove reliable, fire in a high-rise office building will be far less disruptive, with occupants carrying on their normal activities, perhaps oblivious of the fire. This seems to be common in high-rise apartment buildings. Unfortunately, it will be some time before this is generally the case in office buildings and thus the ability of building occupants to move quickly in case of fire is still important.

MOVEMENT ABILITY AND SAFETY

Brief mention should be made of the capability of typical office workers to evacuate to refuge spaces or to the outdoors by means of stairs. If the office workers observed in the Canadian office building evacuations are representative, as they appear to be, it is estimated that about 3 percent of the persons usually present in high-rise office buildings cannot or should not attempt to evacuate by means of crowded stairs. In addition to those with obvious physical disabilities, this minority includes people with heart disorders and convalescents from recent illness, surgery or accident. Movement of these individuals to a place of safety will require additional planning and assistance from other occupants. This could include their descending the stairs behind able-bodied occupants, being carried by others down the stairs, or having elevators, operated by fire department personnel, take them to safety.

Evacuees who responded to a questionnaire after the complete evacuation of a twenty-one-story office building judged their capabilities of descending stairs "without stopping, at a normal speed, and without assistance from others" as follows: 97 percent felt capable of at least three stories of stairs and 64 percent felt capable of descending at least twenty stories. Only 27 percent reported ever having descended twenty stories at one time before the evacuation was held[14]. Nine percent, mostly from the upper half of the building, did not feel capable of descending all the stairs from their normal work floor. (The questionnaire also dealt with normal use of the exit stairs. Currently, the Division of Building Research at the National Research Council of Canada is attempting, through field observations in Ottawa office buildings, to document such normal use which, aside from having economic implications, is relevant to people's ability to use those stairs in emergencies.)

Although people's beliefs about their stair movement capability are important, their actual performance is a more immediate concern in a fire-emergency evacuation. Observing crowds move down stairs, both in office building evacuations and in other situations, one is often impressed by how well people manage, including people with obvious disabilities. It is noteworthy, in this regard, that no injury-causing accidents were reported in the observed evacuation drills in Ottawa, even with observed total stair use exceeding 75,000 person-stories.

Equally noteworthy are some preliminary findings from current Canadian studies of crowd egress from grandstands and other buildings with public assembly occupancies[35]. In the case of a new 17,000 seat triple-tier grandstand in Calgary, the people using the building's 200 flights of stairs had a greater variety of ages and abilities than normally found in office buildings. Even though totally unfamiliar with the building, they used the stairs effectively (a mean flow of twenty-three persons per minute per 22 in. of stair width) and surprisingly safely, particularly in situations where stairs were crowded.

Although these studies suggest a degree of stair safety, they must be regarded with caution. More detailed observations of egress flow by crowds on stairs are needed to assess risk of accident properly and to understand better the factors that cause accidents. In addition to the on-going crowd egress studies by the

Division of Building Research, stair design and safety studies recently done in the United States are proving very useful and should be considered in the design, regulation, and operation of buildings[36-38].

CONCLUDING REMARKS

As the studies reported here deal largely with crowd movement in buildings, the information gained is particularly applicable to traditional total evacuation procedures and facilities. Findings provide an improved basis for making predictions of total evacuation time of tall office buildings and for designing the exit stairs used for total evacuations. This information comes at a time when, increasingly, high-rise buildings are being designed in a more sophisticated manner to reduce the hazards of fire and obviate the need for total evacuation in case of fire. Nontraditional evacuation procedures, some using facilities other than stairs, are being proposed and in some cases adopted[4,13,27,39]. Their testing under field conditions is, however, very limited. Thus, as was the case with total evacuation procedures, overoptimistic assumptions may be made, leading to a false sense of security about their efficacy. For example, the reported observations of evacuation drills using nontraditional procedures indicate that effective fire-emergency organizations, occupant training, and communications are needed to carry out selective evacuation. Currently, aside from government- and institution-occupied buildings, most tall buildings do not have fire-emergency organizations[40] and their occupants are largely unaware of fire-safety facilities and their use in emergencies. Some emergency communication systems, now being installed without adequate standards for either design or maintenance, may fail to function as expected even if trained personnel are available to use them.

In general, neither basic knowledge regarding fire emergency measures, including evacuation, nor related building design and operating practices have kept pace with society's propensity and ability to construct large buildings. More research is needed and the preliminary studies of evacuation reported herein should only be considered part of an initial phase of such research.

REFERENCES

1. Wilson, A. G., and Shorter, G. W. "Fire and High Buildings." *Fire Technology* 6, 22 (Nov. 1970):220-49.
2. General Services Administration. "International Conference on Fire-safety in High-Rise Buildings." Warrenton, Va., 1971. Washington, D.C.: U.S. Government Printing Office, 1971.
3. National Fire Protection Association. "High-Rise Building Fires and Fire Safety." NFPA No. SPP-18, Boston, 1972.
4. Associate Committee on the National Building Code. "Measures for Fire Safety in High Buildings." National Research Council of Canada, Ottawa, 1973.
5. ASHRAE Handbook and Products Directory: 1973 Systems Volume, Chapter 41, "Fire and Smoke Control." New York: American Society of Heating, Refrigerating and Air-Conditioning Engineers, Inc., 1973.
6. City of New York, Local Law No. 5, "Fire Safety Requirements and Controls." *The City Record.* New York, 1973.
7. *America Burning: The Report of the National Commission on Fire Prevention and Control.* Washington, D.C.: U.S. Government Printing Office, 1973.
8. Degenkolb, G. "The Evolution of High-Rise Fire Protection." *Building Official and Code Administrator,* Sept. 1974, pp. 26-32; Oct. 1974, pp. 20-31.
9. Harrison, G. A. "The High-Rise Fire Problem." *CRC Critical Reviews in Environmental Control* 4, 4 (Oct. 1974):483-505.
10. Galbreath, M. "A Survey of Exit Facilities in High Office Buildings." National Research Council of Canada, Division of Building Research, Ottawa, Building Research Note No. 64, Sept. 1968.
11. Galbreath, M. "Time of Evacuation by Stairs in High Buildings." *Fire Fighting in Canada,* Feb. 1969.
12. Pauls, J. L. "Evacuation Drill Held in the B.C. Hydro Building, June 26, 1969." National Research Council of Canada, Division of Building Research, Ottawa, Building Research Note No. 80, Sept. 1971.
13. Bazjanac, V. "Another Way Out?" *Progressive Architecture,* April 1974, pp. 88-89.
14. Pauls, J. L. "Building Evacuation and Other Fire Safety Measures: Some Research Results and Their Application to Building Design, Operation, and Regulation." In *EDRA*

5, Man-Environment Interactions: Evaluation and Applications. The State of the Art in Environmental Design Research—1974, Part 4, p. 147-168. Published by Environmental Design Research Association, Inc. (School of Architecture, University of Wisconsin). (Reprinted as NRCC 14708.)

15. Pauls, J. L. "Evacuation and Other Fire Safety Measures in High-Rise Buildings." *ASHRAE Transactions* 81, part 1 (1975). (Reprinted as NRCC 14808.)
16. National Bureau of Standards. "Design and Construction of Building Exits." National Bureau of Standards, Department of Commerce, Washington, D.C., Miscellaneous Publication M 151, 1935.
17. Joint Committee on Fire Grading of Buildings, Post War Building Study No. 29. "Fire Grading of Buildings (Part 3, Personal Safety)." London: Her Majesty's Stationery Office, 1952.
18. Togawa, K. "Study of Fire Escapes Basing on the Observation of Multiple Currents." Building Research Institute, Japan, Report No. 14, Feb. 1955.
19. London Transport Board. "Second Report of the Operational Research Team on the Capacity of Footways." London Transport Board, London, Research Report No. 95, 1958.
20. Predtetschenski, W. M. and Milinski, A. I. *Personenströme in gebäuden.* Rudolf Muller, Köln-Braunsfeld, 1971.
21. Fruin, J. J. *Pedestrian Planning and Design.* New York: Metropolitan Association of Urban Designers and Environmental Planners, Inc., 1971.
22. National Fire Protection Association, Life Safety Code, Appendix A-5. National Fire Protection Association, Boston, NFPA No. 101, 1973.
23. Bryan, J. L. "A Study of the Survivors' Reports on the Panic in the Fire at Arundel Park Hall in Brooklyn, Maryland, on January 29, 1956." Unpublished paper, Fire Protection Curriculum, University of Maryland.
24. Baker, G. W., and Chapman, D. W. (eds.). *Man and Society in Disaster.* New York: Basic Books, 1962.
25. Wood, P. G. "The Behaviour of People in Fires." Great Britain, Fire Research Station, Fire Research Note No. 953, Nov. 1972.
26. Quarantelli, E. L. "Human Behavior in Disaster." Paper presented at Conference, Designing to Survive Disaster, IIT Research Institute, Chicago, Nov. 1973.
27. Rubin, A. I., and Cohen, A. "Occupant Behavior in Building Fires." National Bureau of Standards, U.S. Department of Commerce, Washington, D.C., NBS Technical Note 818, Feb. 1974.
28. Pauls, J. L. "Fire Safety and Related Man-Environment Studies." *Man-Environment Systems* 5, 6 (Nov. 1975): 386-394.
29. Henning, D. N., and Pauls, J. L. "Building Use Studies to Solve Building Regulation Problems: Some Canadian Examples." Sixth Congress of CIB, Budapest, 3-10 Oct. 1974. (Reprinted as NRCC 14745.)
30. Evans, G. W. "Personal Space: Research Review and Bibliography." *Man-Environment Systems* 3, 4 (July 1975):203-215.
31. Phillips, A. W. "The Physiological and Psychological Effects of Fires in High-Rise Buildings." *Factory Mutual Record,* May-June 1973, pp. 8-10.
32. Hornby, E. S. "Voice Communications Systems in High-Rise Buildings." Paper presented at the Building Design and Communications Seminar, Calgary, Alberta, Sept. 9-11, 1974.
33. Hornby, E. S. "Volunteer Fire Safety Programs Pay High Dividends for Government Officials." *Canadian Consulting Engineer* 16, 11 (Nov. 1974):30-31.
34. Loftus, E. F., and Keating, J. P. "The Psychology of Emergency Communications." Presented at the International Conference on Firesafety in High-Rise Buildings, Seattle, Wash., Nov. 1974, General Services Administration, Public Building Service.
35. National Research Council of Canada, Division of Building Research. "Crowd Egress from Grandstands." *Building Research News* 52 (Oct. 1974):1-3.
36. BOSTI. "Increasing Residential Safety through Performance-based Design—Phase II." Buffalo Organization for Social and Technological Innovation, Inc., 1974.
37. Templer, J. A. "Stair Shape and Human Movement." Ph.D. dissertation, Columbia University, New York, 1974.
38. Archea, J. Personal communication. Center for Building Technology, National Bureau of Standards, Washington, D.C.
39. Stahl, F. I. "Behavior Based Fire Safety Performance Criteria for Tall Buildings." Paper presented at 6th Annual Conference, Environmental Design Research Association, University of Kansas, April 20-23, 1975.
40. Crossman, E. R. F. W., and Wirth, I. "Fire-Safety Organization of Highrise Building Occupancies." Fire Research Group, University of California, Berkeley, Report No. UCB-FRG 74-15, Aug. 1974.

22

Emergency Communications in High-Rise Buildings

Robert A. Glass
Arthur I. Rubin
National Bureau of Standards

INTRODUCTION

It is not often that we can thank Hollywood for producing such a spectacular movie like *Towering Inferno,* which has motivated many people into considering the obvious: their own personal safety in a high-rise building. Although there were technical errors in the movie, such as a virtually smokeless fire, one message was clear: there are inadequate codes and provisions for life safety in high-rise buildings—one being the lack of adequate communications. The potential for a major disaster is real. Hopefully it will never happen, but it could, unless remedial measures are instituted.

Concern for fire safety in high-rise buildings is relatively new. In South America from July 1973 to February 1974 there were three major high-rise fires resulting in 183 fatalities and $9 million in damages (Sharry 1974). None of the buildings involved in these fires followed the NFPA #101 Life Safety Code, but even with such a code the potential for disaster in high-rise buildings in the United States still exists. A major fire at One New York Plaza extensively damaged three floors of the fifty-story building and resulted in two deaths and thirty injuries. This fire focused attention on fire safety, since a major disaster was narrowly missed due to the time of day of the fire (5:45 P.M.). If the building had been fully occupied or the fire had occurred during working hours the life loss would have been much higher.

What problems are associated with occupant safety in high-rise buildings? What are the relationships between communication requirements and some of the latest life safety systems developed especially for high-rise buildings? What design changes in such systems can we expect in the future? We at the National Bureau of Standards' Center for Building Technology are currently looking into fire safety from the viewpoint of building occupants.

Prior to World War II skyscrapers were built primarily of structural steel and concrete and had openable windows, since air-conditioning was not in common use at the time. Most of the "problem" buildings were built during the office building boom of the 1960s and early 70s, since for numerous reasons the most recent trend has been to build taller and taller air-conditioned buildings. In New York City alone Powers (1973) says there are seventy-seven buildings taller than 150 meters—including the two World Trade Center Buildings at 411 meters and the Empire State Building at 381 meters. Of these, the newest buildings present the most fire safety problems because of design changes which include open air spaces, movable walls, modern furnishings, and sealed windows to optimize the effectiveness of central air-conditioning. All of these design features contribute to the rapid spread of a fire after it has started. In addition to the fire hazard, central air-conditioning ducts provide an excellent smoke pathway.

Many of the larger high-rise buildings have thousands of occupants engaged in a variety of activities, dispersed throughout many offices. Each building is likely to constitute a rather complex community, or series of communities, including young and aged, healthy and handicapped, skilled and unskilled, etc. Experts seem to agree that total evacuation of such buildings is no longer thought to be a viable strategy in the event of fire, due to the nonuniformity of people, furnishings, and activities. Instead of this single action to be performed by building occupants, a number of alternative procedures have been developed.

In an editorial in *Fire Journal* Babcock (1971) stated: "Recent fire experience has made it abundantly clear that the conventional concept of what constitutes adequate safety for a building and its occupants just does not work when fire occurs in today's high-rise buildings." Since it takes so long to evacuate tall buildings, the recent trend is to provide "areas of refuge" in which occupants of certain floors (the fire floor and one or two other floors) are directed and instructed to remain in these "safe areas" during an emergency. Thus, depending on the situation a fire safety plan for occupants may call for one group to stay in place, another one to move horizontally to a refuge area, and a third group to move vertically in order to evacuate the building. Under these conditions, the importance of accurate communications becomes evident.

Effective communications assumes not only the capability to transmit a complex set of messages but a high degree of assurance that the appropriate messages are received and understood by those who are directly threatened by the fire. A literature survey by Rubin and Cohen (1974) has shown that scientific research into occupant needs during fire emergencies is nearly nonexistent.

Before addressing particular problems in high-rise buildings in detail, it might be useful to explore the concept of communications in general terms as well as the modes of transmitting information usually encountered.

COMMUNICATIONS

Information provided by signals—general

The receiving of information provided by signals may be divided into at least three separate problems:

1. *Detection problem*—"Is something there?" or "Is something not there?"
2. *Recognition problem*—"If something is there, what is it?"
3. *Discrimination problem*—"Now that I know what it is, is it different from something else?"

This model can be applied to building occupants and their detection of a signal.

Occupants must be alerted as to the presence of an emergency

The signal transmitted must be noticed by building occupants. ("Is something there?" or "Is something not there?"—the detection problem.) People in buildings are engaged in many activities and surrounded by sights and sounds of many types. A warning signal must have sufficient impact to come to the attention of people despite their attention being focused elsewhere.

The signal must be correctly interpreted

Even after a signal has been noticed, it is necessary for the occupant to determine its meaning. ("If something is there, what is it?"—the recognition problem.) Based on training, experience and reasoning, a judgment will be made as to appropriate behavior. The ability to interpret a signal correctly is based on several factors. Perhaps the most important ones are the "message set" (the number of possible messages, and their meanings) and the number of possible interpretations (degree of ambiguity). The more messages and interpretations that are possible, in general, the longer it takes to react to a signal and the greater the likelihood that an error will be made. In the case of fire alarm signals, of special importance is the history or experience of occupants with past alarms that were "fire drills" versus real emergencies.

Deciding what to do and when to do it

Once the signal has been detected and recognized as being a signal the discrimination problem comes into play—"Now that I know what it is (e.g., a signal on a loudspeaker), is it different from something else (e.g., a fire emergency message as opposed to some other message)?" (Once the signal is correctly interpreted, it is still necessary to determine how to respond appropriately.)

A number of alternative actions are likely for the occupant, some of which might lead to safety and others of which are likely to be harmful. Characteristics of the building (such as location of stairways) and clues associated with the emergency (presence of smoke) will naturally influence the decision being made. Once these three questions have been answered only one process is left—doing something about the information obtained.

Performing the action

Finally, the communications system is designed to have the occupant *do* something. The success of the system is largley determined by the appropriateness of the behavior of building occupants, which can be attributed to the effectiveness of the messages transmitted by the system and the previous training of the occupants.

COMMUNICATIONS/CONTROL SYSTEM

For fire safety communication in high-rise buildings, another "variable" must be considered—complexity. The number of messages, possible fire locations, means for conveying information, possible action to be performed, dictate the need for a control center, not a simple communications network.

The federal government through the General Services Administration (GSA) has led the way in emergency communications systems capable not only of directing the movement of people in times of fire emergencies and bomb threats, but also of two-way communication between the control center and firefighters in the building. The establishment of a communications center is part of GSA's systems approach to firefighting, where the major ideas were spawned during the International Conference on Fire Safety in High-Rise Buildings in 1971. The findings of this conference have been summarized as follows (Sampson 1973):

1. Total evacuation is impractical in high-rise buildings.
2. Areas of refuge should be provided for occupants who remain in a building during a fire.
3. Fire size must be limited.
4. Sprinklers should be used more extensively.

5. Fire safety systems must provide structural integrity.
6. Smoke control starts with limiting the size of the fire.
7. An emergency control center should be provided for control of internal firefighting.
8. A total protection plan for occupants should be implemented.

Perhaps the most far-reaching implication of the conference concerned the need for an emergency control center in high-rise buildings. A control center has been the traditional means of implementing complex command and control systems consisting of closely interacting "hardware" and "human" subsystems. The military has used such systems in the past and more recently the National Aeronautic Space Administration (NASA) has been a proponent of this approach, having achieved notable successes in the lunar exploration program. The significance of the communications center is that it accounts for the complexities and difficulties associated with the safety problems and the inadequacy of any *single* approach to fire safety—such as fully automatic sensing and sprinkling devices.

In an article dealing with high-rise safety, Arthur Sampson (1971), director of GSA, stated "in view of the complexity of moving some occupants while others remain in place, it was the consensus that all high-rise buildings require an emergency operation control center, equipped to transmit verbal instructions, zoned emergency communications, two-way communications, and alarms. The emergency operation control center must be in a readily accessible, protected location from which all building emergency systems can be operated."

It is important to make a distinction between a communication system designed to be monitored by an operator only as a means of obtaining information, and a "command and control" system, *one* component of which is the display of the information. A control system for high-rise safety implies an awareness that the solution of fire safety problems is inherently complex. For example, the use of fully automatic sensing and sprinkling devices does not provide a complete solution to the problem of fire safety any more than building evacuation does. Instead, an effective system depends on the integration of the many automatic, semi-automatic, and manually based components associated with the various aspects of fire safety. Above all, a control center is designed to assist a person who is responsible for making decisions as to alternative courses of action open to him in performing his fire safety functions.

PROBLEMS WITH PRESENT COMMUNICATIONS SYSTEMS

Present emergency communications systems have many problems. These problems may be classified into two areas: physical problems due to the system itself; and psychological problems due in large part to the lack of research into the needs of humans in times of emergency.

Physical Design Problems

Transfire capabilities

One of the major physical problems of emergency communications systems is that the control center is typically tied to all sensing and communications devices via separate wire cables. Many of these cables do not have transfire capabilities. That is, they do not function properly when crossing through parts of the building that are on fire. This is a particularly important point, because if a fire takes place in the middle of a building, it is imperative that communications remain open to those people in refuge areas above the fire. This point was emphasized in the following account of a high-rise fire:

> A late night fire that broke out on the twenty-fifth floor of an unsprinklered 80-story building caused moderate damage

and faced fire fighters with ventilation problems before it was extinguished. The fire started in a storage room where computer and theatrical equipment had been stored. About 200 people were in the building at the time, none of them on the fire floor. When the fire entered the cableway carrying wiring for the emergency intercom system, the system was put out of order. This may have accounted for the fact that some 200 occupants did not leave. Fire fighters had to remove some of the windows on that floor and check closely for spread through vertical shafts. The fire was believed to have been of incendiary origin [Anon. 1975].

There are, of course, methods available to solve this problem. Redundant communications lines could be placed in separate locations in buildings as was done in the new GSA Seattle Federal Building. Unfortunately this system might still be vulnerable in a severe fire, and the addition of duplicate wiring adds greatly to the cost. One alternative design might be a wireless system utilizing radios. Of course, there would be many additional problems imposed by such a system. For example, due to the density of building materials, antennae would have to be placed throughout the building. Also, if there were several buildings in close proximity, the radio signals from one system might be picked up in another building. An alternative to a wireless system is a telephone system with transmission lines separated from the communications conduits. Obviously, more work is necessary before any such system is recommended.

Human engineering

As buildings become more and more complex, the fire emergency systems also become more sophisticated. A characteristic shared by these systems is that they have displays (visual and auditory means of communicating information) which are integrated in a console, and manned by an operator located in a control room. The operator's console can be a single simple warning panel and a one-way microphone to notify building occupants of an emergency, or it might be a large console including several major panels of information. In general the more complex systems appear to have been designed on the basis of aggregating many individual displays and controls with such objectives as: minimizing errors, facilitating communications, optimizing controls and displays, ensuring that operators are not overloaded with information. The newer systems appear to be more responsive to proper human engineering in their design. Hopefully the design trend towards a compact, efficient, human-oriented control center will continue.

Operation of system: automatic vs. manual

A major problem with present communication systems is to identify the proper "mix" between manual and automatic modes of operations. Because of the variety of tasks an operator must perform during an emergency, he may be overwhelmed with too many tasks, especially if he also acts as a link between the building communications system and the fire department. At the other extreme many communications-fire safety systems rely on an "automatic first-mode condition." Whenever a fire emergency exists, the computer automatically performs several functions such as sounding alarms and bringing elevators to the lobby floor. In many systems this automatic mode includes the cuing of prerecorded messages to be played on selected floors; the message transmitted being based on the location of the fire.

While automatic cuing of messages was designed to save lives, it could cost more lives than it would save. For example, consider the following hypothetical situation: Suppose that a fire has started on the tenth floor of a building, but because of the building design and placement of the smoke detectors, the smoke drifted up the ventilation system and triggered a detector on the twelfth floor. In this situation wrong instructions will be given and the people on the twelfth floor will actually be moving into the fire rather than away from it to safety. Perhaps a better design would include a period of delay for a few seconds before the tape recorder is turned on. This design would allow enough time for the operator to determine whether any other warning devices on other floors are triggered before he decides what actions would be appropriate. Enabling an operator to override *any* automatic system is essential if his role as a decisionmaker is to be effectively accomplished. Regardless of the amount of planning that precedes the design and installation of automatic communications systems, it is not possible to forecast *all* possibilities. As a result, some provision must be made for those emergencies which were not anticipated. Past experience, such as that gained during the NASA program, demonstrates that a well-trained operator permitted to make and act on decisions provides this critical safeguard.

Operation of system: training of operators

Because of the extreme importance of manning a control center, the training of operators is of concern. No longer can a semi-retired night watchman be relied upon to maintain such a system. Instead these systems require well-trained and well-paid operators, since ultimately the system is only as good as the decisions of the console operator. The job of console operator is a highly technical and skilled position. Only the most competent operators should be selected, and reimbursed accordingly.

Operation of system: equipment malfunctions

Present elaborate communications systems rely heavily on the use of slide projectors and tape recorders. Slide projectors are often used to continuously display floor plans. Most projectors have only a standard projection bulb and are quite prone to burning out. Certainly one margin of safety in this regard would be to have a "hard copy" of all slides available in the control center for easy access. Similarly duplicate "hard copies" of the various tape recorded messages should also be available should the tape recorder malfunction. There is also the possibility that the wrong tape may be selected and played automatically. At present in most instances the control operator does not know whether the correct message was received on the appropriate floor, since he can only monitor the tape recording (in the control center), rather than the speakers on the affected floor.

Fire communications: separate or combined systems

In recent years, there has been considerable discussion as to whether the fire communications system should be maintained as a separate system or combined with existing public address systems.

The advantages of a separate system are that they can be easily monitored and maintained. The major disadvantage is that such a system is costly. A combined system is much less expensive to install and operate, but it has the distinct disadvantage of being more complex and hence more difficult to trouble shoot.

Depending on specific requirements, either approach offers an increased level of life safety over the traditional fire-bell approach.

Psychological Problems

Numerous psychological problems are associated with emergency communications in buildings. The concept of using a public address system for fire emergency warnings is largely traceable to the conference on high-rise fire safety in 1971. It emerged in response to the idea that people needed to be reassured during an emergency to prevent undesirable irrational behavior such as panic. However, if one examines the literature carefully and consults with those who have studied human behavior in disasters, one finds many myths. Dr. Quarantelli from Ohio State University's Disaster Research Unit, reports that people do not panic and do not act irrationally. From his research (on human behavior in mass disasters) Quarantelli (1973:70) concludes that: "Human behavior as such does not appear to be a major problem at times of disaster." Voice communication systems should therefore serve other functions if they are to be maximally useful in fire emergencies. These systems do serve to keep the occupants informed and also presumably help people to find the safer areas of the building. Unfortunately, while these objectives appear to be reasonable, the specifics of how much systems should work have yet to be thoroughly investigated from the standpoint of the needs of building occupants.

Psychological aspects of "the message"

In using a voice communications system two problems are apparent: (1) what type of alarm should be used as a pre-alert signal to let people know that an important message is coming; and (2) what should the content of such a message be? These questions cannot be adequately answered by available research data at the present time. Hopefully, some answers may be provided by the voice system developed for the Federal Building in Seattle. The specific wording of messages and rationale used for the voice system in the GSA Seattle building are presented in a paper by Drs. Elizabeth F. Loftus and John P. Keating, both of the University of Washington. The paper appears in the proceedings of the November 1974 International Conference on Fire Safety in High-Rise Buildings. More laboratory research needs to be performed on the use of verbal directions in emergency stress situations. Before we can be satisfied with any design of such voice communications systems, of particular importance is the need to know what kind of verbal instructions lead to wrong actions, or conversely what instructions lead to appropriate actions. Two examples of confusion in emergency communications have recently occurred. Pauls (1974) reports an incident where there was to be a controlled, videotaped evacuation of a building using an emergency communications system. The office building had twenty-one floors and the third floor was considered to be the fire floor. Pauls (1974:13) reports:

> The evacuation sequence was to be the third floor, fourth floor, second floor, 21st floor, 20th floor, and so on down to the 5th floor until the building was completely cleared of occupants. The exercise started with a general sounding of fire alarm bells throughout the building and await instructions to be given over the buildings' public address system. After about two minutes a somewhat excited voice was heard over the loudspeakers with the following message: "Ladies and gentlemen. We have to evacuate the building. The alarm has been set on the 3rd floor. Please evacuate. Other floors stand by." Use of public address system in this excited and ambiguous fashion resulted in a great deal of confusion in what should have been a highly-controlled evacuation. It was well documented, with observations collected by a team of 15 observers located throughout the building.
>
> In addition, a detailed questionnaire distributed to 200 evacuees immediately following evacuation provided background information about 176 of the 2100 evacuees as well as information about their behavior during the exercise. For example, 17% reported interpreting the situation as a genuine fire emergency when they first heard the fire alarm; but after the ambiguous public address announcement 42% of the respondents reported interpreting it as a real fire emergency. Many respondents even reported that in the announcement they thought they heard "a fire has been reported on the third floor." This example underlines the importance of judicious use of public address systems, which increasingly are being installed in high-rise buildings for use in fire emergencies.

The other example occurred on April 17, 1975, at the World Trade Center. Two small incendiary fires were set on the fifth and forty-ninth floors. Both were small fires and were contained quickly. However, the fifth floor was a storage area and the stairwell door had been propped open causing slightly noticeable smoke to spread up to the twenty-second floor. At the onset of the detection of the fire, verbal messages were sent to the building occupants and they moved to "safe" areas as directed. Apparently the fire was quickly contained and instructions were given for the people to return to their offices. However, because of the presence of smoke, the people refused to return to their offices, despite repeated announcements over the communications system that all was safe.

After much discussion between people on the individual floors and the control center, it was decided to evacuate the 800 people. The communications system did not allow for the tape recording of all communications messages. Thus at this time it is not clear exactly why this situation developed. The National Fire Protection Association has distributed questionnaires and is investigating this incident further.

Selective messages

A number of fundamental psychological problems can be illustrated in the present system in the GSA Seattle Federal Building.

When a fire alarm starts, the elevators are automatically "captured" and brought to the ground floor for fire department use. In the Seattle building this procedure entails capturing twenty-two elevators and returning all of them to the ground floor. Under the present system if a fire breaks out on one floor, the floor above, the fire floor, and the floor below are evacuated to two separate floors. Thus a total of five floors are affected and receive the appropriate messages. The rest of the building is undisturbed (except for the loss of elevator service) unless of course, the fire becomes more severe. All occupants of the building would be affected when they try to use the elevators, and cannot get them to respond. An undue amount of anxiety might be generated since the individuals involved would realize there was a fire emergency but not be aware of its location. In this situation one person might tell a few fellowworkers about the emergency with the result that they might move to the nearest stairwell, thus presenting problems if the wrong exit pathway is accidentally chosen.

A possible alternative design might be to have warning messages on all floors near the elevators to the effect that the elevators are in a fire mode. In some buildings all fire floor fire wardens are notified during emergencies, and supposedly station themselves in the elevator lobbies to discourage use. This latter procedure is also likely to induce anxiety since occupants will be alarmed, but unaware of the nature and extent of the problem, and who might be affected by it.

COMMUNICATION SYSTEMS

Research needs

Virtually no research has been performed into the needs of building occupants in an emergency utilizing an emergency communications system. Some of the questions that research should be designed to answer include:

1. How do we best attract the attention of occupants? (What characteristics should the messages have to ensure that occupants are aware of them regardless of where they are?)
2. What should the signal to noise ratio be for auditory and visual messages.
3. What particular messages should be transmitted under what conditions?
4. Which message should be prerecorded, and which ones should be transmitted "live"?
5. What capability is needed for two-way communications—between control center and occupants, between control center and fire department?
6. What information should be transmitted visually (signs, lights), by auditory means (signals, voice) and by both means?
7. What message should be automatic? How should they be transmitted?
8. What backup systems are needed for manual override or substitute?

SUMMARY

This chapter looked at the history of the development of high-rise buildings and problems in life safety related to fires. Information provided by warning signals and the needs of building occupants are discussed. High-rise emergency communications systems are examined as well as the general approach mentioned. Some suggestions on system improvement have been made. However, answers are not offered, rather potential areas of research are identified.

Today's emergency communications systems are likely to improve the chances of survival in a high-rise building fire, but the level of safety offered could be improved even further by research into specific areas identified in this chapter.

REFERENCES

Anon. *Fire Journal* 69, 1 (1975):54.

Babcock, Chester I. "Safety at Any Height." *Fire Journal* 65, 4 (1971).

Loftus, E. F., and Keating, J. R. "The Psychology of Emergency Communications." Proceedings of the Public Buildings Service, International Conference on Fire Safety in High-Rise Buildings, November 1974.

McCormick, Ernest J. *Human Engineering.* New York: McGraw-Hill, 1957.

Pauls, J. L. "Building Evacuation and other Fire-Safety Measures: Some Research Results and Their Application to Building Design, Operation and Regulation." Presentation —5th Environmental Design Research Association Conference, June 1974.

Powers, W. Robert. "The Causes of the Problem: As Seen in the Loss Experience of New York City." *Factory Mutual Record*, May-June 1973.

Rubin, Arthur I., and Cohen, Arthur. *Occupant Behavior in Building Fires.* National Bureau of Standards, Washington, D.C., Technical Note 818, February 1974.

Quarantelli, E. L. "Human Behavior in Disaster." Conference on Designing to Survive Disaster, November 1973.

Sampson, Arthur F. "Firesafety: A Management Concern." *Business Week*, October 6, 1973.

Sampson, Arthur F. "Life Safety Systems for High-Rise Structures." *Fire Journal* 65, 4 (1971):8–9.

Sharry, John A. "South America Burning." *Fire Journal* No. 68 (1974):23–33.

23

Emergencies in Tall Buildings: The Designers Respond to the Human Response

Walter A. Meisen
Ronald E. Reinsel
General Services Administration

INTRODUCTION

The U.S. General Services Administration's Public Buildings Service (PBS) has traditionally addressed various emergencies, disasters, and panic situations during the building design stage. Among these emergency types are security problems such as bombings and demonstrations and natural disasters such as earthquake and windstorm. Other emergencies which have received much attention by GSA involve fire and explosions.

This particular problem of tall buildings has received emphasis within the fire profession over the last five years. PBS began serious analysis of the problem when two frightening fires broke out in high-rise buildings in New York City in 1970. These fires brought to public attention the acute fire safety problems in these structures, and pointed out that high-rise building life safety designs in the recent past have not been adequate.

A new approach had to be developed for fire protection. As a start, GSA convened an International Conference on Firesafety in High-Rise Buildings in April 1971. At this conference GSA and the other participants recognized that you cannot treat a "tall building as a small building" and that human behavior, and problems cannot be addressed and solved after-the-fact or even during emergencies. At this high-rise conference the participants identified three predominant tall building constraints as related to fire emergencies:

1. Total evacuation in emergencies is impractical.
2. Some floors are beyond the reach of fire department ladders.
3. A potential exists for upward smoke movement due to the well-known "stack effect."

Since 1971 GSA has sponsored three major high-rise fire safety conferences. The first conference inspired a total fire safety systems decision analysis approach to be included at the design stage of all future high-rise buildings and other major projects. As an additional requirement, the contractor for each job must hire a qualified fire safety consultant to ensure completion and performance of the system.

In July of 1973 GSA, along with the Department of Housing and Urban Development, the National Bureau of Standards, and the National Science Foundation sponsored the second international high-rise conference. The initial goal of this conference was to produce interaction of value both to the researchers in guiding the direction of their research projects and to the designers in knowing how and where to obtain data for their design projects.

The November 1974 high-rise conference in Seattle, Washington, provided information on some recent state-of-the-art advances in fire safety technology. Among the subject areas discussed were test and evaluation of the smoke control features of the Seattle Federal Building, the voice emergency message system for the Seattle Federal Building, discussions by the fire department and by a systems analyst on a study of fire loads and live loads in buildings.

The Seattle Federal Building which was dedicated in November 1974, was designed as a prototype of the elements of a Building Firesafety System that GSA employs to account for human and structural survival in tall buildings. The keystone of the system is that the designer acknowledges and anticipates the constraints and capabilities of both the building and its occupants. The function of the design should be to anticipate, channel, and control a variety of human responses to tall building emergencies. The product of design merges the human and mechanical elements to provide for maximized fulfillment of survival needs.

The first priority in this systems approach is to provide early warning detection and automatic suppression capability. These systems will initiate an automatic building response in addition to alarming the fire department. Among the functions automatically initiated by alarm are:

1. Protected ways of egress for occupants and also ingress for firemen (e.g., stairwell pressurization and elevators dedicated for fire department use).
2. Voice and visual communications to occupants to direct staged movement of persons within a building to safe refuge areas (either on the interior of the exterior to the building).
3. Two-way communications for follow-up to the fire report and for the use of firemen.
4. Automatic elevator capture—to prevent people using elevators to exit.
5. Smoke control systems to maintain the supply of noncontaminated air for occupants who necessarily remain in the building during the fire.

Requirement has been made for installation of total automatic sprinkler protection in all new high-rise buildings and a control center provided with the capability to monitor and manually override the automatic response.

The Facilities Self-Protection-Plan for the Seattle Federal Building preplans and designates the duties and responsibilities of officials and occupants to assure personnel movement during emergencies. Among the items in this plan are detailed actions that handicapped persons monitors should take during all emergencies.

GSA feels that a key to a designed human response to fire emergencies in tall buildings is Division 17 of the national construction specification system. Division 17 deals with control and monitoring systems to insure that required system functions and interfaces (such as emergency communication) are addressed and incorporated early in the design process to produce an integrated design package that precludes "add-on" costs or a piecemeal approach to design.

GSA approaches design as fulfillment of stated goals through performance-based specifications. Given that our ultimate goal is life safety during emergencies, our immediate task is to develop a system which in its performance accounts for the potential performance of its users.

In order to design for people affected by a protective system we must recognize:

1. the needs of the persons involved and
2. the behaviors and characteristics of the persons involved.

While the first consideration is largely straight forward in physical detail (needs for removal from the hazardous area, needs for movement to safety, needs for elemental protection) it is further defined by the psycho-social details of the second factor. The person requirements and person potentials cannot be addressed after the fact or left to random resolution during emergencies; they must be considered and responded to by the designer and provided for within the comprehensive planning.

THE HUMAN RESPONSE

To achieve a functional design we must approach existent functional relationships. We must define the population by the factors which determine responsiveness, develop a catalog of potential responses, and devise an instrument which will channel potential responses to the desired response. Inherent in the design of the successful channeling instrument will be the fulfillment of the personal needs which motivate the potential responses.

Responsiveness is dependent upon an individual's capability to actively respond to external stimuli. Capability may be divided between physical capability and mental capability. The physical dimension accounts for the degree of ambulatory mobility, physical restraint, chronologic age, and consciousness. The mental dimension accounts for the degree of apathy, excitability, rationality, mental age, consciousness to and knowledge of the environment.[1] Given the individual's capability to respond, what factors determine the content of the behavioral response? Glass states that behavior under emergency conditions is dependent upon such variables as the perceived nature and intensity of the traumatic agent, the preset attitude of the individual, variations in individual ability and speed of perception, comprehension and action, and the composition of the group presented with the emergency condition.[2]

A state of emergency is subject to differential perception. While the threat is common its perception is relative. Threats which are seen as mild to moderate by one individual may be deemed severe to another and will produce corresponding degrees of apprehension, concern, or tension. It is the degree of arousal produced by the perception which motivates response.

Response may either hinder or facilitate production of appropriate individual behaviors according to the individual's level of arousal intake and analysis of relevant information, and perception of behavioral options. Janis describes these factors as the preset to behavior, actualized as either fight or flight.[3]

Over-arousal will tend to produce nonadaptive physical and psychological reactions based upon flight. Beyond a physical response, flight is psychologically manifested as rationalization for inappropriate behavior. Individuals with high continued arousal will overreact to ambiguous signals or information and will be unable to utilize skills or mobilize correct responses to the emergency condition.

Ambiguous information leads to wrong responses when it is incorrectly processed. This is often the case when an individual in a highly aroused state, perceiving limited behavioral options, is given limited information regarding the cause of arousal. The ambiguity of the stress is heightened, tension is increased, and irrational flight is produced.

The desired pattern is that of a contingency response of acquiring knowledge and acting without undue alarm. This constitutes the most adaptive survival response in that the individual learns enough about the danger to permit the arousal of appropriate concern, is alert to pertinent information, discriminates between options, responds with appropriate behavior and avoids indiscriminate worry.

The range of ability and speed of perception, comprehension, and action is distributed within a population similar to a bell-shaped curve.[4,5] Individuals may be categorized within this frequency distribution to predict group responsiveness:

1. *Trained or emergent leaders*—15%-20% of the population—quickly grasp available environmental information, integrate the situation with past experience, and make decisions which are realized in effective action.
2. *The easily led*—approximately 50% of the population—have adequate environmental perception, but are not able to produce adequate solutions or action. While unable to produce actions, they are highly suggestible and will respond to either effective leadership of join others in mass flight.
3. *The poorly effective or dependent*—10%-15% of the population—have imperfect perception and difficulty in responding. They require more direct external structuring of their responses.
4. *The ineffective and stunned*—10%-25% of the population—have impaired perceptions and give inadequate or irrational responses.
5. *The withdrawn from reality*—no more than 1% of the population—show primitive behavior with illogical responses or no response. Unable to cope in any manner, they manifest complete psychologcial withdrawal.

Two factors will greatly affect the proportions of individuals within these categories for a specific occasion:

1. The adaptive time factor: At the onset of the emergency stress approximately 100% of the population may be noneffective; with the passage of time the ability of the majority of individuals to react effectively shows dramatic increase.
2. The group composition factor: An untrained heterogeneous group will contain a larger proportion of individuals producing less effective behaviors. A trained and homogeneous group will produce a higher proportion of effective and adaptive behavior.

Given these yardsticks of behavioral determinants, how can the designer most effectively manipulate the environment to maximize the production of effective behavior during a fire emergency?

THE DESIGNERS RESPOND

The occupant population within a Federal Office Building will be primarily composed of ambulatory, nonrestrained, conscious adults. They will be nonapathic, normal in mental age, conscious to the environment. They will be representative of the greater population in excitability and rationality of response and will be mixed in knowledge of the environment due to the presence of both permanent workers and transient occupants.

From this definition of the concerned population it is determined that the majority of persons are able to respond in a "normal" manner and will respond in an "effective" manner given the proper leadership.

The most available and effective means of behavioral determination is control over the inputs to perception through control of communication and its content. This approach has been followed based upon the system suggested by Dr. Gilbert Teal[6] and has been realized as an essential component within the GSA fire safety prototype as the Vocal Alarm System (VAS).

The attributes of the system are:

1. Automatic initiation of verbal communication to affected occupants over a public address system.
2. Alert of occupants to receive information.
3. Provision of preprogrammed situational information for varying preplanned conditions.
4. Provision for differing instructions for differing occupancy zones.
5. Provision of leadership toward a single behavioral option.
6. Provision for manual override to update or cancel automatic messages.

A VAS is further necessitated by the amount of information which is required for personnel movement within a tall building. Since total immediate evacuation is deemed impractical, the present prototype calls for staged movement from the fire-affected and adjacent floors to areas both above and below the

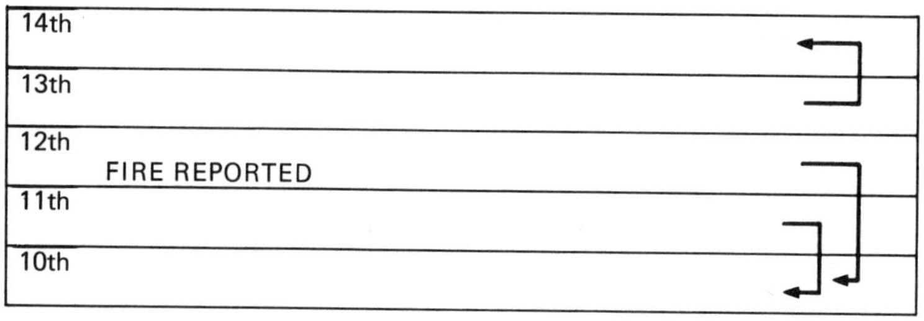

Figure 23-1
Staged evacuation movement: Fire on 12th floor.

danger zone. Staged movement creates an evacuation zone surrounding the fire in order to remove occupants from immediate danger and to allow for freedom of movement for fire fighting personnel. Occupants may be further evacuated from the staging areas if conditions warrant.

Such staged movement requires greater floor-specific instructions that can be given by a traditional single information device. Single command systems would require complex coded signals to convey proper information. Such a coded system would require rigorous training unavailable to the transient population and easily forgotten by the permanent population.

THE VAS

The content of the Vocal Alarm System has been developed by psychologists Keating and Loftus[7] of the University of Washington. Message content is divided into three sections: Alert Tone, Introduction, and Instruction.

Alert Tone

Occupants should be prepared to receive information by a signal which alerts the population to the data input. The qualities of such a signal should include: audibility (easily heard above background noises), capability of evoking quick response, alertive, discriminability from other signals, informative, nonmasking, nonpainful, and nondamaging.[8]

Research indicates that an oscillating, pure tone signal is recommended as a warning device if presentation is intended over an intercom system followed by speech.[9] Tone presentation should be made in the range of maximum auditory sensitivity (between 500–3000 Hz) and below the pain threshold (approximately 110 db at 1000 hz).

For this purpose the standard FCC broadcast alert tone (1000 hz. pure sine wave) was selected as the most efficient device which embodies all of the stated desirable qualities when presented 25–30 db above the expected ambient noise level of 65 db. The resultant sound pressure delivery of 90–95 db will act as a sufficient alerting stimuli without damage to hearing ablity.

Introduction

The alert tone should be followed by a verbal request for attention. This request serves as a transition between pure tone presentation and speech content information by focusing the alerted auditory system to verbal input.

Introduction given by a female voice will counteract any tendency toward "false alarm behavior" due to previous exposure to the FCC tone over radios.

Content of the introduction should reflect a "softness" of presentation least likely to induce panic. For this reason the phrase "May I have your attention please" was chosen over such options as "Your attention please" or "Attention." The introductory phrase is repeated to increase attention to the verbal content. In messages to elevators and receiving floors the phrase is used only once without the prior alert signal due to lower ambient noise levels and the need for quicker message transmission.

Instructions

Instructions are given by a male voice. The majority of the content should be presented in the most easily understood range of voice delivery (1000+hz).[10] Research has noted that a switch from a female to male voice will be noticed even when people are not paying attention to the message.[11] Thus the voice switch insures that the emergency message content will penetrate the attentional barrier of all affected occupants. The male voice capitalizes on the societal preconditioning to expect a male to have control over the situations and to exert leadership.

The message content is delivered in clear and concise language employing nonconfusing, high content words, chosen for high frequency occurrence in normal written and verbal communication.[12] Instructions are given to occupants in a nonemotional voice telling what has happened (correct information), what they are to do (leadership toward a single behavioral option), and why they should not attempt undesirable options (avoidance of noneffective behavior such as use of elevators).

—Message to Fire Floor and Floor Below (Fire Reported on 12th Floor).
[Alert Tone]
FEMALE VOICE: May I have your attention please. May I have your attention please.
MALE VOICE: There has been a fire reported on the 12th floor. While this report is being verified, the building manager would like you to proceed to the stairways and walk down to the 10th floor. Wait on the 10th floor for further instructions. Please do not use the elevators, as they may be needed. Please do not use the elevators, but proceed to the stairways.

Information is given in familiar word patterns.

The phrase "a report of a fire" is used rather than the word "Emergency." Emergency is a highly ambiguous term, and ambiguity can induce panic. Fire is the true situation.

"While this report is being verified" implies that immediate official response to the situation has been initiated.

"The building manager would like you to . . ." gives the impression that an actual person is in control of the situation and is directing their actions.

"Proceed to the stairways and walk down to the 10th floor. Wait on the 10th floor for further instructions." The word "evacuate" has been avoided since it may mean to some of the occupants that they should leave the building. "Walk" is a much more familiar word and will be better understood.

"Please do not use the elevators, as they may be needed. Please do not use the elevators, but proceed to the stairs." The destination, means of movement, and the message to avoid the elevators are given twice thus providing a redundancy of information. Rationale is also provided for why the elevators should not be used, making it less likely that occupants will attempt to use them.

—Message to Floor Above.
[Alert Tone]
FEMALE VOICE: May I have your attention please. May I have your attention please.
MALE VOICE: There has been a fire reported on the 12th floor. While this report is being verified, the building manager would like you to proceed to the stairways and walk up to the 14th floor. The 14th floor is a safe area where you should wait for further instructions. Please do not use the elevators, as they may be needed. Please do not use the elevators, but proceed to the stairways.

Where upward movement is required, occupants are told that it "is (to) a safe area" in order to overcome the natural desire to move downward. Instructions to "wait (there) for further instructions" reinforces the idea of temporary refuge from which the evacuees may be moved if necessary.

–Message to Receiving Floors.
[Alert Tone]
FEMALE VOICE: May I have your attention please .
MALE VOICE: There has been a fire reported on the 12th floor. People from other floors will be entering your area. Please remain at your desks while they are in your area. You are safe in your area.

Receiving floor occupants are told to expect the influx of persons to their floor to avoid possible panic due to their sudden appearance. The word "people" is used, rather than "occupants" because it is a much more familiar word, occurring almost 100 times more frequently in normal speech.

It is emphasized that receiving floor occupants "are safe in (their) area" to counter the possible desire to join in evacuation; such movement beyond the containment zone could begin a snowballing of movement throughout the building.

–Message to Elevators.
[Alert Tone]
FEMALE VOICE: May I have your attention please.
MALE VOICE: The building manager has directed all elevators to the entrance lobby. There has been a fire reported in the building and the elevators may be needed. Please proceed to the lobby area for further instructions.

The elevator message begins with the explanation that "the building manager has directed" their movement before they are told of the reasons for the movement so that they will not be alarmed by a change in elevator direction or the bypassing of destination floors.

The reference to "all elevators" is made so that passengers do not feel that their elevator has been singled out for any reason.

The correct information "report of a fire" is given so that passengers may disseminate this accurate information to prospective users in the lobby. "The elevators may be needed" has a calming effect and provides the occupants with a rationale for why the elevators have been directed to the lobby.

RESULTS OF THE VAS FIELD TEST

In field testing the system under simulated emergency conditions the VAS has been shown to be highly effective in directing personnel evacuation.[13]

Comparison was made between groups with prior instruction to the alarm and evacuation model and with persons receiving no prior orientation (as would be the case between permanent occupants and transients). No observable or statistical differences were found between groups in time to respond, orderliness of response, or correct compliance to instructions.

In questionnaire evaluation of the test 95.2% of the occupants stated correct identification of the means of evacuation instructed; 97.2% of the evacuating population correctly identified the floor to which they were instructed to go; 98% indicated that they needed no other help to understand the directions, understood the reason for the evacuation, and actually went where they were instructed to go. Clarity, rationale and confidence in the messages were rated positively without statistical differences by both groups.

In comparing performance of the VAS with evacuation systems in similar high-rise buildings superiority of the automatic system is again demonstrated. Comparison was made with a commercial office employing a similar movement system but with instruction given by floor fire wardens. In the commercial building, four minutes after the alarm people were still attemptingt to gain access to captured elevators. Six minutes after the alarm people were still leaving floors which were to be evacuated and 100% evacuation was never achieved. In the VAS test, total evacuation was accomplished for both groups within 1.5 minutes.

The superiority of the VAS as an effective signaling device for swift and complete emergency evacuation has been reasonably identified. By fulfilling the need for accurate information and leadership the system channels behavior and directs effective responses. Movement is accomplished without confusion and confidence is instilled in occupants that emergencies are properly handled.

The VAS, as a product in prototype, acts as an effective tool to merge the human population with the total safety system and becomes the essential element of the system. By designer response to the needs of human response we are able to increase the potential for the most significant behavioral consequence—that of survival.

Because the General Services Administration recognizes that there are definite social and psychological impacts of tall buildings on their occupants, we have been concerned with the design and construction of protective systems which confront these impacts headon. We look for greater research and development by all segments of our industry to continue in this area of human response to the environment.

NOTES

1. G. Clairborne, "Occupant Activity Classification," in GSA, Public Buildings Service, *International Conference on Firesafety in High-Rise Buildings,* Washington, D.C., May 1971, p. A-24.
2. Albert J. Glass, "Mass Psychology—The Determinants of Behavior Under Emergency Conditions," in National Academy of Science, *Proceeding of a Workshop on Mass Burns,* Washington, D.C., 1969, pp. 11-24.
3. Irving L. Janis, "Psychological Effects of Warnings," in G. W. Baker and D. W. Chapman (eds.), *Man and Society in Disaster* (New York: Basic Books, 1962), pp. 55-92.
4. S. L. A. Marshall, *Men Against Fire* (New York: Wm. Morrow and Company, 1947), pp. 764-769.
5. J. S. Tyhurst, "Individual Reactions to Community Disaster," *American Journal of Psychiatry* 107 (1950-51): 764-769.
6. G. Teal, "Occupant Protection—Psychological Factors," GSA, PBS, *International Conference of Firesafety in High-Rise Buildings,* Washington, D.C., 1971, p. A-19.
7. John P. Keating and Elizabeth F. Loftus, "The Psychology of Emergency Communications," University of Washington, Department of Psychology, Seattle, 1974.
8. E. J. McCormick, *Human Factors Engineering* (New York: McGraw-Hill Co., 1964).
9. *Human Engineering Guide on Equipment Design* (Washington, D.C.: U.S. Government Printing Office, 1972).
10. P. B. Danes and E. N. Pinson, *The Speech Chain* (Baltimore, Md.: Bell Telephone Laboratories, 1963).
11. E. C. Cherry and W. K. Taylor, "Some Further Experiments on the Recognition of Speech with One and Two Ears," *Journal of Acoustical Society of America* 25 (1953):975-979.
12. *Human Engineering Guide on Equipment Design,* pp. 222-223.
13. J. P. Keating and E. F. Loftus, "Evaluation of the Effectiveness of the Vocal Alarm System of the Seattle Building," University of Washington, Department of Psychology, Seattle, 1974.

24

High-Rise Fire Safety/Human Response

W. Gene Williams
W. G. Williams and Associates, Inc.

Byron Hollander
Oklahoma City Fire Department

As the United States celebrates its illustrious second-century birthday, we have learned very much about many things to prove that ours is now the greatest nation on the earth.

Despite our present greatness, we are still plagued by an age-old nemesis—*fire.* This chapter will address itself to telling about fire, what it is, its nature, its cost, the spread of fire, brief reviews of past fires and lastly—what we can do with our present knowledge and technology to make our high-rise buildings as fire-safe as possible.

WHAT IS FIRE?

Fire is the result when fuel and heat are added to air. All three must be present; without any one, the fire goes "out." Air is essential to support a fire because approximately 21% of air is oxygen, and oxygen is highly flammable. Fire (and people) cannot survive if the oxygen level drops below 16%. Fuel is necessary as the source of flammable vapors. Fuels do not burn; when they reach their kindling temperatures, they release vapors which, when mixed with correct amounts of air or oxygen, ignite and burn. Heat is necessary to cause fuel to interact with air. Heat can be generated from several things, flame, chemical action, heat filament or electric arc.

THE HIGH COST OF FIRE

Almost 12,000 people in our nation are killed by fires each year, and most of these deaths occur from suffocation—or the inhalation of toxic fumes. In addition, some 300,000 Americans each year are injured by fire.

U.S. fires consume more than $3 billion in furniture, building materials, and equipment. Additionally, fire prevention costs, fire fighting, insurance, and other related expenditures, bring the actual costs to over $12 billion per year. To this figure must be added the horrendous cost of *human suffering,* not to mention the loss of business profits, records, and documents, plus rebuilding and replacement costs.

Within the United States in the next hour, probably 300 fires will be started, causing some $300,000 in property damage—and probably one human life will be extinguished. Some thirty-four more Americans will have been injured, perhaps maimed, crippled, and disfigured for life.

THE SPREAD OF FIRE

Fires don't usually start out big—except in explosions—they start small, sometimes smoldering for days, before bursting into flames. However, once the flame stage commences, it can spread 100% within the next four minutes.

It is commonly thought that most fires have four stages, as outlined below:

1. *Incipient stage.* Invisible gases are emitted as the fire begins. There is no visible smoke or flame, and even though no significant amount of heat is given off—a fire is beginning.
2. *Smoldering stage.* Combustion products appear in smoke form, consisting of various gases and small amounts of liquids and solids—solid particles usually consist of ash, iron oxide and various other noncombustible materials. Neither flame nor significant heat is present.
3. *Flame stage.* Fire becomes flame. While no great degree of heat is present, it will follow almost immediately.
4. *Heat stage.* High temperature uncontrolled heat appears which generates more combustible gases, forcing the air which contains these gases to expand rapidly. A near-explosive atmosphere is reached in which the spread of fire can be rapid.

A REVIEW OF HIGH-RISE BUILDINGS PAST AND PRESENT

"They don't build buildings like they used to." How many times have we heard that saying? Of course, the saying is absolutely true—we do build them differently.

At this point, it should be stated that a high-rise building can be defined as a building containing many floors above grade level into the sky; a building higher than safety ladders can reach; or, any building over six stories or 75 feet in height.

The early fifties saw changes in the methods of erecting high-rise buildings. Before this time, buildings were generally constructed of steel encased in concrete. Floors were usually of concrete and the walls were built as an integral part of the structure. Steam heat was used in winter, and summer air-conditioning as a building system was almost nonexistent—windows were operable and were used to allow cooler air to enter the building. Wall and ceiling surfaces were usually hard finish plaster, and "dropped" ceilings and their respective ceiling voids were unknown. Very little space was provided for power, utilities, and communications—*hence not many openings penetrated the respective floors as "shafts."*

Also, the various building codes around which these buildings had been constructed, outlining minimum acceptable standards of construction, apparently produced reasonably fire-safe buildings, and the facts have tended to support this assumption. Because of an apparent set of codes that delivered fire safety, a complacent attitude seemed to develop that buildings were "fire safe." This complacency coupled with the current construction methods were to "out-of-step" with the new breed of high-rise buildings.

Today's high-rise buildings have large sections of their panel walls actually hung from floor slabs. New insulating materials do not tend to absorb heat, as masonry and concrete do, *but tend to reflect the fire's heat.* No longer do we see operable windows.

Instead, they are inoperable, or "fixed." Multiple openings penetrate floors and walls for duct work, power and communications systems, thereby creating air spaces which can sustain and feed fires and allow it to spread throughout a building, rapidly, and sometimes tragically.

HISTORY

"Then the Lord rained upon Sodom and Gomorrah brimstone and fire from the Lord out of heaven" (Gen. 19:24).

Did Nero actually burn Rome? What a sight of destruction that must have been. Imagine an entire city ablaze! Think of the great earthquake that set San Francisco afire . . . and is it true, that Mrs. O'Leary's cow was discontent enough to upset the burning lantern and turn Chicago into ashes?

The world has known great calamities by fire—Pompeii (molten lava), many volcanic eruptions around the globe—and yet, there are recorded others in the last quarter-century that are fresh on our minds: the 29 story Andraus Building in Sao Paulo, Brazil—16 people killed, 375 injured; Rault Center, New Orleans, this 15th floor fire caused 6 people to jump to their deaths; another fire in a New Orleans motel caused six deaths by smoke inhalation; the Tae Yon Kak Hotel in Seoul, Korea, took 163 lives; and the Dale's Penthouse Restaurant fire in Montgomery, Alabama, killed 25 persons. Lest we forget, the 1942 Cocoanut Grove fire in Boston, Massachusetts, took 492 people.

In 1971, the General Services Administration convened its 1971 conference in open forum to determine problems concerning high-rise fire safety, which include:

1. *High-rise construction popularity.* People enjoy the status symbol of living and/or working in a tall building. Lack and high cost of land causes owners to go up, up, and up.

2. *New types of construction.* More punched holes in new buildings cause fires to penetrate other spaces quite rapidly.

3. *Materials.* Many materials are highly combustible, and emit toxic fumes when burned. Other materials are untested for fire safety.

4. *Location.* High-rise buildings and densely populated urban areas exist simultaneously. Crowded streets and traffic congestion are a part of this scene. Firefighting vehicles and equipment sometimes can hardly get near enough to a burning building to extinguish it. Plaza areas around some buildings including changes in grade levels plus courtyard sculptures also prevent firefighter's equipment from getting close to the fire.

5. *Height.* If a building is higher than fire ladders, height becomes a major problem for extinguishing fires.

6. *Inside firefighting.* Some building fires must be fought from inside the building. Carrying heavy hoses up stairways is difficult—firefighters must be replaced due to the intensity of heat and smoke.

7. *Evacuation.* Many buildings have several thousand occupants, and their evacuation from the building is almost impossible in many instances.

8. *Elevators.* Building occupants habitually use elevators for vertical travel, even from one floor to the next. As they are conditioned to this mode of vertical travel, it is no wonder that their first impulse is to evacuate by elevator. This should not be done, because in many instances, the elevators will rise or descend to the floor where fire exists, the doors will open and the elevator cab becomes a death box.

9. *Panic.* The inability to evacuate, and the lack of directions for doing so, causes people to panic in high-rise fires. Actually, most high-rise building occupants know very little about the structure's facilities. In general, they know about the lobby, elevators, hallways, their office, coffee shop, and restrooms—and that is about all. Many do not know the locations of the stairs, and that the stairs *only* must be sought out when emergencies arise. Panic causes people to do strange things . . . many perish because they have never been instructed *what to do,* and *what not to do.*

The foregoing has led us to the following conclusions:

1. It is almost impossible to completely evacuate a building.
2. Areas of refuge must be provided for occupants who must remain in the building.
3. The fire size must be limited and controlled.
4. Smoke control starts with limiting the size of the fire itself.
5. A grade-level "command-post" control center *must* be provided for the control of internal firefighting.
6. A total protection plan for occupants must be implemented.
7. Fire safety systems must provide structural integrity.
8. Sprinklers must be used more extensively, and they must have the volume and pressure of water to adequately perform their functions.

A NEW CONCEPT—FIRE SAFETY MANAGEMENT

Fire safety management means the application of *all* building systems to enable utilization of the structure itself as a primary source for preventing and controlling fire.

Objectives

1. *Fuel control.* Potential fuel for fire must be controlled by considering both direct potential for combustion and the development of smoke and toxic gases produced by combustion. Wall and floor coverings, ceiling materials, furnishings and decorations must be thoroughly considered before installation and/or placement.
2. *Compartmentation.* Structural elements having integral fire resistance should be used to compartment areas, thereby containing combustion.
3. *Early detection.* Fire must be detected as early as possible—at the incipient stage.
4. *Heating, ventilating, air-conditioning (HVAC) control.* These systems must be controlled and utilized to contain fire and smoke, and direct its movement. This could provide the creation of safe or "haven" areas for building occupants.
5. *Occupant movement control.* Occupant movement should be controlled and directed by using voice communication systems.
6. *Access.* Firefighters must have rapid access to fire areas by *all* available means.
7. *Elevator control.* Firefighters and other fire safety personnel *must* have control and manual override of elevators in emergencies.
8. *Electronic sprinkler system supervision.* This is needed for supervising the sprinkler systems and maximizing control of fire and smoke.
9. *Control center.* A central "command post" control center for use by building and fire department personnel during a fire emergency is necessary to provide for fire department communications within the building; announcement and identification of fire conditions within a building; supervision and activation of fire suppression systems and provisions for a central control panel which can coordinate building fire safety and other systems.

Fire safety management calls for the integration of all systems within and all those involved in planning, design, construction, and operation of high-rise buildings.

Elements of a Fire Safety System

1. Automatic smoke control. Air-conditioning operation to keep building smoke-free.
2. Fire and smoke detectors:
   a. fixed temperature and rate of rise thermal detector;
   b. fixed temperature, replaceable element;

c. plug-in detector—combination fixed temperature/rate of rise and fixed temperature only;
d. air duct detectors;
e. ionization smoke detector;
f. visible smoke detector;
g. infrared flame detector.

3. Fire doors. Specially constructed fire-rated doors that are programmed to close under various emergency conditions. These automatic closing units enable compartmentation—to divide a building into separate compartments, isolated by electronically controlled fire and smoke barrier doors.
4. Fire-resistant building materials. The use of building materials that are incombustible, or nearly so.
5. Fire-safe stairwells. Incombustible materials, four-hour construction, nonslip treads, proper widths, handrails, lighting, and emergency lighting.
6. Two-way communication systems:
   a. It is necessary that occupants be moved or instructed to move within the building to safe "haven" areas.
   b. Communications must be capable of specific application—zoned to reach a specifically given area;
   c. Communications must be incorporated with other controls, HVAC, elevators, automatic doors, so that areas of safety can be created and the passageways to these areas kept open;
   d. Data gathering/decision-making/control depends essentially on two-way communications to control affected areas and control nonaffected areas plus the ability to inform, dissenminate, and relay undated messages when and where needed.
   e. A fire command station must be designated so that all controls can be centralized and operated from one given area.
7. Water stand pipes. Wet or dry or combination fire hose cabinet locations clearly marked for ready usage.
8. Safety floors. Incombustible, *with no unnecessary leakage holes.*
9. Twenty-four-hour fire control center (command post), monitoring control and information of all systems.
10. Emergency generator. To provide auxiliary power throughout the building if the primary source of power is lost.
11. Mechanical equipment monitoring. To assure that this function is operating satisfactorily, a central monitoring facility for remote equipment should be provided.
12. Voice alarms. Live and taped messages to inform occupants of routine or special directives. Both men's and women's voices should be used.
13. Fire extinguishers. Well-located, current, adequate fire extinguishers are a necessity.
14. Automatic sprinklers. To be installed overhead for rapid response to fires in providing a deluge water extinguishing system.
15. Fire walls. Fire-safe walls for compartmentation of floor areas.
16. Safety areas. Fire-safe zones for occupants during a fire.
17. Automatic elevator recall. To control elevators for fire safety/firefighters' use.
18. Fire protection plan. Each high-rise building should have the following:
    a. twenty-four-hour designated disaster (fire) controller;
    b. an implemented plan of action in case of emergency;
    c. floor fire wardens;
    d. assistant fire wardens;
    e. fire drills;
    f. fire preparedness plans;
    g. education program;
       i. "What to do!"
       ii. "What not to do!"
    h. site and building plans available to fire de-

partment before fire occurs. Also, the building fire controller should arrange to have firefighters acquaint themselves with the building in case fires start there—a "dry-run" could be helpful.

Finally, no building is absolutely fire safe. However, a total fire safety system designed and integrally constructed within a structure *can improve* its relative safety. Much research can and must be done in high-rise fire safety. The resulting "best methods" should be implemented to make buildings "as safe as possible."

REFERENCES

Bazjanac, Vladimir. "Another Way Out: Elevators in Evacuating High-Rise Buildings." *Progressive Architecture,* April 1974, pp. 88, 89.

Bose, Vilmar K. "Highrise Living: How Safe?" *AIA Journal,* January 1972, pp. 32-34.

Harmathy, T. Z. "Design Approach to Fire Safety in Buildings." *Progressive Architecture,* April 1974, pp. 82-87.

Jensen, Rolf. *Fire Protection for the Design Engineer.* Boston: Cahners Books, Division of Cahners Publishing Company, Inc., 1975.

Lyons, Robert J. "Automatic Heat and Smoke Venting." *Progressive Architecture,* April 1972, pp. 114-117.

Macsai, John. "Fire Safety." *Building Design Construction,* May 1975, pp. 59-61.

NECA. Electrical Design Guidelines, "High Rise Fire Safety." June 1974, pp. 1-16.

Villecco, Marguerite. "Technology." *Architectural Forum,* March 1972, pp. 52-55.

25

Simulation of Elevator Performance in High-Rise Buildings under Conditions of Emergency

Vladimir Bazjanac
University of California, Berkeley

INTRODUCTION

Elevators comprise the single most expensive mechanical system in any regular high-rise building. The elevator system for the Bank of America headquarters building in San Francisco cost 6.39% of the total construction cost; for the Alcoa Building it cost 7.98%. The average cost of elevators in a high-rise building varies between 7-8% of the total building construction cost.* Yet, elevators are taken out of service and cannot be used by the building population when they are needed most: in cases of emergency when escaping *fast* may mean the difference between life and death!

Most cities in the United States have appended their building codes to require automatic grounding of all passenger elevators in cases of emergency:

> [In emergency mode] elevators which are in normal service . . . shall return non-stop to the main floor. An elevator travelling away from the main floor shall reverse at the next available floor. . . . Elevators standing at a floor other than the main floor with doors open, shall close their doors without delay. . . . Elevators on emergency service should not respond to corridor calls. . . .[1]

This means that people cannot use elevators to escape from danger and must find another way to reach safety (Figure 25-1).

The danger of elevator failure, the need for the emergency personnel to get to the area in danger without delay, and the opinion that existing elevator configurations cannot evacuate people fast enough are reasons given most frequently for the elimination of elevator service.

The use of elevators in past emergencies often required travel through zones of danger, which sometimes caused mechanical failure or malfunctioning of

*The portion of the total building cost spent on elevators depends on the future use of the building, concern for elevator service, type of high-rise, etc. Quoted percentages apply to high-rise office buildings and were obtained by courtesy of Skidmore, Owings and Merrill, San Francisco, Calif.

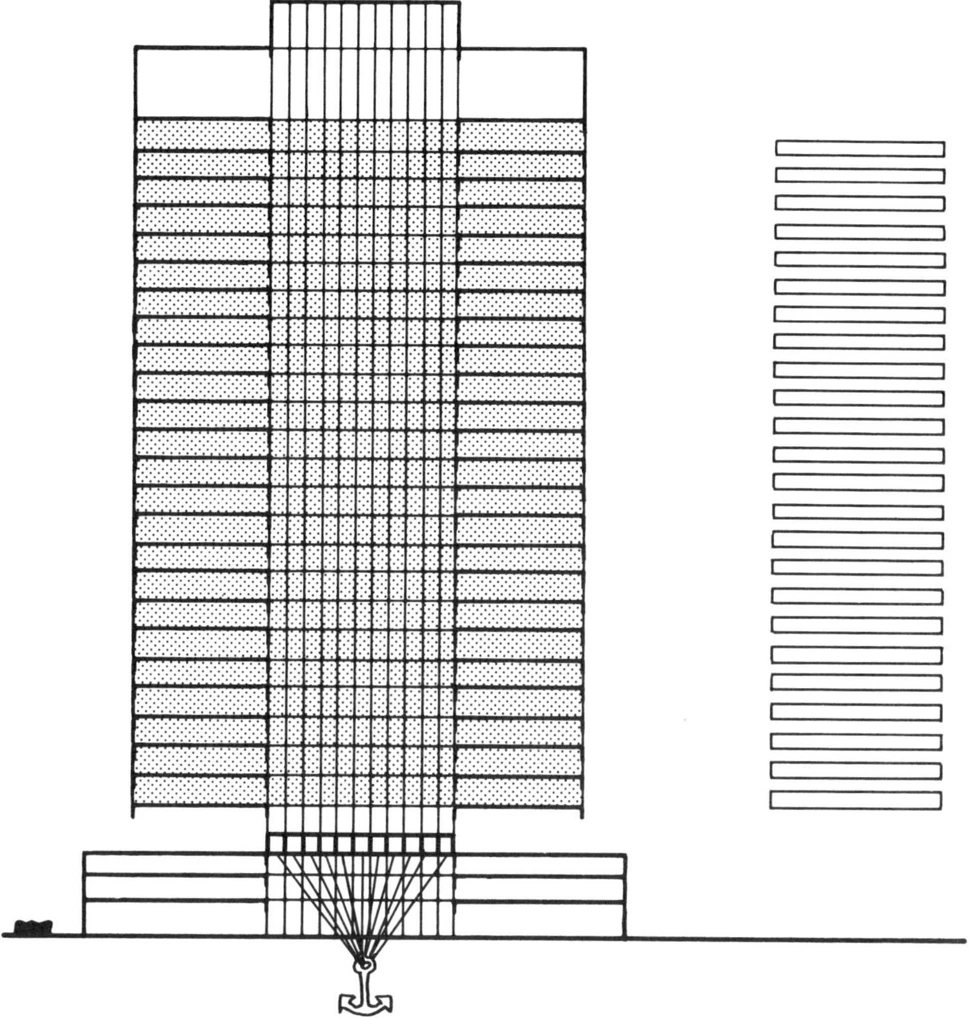

Figure 25-1
When elevators are grounded, no floor calls can be answered.

elevators in which lives were lost (e.g., unscheduled opening of elevator doors on floors engulfed in fire, false floor calls, failure of elevators to close doors and depart because of smoke, etc.). Possibility of power failures, destruction of elevator control mechanisms and wiring, and damage to equipment in general further compound the risk of using elevators in emergencies. Naturally, building codes which require the grounding of elevators eliminate such risk.

The use of elevators by the building population during an emergency might interfere with operations of emergency personnel (primarily the Fire Department and building operations personnel). People trying to escape may congest the elevator system, and emergency personnel and equipment may find it difficult to reach the floor of danger. The competition for elevator service and delays in reaching emergency areas is completely avoided if elevators are automatically taken to the main floor and parked there at the disposal of emergency personnel.

The opinion that elevators cannot provide evacuation service is founded in experiences with the *normal* use of elevators during periods of peak demand for service. Elevators make numerous stops (floor after floor) on a trip and take extended time to reach the last floor of service. Under such conditions they cause long waiting on many floors, and their numbers and service appear insufficient to frustrated people who are waiting for elevators.

The automatic grounding in emergencies required by most building codes is an extremely simplistic answer to aforementioned problems. It fails to recognize that most emergencies do not start in elevator shafts or lobbies and that most elevators fail only considerably later after the beginning of an emergency. It ignores the fact that Fire Departments and other emergency personnel in most cases use only one elevator at the time to reach the area of emergency and that they prefer to use service elevators (the main loading floor for service elevators is usually different from the main floor of the building!). It does not consider the avoiding of multiple stops on elevator trips which, together with organized and controlled elevator loading procedures, can increase the efficiency in the use of elevators by an order of magnitude. In addition, the automatic grounding of elevators discriminates against the handicapped and the elderly: it takes away their only means of escape to safety.

With elevators grounded, people are expected to escape on foot through stairs. The requirement to ground elevators implies that escape on foot using stairs is always safer then escape with elevators. Yet, as the calculations of a member of the National Research Council of Canada show,[2] the congestion in stairwells during total evacuation of high-rise buildings may often reach such proportions that all movement of people comes to a complete stop. In other words, escape through stairs may become no escape at all!

Elevators have characteristics which make them very desirable, and perhaps the best means of movement of people in emergencies. They are fast and they are equally suitable for use to the young, the old, the handicapped, to the frequent and to the occasional users of the building. Elevators can be controlled from the outside of the emergency zone and their operation can be made independent of the psychological states of those who are being transported. The potential and the limitations of the use of elevators in evacuation of high-rise buildings should be reevaluated with much more courage and confidence than is contained in the requirement to automatically ground elevators.

HOW MUCH TIME IS NEEDED FOR EVACUATION WITH ELEVATORS?

Analyses of fires in high-rise buildings of the past show that elevators are safely operable for a considerable period of time at the beginning of fires, and often are not seriously damaged by the fire at all. Even fires that burn out of control and damage the whole building, like the fire in Sao Paulo in 1972, do not always destroy the elevator system. In the Sao Paulo fire a number of people apparently escaped to safety with elevators.[3]

Chief E. D. Condon of the San Francisco Fire Department classifies all high-rise buildings in three groups: modern buildings with a life-safety system (those which have elevator lobbies enclosed with non-combustible walls on each floor), modern buildings without life-safety system, and old buildings which have been designed with total lack of understanding of fire safety (such buildings might even have open elevator shafts). In modern buildings without life-safety systems the elevator system can be expected to operate reliably for more than five minutes after the beginning of the fire. For modern buildings with life-safety systems this expected safe operating time can be extended to well over ten minutes and, barring disastrous fires within the elevator core iself, it could easily be half an hour or more. This means that in modern buildings there is a period of time at the beginning of the fire during which elevators can be safely used to get people away from danger.

We experimented with a number of existing high-rise buildings to find out how to use elevators during these brief, but safe periods of time, and to define possible strategies of evacuation. The experiments were conducted in the Department of Architecture at the University of California under the sponsorship of the National Science Foundation; they were done with the help of a computer-based elevator simulator which was designed to simulate partial or total evacuation from buildings. The simulation was used to generate the information on how evacuation could be accomplished, without causing the interruption of operation of any real building. The generated information included the numbers of people and times of evacuation for different strategies of evacuation.

Partial Evacuation

Two types of emergency conditions were investigated: emergencies on one floor, and emergencies in the entire building. In emergencies in which the fire is contained within one floor the actual evacuation zone includes three floors: the floor of fire, the floor above (which may be infiltrated by smoke), and the floor below (which may receive a lot of water from firefighting above). Fires were assumed on every floor one by one (from the bottom to the top of every building used in experiments) to determine which three-floor area in the building takes most time to evacuate completely.

The simplest strategy of the use of elevators we investigated was an extension of what takes place under present code requirements. After elevators are all automatically dispatched to the ground floor lobby, they are re-activated under normal "down-peak" operating mode* and allowed to answer calls from the three floors in the evacuation zone. People found in the three floors are taken to the main lobby (Figure 25-2). Using this strategy the experiments show that in most buildings the last person is evacuated from any three-floor zone in less than eight minutes. Evacuation time can be improved if, instead of taking people to the ground floor lobby, they are unloaded at the edges of the elevator zone (i.e., at the bottom or top floor of the elevator zone, whichever is closest to the emergency zone). Using this elevator operation strategy (Figure 25-3) the last person can be evacuated from a three-floor emergency zone in less than five minutes. The evacuation time can be further reduced to a little over four minutes if the elevators unload people on floors just below and just above the emergency zone (Figure 25-4).

The time of evacuation obviously varies from one building to another and is, in general, a function of the number of people to be evacuated, the number of elevators, the distance and speed elevators travel, elevator capacity, and the number of elevators in actual use.

The number of people to be evacuated from a floor is defined as the expected number of people found on that floor. This number is not decreased by the number of people that might escape through the stairways or other means, because it is impossible to predict what percentage of the floor population might escape through means other than elevators in an actual emergency in which elevators *are available.* This assumption therefore represents the worst condition that can be encountered and any reduction in the number of people on the floor (because of escape using other means) will shorten the time needed for evacuation with elevators.

One of the major causes of delay in elevator service are multiple stops (i.e., more than one stop for

*In "down-peak" operating mode elevators respond to the call for service under the assumption that the traffic is directed out of the building. Calls for service downwards (if the main lobby is in that direction) are given priority over calls for service upwards.[4]

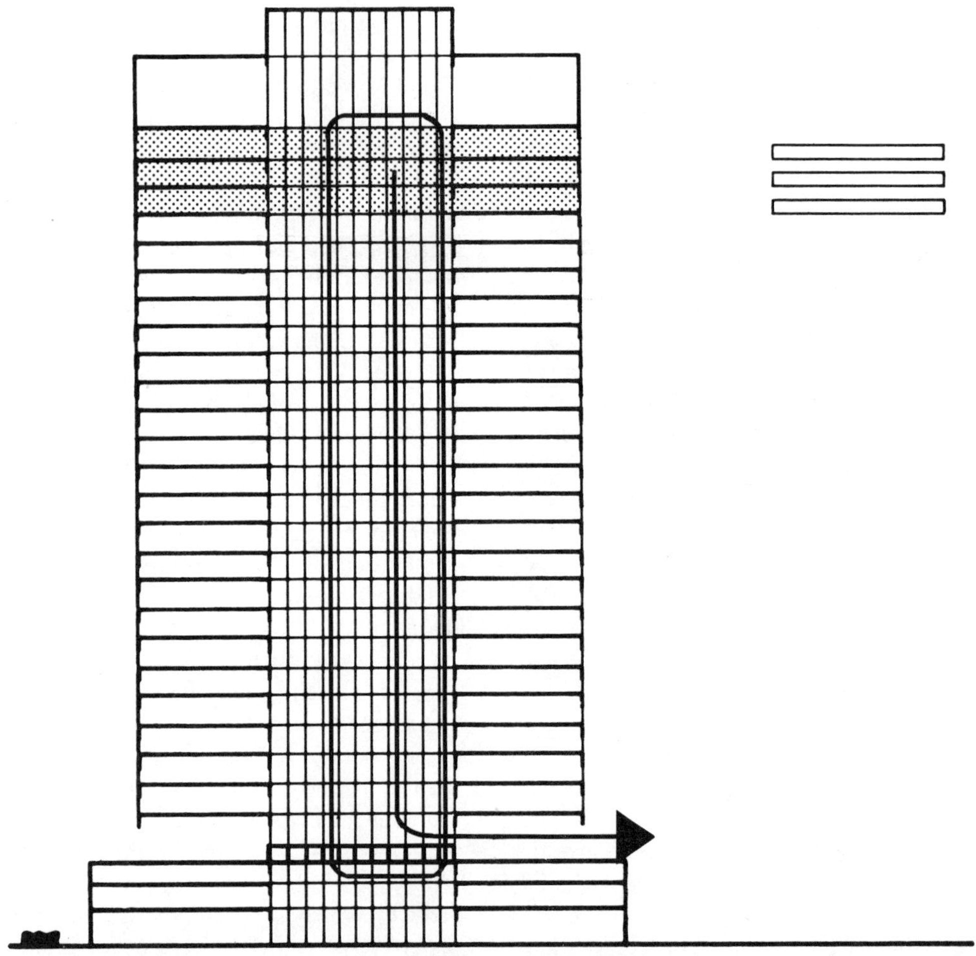

Figure 25-2
Three-floor area of emergency is served by all available cabs in elevator zone. Service elevator is grounded for the disposal of Fire Dept. Evacuees unload in main lobby.

loading and unloading on the same trip). All unnecessary stops *must* be eliminated for efficient evacuation with elevators. Multiple stops were avoided in the experiments by sending all filled cabs automatically to the unloading floor.

The performance under normal "down-peak" conditions also depends on distance elevators have to travel and the speed at which cabs travel. Obviously, the shorter the distance of travel the shorter the evacuation time. However, the distance of travel can be offset by higher elevator speed which in many buildings causes the lower floors of the higher elevator zones to be evacuated sooner than the higher floors of the lower zones. This means that in buildings which do not have well-balanced distance and speed of travel of elevators, some floors may take

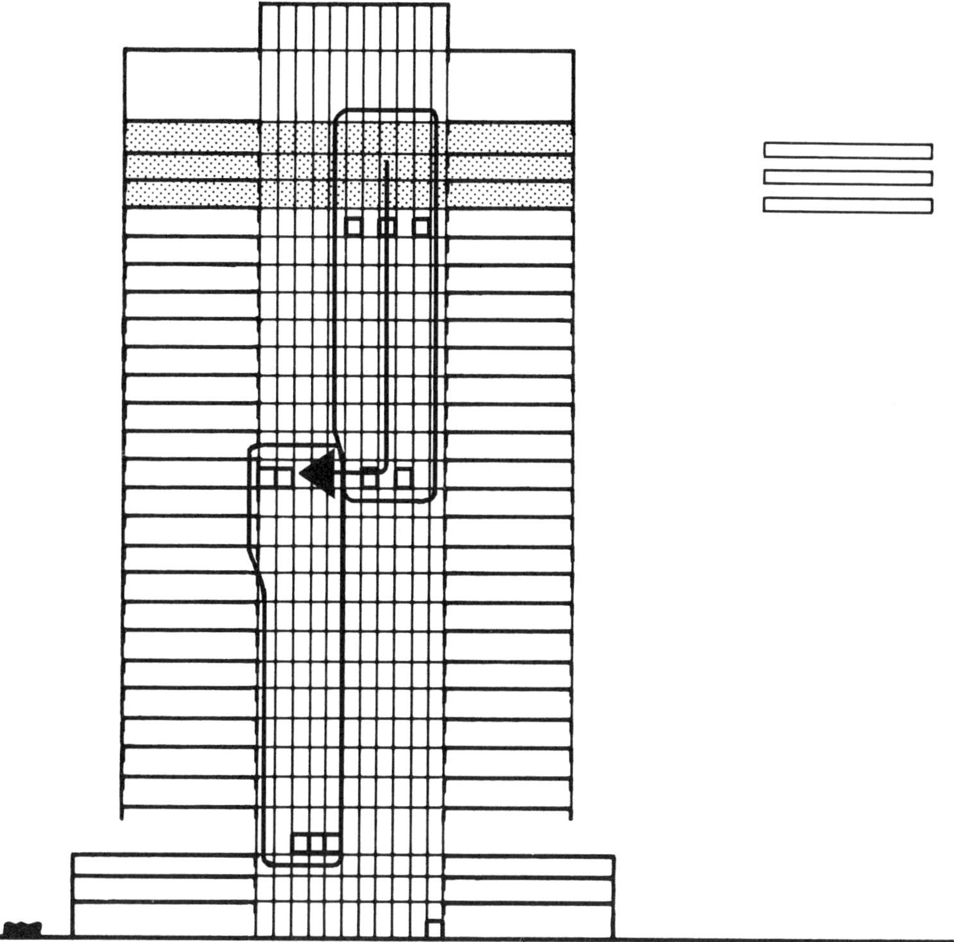

Figure 25–3
The three-floor zone of emergency is served by all elevators in zone. These elevators travel only to the bottom or top of their zone. Passengers unloaded there are picked up by elevators from the other zone.

considerably longer to evacuate than others. Under normal "down-peak" operating mode when all elevators which can serve the three floors in the evacuation zone are dedicated to serving only those three floors, some elevators may actually be idle some of the time. Elevators are dispatched to those floors only while calls on those floors are active. Calls on a particular floor are inactive while an elevator is in the process of loading on that floor. This means that a larger number of available elevators will not necessarily reduce the evacuation time.

This has another interesting implication: when one elevator is idle it can be used by building operations and firefighting personnel without significantly affecting the evacuation from the three-floor zone. Since the Fire Department rarely needs the services

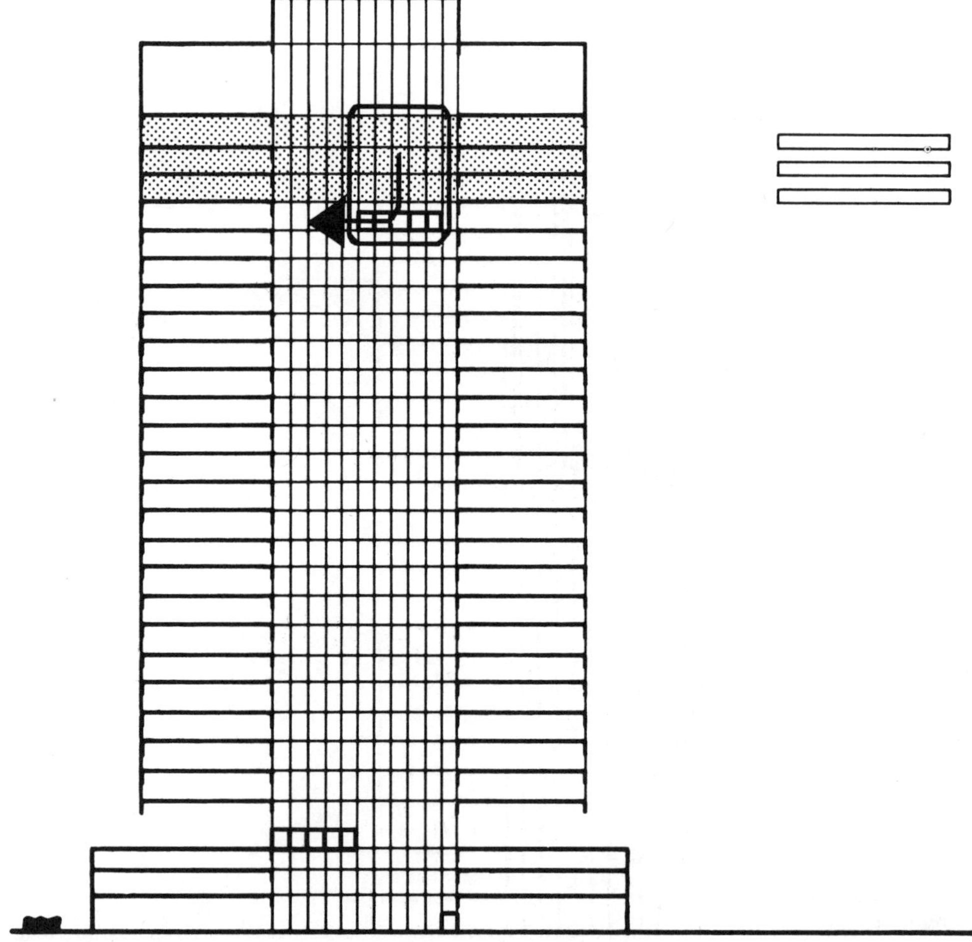

Figure 25–4
Elevators in the zone travel only within the floor below and the floor above the three-floor evacuation area.

of more than one elevator, this indicates that making elevators available for evacuation will not hamper the use of elevators by the Fire Department and other firefighting personnel. At the same time, the dedication of one elevator to the Fire Department and the resulting reduction of the number of available elevators will not significantly affect the evacuation of people in danger.

The results from experiments indicate that evacuation of three-floor areas with elevators can be safely accomplished in modern buildings if it is started without delay. The selection of a particular strategy will depend on the estimate of how much time is left to safely operate the elevators. If enough time is left, people should be taken to the ground floor. This will diminish the demand on elevator service should it later become necessary to evacuate the rest of the building as well. The difference in evacuation time between taking people out of the building and lowering them to the edge of the elevator zone (if not the same) might vary up to three minutes and in most cases will be less than two. This difference may not be significant enough to cause not to try to take all the people out of the building, especially in view of the fact that these evacuation times are based on maximum occupancy figures, and that in a real life emergency it may take less to evacuate the three floors.

If the expected remaining time to safely operate the elevators is less than five minutes, one should remove people from the endangered three-floor zone to the floor at the closest boundary of the elevator zone. If the building was designed with foresight, that floor will also be served by elevators from the adjacent zone (it will be a sky lobby or the floor at which two zones overlap), and the evacuees will board different elevators which will take them to the ground floor. If the elevator zones do not overlap, evacuated people are still only one floor from the other elevator zone.

Very little time is saved if people are unloaded at floors immediately below or above the three-floor evacuation zone rather than at the border floors of the elevator zone. Our experiments show evacuation times become about 30 seconds shorter, and the difference is never more than 45 seconds. Since it is very difficult to predict the exact amount of elevator failure, such small difference in evacuation time is not very significant.

By far the fastest method of evacuation of any individual floor is the simultaneous dispatch of all available elevators to that floor (Figure 25-5). Such dispatching is not possible in the normal (automatic) "down-peak" operating mode and in most buildings can be done only manually from the central control post. When elevators are dispatched simultaneously, and if the total number of people per floor does not exceed the combined capacity of all available elevator cabs, the entire floor might be evacuated at the same time. The evacuation time then becomes a function of when the last elevator can reach the floor and the time it takes to load the cabs. The former in turn depends on where the elevators are at the time of the switch to the simultaneous dispatch mode; the latter, and the success of this strategy depends entirely on the ability to get everybody on the floor to the elevator lobby in the short time it takes the elevators to reach the floor and load people.

Total Evacuation

Experiments with *total* evacuation of buildings (where all people are removed from the entire building) have shown some surprising results. The total evacuation time of some smaller buildings, which have half as many floors as some larger buildings, was more than twice as long as evacuation time of some of the largest buildings.

Time of total evacuation from a building depends primarily on the number and distribution of people in the building, the design of the building and the characteristics of the elevator system (Figure 25-6). Nothing can substitute for a low number of people in the building and a large number of elevators to serve them. The smaller the people/elevators ratio (i.e., the more "elevatoring" per person) the faster the evacuation of the building.

Slow elevator speeds and poor balance between elevator speed and distance of travel cause considerable extension of evacuation time. Most significant are the number of floors in the elevator zone and the number of elevator cabs serving that zone. Some smaller buildings are divided in two zones only, which are served with relatively few elevators. These elevators tend to have slow top speeds because of the relatively low height of the building. Some of the tallest buildings will often have up to eight elevators serving a ten- to twelve-floor zone at high speeds, which is the main reason why such buildings can be evacuated much faster than the smaller ones.

All buildings were completely evacuated in the experiments in less than 30 minutes. It appears that one can expect any "normal" building (that is, any

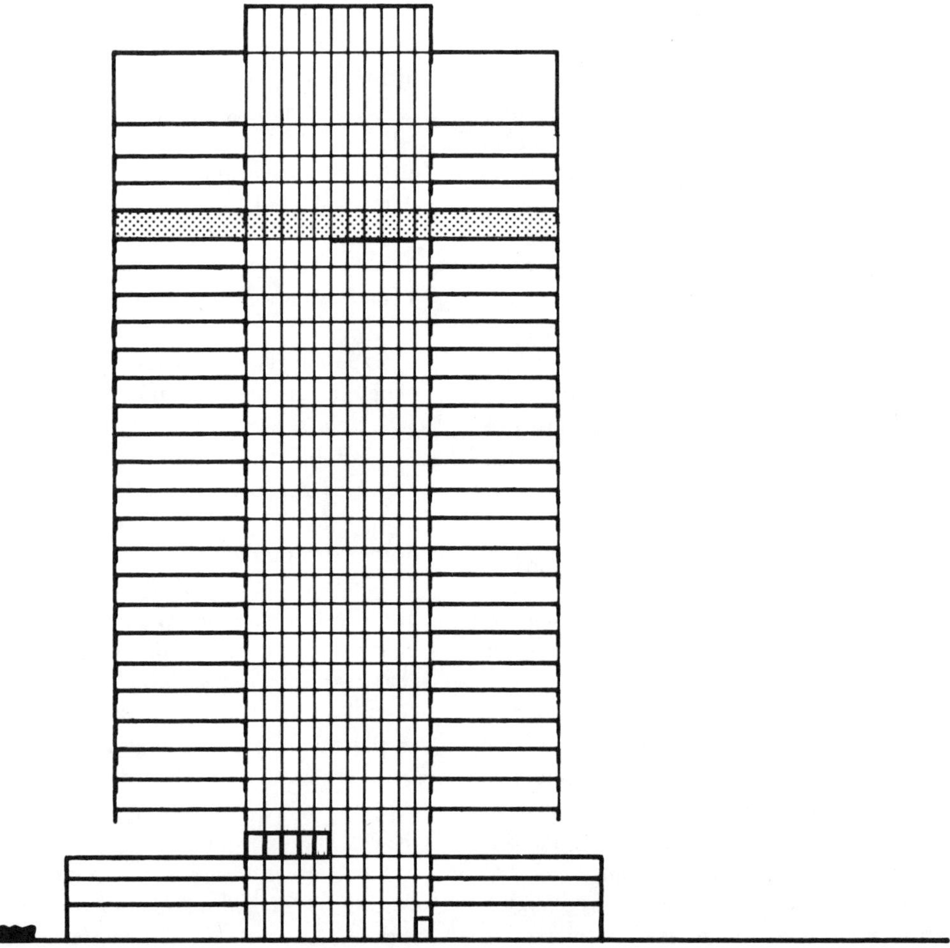

Figure 25-5
All elevators in the zone are dispatched simultaneously to the one floor of evacuation. People are evacuated in the time it takes to load the last cab. Service elevator is left to the disposal of Fire Dept.

building which has a satisfactory elevator system under normal day-to-day conditions of operation) to be totally evacuated with elevators within one-half hour. Buildings which have very efficient elevator systems can be sometimes completely evacuated in less than 10 minutes.

There was a fire on the mechanical floor of a twenty-two-story office building in downtown San Francisco a few years ago. The fire was not a serious one and was contained within the mechanical floor. The smoke, however, spread through the mechanical system into the rest of the building, which necessitated the total evacuation of the building. Using both elevators and stairwells it took over half an hour to evacuate the building. The evacuation caused a lot of confusion and was far from efficient. The use of

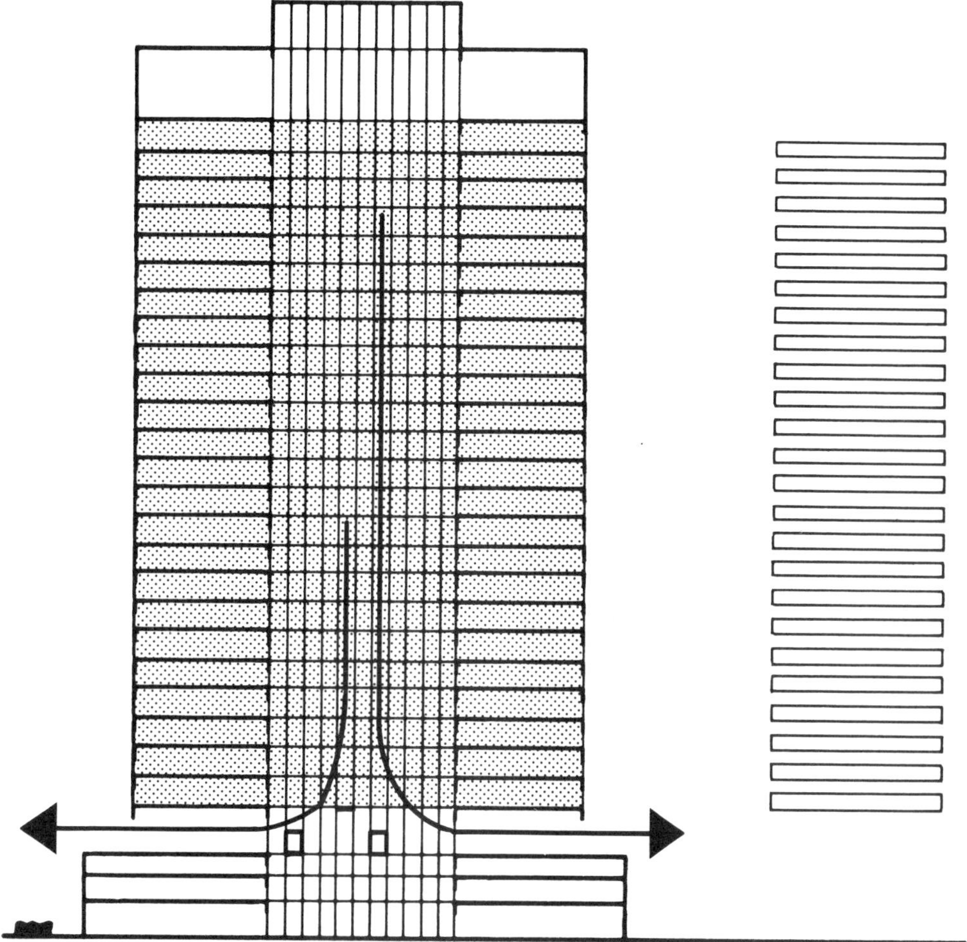

Figure 25-6
All elevators in the building are employed in total evacuation. Evacuation time depends on number of people and elevators, and elevator performance characteristics.

elevators was "ad-hoc," with cabs stopping practically at every floor in each trip.

This evacuation was duplicated with the elevator simulator using controlled elevator operations in "down-peak" mode. The simulated evacuation of the entire building (with no use of stairwells) was accomplished in 8 minutes and 20 seconds (Figure 25-7).

The discrepancy between the real-life emergency and the result from the experiment with the elevator simulator is caused by the difference in the extent of control exercised in the evacuation procedure. While in the real-life emergency there was very little understanding and control of evacuation, total control was assumed in the experiments. In fact, all experimental results are based on the assumptions of a steady flow of people to be evacuated to the elevators and the

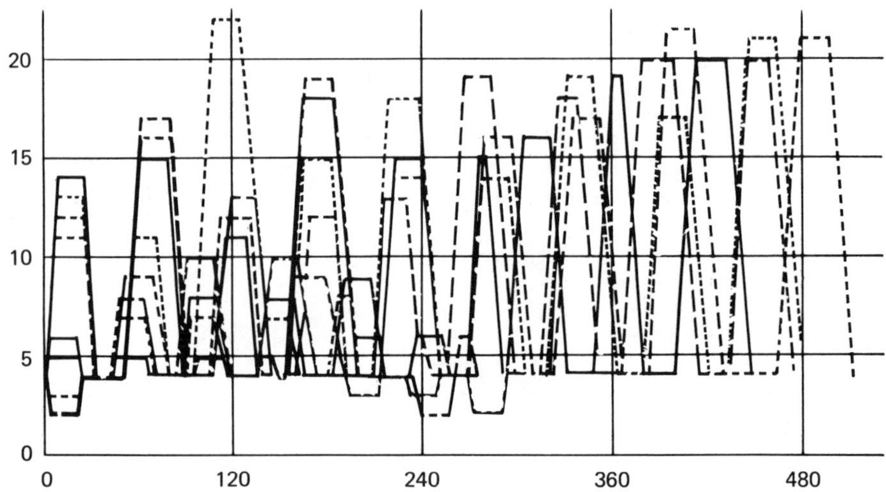

Figure 25–7
Total evacuation of a two-zone building with very efficient elevator system.

smooth loading of elevators without any delay. Any deviation from these assumptions, i.e., any inability to secure such steady flow of people and smooth loading of elevators in real-life emergencies, will considerably extend real-life evacuation times.

Such maximum control of evacuation can be accomplished in reality only if the flow of people to elevators and loading of cabs is planned for, well organized, and supervised by trained personnel. To achieve such level of control it will be necessary to place trained wardens on each floor of evacuation, who will direct people and make sure that there are no delays in the loading of elevators. In fact, the ability to provide such controlled loading of elevators is by far the most critical factor for accomplishment of fast evacuation. Without it, even the most efficient elevator system and best evacuation-minded building design will be of little value.

BUILDING DESIGN CONSIDERATIONS

The concept of refuge areas, i.e., the selective distribution of safe and life supporting areas within the building, has little effect on evacuation. Refuge areas are critical in maintaining safe environments for people who cannot be evacuated. Our experiments demonstrate that if there is enough time to remove people from the zone of immediate danger, the difference between taking them to other floors or all the way out of the building is not significant for modern buildings. In such buildings one can expect to maintain safe elevator operations for more than five minutes at the beginning of fire, and there is enough time to evacuate people from any three-floor emergency zone all the way out of the building, provided that the evacuation starts immediately. This makes evacuation with elevators a factor of lesser importance in locating refuge areas.

The best location for refuge areas (as far as elevators are concerned) are sky lobbies of floors at which two elevator zones overlap. Such floors are directly accessible to a larger number of elevators and therefore more people can be unloaded there faster than on other floors. If the building has no sky lobbies or floors at which elevator zones overlap, the best location for refuge areas are floors at the border of elevator zones. Refuge areas on such floors are most accessible to people coming from floors served by adjacent elevator zones.

Elevator zoning has a major significance in accomplishing fast evacuation. Overlapping zones, i.e., servicing of one floor by two elevator zones, is one of the most desirable and most important features for safe evacuation from high-rise buildings. Overlapping zones have the effect of sky lobbies: people from one zone can be unloaded at the floor of overlap and picked up by elevators from the other zone to be taken out of the building. Without overlapping floors, each zone acts as a separate building. Elevators from the first zone do not have to travel all the way to the ground floor lobby, their travel distance (and time) is shortened and the evacuation is accomplished faster.

The speed of evacuation depends partially on how well the speed of travel is balanced with the distance cabs have to travel. If this balance is poor it can be improved by modifying the distance of travel. This is possible only if the zones overlap in the building: another very important building design feature is the actual division of elevator zones in the building. The more zones in the building the faster the evacuation; also, the more elevators in a zone the faster the total evacuation of the zone.

Mode of elevator operation is yet another factor. Partial evacuation accomplished with the normal "down-peak" mode of operation can be significantly shortened by sending elevators simultaneously to the emergency floor. At present, in most high-rise buildings, this is achieved by switching from automatic to manual control, which allows the simultaneous dispatch to the same floor. Emergency operating mode should include *automatic* simultaneous dispatching to the same floor as one of the standard features.

Evacuation could be improved by an order of magnitude if it were conducted with a good understanding of what is actually happening in the entire building. If one could observe the population of each floor and assess the progress of evacuation, one could adjust the evacuation strategy from floor to floor and from one minute to another. This calls for intelligence systems for buildings which would inform central control posts about the conditions of the emergency and the population throughout the building and would permit direct communication between command posts and elevator lobbies on each floor.

With such intelligence systems available one could design intelligent elevator dispatcher mechanisms which would be capable of receiving and interpreting the information about the conditions on every floor in the building. Such intelligent dispatchers could weigh the assignments for service to floors in terms of the number of people to be evacuated and the extent of immediate need for evacuation; in that way elevators would be automatically sent to floors with the most pressing need for service and would operate under the most efficient strategy of evacuation for the detected conditions.

CONCLUSION

It is clear that the automatic elimination of elevators from service in case of emergency is wrong: it eliminates a method of evacuation which is safe for a period of time and which could provide all the necessary means to evacuate the building. Preventing the use of elevators when they are needed most is not only extremely wasteful—it aggravates the evacuation problem and is counterproductive.

Elevators should be used only when their operation is safe. However, the decision to pull elevators out of service should be made according to the spread of danger in each individual case by an authorized person on location—not a priori through legislation. If it is too dangerous to operate elevators in the zone of emergency, but still safe in the rest of the building, elevators should be used in conjunction with evacuation on foot. People can escape from the emergency zone to the floor below on foot, and elevator service can be concentrated to evacuate people safely from that floor.

With proper planning and control of evacuation procedures, elevators can accomplish safe evacuation of modern buildings. In most modern buildings the performance of elevators themselves is totally adequate; lacking are the planning of how to act in emergencies and the control of population which is evacuated, as well as intelligence systems to monitor the progress of emergencies. While intelligence systems and intelligent dispatchers might require technological developments of the future, better planning and control of evacuation procedures can be achieved in existing buildings immediately. If the thinking about the use of elevators in emergencies becomes positive, high-rise buildings will become safer soon after that.

NOTES

1. Excerpted from the *Building Code of the City of New York,* 1970, Chapter 26.
2. J. Brooks Semple, "Smoke Control in High-Rise Buildings," *ASHRAE Journal,* April 1971, p. 31.
3. A. Elwood Willey, "High-Rise Building Fire," *Fire Journal,* July 1972, pp. 7–108.
4. See George R. Strakosch, *Vertical Transportation: Elevators and Escalators* (New York: Wiley, 1967), Chapter 6.

26

Sociological Aspects of Natural Disasters

J. Eugene Haas
University of Colorado

Some time ago several of us received a request to put together a compendium of the findings available to answer the question: "What is known about human behavior in natural disasters?" In the process of reviewing all of the published empirical work that we could find, it became clear that there were many gaps and that most of the findings were from individual case studies of a single disaster event. Systematic comparative studies were few in number and more sophisticated research designs were almost never used.* But at least we now have a better notion of where the research needs are. A quantitative overview of the findings may be seen in Table 26-1.

It has also become clear that research on human aspects of natural disasters has been poorly funded in the United States. Such funding represents perhaps 2% to 3% of the amount spent on physical science and engineering research related to natural hazards. So our progress has been slow, but there has been progress. Furthermore, there has been increasing communication between behavioral scientists and members of the other relevant professions.†

RESEARCH FINDINGS

The title of this chapter is really too broad for a short presentation so I will stick with some of the re-

A number of the findings noted herein were developed or refined during the course of research efforts at the University of Colorado. Financial support for the research was provided by NSF-RANN (Grant Nos. GI-32942, GI-39246 and AEN 74-24079), the Federal Disaster Assistance Administration, NOAA, and the National Academy of Engineering Committee on Natural Disasters.

*Dennis S. Mileti, Thomas E. Drabek, and J. Eugene Haas, *Human Systems in Extreme Environments: A Sociological Perspective*, University of Colorado Institute of Behavioral Science, 1975, 165 pp. Many of the conclusions presented in this chapter are drawn from this volume.

†This has been a special emphasis of the Institute of Behavioral Science at the University of Colorado in the conduct of its natural hazards conferences. Recently the Earthquake Engineering Research Institute (EERI) has taken steps to encourage similar interaction.

TABLE 26–1
Distribution of Published Hazard/Disaster Findings When Each Finding Is Tallied in All Relevant Cells of the Matrix (N = 1,399)

	Knowledge Matrix Time						
	A	*B*	*C*	*D*	*E*	*F*	
System Level	*Preparedness/ Adjustment*	*Warning*	*Pre-Impact Early Actions (Mobilization)*	*Post-Impact Short-term Actions*	*Relief Restoration*	*Reconstruction*	
Individual	96/*N* .07	93/*N* .07	87/*N* .06	162/*N* .12	50/*N* .04	31/*N* .02	*N* = 519 % = 38
Group	16/*N* .01	28/*N* .02	30/*N* .02	77/*N* .06	15/*N* .01	17/*N* .01	*N* = 183 % = 13
Organization	25/*N* .02	11/*N* .01	8/*N* .01	126/*N* .09	43/*N* .03	9/*N* .01	*N* = 222 % = 17
Community	104/*N* .07	4/*N* .00	8/*N* .01	129/*N* .09	72/*N* .05	45/*N* .03	*N* = 362 % = 25
Society (Nation)	56/*N* .04	4/*N* .00	7/*N* .01	27/*N* .02	12/*N* .01	6/*N* .00	*N* = 112 % = 8
International	1/*N* .00	0 .00	0 .00	0 .00	0 .00	0 .00	*N* = 0 % = 0
	N = 298 % = 21	*N* = 140 % = 10	*N* = 140 % = 11	*N* = 521 % = 38	*N* = 192 % = 14	*N* = 108 % = 7	*N* = 1,399 % = 101

Source: Mileti et al., 1975, p. 13.

search findings which hopefully will be of greatest interest to professionals in engineering and architecture.

Although a capsule version of "what is known" about the following topics is presented here, the reader should be aware, however, that in some instances, educated speculation has to be substituted for nonexistent systematic empirical evidence.

Level of community preparedness

Why are some cities less vulnerable than others? After disaster impact, why do some respond more quickly and effectively than others?

Figure 26-1 provides some indication of the complexity involved. No simpler answers are known. For example, it appears that prior disaster experience can have several consequences for level of preparedness. If the disaster experience has been recent and large scale, level of preparedness tends to be higher. If prior disasters have been small in impact or if it has been many years since the last one, then the city will be relatively unprepared.

But that is only one factor affecting preparedness. For many areas land use is a critical factor determining vulnerability and preparedness. If the principal economic power centers within a city stand to profit significantly from largely unregulated land use, then the ability of the community to avoid losses will be low. This is especially obvious for hurricane, flood, and earthquake hazards.

Perception of hazard

Individual citizens, business executives, and most public officials tend to underestimate the hazard. Factors related to accuracy of hazard perception are indicated in Figure 26-2. The findings suggest that

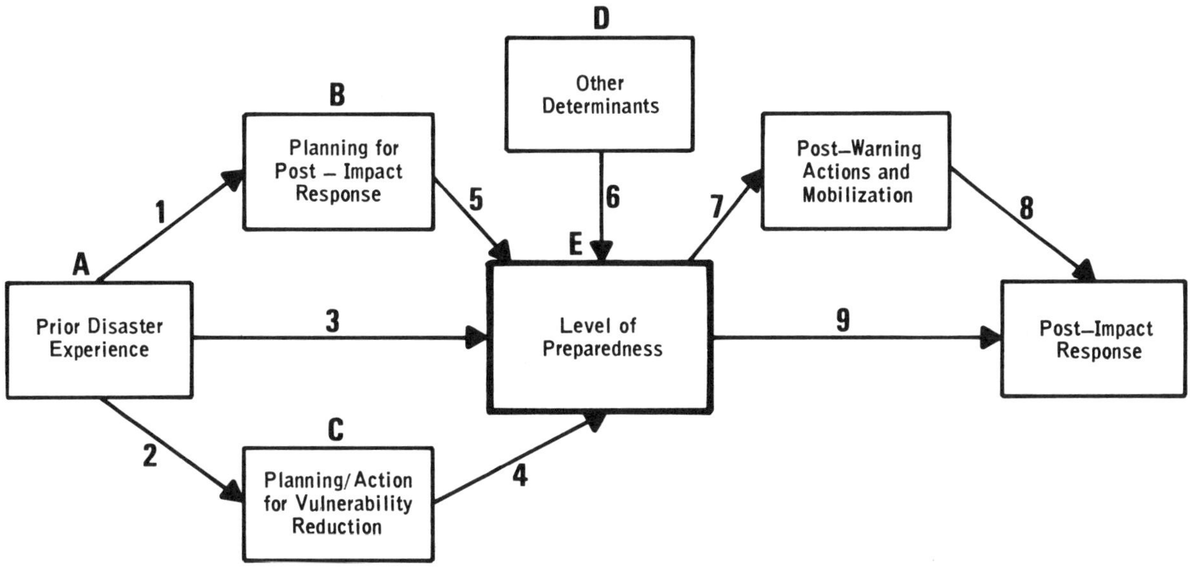

Source: Mileti et al., 1975, p. 16.

Figure 26-1
Outline of components and links relating to level of preparedness.

Related:

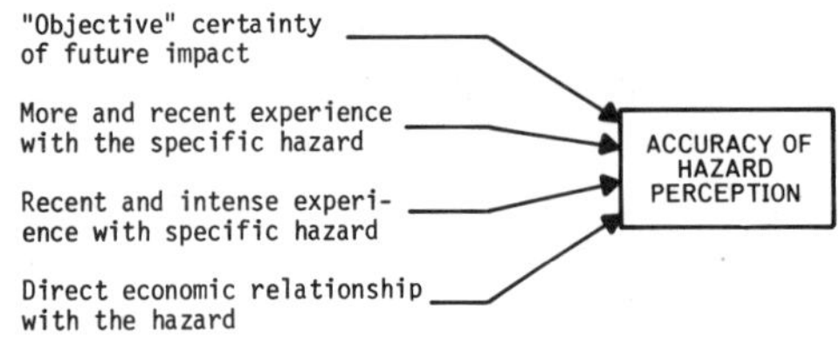

Not Related:

Educational level

Sex

Income level

Age (one known exception)

Risk taking propensity

Knowledge of protective structures (floods only)

Source: Mileti et al., 1975, p. 25.

Figure 26-2
Outline of findings of variables related to accuracy of hazard perception.

the perceived fire and earthquake hazard to the individuals living or working in tall buildings is not likely to be very accurate in most instances.

Panic and flight

In Western, industrialized societies panic and flight in the face of catastrophes (excluding civil disturbances) is almost unknown. They are not typical responses to perceived physical threat so far as we know. There may be special circumstances, such as fire in tall buildings, where exit routes appear to be limited or blocked, which tend to produce panic and flight. Given the frequency of fires as contrasted to earthquake or hurricane strikes, it would appear that carefully designed research on this topic is in order.

Convergence

Rather than running away from unusual and threatening scenes, people tend to converge as though they were drawn by a magnet. The same may be said for materials and communications. While this convergence does help to solve some problems, e.g., search and rescue of victims, it also creates additional ones, e.g., overloading of lines of communication. The more visible or publicized the unusual event the more the convergence. It is not known whether this tendency holds among occupants within a tall building or not.

Looting

Under nondisaster conditions "looting" is recorded as burglary, breaking and entering, and shoplifting. The same behavior has a different name in the disaster context. The meager evidence available suggests that reported crimes against property decrease sharply during the emergency period following disaster impact. It is our observation that the news media vastly overplay the incidence of looting. It appears that police officials believe that potential looting is a pressing problem to be given highest priority and they assign their personnel accordingly during the first few days after impact. Those actions may partially explain why looting is in fact relatively rare. Managua, Nicaragua, after the 1972 earthquake was an exception and appears to be a special case (Kates et al. 1973).

Helplessness and disorientation

Many, but by no means most, disaster victims do appear to be stunned for a few hours following impact. But being stunned by no means implies that they are incapacitated, disoriented, or helpless. Indeed, one of the most obvious characteristics of human behavior after impact is problem-oriented activity of a very altruistic type. People seldom sit around waiting for government help. They see what needs to be done, or at least the more obvious needs, and they tackle the problems with whatever skills and tools are available.

Price gouging/selfishness/antisocial behavior

Altruistic behavior is the mode during the emergency period. There is a pervasive feeling that much "normal" economic behavior is not appropriate. Those who had few or no losses, usually the great majority, express a sense of guilt for "having been so lucky." They can assuage those feelings in part by giving generously of their time, talent, and money, which most of them do. But quite apart from any guilt feelings, when disaster needs are so obvious and often dramatic, most people want a piece of the action. They want to help their fellow man and fellow woman. And they help with great enthusiasm. Price gouging in particular is severely frowned upon.

Significance of kin

When a family has been hard hit in a disaster, kinship takes on a new meaning. Other members of the immediate household are the very first concern during the warning period. Indeed, decisions to evacuate or stay are typically family decisions rather than individual ones and all members tend to abide by the outcome of the discussions among the members that can be located.

After impact the first action is to locate all members of the immediate family and to care for their most obvious needs. If one or more of the adults in the family have organizational responsibilities, the organization will usually just have to wait until the safety and location of family members has been taken care of.

When the family dwelling has been damaged or destroyed the extended family often becomes very important. Uncles, aunts, adult brothers and sisters, as well as parents, provide food, shelter, and emotional support to the victim family. In developing countries the kinship system is the primary source of assistance and support for disaster victims. In Nicaragua it served as a huge, dispersed, mass care operation during the emergency period and for months thereafter. In the United States the family is less dominant and the organized support of government and voluntary agencies takes precedence in supplying the physical needs of family victims. Some families look to neither kin nor organizations for assistance but rather follow an "autonomous" mode (Haas, Kates, and Bowden 1976).

Use of mass care centers

In the United States refugee care centers are usually opened up quickly. Shelter, food, and simple medical care are normally available as is information on how to get government assistance for various needs. But normally no more than one-third of the displaced come to such centers. Family and friends appear to be the primary locational alternatives. The more affluent often stay in hotels and motels in surrounding areas. It is this dispersion of victims that makes it difficult to get rapid, accurate estimates of the total needs of the community.

Significance of neighboring

In a society where adult kin tend to be scattered to the four winds, neighbors may partially substitute for nearby relatives. That will be possible, of course, only when neighbors know each other as persons, where some kind of a personal relation has been established. On the whole, such personal relations are less likely to exist in large apartment buildings, tall or otherwise, than in single family and other lower density residential areas. Neighbors who are "personal neighbors" will help each other in times of need such as disaster. This is true both before and after impact. Neighbors who are strangers tend to act like most other strangers (Drabek and Key 1975).

Horizontal and vertical evacuation

When warnings are received in time, evacuation becomes possible. It is by no means automatic, however.

We normally think of hundreds or thousands of persons streaming out of an area by car—horizontal evacuation. This now occurs in varying degrees in the face of approaching hurricanes and riverine floods. In the near future it will happen in the last few weeks prior to a damaging earthquake (Haas, Mileti, and Hutton 1975).

As the population density continues to increase along the Atlantic and Gulf Coasts, the possible need for vertical evacuation becomes more apparent. Many heavily populated coastal areas have only a few highways permitting exit to inland, safer areas in the face of a threatening hurricane. Given a late shift in direction of the hurricane just prior to landfall or widespread tardiness in response to warning messages, the few exit routes may well not be adequate to permit evacuation of the population. Many persons will be caught as those routes go under water from the storm surge. A possible alternative is to have vertical evacuation to the higher floors of predesignated tall buildings along the coast. The idea sounds feasible until you inquire about how an owner is likely to respond to a request to open his building to an undetermined number of unknown persons to "camp out" in his halls, etc. for perhaps twenty-four to thirty-six hours. Would toilet facilities be adequate? Who would pay for any damage or soiling of carpets by the vertical evacuees? Who would be legally liable for any injuries that might occur? And what of the preferences of the paying tenants regularly using the building?

The basic idea is attractive until the many complications are considered.

FACTORS AFFECTING HAZARD PREVENTION/MITIGATION

In the United States, land development, land use management, and building code adoption and enforcement are considered to be prerogatives of local government. Those decisions are the *primary factors* determining deaths, injuries, losses, and disruption from natural disasters. Yet when the disaster comes (a disaster is a hazard that has gotten out of control), it is primarily the federal government, using the U.S. taxpayer's money, that picks up the disaster relief price tag. The land speculators, developers, builders, bankers, and realtors operating in the local area set the city up for a disaster as a by-product of conducting their businesses. They can do so with a large measure of impunity because they seldom have to bear the losses (White and Haas 1975).

Only in the last few years have we seen the few tentative first steps taken toward making those who would profit from the development and sale of real property begin to carry a share of the responsibility for the hazard related outcomes. The National Flood Insurance Program and the 1974 Federal Disaster Assistance Act represent significant first steps.

UNANTICIPATED CONSEQUENCES OF THE TECHNOLOGICAL FIX

In the 1930s this nation decided to reduce future losses to floods by designing and constructing massive flood control works. That effort has been underway now for some forty years. Expenditures for those engineering works have continued to mount over the years. And what of the trend in losses to floods? Those losses have continued to rise and are still doing so. The more we invest in flood control works, the greater our national flood losses (White 1975).

How can that be? There are apparently a number of factors involved, but one stands out. When the flood control works are in place, many persons come to believe that the formerly dangerous flood plain is now safe. Undeveloped land mushrooms into costly development of all types. The flood control works do indeed preclude most small and moderate flood situations but inevitably the "larger than normal" flood comes and the flood works are inadequate. Now the flood plain is filled with hundreds of millions of dollars worth of capital investment and the losses are staggering. The sense of safety turned out to be false.

TALL BUILDINGS IN AN EARTHQUAKE

It is not enough that tall buildings refrain from collapse in an earthquake. At a minimum they must make possible the very rapid evacuation of the building occupants. When elevators stop working and stairwells are covered here and there with fallen materials, the situation is ripe for a fire holocaust, especially if panic develops.

Think for a minute of the billions of dollars invested in the United States in tall buildings in areas designated seismic zone three. How do the occupants of those buildings respond when there is marked shaking of the earth? Do people immediately jam halls and stairwells? Or do the occupants simply stay in the area where they were when the shaking started? Does behavior change if the shaking continues for more than ten seconds? Since fire often follows earthquake, are people in tall buildings generally aware that there is increased fire hazard in such a setting?

We have invested billions in such buildings but to my knowledge not a single systematic empirically based study has been conducted by behavioral scientists on any of these questions. The Earthquake Engineering Research Institute is developing a set of guidelines for data collection following earthquakes, which includes some mention of these matters (EERI 1975). If tomorrow, however, an earthquake hit a metropolitan area of the United States, no one would be ready to collect relevant data promptly and above all, there would be no research funds available for such efforts in less than six months, if at all. That is deplorable. Such a situation should not be allowed to continue.

REFERENCES

Drabek, Thomas E., and William H. Key. "The Impact of Disaster on Primary Group Linkages," *Mass Emergencies* (forthcoming). Also presented as paper at the Annual Meeting of the American Sociological Association, San Francisco, August 1975.

Earthquake Engineering Research Institute. *Learning From Earthquakes.* Vol. IV Social Science Field Guide, 1975.

Haas, J. Eugene, Robert W. Kates, and Martyn J. Bowden (eds.). *Reconstruction Following Disaster.* Cambridge, Mass.: MIT Press, 1976.

Haas, J. Eugene, Dennis S. Mileti, and Janice R. Hutton. "Uses of Earthquake Prediction Information." Paper presented at XVI General Assembly of the International Union of Geodesy and Geophysics, International Association of Seismology and Physics of the Earth Interior, Symposium No. 4: Geophysical Phenomena Preceding, Accompanying and Following Earthquakes. Grenoble, France, September 2, 1975.

Kates, Robert W., et al. "Human Impact of the Managua Earthquake Disaster: Transitional Societies are Peculiarly Vulnerable to Natural Disasters." *Science* 182 (December 7, 1973):981–990.

Mileti, Dennis S., Thomas E. Drabek, and J. Eugene Haas. *Human Systems in Extreme Environments: A Sociological Perspective.* Monograph #021. Boulder, Colo.: Institute of Behavioral Science University of Colorado, 1975.

White, Gilbert F., et al. *Flood Hazard in the United States: A Research Assessment.* Monograph #006. Boulder, Colo.: Institute of Behavioral Science University of Colorado, 1975.

White, Gilbert F., and J. Eugene Haas (eds.). *Assessment of Research on Natural Hazards.* Cambridge, Mass.: MIT Press, 1975.

27

Panic Behavior: Some Empirical Observations

E. L. Quarantelli
Ohio State University

INTRODUCTION

While my interest is in depicting panic behavior, the phenomenon cannot be understood unless it is seen in a balanced perspective. That is, the behavior must be seen in the larger context of how human beings react under stress. I will try to show that there is a very widespread misconception about behavior under stress. Unless there is a recognition of this, the problem of panic behavior and what to do about it cannot be addressed.

Planning can reduce human casualties, personal losses, property damage and the general social disruptions which occur as a result of natural catastrophes or technological accidents.[1] Whether it is overall community disaster planning or whether the plans involve management or designing of space use in emergencies in a specific high-rise building, the planner must proceed with accurate knowledge and understanding if any success is to be achieved. Thus, plans based on major incorrect assumptions or faulty suppositions about human behavior in the situation for which planning is developed will be useless.

Much thinking about human behavior in extreme stress situations is wrong. It is wrong in the sense that it does not agree with what has been established by systematic and wide ranging studies by social scientists doing research in the United States and elsewhere around the world. However, the prevalence of mythologies about human responses in disasters is understandable. The empirically based knowledge developed in the last several decades by sociologists, social psychologists and other behavioral scientists does not yet have wide currency.[2] The existing base of knowledge has not generally entered into the mainstream of either popular thought or the non-social science and engineering worlds.

Misconceptions About Disaster Behavior

The general view that prevails is that human beings are very likely to do badly in the face of extreme danger or threat. Behavior in disasters is thought to be characterized by illogical actions, irrational decisions, personal and group disorganization culminating in the worst of situations in widespread "hysteria" and "panic." The imagery that is conjured up is clear and can be evoked by asking the average person to associate freely what comes to mind when one thinks of disaster behavior.

Actually the evidence for what can be said to be prevailing general beliefs rests on something more than personal illustrations. For instance, two recent large-scale population surveys, one in Delaware[3] and another in Ohio,[4] found that a large majority of those interviewed agreed with the following statement. "A major problem community officials confront when faced with a natural disaster is controlling the panic of people fleeing from the disaster area." About 84 percent of each sample agreed with the statement. Most people have little faith in the abilities of others to react well in an extreme crisis. It is not an insignificant matter that people in general are so dubious of the abilities of others to bear up well under extreme stress. On the other hand, the existence of a belief does not mean that it necessarily has an overt behavioral counterpart, in this instance that human beings will actually react poorly in severe crisis situations. But the view is widely held and with considerable tenacity.

Part of the tenaciousness of the belief that people will not behave well when facing danger is rooted in literary and journalistic accounts of the actions of people in major emergencies. The current wave of "disaster movies"—*Earthquake, Poseidon Adventure, Tidal Wave, Towering Inferno, Airport,* etc.—is a recent expression of a genus that has been long standing in the area of art. It is part of a general class of story that depicts the "cracking up" or the "breaking down" of large numbers of human beings when under pressure. Scenes of hysteria or frantic flight are almost mandatory in such literary or cinematic accounts. In fact, the heart of the drama in most such depictions is the hero or heroine almost single-handedly attempting to stem the tide of panic or hysteria which is engulfing most others. Recent artistic depictions differ from the past only in that the black and white portrayals of behavior in past artistic productions are currently vivified by technicolor.

Journalistic accounts of supposedly real (as opposed to fictional) responses to disasters do little to counter the general imagery. Press or news accounts, while they may occasionally spotlight heroic acts, tend to stress the "panic" in the situation presumably manifested in wild flight or hysterical actions; or if wild behavior is not projected, the emphasis then is on the "shock" or "stun" reaction or people who are so overwhelmed by danger that they are immobilized from "panicking." Elsewhere I have characterized this as a Dr. Jekyll-Mr. Hyde assumption about the nature of human beings.[5] The implicit notion is that the latter—the darker, impulsive, irrational, more animal-like side of the human creature—will break through in highly stressful situations. The imagery again is clear—human beings are not reeds that bend easily with the wind; instead they are even more fragile saplings that will break and snap under the surge of a very threatening event.

The media, be it radio, television, newspapers, or magazines, also have succeeded in implanting in the thinking of many people certain images of particular news events. Thus, to mention to almost anyone the Orson Welles' "War of the Worlds" broadcast, the Iroquois theater or Cocoanut Grove nightclub fires, or more recent high-rise hotel or office building fires in Brazil or Korea is to evoke an image of stressful human behavior that is not exactly edifying or laudable. A frequent accompanying notion is that while the reports mirror admittedly extreme cases, it is implicitly assumed that other stressful events are on the same continuum insofar as behavioral responses are concerned.

Furthermore, it is not impossible to see the same image assumed in the thinking and behavior of officials and others who have planning, operational or policy positions of responsibility at times of large-scale emergencies. This can be seen in what planners, officials, and administrators sometimes actually do an decide about disaster problems. Let me give some illustrations both from my studies[6] or, when specifically cited, the research of others.

Indicative of the image held is the occasional failure of responsible officials to take appropriate actions during pre-impact periods of possible catastrophes because of their concern about generating panic. For example, city officials and the state police refused to order the evacuation of an ocean resort town, despite strong urgings by the Weather Bureau and the Coast Guard, because they thought such action on their part might precipitate a panicky flight. They preferred to chance the danger of inaction, even though they knew that the only two evacuation routes would become impassible if the hurricane heading for their low-lying area was as intense as predicted.

Very recently, local and other officials argued behind the scenes about evacuating some or most of a large American city because of the possible threat of a chlorine gas leak from a grounded barge. A reason advanced for having no public evacuation at all was the fear of starting a panic. The response of some local officials to the earthquake prediction capability currently being developed is that they would hesitate to order evacuation because it might generate a wild flight from the area.

Concern over evoking panicky reactions sometimes hinders even alerting people to possible dangers. Thus, during floods on the Rio Grande, some Mexican and American officials felt that they had to play down warnings, otherwise people would panic.[7] Italian officials with knowledge of the flood threat facing Florence refused to issue warnings because of their concern that the ensuing disorderly flight that was envisioned would be more destructive than the flood waters could possibly be. Because of a similar concern, forecasts of tornado conditions were not issued prior to a tornado in New England a few years ago. In the very recent 1974 Xenia disaster, a television station, showing on the screen the radar indicators of a tornado cloud about to hit the area, failed to activate the emergency broadcasting system because "that thing has been built up into a serious type warning and I'm afraid if people heard it come on, there might be panic."[8] In a much more circumscribed crisis situation, but because of this same fear of initiating panic, alarm bells were not rung on the collision-doomed ship, *Andrea Doria.*

Until there was an absorption of the results of much social science research put out by the Disaster Research Center at Ohio State University,[9] civil defense planning in this country also assumed that not only was flight withdrawal inevitable in the case of enemy attack, but that it was going to be markedly maladaptive, unthinking, and contagious behavior. For years the major control problem was seen as one of stopping a panicky exodus from a threatened area. In the last five years or so, the official civil preparedness agency has swung 180 degrees away from this position, but this old image still exists in the thinking of many other government officials.[10]

The imagery involved, of course, as we have already implied, is neither peculiarly American nor is it a new idea. For example, British planners prior to World War II assumed that in the event of war

> . . . a large exodus from London and other cities was inevitable; panic would send the people out and unless the Government took firm control . . . chaos and confusion were bound to ensue. . . . In its deliberations, the question was viewed not as a problem of getting people away, but as a problem of preventing panic flight. This led . . . to the suggestion that the (police) force should be enlarged and a cordon thrown round London. So convinced was the committee . . . that a "disorderly general flight" would take place that it felt it could not carry its study further until a decision had been reached on "how control of the population was to be exercised."[11]

The general picture of how people are expected to behave in disasters could be detailed further using examples and illustrations involving different types of disaster agents and different kinds of social settings. But the additional details would not alter the picture of disaster behavior that we know exists in the minds of most people. There is a high degree of expectation that behavior under extreme stress is impulsive and not controlled, that it is irrational in that means are not appropriately adjusted to ends, and that it is disorganized with personal and social chaos always threatening to engulf the situation.

I have briefly sketched the general image of behavior expected in disasters to emphasize that it is widely believed and accepted as being a true picture of what occurs, that examples—real or imagined—of the behavior can be pointed to, and that the acceptance of such an image has definite implications for planning, policies, and practices. If the image is a true one, then it carries certain implications of how one even thinks of behavior in disaster. One implication is that the study of panic behavior becomes equivalent to the study of, if not the most frequent, at least the ever present and most prevalent possible human response under extreme stress.

However, as already said, the empirical evidence clearly indicates that the general belief is fundamentally incorrect. The popular image of human behavior under stress is widely at variance with the scientifically based picture developed in sociological and other social and behavioral science research into the area of disaster response. The empirical evidence and systematic studies simply do not support the widely believed, acted upon, and probably to many people, the "obvious" conception or image. But this is another instance in which research has shown that what "everybody knows" is just not true when carefully examined by social scientists.

Social Science Research on Disaster Behavior

A word should be said about this body of social science research to indicate its range, depth, and directions. Unknown to most people, a steady stream of actual field research into natural and technological disaster situations has been going on for about two and a half decades. The work started in the early 1950s and has continued to the present. Social scientists, mainly sociologists, have been going to actual disasters, sometimes before they even occur, as in forecasted or predicted floods and hurricanes, and have studied in the field the actual response of people and groups to sudden stressful situations. While the focus has more often been on large-scale community disasters, more localized catastrophes such as explosions and fires have not been totally neglected.

The Disaster Research Center,[12] for instance, has engaged in a variety of sociological research studies on the reactions of groups and organizations in communitywide emergencies, particularly natural disasters. Since its inception, 267 different field studies have been carried out. Teams have gone to earthquakes (in Japan, Chile, Yugoslavia, Italy, Iran, El Salvador, Greece, California, and Alaska), hurricanes (in the southern and eastern United States as well as Japan), floods (in Italy, Canada, and more than a dozen states), as well as tornadoes around the country. Large explosions and forest fires, toxic spills and lake shore erosion incidents, destructive seismic waves and major dam breaks and great blizzards have also been studied in Australia, Italy, Canada, and different regions of the United States. For purposes of comparison, Center personnel have examined organizational responses to civil disturbances in about a dozen American cities as well as Curaçao in the West Indies.

While we are the oldest, the most widely ranging in terms of the kinds of disaster events studied, and have the biggest field data bank as well as the most continuous social science disaster operation in the world, we are not alone. Apart from the very large-scale, extensive, interdisciplinary and applied work recently initiated at the University of Colorado,[13] and a few more localized points of disaster studies in the United States, there are some major centers of research in France, England, Japan, and Italy as well as some social and behavioral scientists actively at work in Sweden, Australia, Belgium, and New Zealand. In addition, Canada is in the process of developing a major research capability.[14]

Among the major centers elsewhere outside of the United States, the French center has particularly focused on human behavior in fire situations and problems relating to high-rise buildings. (However, probably the most systematic study on human behavior in fires has been undertaken in England.) The Japanese also have done studies on department store and nightclub fires.

As a result of informal linkages between the centers and other researchers, meetings and conferences,[15] the production of bibliographies on disasters[16] as well as publication series,[17] the existence of a newsletter[18] and a professional journal, *Mass Emergencies,*[19] the exchange of information on the social and human aspects of disasters has accelerated rapidly in the last few years. Apart from wanting to call attention to this body of knowledge, scientific workers, and research locales to those who might not be aware of their existence, I mention it to emphasize the widely based nature of my initial remarks here. There is general consensus among this cluster of researchers around the world that their studies in different societies of human behavior in a variety of disasters generally support the proposition that human behavior under stress is relatively controlled, rational and adaptive. This is the general conclusion independently reached by those who have been studying disasters. Basically, human behavior under extreme stress is controlled rather than impulsive, uses appropriate means for the perceived ends, and is organized and functional for the most part.

I hasten to add that this is not a Dr. Pangloss view of the world; it neither implies nor does it mean that there are no problems in disasters. In actual fact, there are a great number of them, such as the activation of disaster plans, the alerting of populations about dangers, the mobilization of emergency organizations, the coordination of response among key groups, the allocation of resources to long-run recovery. Also, there are problems regarding specific tasks such as search and rescue, assembling of lists of missing persons, controlling outside convergence on impacted areas, appropriate distributing of casualties to hospitals, and delivering mental health services. But if most researchers were asked to rank problem areas in relation to disasters, the general behavior of human beings under extreme stress situations would not be rated high, either as a practical matter or as an issue of theoretical concern. The difficulties that exist in disaster planning and disaster operations, and there are many such difficulties, emanate more from other factors and aspects than from the response of human beings as such to extreme stress.

I would be the last to deny that cases of very unusual and certainly dysfunctional behaviors can be found at times of disasters. It would be possible for me to spend pages regaling you with dramatic and colorful anecdotes and examples of such behavior. But to emphasize them would be to distort the general picture, the modal responses, the statistical frequencies upon which both disaster planning and disaster research have to focus.

Let me briefly discuss this in more concrete terms. Take the matter of frequency of "irrational behavior." You can take practically any category of such behaviors, and in the most extreme of cases, it is only a very, very tiny fraction of all the range of behaviors involved. One reason this is not understood and recognized is that many misconceptions circulate about such matters. Take the "War of the Worlds" broadcast alluded to a little earlier. The general belief is that this involved many people being disturbed and fleeing in panic. Even very recently, a discussion of mass communication influences observed that the broadcast "triggered panic in hundreds of thousands of listeners across the nation, actually sending many into physical flight."[20] However, a study conducted right after the event showed that 84 percent of the audience of 34 million people never thought of it as anything but a dramatic show.[21] This does not mean that the other 16 percent got hysterical or even overtly reacted very much. In the vast majority of these cases, the fleeting thought did occur that perhaps it was an actual news broadcast. But the number of people who actually did anything that could be considered "panicky" in any sense of the term was a miniscule fraction either in absolute or relative terms.

A recent Swedish study suggests how small the number may have been. In 1974 there was a radio broadcast in Sweden which made reference to a nuclear plant accident which generated a radioactive cloud drift. As in the instance of the "War of the Worlds" broadcast, this too was purely a fictional account. News accounts described fleeing and hysterical persons. In fact, an Associated Press International wire service story, headlined "Fake nuclear disaster causes panic in Sweden," reported that "thousands panicked, running to closed fallout shelters, and it took several hours to restore calm."[22] There was a debate in the Swedish Parliament that broadcasts of such a kind should be prohibited because it was unjustified that thousands of Swedish citizens should be disturbed, that they should clog thte roads in flight, etc. A team of Swedish sociologists decided to make an intensive study of the reactions of the population in the affected area.[23] They undertook an intensive interview sample of the population in the affected area, examined records, police reports and thoroughly looked into all the behavioral reactions. *They found not one single case of flight in their sample.* Since the study involved a sample, we cannot be certain that no one actually fled, but it is obvious, despite the press accounts and the Parliamentary debates, that very few, if any, Swedish citizens fled in panic or otherwise fled with respect to that broadcast.

Careful analyses of panic flight where it has occurred show that it is seldom if ever the modal category. Nearly 500 people did die in the Cocoanut Grove nightclub fire, and there was panic behavior in that situation without question, but it seems questionable on the basis of the available data that more than a third of those at the very most may have engaged in panicky behavior. A French study of panic behavior in a 1970 dance hall fire which killed 144 people, as well as similar Japanese studies of nightclub and department store fires, do not support the notion that panic behavior was the prevailing mode of response in those situations either. Wood, in England, in his very careful study of nearly 1,000 fire incidents similarly concluded:

> In general terms the majority of people appeared to have behaved in what might be considered an appropriate fashion, although some five percent of the people did something which was judged to "increase the risk." There was little evidence of true "panic."[24]

Overall, my point has been that in both absolute and relative terms, human behavior in disasters in modern, industrial societies is fairly good by almost any reasonable criteria one could use. There is little evidence beyond anecdotal stories, and none of a systematic, comparative and quantitative nature that suggests that behavior under stress is any more illogical, irrational or dysfunctional than everyday behavior. Part of the problem is that sometimes the behavior under stress is compared not with everyday behavior but with an idealized conception of behavior. Of course along that line it does not come out well. But this is a match of real disaster behavior with the ideal, when the honest comparison should be between real disaster behavior and actual everyday behavior. If the last kind of match is made, there is not that much difference between the two.

THE NATURE OF PANIC BEHAVIOR

With this as background we can now turn to a consideration of panic behavior. If it is understood, as we have emphasized in the previous pages, that panic behavior represents a statistically infrequent behavior, we can better consider what it might involve and what its distinguishing characteristics might be. If it is understood that panic is a very atypical response pattern, we can better determine the specific conditions required for its occurrence. I therefore want to turn now to a detailing of the characteristics of panic and a somewhat more general look at what seems to be associated with its occurrence.

My remarks are distilled from an analysis of two major sources of data: (1) my own studies on this topic initiated in 1950, a quarter of a century ago; and (2) the work of others not only in this country but also in France, England, and Japan.[25] Thus, this is not a report on a single, empirical study, but concerns the general findings derivable from an examination of most of the focused and systematic research undertaken on this topic.[26]

Panic behavior is characterized by six features, three of a covert nature and three of an overt nature. Covertly, panic involves a very acute fear reaction of an anticipatory danger and in response to a specific threat. Overtly, panic involves flight behavior of a nonsocial and a nonrational kind. When all six features are present together, it is a clear instance of panic behavior.

Covert Features

Covertly, panic involves fear, not anxiety, a projection into the future rather than a view of the past, and a perceived place of danger rather than a generalized threat.

Panic participants invariably define the situation they are in as highly and personally dangerous. Whether this is arrived at individually or collectively, panic participants always perceive a direct threat to their own physical survival. This experiencing of extreme danger to bodily safety is illustrated in the remarks by a man who looked up and saw a flaming plane diving toward the street where he was pushing a wheelbarrow:

> This thing seemed to me as if it was coming right at me. I ran like a scared rabbit across the street. My pushcart—I abandoned that to save my neck. I was scared. This thing went up in a big puff of flame and gasoline. It exploded. All I was thinking was that this big ball of gasoline was coming down on top of me and I was making a run in order to get away from it. I was running pell-mell across the street. I was looking at this big ball as I was running like a scared rabbit for fear it was going to pounce on my head, you know. The only thing I was thinking as I was running across and I was looking up at this big ball of fire, I was thinking to myself, I wonder if any part of this is going to hit me?

This kind of response is unlike those situations in which there is perception of great personal threat, but the danger is not conceived of in direct bodily terms (e.g., in possibly becoming bankrupt). In panic the physical self is seen as seriously threatened.

However, it is not just personal danger per se that is involved in a panicky reaction. A person may envision a threat to self-existence, for example because of environmental pollution or cigarette smoking, but that is a perceived danger and reaction of a different order. Instead, panic participants see the potential threat to their physical existence as very immediate and survival as dependent on a very rapid reaction. A laborer caught in a plant explosion who fled in panic after recovering consciousness said: "When I came to, the dust and minerals and everything was crashing all around. My first thought was that something would fall on me and finish me. My main thought was to figure a way to get out." Thus, in panic there is a perceived immediate danger to physical self.

But people do not usually flee in panic from a dangerous situation. In fact, as we have stressed, such a response is rare. Individuals may feel themselves extremely and personally threatened, and yet engage in a variety of nonpanic behaviors including, for example, direct actions against the danger. To the extent they do so, it is because they check their fear, i.e., their impulse to run from the threatening situation (and as Young points out, "for human subjects to designate an experience as *fear,* the presence of an escape impulse is required"[27]). Self-control is maintained.

Thus, the panicky reaction is characterized not so much by the presence of fear as by unchecked fear. Persons may feel extreme fear for their actual physical safety and yet maintain a high degree of control over their activities. This is well illustrated by soldiers involved in combat. Usually they maintain control over their fears. Conversely, in panic there is a collapse of existing curbs on the impulse to flee. The participant is the individual who has lost control over fear. One woman described her fear just before she fled in panic as follows:

> You wanted to just get away. I felt I wanted to go. I wanted to run. Get away. Get away. I thought if that house goes the

one next to me is going to go too and I'd be in the center of it. I heard the crash, the house went up (i.e., exploded) and I went.

The orientation of attention of panic participants is always to the future, to what subsequently may be endangering to the physical self. Concern is not directed to what has already happened; it is focused on what may happen to self. Thus, during an earthquake a panic participant perceives (to paraphrase many) "if I stay here I will be killed." It is the anticipatory rather than retrospective perceptions of danger that accompany panic activity. Thus, a woman on a cruise ship that caught fire noted that waking up in the middle of the night: "I smelled smoke and I opened the door of my cabin. But the corridor was full of smoke. You just couldn't see a thing. I smashed the porthole out with my fist. It was the only way to get out. It was either that, or stay and die."

Furthermore, the potential threat is seen as having immediate consequences, at most within the time span of several minutes. A rapid reaction of some sort is viewed as necessary in order to survive the quickly anticipated perilous effects. In fact, an almost necessary concomitant of the loss of self-control is that the orientation of activity of the participant is highly self-centered, both temporally and psychologically. The fleeing individual thinks only of saving oneself quickly. Subjectively, it involves a complete focusing upon the idea of getting oneself immediately out of the threatening situation. "All I thought about was getting out of there," said a woman who fled in panic from a building during an earthquake. Another person after an initial explosion in a fireworks factory observed that she was expecting another explosion, that she was crawling and

I didn't think I'd ever get up and I thought that explosion would get me before I could get up. I just wanted to get out of there alive. I never wanted to be blown to pieces. I think that's a horrible death. I thought of that at the time. After I got to my feet I started running as best as I could.

The idea that there is an immediate threat (and not a past danger) leads to a complete focalization upon the idea of getting oneself quickly away from the immediate area of danger.

However, that panicky individuals react toward very immediately rising threats rather than retrospective dangers does not mean that there necessarily exists an objective peril. In fact, the realness of illusoriness of the threat is, as far as a panicky reaction is concerned, of little import. Regardless of the objective circumstances, it is how the persons define the situation that determines the reaction. Thus, panicky reactions will occur in situations involving no real threat simply because a danger is perceived as possible. This very often happens after an explosion. Similarly, the calmness of people in certain objectively threatening situations frequently stems from a discrepancy between the objective situation and the subjective definition of it as nonthreatening.

Panic participants are not only aware of what they are immediately afraid *for* (which is their own physical survival) but they also know what they are afraid *of.* The fear experienced in a panic reaction is of something specific, of something that can be designated. The covert response of the person in panic is never in regard to the unknown or the incomprehensible as such. The reaction is always regarding a specific threat, the particularization of which may be arrived at individually or through interaction with others. For example, a sailor caught in an explosion on an American aircraft carrier noted:

I went down to Hanger Bay One. Then the explosion occurred, quite a blast. The heat was terrific. I got a little panicky. I was on Hanger Bay One and I started thinking of those planes going on fire. It was pretty dangerous with all those planes and gasoline around and stuff to come down on top of me. I was thinking of getting out of there as soon as possible.

Implied in the quotation is the related point that in defining the dangerousness of the situation, panic participants perceive the threat as associated with a specific place or locale.

Consequently, flight continues only to the extent people believe themselves well within a danger area.

Fleeing stops when there is the belief that one is no longer exposed to the consequences of the threat as illustrated in the remark of a factory worker after an explosion: "My idea was to get away from the building because I had in mind it might fall. At the time I knew I was in danger of death, but after I got out of the building I felt I was out of danger." Outside he stopped running. Far from running until they are physically exhausted, panic participants generally stop quickly. The characteristically short duration of panic flights stems from this fact that panicky persons run only as far as necessary to get outside of the perceived zone of danger. (Actually, danger in panic is not necessarily associated with being inside a building; an open area during a machine gun strafing could also be viewed as a place of danger.)

Overt Features

Overtly, panic involves directional rather than purely random flight, nonsocial rather than antisocial activities, and nonrational rather than irrational behavior.

Flight is the outstanding feature of panic insofar as outward manifestation is concerned. While such physical behavior is not peculiar to panic, it is nonetheless an ever present feature of the phenomenon whenever it occurs. The flight most frequently takes the form of actual physical running. However, it may also be expressed in roughly equivalent activities such as driving vehicles, swimming, crawling, riding horses, rowing, climbing, jumping, digging, etc. Varying combinations of all the possible physical actions can sometimes be seen in those rare instances of panic among military units. This variety in the expressions of flight is possible because most socially learned and ingrained motor patterns of action continue to be available to individuals in panic. Participants do not regress to acting in infantile or purely biologically patterned ways. But since the majority of situations wherein panic occurs do not lend themselves to nonrunning activities, panic flight is generally manifested in running.

The loss of control over fear and the focalization of thought on escaping does not mean a panicky person is completely unresponsive to other aspects of the situation or that there is just blind fleeing. On the contrary, a panicky individual orients the fleeing and modifies the flight behavior in terms of the perceived circumstances. Thus, a panic participant does not blindly run into objects; if possible, an attempt is made to go around obstacles in one's path. An attempt is made to go through a door before an effort is made to flee through a window, etc.

Panic flight is not a random or headlong stampede. It is directed towards the goal of getting away from the area of danger. Thus, the flight behavior is always oriented with reference to a location of danger; that is, panicky people flee from particular locales, such as a collapsing building or a gas-filled house. Usually this involves movement away from specific points of danger; panic participants thus run away from, for example, the flaming section of a building. However, if some danger lies between presumed safety and the endangered persons, the flight may be in the direction of that specific peril. Thus, panicky persons may run toward dangerous objects if escape from the threat lies in that direction (e.g., toward sheets of flame if the only known exit from a building is on the other side). Much panic fleeing which appears to an outside observer as blind fleeing into danger is of this nature. The behavior is not, as some have asserted, characterized by "blindness to reality."[28] Instead, as one person who fled in panic observed: "Since my escape through the door was cut off, I shielded my face with my hands and crashed head first through a window. It was my only hope of getting out."

At any rate, panic flight is not helter-skelter; participants do not run every which way but instead take their general orientation for flight from specific referent points. Two factors are often involved in the determination of the particular direction of flight (e.g., through which exit an individual will attempt to escape). These are (1) habitual patterns and (2) the social interactional pattern following the definition of the situation as dangerous. The former factor is exemplified in the tendency of panicky housewives to flee out of the frequently used but more distant back doors, rather than the infrequently used but nearer front doors of their homes. The latter factor is illustrated in the remarks of a worker after a plant explosion. He noted: "There was a gush of flame and smoke coming up the elevator shaft. I just started running. Lots of other people were running too. That's how I knew where to go." This interactional factor, however, is influential only within the confines of the actual setting participants find themselves in at the time of crisis. If there is only one apparent or known exit, people will flee in that direction.

The flight behavior in panic always takes on a nonsocial character. However, such behavior is not necessarily antisocial. This is more than a play on words. The panicky person acts in a nonsocial rather than antisocial way by disregarding the usual relationships and expectations. Even the strongest primary group ties may be shattered and the most socially expected behavior patterns may be ignored. Thus, there is the example of the mother who, thinking a bomb had hit her home, fled in panic, leaving her baby behind, and returned only when she redefined the situation as an explosion across the street. As she stated it, the explosion

> shook the house. The first thing I thought of was a bomb. I just felt it was a bomb and I ran out. I was in my bathrobe. You don't think of anything save to get out—just to get out. I ran out and the house over there was flames from the bottom to the top so I ran back and grabbed the baby out of his crib.

This illustration might be interpreted, indirectly at least, as an instance of antisocial behavior.

There are many situations where panic flight, in which a number of persons are engaged simultaneously, is not only appropriate in itself but also has no antisocial consequences. For instance, the mass fleeing of separated householders from their gas-filling houses in one disaster was no hindrance to the fleeing of any other person. There was no physical contact of a destructive sort on the part of the individuals running out of their homes. The flight behavior, as it is in many and probably most panics, was personally functional and in no way socially maladaptive to the situation. It is only in the very rare instance that panic takes the form of a mass of individuals trampling over one another in a wild stampede.

The nonsocial aspect of panic behavior tends to be short-lived, but it is this feature which, even at an overt level, distinguishes many cases of panic from controlled withdrawal behavior. In the case of the latter, there may be confused, random, ill-coordinated activity, but the conventional social roles and normal interactional patterns are not totally disregarded. For example, when a plane crashed into an apartment house in one disaster, most families evacuated as units, neighbors were warned, alternative courses of action were discussed, etc. People acted in an erratic and partially unorganized fashion, but unlike when persons are panicky, most of their behavior was in terms of the group norms that ordinarily guided their activities. Such excited flight should not be confused with panic flight.

Panic flight represents very highly individualistic behavior. It involves completely individual as opposed to group action in coping with the problem of escape from danger. In panic there is no unity of action, no cooperation with others, no joint activity; there is a total breakdown of corporate or concerted behavior. In short, panic flight is the very antithesis of organized group behavior; it is the manifestation of nonsocial behavior at its zenith.

Just as panic is nonsocial rather than antisocial, so it is nonrational rather than irrational behavior. Again this is more than a mere play on words. The panicky person retains not only the learned neuromuscular coordinations required for the carrying out of complex motor activities, but also the capacity for perceiving, remembering, thinking and all the other socially acquired processes necessary for a human being to act. There is not a regression to infantile reaction patterns, or a reverting to purely reflexive or unlearned ways of reacting. The human being remains mostly a human being even at times of panic.

To be sure, as said earlier, there is a focusing of perception at times of panic behavior. However, this does not mean or imply that the participant acts only reflexively or instinctively and is totally unaware of anything else. For an individual to engage in flight at all there has to be sufficient awareness to perceive *and* to continue to define a situation as a highly threatening one. A certain minimal awareness is also indicated by the fact that panicky persons do not run blindly into walls; they head for doors; and they go around objects and obstacles in their path if at all possible instead of attempting to crash through them. Moreover, when fleeing in a collective panic, participants are at least partially aware of the presence of others although they do not respond to these other individuals in terms of their usual social roles.

However, to state that panic flight involves a degree of awareness on the part of participants is not to suggest in any way that it is a highly rational activity. It certainly does not involve the weighing of alternative courses of action that might be followed in the situation. As a woman who fled in panic during an earthquake said: "The first thought you have is to run. I had that thought. I ran." On the other hand, the thinking of the panicky person is not "irrational" if by that is meant anything in the way of faulty or illogical deductions from given premises. From the position of an observer with a much broader perspective of the situation this may appear to be the case. However, from a participant's viewpoint, given the necessarily more limited perspective of only certain portions of all the circumstances involved, no such interpretation of irrationality is warranted. To the panicky person the flight appears quite appropriate to the situation as perceived at that time; however, it may be evaluated differently in retrospect.

Rather than being rational or irrational, the behavior of a panic participant is nonrational. Faced with the immediate possibility of personal annihilation, a panicky person does not consider possible alternative lines of action other than flight which might be followed. In the face of a threat, the potential courses of action available range from direct attack to movement away from the endangering object. However, the panicky person makes no overt attempt to deal directly with the threat itself; there is no attempt to bring the threat under control, to act towards it, or, where physically possible, to manipulate it in any way. The panicky person just thinks of escaping, making no attempt to cope with the threat other than to flee from it. Furthermore, there is no account taken of the possible consequences of the fleeing behavior. In certain infrequent circumstances this may be even more dangerous than the panic-inciting threat itself. The behavior of the panicky person thus is nonrational in the sense of not considering alternative courses of behavior to fleeing and of not foreseeing the possible consequences of panic flight.

Because a panicky reaction is nonrational, it is not always necessarily personally or collectively inappropriate to the situation. That a panicky person flees and makes no direct attempt to cope with the threat does not make the behavior necessarily nonfunctional. It often is not. Frequently, running away is the most adaptive course of action that the person could take in the particular situation. Thus, to flee from a building where the ceiling is threatening to collapse as a result of earthquake shocks is, on most occasions, an appropriate and effective response. In such instances the panic flight is functional, if functionality under such circumstances is thought of as behavior which from an objective viewpoint is appropriate to the maintenance of the life of a threatened individual.

Likewise, the behavior of panicky persons is not necessarily collectively maladaptive. There are many occasions where flight, in which a number of persons engage simultaneously, not only is appropriate in itself but also has no inappropriate consequences of a social nature. People can run out of houses or buildings without having any or very little bodily contact of a destructive sort with one another. In fact, it is only rarely, and almost always because of the presence of physical barriers, that panicky individuals may proceed to knock one another down and to trample over each other. Such collectively maladaptive activity, however, is highly atypical and is definitely not a common characteristic of the behavior of panicky persons.

The conception of panic flight as being always nonfunctional or maladaptive conceals a normative judgment the basis of which we cannot consider here. It would be actually stupid and foolish in many dangerous situations to fight or confront the threat involved. As an old, pre-Mao Chinese proverb says, "Of 36 ways to escape danger, running away is best." Suffice it to say that panic behavior sometimes is functional and adaptive and sometimes it is not. If it is the latter, it is generally because of specific physical circumstances.

In summary, panic is an acute fear reaction marked by flight behavior. Subjectively, there is an intense fear reaction, i.e., a strong impulse to flee from a threatening danger. Panic participants are seized by fear of a specific object perceived as involving an immediate and extreme threat to physical survival. Overtly, the flight behavior always involves an attempt to remove oneself physically from the endangered area. In fleeing, the participants do not weigh the social consequences of their action and are highly individualistic and self-centered in their flight with regard to one another; thus, the behavior is nonrational and nonsocial, although not necessarily nonfunctional or maladaptive. Since there is no consideration of alternative courses of action to flight, with the thought being focused on the removal of oneself from danger, usual social relationships and role patterns are ignored and there is no possibility of group action.

CONDITIONS FOR PANIC

What accounts for the behavior whose characteristics we have just described? In general terms, of course, panic occurs in a crisis situation, where the traditional socio-cultural framework is not adequate enough to guide behavior along everyday, routine lines. In such situations, technically and in sociological terms, collective behavior occurs.[29] However, panic flight is only one of the possible collective behavior outcomes in such situations. Thus, there must be more specific conditions other than a general crisis setting for panicky behavior to develop. My own view is that there are two contextual and three immediate conditions that are responsible for the phenomenon. I will merely sketch these factors.

Contextual conditions

Panic seems to be particularly facilitated by the presence of two kinds of contributory factors. One is the existence of a pre-crisis definition of certain kinds of crisis settings as having high potential for evoking panic flight. People do have preconceptions of the danger of certain situations, and in particular have images of the probable behavior of others in such circumstances. The simplest example is the widely shared belief that a fire in a crowded and enclosed area is especially dangerous because, among other things, panic flight is probable. Two sociologists a long time ago wrote that individuals "become panicked in situations which have previously been linguistically defined as fearful or terrifying."[30] My point is simply an extension of their view.

Another contextual condition that facilitates panic flight is the absence of pre-crisis social ties among the potential participants. Social links or bonds to others are very powerful anchors against getting involved in panic flight. Both sides of this factor are very well illustrated in the following retrospective observations by a man sitting with his son in a large theater with only one exit down a long narrow passageway when there was a shout of fire and people started to flee. "With me was my young son. If he had not been there I should have been one of those scrambling, screaming madmen. . . . But the thought held my mind that I could not bear to have my son see me as those others were; that if he did see me so, I never should be able to face him again. . . . Also . . . I was responsible for him, that he came before myself. . . .[31]

Immediate conditions

There are three immediate conditions which seem to activate panic flight. The first is a perception of possible entrapment. The second is a sense of powerlessness or impotency in the situation. And the third is a feeling of social isolation or sole dependency upon onself in the crisis.

A crucial and immediate factor for the occurrence and continuance of panic is the perception on the part of participants that they may be unable to escape from the impending threat. Whether this perception is individually or collectively reached, the idea of possible entrapment predominates from the initiation of panic flight. As one panicky person reported: "I didn't even think of anything except getting myself out. From the time I left my bed to the door, that's the only thing I could think of. Am I going to get out? Am I going to be trapped?"

It is very crucial to recognize that what is involved here is the perception of possible entrapment. If individuals think or believe that they are trapped absolutely and unconditionally, they will not flee. A sailor trapped in an aircraft carrier explosion interestingly describes both these different kinds of perceptions:

> I couldn't go anywhere. I couldn't run anywhere. After I saw I couldn't get out, I figure nothing I could do about it. It was my time to go. I was calm, I didn't get excited. I was hoping it wouldn't take too long to die because I didn't think we had a chance. I had given up. I figured there was no way of getting out. . . . But I did get scared after I thought I had a chance to escape.

Panic flight only occurs when avenues of escape are evident, when being trapped is sensed or thought of as a possibility rather than an actuality.

Also important as an immediate condition for panic flight is a sense of powerlessness or helplessness in the face of the danger. Seeing themselves faced with the necessity of reacting, persons may feel that they are unable to prevent the consequences of the impending threat from occurring. This sense of impotency has nothing to do with the capability of a fear-stricken individual to flee. Panicky persons may feel helpless in bringing the threat itself under control, but the sense of impotency does not extend to their possible flight. As one woman who fled in panic said:

> When I realized the gas was escaping from the hot-water heater, I knew it wasn't anything to monkey with, something not to play with. I *knew* that an accumulation of gas would blow up. I mean water you could cope with, dumping it out or something, but with gas I don't know anything. I thought my house was going to blow up. I was really scared. I ran out.

The third immediate condition which seems to generate panic flight is a feeling of social isolation in coping with the danger. The physical presence or absence of others around the person is not the crucial matter in this respect. It is rather whether the involved person perceives that if anything is to be done, it will have to be done by himself. In all instances of panic flight, this feeling of "solitude" or dependency solely on one's own actions is present to some degree. This dimension is illustrated partly in the remarks of a woman working in a plant with a number of other women when an earthquake occurred. She said:

> When it started shaking so bad I noticed that I was there by myself. I felt even more scared. When you're by yourself in something like that and there's nobody to depend on. There was nobody around. I don't know where they disappeared to. I didn't see nobody. I ran.

THE FUTURE

I have described the major characteristics of and alluded to the conditions associated with a relatively infrequent but nonetheless occasional human response to a crisis or disaster situation. Unfortunately, there is no reason to anticipate anything except an increase of such behavior in the future. The reason is simple and twofold. We are going to have more disaster events in the future, and the more of them the more likely there will be additional panic incidents. In addition, different developments in the future are almost certain to create more or reinforce existing panic-producing conditions. Whether it be high-rise and windowless buildings, nuclear plants with radioactive spill potentials, vast underground malls or domed stadiums, or many other technological developments that could be mentioned, they are all raising the panic potential.

There is irrationality associated with panic, but it is not as said earlier in the behavior itself; it is rather in the acts of human beings who are continually increasing the probabilities of disasters and of specific panic-producing conditions. This is not to argue against technological development as much as it is a plea for careful consideration of the public policy implications of matters which are sometimes treated solely as engineering problems or questions.

NOTES

1. See R. R. Dynes, E. L. Quarantelli, and G. A. Kreps, *A Perspective on Disaster Planning* (Columbus, Ohio: Disaster Research Center, 1972); G. White and J. E. Haas, *Assessment of Research on Natural Hazards* (Cambridge: MIT Press, 1975); and H. Beach, *Management of Human Behaviour in Disaster* (Ottawa, Canada: Department of National Health and Welfare, 1967).
2. See E. L. Quarantelli and R. R. Dynes (eds.), "Organizational and Group Behavior in Disasters," *American Behavioral Scientist* 13 (January 1970):323–456; and A. Barton, *Communities in Disaster* (New York: Doubleday, 1969).
3. D. Wenger et al., "It's a Matter of Myths: An Empirical Examination," *Mass Emergencies* 1 (October 1975).
4. Personal communication from Professor Sue Blanshan, Department of Sociology, Wittenberg University, June 7, 1975.
5. E. L. Quarantelli, "Images of Withdrawal Behavior in Disasters: Some Basic Misconceptions," *Social Problems* 8 (Summer 1960):63–79.
6. Unless otherwise cited, all illustrations in this chapter are from my own research. Among my publications from which I draw some of the specific examples are: "The Nature and Conditions of Panic," *American Journal of Sociology* 60 (November 1954):267–275; "The Behavior of Panic Participants," *Sociology and Social Research* 41 (January 1957):187–194; (with T. Drabek), "Scapegoats, Villains and Disaster," *Transaction* 4 (March 1967):12–17; (with R. Dynes), "When Disaster Strikes," *Psychology Today* 5 (February 1972):66–71; "Human Behavior in Disaster," *Proceedings of the Conference, Designing to Survive Disaster* (Chicago: ITT Research Institute, 1973), pp. 53–74; and (with V. Taylor and A. Ross), *Delivery of Mental Health Services in Disasters: The Xenia Tornado and Some Implications* (Columbus, Ohio: Disaster Research Center, 1976).
7. R. Clifford, *The Rio Grande Flood* (Washington: Committee on Disaster Studies, 1956).
8. R. Heiland, "Tornado Warning: How Good?" *Xenia Daily Gazette*, June 12, 1974, p. 2.
9. See R. R. Dynes and E. L. Quarantelli, *The Role of Local Civil Defense in Disaster Planning* (Columbus, Ohio: Disaster Research Center, 1975).
10. Points in this paragraph are all discussed in my *Social Problems* article cited above.
11. R. Titmus, *Problems of Social Policy* (London: Longmans Green, 1950), p. 23.
12. For a description of Center activity, see R. R. Dynes and E. L. Quarantelli, *Report on the Activities of the Disaster Research Center, Preliminary Paper No. 15* (Columbus, Ohio: Disaster Research Center, 1974).
13. Information about the Colorado work can be obtained from Professor J. Eugene Haas at the Institute of Behavioral Science at the University of Colorado.
14. A listing of major social science centers and researchers is provided in *Unscheduled Events* 8 (1974), put out by the Disaster Research Center at Ohio State University.
15. For details on a week-long conference between social scientists from the two countries, see *Proceedings of the Japan-United States Disaster Research Seminar: Organizational and Community Responses to Disaster* (Columbus, Ohio: Disaster Research Center, 1972).
16. See the one issued by the Disaster Research Center entitled *An Annotated Bibliography on Disaster and Disaster Planning* (Columbus, Ohio: Disaster Research Center, 1972); also, the listing of items by the Disaster Research Unit at the British disaster research center entitled *A Bibliography of Disaster Reference Material;* and A. Cochran, *A Selected Annotated Bibliography on Natural Hazards* (Denver: Institute of Behavioral Science, University of Colorado, 1972).
17. The Disaster Research Center at Ohio State University, the Institute of Behavioral Science at the University of Colorado, as well as the French, English and Japanese centers have their own publication series. Lists of their publications can be obtained from the first two sources.
18. As noted in note 14, a limited circulation quarterly newsletter, *Unscheduled Events,* is issued by the Disaster Research Center.
19. The first issue of this journal will appear in October 1975 and is published by Elsevier Press in Amsterdam, The Netherlands (P.O. Box 211). The co-editors of the journal are myself and Professor J. Nehnevajsa of the University of Pittsburgh.
20. F. Kline and P. Tichenor (eds.), *Current Perspective in Mass Communication Research* (Beverly Hills: Sage, 1972), p. 236.
21. H. Cantril, H. Gaudet, and H. Hertzog, *The Invasion from Mars* (Princeton: Princeton University Press, 1940).
22. Associated Press Wire Service, December 15, 1973.
23. K. Rosengren, *The Barseback Panic* (Lund, Sweden: University of Lund, 1974).
24. P. G. Wood, *The Behaviour of People in Fires* (London: Loughborough University of Technology, 1974).

25. For references, see previous footnotes on my work and the research of others. See also, for discussion of panic, P. Foreman, "Panic Theory," *Sociology and Social Research* 37 (1953):295–304; D. Schultz *Panic Behavior* (New York: Random House, 1964); C. Chandessais, "Practical Measures Against Panic," *International Civil Defense Bulletin,* no. 203 (May 1972):389–395; and, S. Guten, and V. Allen, "Likelihood of Escape, Likelihood of Danger, and Panic Behavior," *Journal of Social Psychology* 87 (1972):29–36.
26. Quotations and examples, unless otherwise cited, are drawn from my own studies, some of which have been used in the previous publications listed in note 6.
27. T. Young, *Emotion in Man and Animal* (New York: Wiley, 1943), p. 197. For a more recent discussion of the escape impulse in fear, see J. McDavid and H. Harari, *Social Psychology* (New York: Harper, 1968), p. 46.
28. J. Lowry, "The Psychological Problem in Disaster," *International Civil Defense Bulletin,* no. 165 (May 1969): 83.
29. For discussions of collective behavior, see E. L. Quarantelli, J. Weller, and D. Wenger, *Collective Behavior* (forthcoming); R. Turner and L. Killian, *Collective Behavior* (Englewood Cliffs, N.J.: Prentice-Hall, 1972); and J. Weller and E. L. Quarantelli, "Neglected Characteristics of Collective Behavior," *American Journal of Sociology* 79 (November 1973):665–685.
30. A. Lindesmith and A. Strauss, *Social Psychology* (New York: Dryden, 1949), p. 332.
31. C. Kelland, "Panic: How Men and Women Act When Facing Terror," *American Magazine* 109 (1930):92.

Index